In this important study, Damon L. Perry provides an insight-laden and up-to-date account of the Islamist movement that operates today in Britain. At a time when the British Government is thinking hard about how to deal with 'non-violent extremism', this book is valuable reading for policymakers and academics alike.

Dr. Martyn Frampton, Reader of Modern History at Queen Mary University of London and the author of *The Muslim Brotherhood and the West: A History of Enmity and Engagement* (Harvard University Press)

This book provides a most comprehensive and nuanced analysis of 'participationist' Islamism in Britain associated with the Muslim Brotherhood and Jamaat-i-Islami. It is sharply observed, grounded in scholarship and will be of great use to anyone studying Islamism or working in counter-extremism, counterterrorism, or social policy.

Professor John Bew, Professor in History and Foreign Policy at the War Studies Department, King's College London, and former co-Director of the International Centre for the Study of Radicalisation and Political Violence

The Global Muslim Brotherhood in Britain

Since 2011, with the British Government's counter-radicalisation strategy, Prevent, non-violent Islamist groups have been considered a security risk for spreading a divisive ideology that can lead to radicalisation and violence. More recently, the government has expressed concerns about their impact on social cohesion, entryism and women's rights. The key protagonists of non-violent Islamist 'extremism' allegedly include groups and individuals associated with the Muslim Brotherhood and Jama'at-i-Islami. They have been described as part of the 'global Muslim Brotherhood', but do they constitute a singular phenomenon, a social movement?

This book shows that such groups and individuals do indeed comprise a movement in Britain, one dedicated to an Islamic 'revival'. It shows how they are networked organisationally, bonded through ideological and cultural kinship, and united in a conflict of values with the British society and state. Using original interviews with prominent revivalist leaders, as well as primary sources, the book also shows how the movement is not so much 'Islamist' in its ambitions for an Islamic state, but concerned with institutionalising an Islamic worldview and moral framework throughout society. The conflict between the government and the global Muslim Brotherhood is apparent in a number of different fields, including education, governance, law and counter-terrorism. But this does not simply concern the direction of government policy or the control of state institutions. It most fundamentally concerns the symbolic authority to legitimise a way of seeing, thinking and living.

By assessing this multifaceted conflict, the book presents an exhaustive and up-to-date analysis of the political and cultural fault lines between Islamic revivalists and the British authorities. It will be useful for anyone studying Islam in the West, government counter-terrorism and counter-extremism policy, multiculturalism and social cohesion.

Damon L. Perry, PhD, is an independent policy and security analyst specialising in violent and non-violent Islamist extremism.

Routledge Studies in Political Islam

This series provides a forum for the latest research on all aspects of political Islam. It includes a range of approaches and studies on individuals, movements, theory and practice.

For a full list of titles in the series: https://www.routledge.com/middleeaststudies/series/SE0520

6. The Muslim Brotherhood
Hasan al-Hudaybi and Ideology
Barbara Zollner

7. Islamic Revivalism in Syria
The Rise and Fall of Ba'thist Secularism
Line Khatib

8. The Essence of Islamist Extremism
Recognition through Violence, Freedom through Death
Irm Haleem

9. Religious Authority and Political Thought in Twelver Shi'ism
From Ali to Post-Khomeini
Hamid Mavani

10. Islamism and the West
From "Cultural Attack" to "Missionary Migrant"
Uriya Shavit

11. Islamists of the Maghreb
Jeffry R. Halverson and Nathaniel Greenberg

12. The Global Muslim Brotherhood in Britain
Non-Violent Islamist Extremism and the Battle of Ideas
Damon L. Perry

The Global Muslim Brotherhood in Britain

Non-Violent Islamist Extremism and the Battle of Ideas

Damon L. Perry

Routledge
Taylor & Francis Group
LONDON AND NEW YORK

First published 2019
by Routledge
2 Park Square, Milton Park, Abingdon, Oxon OX14 4RN

and by Routledge
52 Vanderbilt Avenue, New York, NY 10017, USA

First issued in paperback 2020

Routledge is an imprint of the Taylor & Francis Group, an informa business

British Library Cataloguing-in-Publication Data
A catalogue record for this book is available from the British Library

Library of Congress Cataloging-in-Publication Data
Names: Perry, Damon L., author.
Title: The global Muslim Brotherhood in Britain : non-violent islamist extremism and the battle of ideas / Damon L. Perry.
Description: New York, NY : Routledge, [2018] | Series: Routledge studies in political Islam ; V. 12 | Includes bibliographical references and index.
Identifiers: LCCN 2018009061| ISBN 9781138564015 (hbk) | ISBN 9781315122144 (ebk)
Subjects: LCSH: Ikhwan al-Muslimun –Great Britain. | Islamic fundamentalism–Great Britain. | Muslims–Great Britain.
Classification: LCC BP65.G7 P47 2018 | DDC 320.55/70941–dc23
LC record available at https://lccn.loc.gov/2018009061

ISBN 13: 978-0-367-58846-5 (pbk)
ISBN 13: 978-1-138-56401-5 (hbk)

Typeset in Times New Roman
by Taylor & Francis Books

MIX
Paper from responsible sources
FSC™ C013985

Printed in the United Kingdom
by Henry Ling Limited

Contents

Figures

Acknowledgements

This book began as a doctoral thesis in the Department of War Studies at King's College London, but has been restructured, revised and updated for publication with Routledge. It is fitting, then, that I first express my gratitude to John Bew, my former supervisor at King's, whose valuable and constructive advice throughout the process of research and writing helped me to plot a clear course to completion and gave me the confidence to bring my doctorate to fruition.

I would like to thank a number of other inspiring and generous people who encouraged me during my work on this project. I am particularly grateful to Lorenzo Vidino, who saw the potential value of an in-depth study of the global Muslim Brotherhood in Britain and provided valuable feedback on an early thesis plan. I am also grateful to Patrick Sookhdeo for first encouraging me to embark on a doctorate and for opening the doors of the Barnabus Fund library in the beautiful village of Pewsey. I'd also like to thank Stephen Vertigans, who read the entire thesis, provided me with constructive feedback, and encouraged me to publish it as a book.

A special thanks is owed to all of the people who agreed to give up their time to talk with me about Islamism and 'non-violent extremism' in Britain before, during and after my doctoral studies. These include leaders of various Muslim groups, revivalist and secular, as well as analysts and other observers: Mohammed Abdul Aziz, Muhammad Abdul Bari, Daud Abdullah, Iftikhar Ahmad, Anas Altikriti, Irshad Baqui, Martin Bright, Abdullah Faliq, Paul Goodman, Omer El-Hamdoon, Suhaib Hasan bin Abdul Ghaff, Usama Hasan, Dilwar Hussain, Eric Kaufmann, Tehmina Kazi, Shiraz Maher, Sheikh Maulana Abu Sayeed, Sheikh Ibrahim Mogra, Farooq Murad, Pragna Patel, Suleman Nagdi, Anas al-Shaikh-Ali, Sam Westrop and Michael Whine.

A number of academics that I approached for access to certain journal articles were incredibly kind and prompt in replying with the materials and answering questions. For this, I would like to thank Nick Crossley, Barry Markovsky, David Snow, Cihan Tuğal and Loïc Wacquant. During the course of conducting the preliminary research for this thesis, I was fortunate to benefit from feedback on some of my writing from two great (but unrelated) scholars of Islam based in the United States, David Cook and Michael Cook. At this time I was also lucky to receive an unpublished paper on Islamism in the West by Jeffrey Bale. I would like to thank each of them for their generosity and insights.

The support of several friends cannot be overlooked while thanking those that have been of help to me during the process of research and writing. Scott Biagi, in particular, has been a constant inspiration and a much-valued critical friend. I am grateful to Veronique Pin-Fat for giving me solid, practical advice at the onset of my doctorate, and to Daniel Burn, Andy McElroy and Nick Prendergast for numerous engaging discussions on issues relating to the subject of this book.

Lastly, but most importantly, I want to express my sincere thanks to my family. I am very grateful for having such loving parents, Margaret and David, who have supported my education and kindled my intellectual curiosity from a young age. I owe a special thanks to Satoko for making it possible for me to undertake this project by supporting me and our wonderful children during the entire process. I cannot thank them all enough for their patience with my distractions and absences.

Organisations' acronyms

Not all of the organisations mentioned in this book refer to themselves in terms of acronyms. The Islamic Foundation, the Islamic Sharia Council, Muslim Aid, Muslim Welfare House and the Palestinian Return Centre, for example, are all important nodes in the global Muslim Brotherhood network, but are generally not referred to by acronyms. Many others, however, are commonly referred to as such. These are listed below.

AML	Association of Muslim Lawyers
AMS-UK	Association of Muslim Schools UK
AMSS	Association of Muslim Social Scientists
BMI	British Muslim Initiative
CST	Centre for the Study of Terrorism
ECFR	European Council for Fatwa and Research
ELM	East London Mosque
FIOE	Federation of Islamic Organisations in Europe
FOSIS	Federation of Student Islamic Societies
IBERR	International Board of Educational Research and Resources
iERA	Islamic Education and Research Academy
IFE	Islamic Forum of Europe
IHRC	Islamic Human Rights Commission
IIIT-UK	International Institute of Islamic Thought UK
IUMS	International Union of Muslim Scholars
Interpal	Palestinian Relief and Development Fund
ISB	Islamic Society of Britain
MAB	Muslim Association of Britain
MCB	Muslim Council of Britain
MEMO	Middle East Monitor
MEND	Muslim Engagement and Development – formerly iEngage
MET	Muslim Educational Trust
MINAB	Mosques and Imams National Advisory Board
MRDF	Muslim Research and Development Foundation
MSF	Muslim Safety Forum
NAMP	National Association of Muslim Police

NICMU	National Interim Committee on Muslim Unity
PSC	Palestinian Solidarity Campaign
RMCG	Rohingya Minority Crisis Group
UG	Union of Good
UKIM	UK Islamic Mission
YMOUK	Young Muslims Organisation UK
YMUK	Young Muslims UK

Introduction: the global Muslim Brotherhood and 'non-violent Islamist extremism' in Britain

This book is the first sustained analysis of one particular strand of 'Islamist' activism in Britain. Islamism of various hues in Britain has been the topic of many studies in recent years, but none has explored in such detail the organisational and ideological connections of the groups and individuals associated with 'participationist' Islamism. Moreover, none has explicitly raised the question as to whether and how these individuals and groups collectively comprise a movement in Britain. Lorenzo Vidino's book from 2010, *The New Muslim Brotherhood in the West*, provides the most explicit conceptualisation and detailed analysis of such a movement in Europe and America, but the sole chapter dedicated to Britain, while informative, is relatively limited and somewhat dated. Studies of participationist groups in Britain have appeared in various articles and think tank reports, and they provide some valuable insights for this book, but this is the first study to analyse such groups so comprehensively and to do so with specific focus on their collectivity.

Participationist Islamism, it should be said at the outset, is a term borrowed from a taxonomy provided by Jeffrey Bale.[1] It is also shared more widely by Vidino and others.[2] Characterising Islamism in fairly typical terms as a 'political ideology' that insists on the establishment of an Islamic world order or Islamic state,[3] Bale divides Islamists between those who reject and those who accept participation within democratic political systems.[4] The 'rejectionists' are sub-divided into violent jihadist groups, such as al-Qaeda, and 'ostensibly non-violent groups', such as Hizb ut-Tahrir. Both, he says, 'openly disparage the institutions and values of Western host societies', which they ultimately aspire to destroy.

Separate from these are the 'participationists', who are understood to seek an Islamic world order or state through non-violent means. These include groups and individuals alleged to have historical and ideological connections with the Egyptian organisation founded by Hasan al-Banna in 1928, *al-Ikhwan al-Muslimun* (The Society of the Muslim Brothers), and the organisation established in colonial India by Abu al-A'la Mawdudi in 1941, *Jama'at-i-Islami* (The Party of Islam). Since al-Banna and Mawdudi considered the purpose of their work as the revival of Islam's pre-eminence and glory, the Ikhwan, Jama'at and the groups associated with them are also referred to as 'Islamic revivalists'.

This book uses both terms, 'participationists' and 'revivalists'. The former is used mainly because this is how many observers refer to the individuals and groups associated with the Ikhwan and Jama'at. It correctly describes their preference for engagement in democratic politics and thus distinguishes them from Muslim activists that reject involvement in what they see as corrupt and forbidden 'man-made' systems of government. The term 'revivalists' is also used, since this is how the individuals and groups in question tend to see themselves. This book tends to use this term more frequently, since it assumes less about the importance of the Islamic state as a goal than the term 'participationist' does. In itself, 'participationist' merely reflects a chosen approach to activism, but it derives from a taxonomy of Islamism, described briefly above but elaborated upon in chapter 1, in which all protagonists are deemed to be striving for an Islamic state. The term 'revivalist', however, leaves open the question of the extent to which the conceived revival of Islam is directed to a political state of affairs – an Islamic government – or a society infused with Islamic values.

'Non-violent extremism': a conveyor belt to terrorism?

Over the last few years, the relevance of this book's topic has become more evident as the British government has become increasingly concerned about non-violent forms of Islamism in Britain. Although the government does not distinguish between rejectionist and participationist non-violent Islamism, it nevertheless sees a significant problem in what it calls 'non-violent Islamist extremism'. The government's concern is primarily driven by security interests. Although not universally shared amongst government officials, the notion that non-violent Islamist extremism may act as a pathway to violent extremism, i.e. terrorism, has been officially endorsed by the current Conservative government.[5] Some senior government leaders, including the former prime minister David Cameron and the current prime minister Theresa May, have expressed a broader concern regarding the detrimental effects of such extremism upon community cohesion and human rights, yet the overriding preoccupation with it relates to its potential radicalising influence upon British Muslims who may end up involved in planning, preparing or conducting terrorist attacks.

In February 2011, at the Munich Security Conference, Cameron identified a spectrum of Islamist extremism, stretching from non-violent to violent ideological orientations. He declared:

> Islamist extremism is a political ideology supported by a minority. At the furthest end are those who back terrorism to promote their ultimate goal: an entire Islamist realm, governed by an interpretation of Sharia. Move along the spectrum, and you find people who may reject violence, but

> who accept various parts of the extremist worldview, including real hostility towards Western democracy and liberal values.[6]

He added that the 'radical beliefs' of many convicted terrorists were initially influenced by 'non-violent extremists'. The Munich speech marked a significant shift in government security policy. Several months later, the government launched its revised counter-radicalisation strategy, Prevent, which emphasised the importance of targeting the ideology shared by both violent and non-violent Islamist extremists. For the first time, it provided a definition of extremism as 'the vocal or active rejection of British values'.[7]

Heightened fears regarding the dangers of 'non-violent Islamism' in Britain have been stoked more recently by several international developments. The first is the rise of the Islamic State (IS) in Iraq and Syria. From mid-2014, non-violent Islamist groups in Britain, including those linked to the Muslim Brotherhood and the rejectionist Hizb ut-Tahrir, came under heightened scrutiny for their alleged role in providing the 'mood music' for the radicalisation of British Muslims joining IS's insurgency.[8] The gruesome beheadings of British and American journalists and aid workers by a British IS jihadist, Mohammed Emwazi, beginning with that of James Foley in August 2014, increased concerns about the possible radicalising influence of these groups. Such concerns were intensified by estimates that hundreds of Britons had joined the ranks of IS in Syria and Iraq. Indeed, fears of the return to Britain of substantial numbers of British jihadists to conduct acts of terrorism, supported by direct threats to Britain issued by British IS members,[9] led the government to elevate the terrorism threat level from 'substantial' to 'severe', the second highest of five levels.[10]

The second international development to stimulate concern over non-violent Islamists in Britain was the rise to power of the Muslim Brotherhood in Egypt after the 2011 'Arab Spring' and its ousting from office almost a year later. In April 2014, reportedly prompted by the United Arab Emirates and Saudi Arabia, Cameron ordered an internal review of the Muslim Brotherhood to understand the group's 'philosophy, activities, impact and influence on UK national interests, at home and abroad'.[11] After a considerable delay, a summary of the review's main findings was published in December 2015.[12] The full report has been withheld from publication. In addition to the organisation headquartered in Cairo and its offshoots abroad, the review also considered British groups associated with Jama'at-i-Islami, indicating that the government sees the Brotherhood in Britain as a broad-based ideological movement. Supporting this interpretation, the summary document clusters Ikhwani- and Jama'ati-associated groups together in what it calls 'the UK Brotherhood movement'.[13]

The review appears to have been commissioned amidst concerns that the Brotherhood may be harmful for social cohesion and even linked to terrorism.[14] Indeed, although the main findings summary states that the Muslim Brotherhood 'has not been linked to terrorist related activity in and against the UK', and 'has often condemned [Islamist] terrorist related activity in the UK', it notes that 'Muslim Brotherhood-related organisations and individuals in the UK have openly supported the activities of Hamas'.[15] More importantly, it cautions that 'aspects of Muslim Brotherhood ideology and tactics, in this country and overseas, are contrary to our values and have been contrary to our national interests and our national security'.[16]

The view that non-violent Islamists pose a problem for national security and social cohesion has long been expressed by Quilliam, a London-based think tank. In 2010, Maajid Nawaz and Ed Husain of Quilliam wrote to Charles Farr, the director general of the Office for Security and Counter Terrorism, providing an extensive analysis of what they referred to as 'the UK's counter-extremism strategy' with a view to 'mak[ing] it more effective both at preventing terrorism and at fostering greater integration and national cohesion'.[17] The 'non-violent, yet extremist, ideology' of groups related to the Muslim Brotherhood and Jama'at-i-Islami, they suggested, has been 'increasingly recognised as a root cause of Islamist extremism and terrorism'.[18] The kick back against Prevent by such groups, they claimed, was attributable to this recognition.

Quilliam appears to have an influential role advising the British government. Nawaz claimed credit for helping draft Cameron's speech delivered in Birmingham in July 2015, in which the prime minister reiterated the view that non-violent extremism serves as a possible precursor to involvement in terrorism. 'I'm proud to have helped with UK PM Cameron's speech that names and isolates Islamism,' Nawaz wrote. 'Our work is taking root'.[19] Quilliam's influence may be significant, though Cameron had expressed similar views prior to becoming prime minister. In 2008, he warned against the 'extremist mindset that gives succour to terrorists by excusing their actions', noting the role of non-violent apologists for terrorism, including government officials and academics.[20]

Quilliam is not the only voice outside government suggesting that there is a relationship between non-violent extremist groups and terrorism. In 2011, Michael Whine of the Community Security Trust similarly contended that the ideologies of the Muslim Brotherhood and Jama'at-i-Islami in Britain promote 'extremism' and act 'as a conveyor belt or springboard that enable some activists to become terrorists'.[21] This view has been expressed more recently by Samuel Westrop of Stand for Peace. The role of non-violent extremists 'within the conveyor belt', he has argued, is not equivalent to the influence of a single preacher, activist or group, but is found in the production of 'a culture of extremist Islamic thought' perpetuated by a network of schools, mosques and other social institutions.[22]

For the government to tackle 'non-violent extremism', it is surely important for it to identify which groups and individuals to be concerned about. Yet, at least to the public, the government usually talks of non-violent Islamist extremism in general terms, rather than singling out particular groups or individuals. There have been some exceptions. In 2007, for example, Cameron advocated the banning of Hizb ut-Tahrir, as had former prime minister Tony

Blair two years earlier.[23] He reiterated this call a year later, describing the group in unequivocal terms as 'a conveyor belt to terrorism'.[24] In 2011, however, David Anderson QC, the independent reviewer of terrorism legislation, told Parliament that he does 'not recommend changes to the system for proscription' that would allow Hizb ut-Tahrir to be banned.[25] The group continues to operate legally in Britain, although other rejectionist groups have been banned under the Terrorism Act 2000, including al-Muhajiroun and Islam4UK.[26]

The notion of non-violent Islamist extremism serving as a conveyor belt to terrorism, as well as the singling out of Hizb ut-Tahrir as an exemplary group to be proscribed, has met with some criticism. Robert Lambert and Jonathan Githens-Mazer, for example, state: 'Approaches that emphasize specific forms of Islamic ideology or theology as causal "mood music" for terrorism are, at best, existentializing red herrings that are prone to miss the point, no matter how politically faddish.'[27] They note that 'ideology, whether defined rather broadly as one of "Islam under threat" or more specifically as a "Salafi-jihadi" orientation, is present in a variety of cases where individuals don't become terrorists. It is therefore illogical and dangerous to assume that identity issues and/or ideology in and of themselves are causing terrorism'.[28] Similarly, Arun Kundnani writes, 'the official narrative implies that, once an individual has adopted an extremist religious ideology, terrorism will result, irrespective of the political context or any calculation on the part of an organisation or social movement'.[29] Rather than a religious ideological outlook, Kundnani argues that the factors that lead to terrorism are political, the most important being grievances such as those relating to the American and British 'occupation' of Iraq.

Critics of the notion that non-violent extremism leads to violence, including the leader of Hizb ut-Tahrir in Britain, Abdul Wahid, also point to leaked classified papers prepared in 2010 for the Cabinet's home affairs committee. One of these papers, apparently produced with the assistance of Mohammed Abdul Aziz, a former representative of the revivalist-led Muslim Council of Britain (MCB), stated:

> It is sometimes argued that violent extremists have progressed to terrorism by way of a passing commitment to non-violent Islamist extremism, for example of a kind associated with al-Muhajiroun or Hizb ut Tahrir … . We do not believe that it is accurate to regard radicalisation in this country as a linear 'conveyor belt' moving from grievance, through radicalisation, to violence … . This thesis seems to both misread the radicalisation process and to give undue weight to ideological factors.[30]

Such criticisms are part of a complex debate on non-violent Islamism in Britain. It would be an oversimplification to portray this debate as one between the government and its detractors. Within government there are, or have been, some officials who endorse the view shared by Cameron's critics.

In 2010, for example, Robert Mason, a senior official of the Department for Communities and Local Government, wrote a 'restricted' memorandum to communities secretary Eric Pickles, asserting that the papers mentioned above present 'a clear assessment that individuals do not progress through non-violent extremist groups to violent groups'.[31] He added, 'Extreme groups may also provide a legal "safety valve" for extreme views.'

And there are others outside government – academics and journalists – who, like Cameron, see non-violent Islamist groups as playing a significant role in radicalisation and terrorism. Whine, Westrop and Nawaz have already been mentioned. Peter Neumann and Brooke Rogers of King's College London have also expressed concern regarding Islamist 'gateway organisations' that they say 'form part of a "conveyor belt" through which people are primed for their later involvement in terrorism'.[32] According to Neumann and Rogers, such organisations provide individuals with 'the ideological framework – the mindset – which leads to involvement in violence', as well as the 'social networks with violent extremists' that enable violent action.[33] They identify three gateway organisations in Britain – Tablighi Jama'at, Hizb ut-Tahrir and al-Muhajiroun – all of which are rejectionists, not participationists.

Participationist groups associated with the Muslim Brotherhood have not featured as prominently in the debates concerning non-violent Islamism in Britain as rejectionists have. This is probably because the primary concern with non-violent Islamism is with its potential for radicalising Muslims and thus its function as a way station for Islam-inspired terrorism. There is no hard data regarding terrorism arrests and convictions in Britain that compares the number of terrorists linked with rejectionist groups to the number linked with participationists. This data would be useful. But it is likely that far more terrorists are linked to rejectionist than to participationist groups. According to Raffaello Pantucci, almost half the terror plots carried out or foiled by police in Britain in the last two decades have been connected to al-Muhajiroun.[34] Brotherhood-associated groups in Britain, while supporting the terrorism campaigns of Hamas in Israel and other insurgencies they consider as defensive in nature, generally condemn terrorism in the West and refrain from openly promoting hostility between Muslims and secular, Western culture.

Although some analysts, such as Whine, have expressed concerns regarding Brotherhood-linked groups' potential for radicalising Muslims in Britain, such concerns are less pronounced compared with those regarding groups that openly reject Muslim political participation, publicly affirm Britain's future status as part of a global Islamic caliphate, and – without believing they need an intermediary role with government – have less to lose by stridently denouncing government policy.

Beyond radicalisation: matters of social cohesion and entryism

The government's concerns regarding non-violent Islamism may have centred on radicalisation and terrorism, and the debate on the role of non-violent

Islamism as a precursor to violence may have focused more on rejectionist groups than on participationists. But in the last few years, the government has begun to express serious concerns about non-violent Islamism's impact on social cohesion and civil liberties, including women's rights. It has also begun to express the need to safeguard against non-violent Islamist extremism and entryism within key British institutions. It is in relation to these concerns that participationist groups and individuals have played their most significant role in the debate on non-violent Islamism in Britain.

In December 2013, a government report identified schools, universities and prisons as institutions vulnerable to 'the ideology of Islamist extremism'.[35] Building on the findings of this report, a new statutory duty came into force on July 1, 2015, requiring all public bodies, including schools, prisons and local councils 'to take steps to identify and tackle radicalisation'.[36] The 'Prevent duty', as it is known, has its legal basis in the Counter-Terrorism and Security Act, which came into effect in February 2015.[37] Official guidance notes for this duty state that the staff of the 'specified' public institutions 'need to know what measures are available to prevent people from becoming drawn into terrorism and how to challenge the extremist ideology that can be associated with it'.[38]

Extremism in British schools has been a special concern of the government. New teachers' standards were introduced in 2012, stipulating that 'teachers must not undermine fundamental British values, including democracy, the rule of law, individual liberty and mutual respect, and tolerance of those with different faiths and beliefs'.[39] Prior to November 2014, all schools were required to 'respect' these values. Now, however, they have a responsibility to 'actively promote' them, as a bulwark against extremism and for the 'spiritual, moral, social and cultural development of pupils'.[40] Whilst the Prevent duty focuses on vigilance and the prevention of radicalisation, this responsibility to promote 'British values' in schools is geared to the more positive task of ensuring knowledge of and identification with democratic, progressive culture.

One event that encouraged the government to introduce these changes was the 'Trojan Horse' scandal in Birmingham, where a government-commissioned inquiry found city schools had been targeted by a 'co-ordinated, deliberate and sustained' campaign to introduce 'an intolerant and aggressive Islamic ethos'.[41] Of particular controversy was the central involvement of a senior member of Britain's largest Muslim umbrella group, the Muslim Council of Britain (MCB), who has now been banned from any involvement in British schools.[42]

This 'plot' – and the problem of a rejection of British values within religious supplementary schools – was mentioned by the then home secretary Theresa May in a speech she gave in March 2015.[43] Calling for a partnership between government and civil society to combat extremism, she identified the problems with non-violent extremism in universities, charities, local government and religious arbitration tribunals. Specifically, she identified the discrimination against women in *shari'a* courts across the country as a problem to be investigated by an independent commission. This follows similar concerns raised in three separate reports produced by the think tank Civitas, the advocacy group One Law for All, and the former deputy speaker of the House of Lords, Caroline Cox.[44] Two further studies, by Elham Manea and Machteld Zee, have since echoed these concerns.[45]

In her March 2015 speech, May also singled out the London Borough of Tower Hamlets for 'allegations of corruption, cronyism, extremism, homophobia and anti-Semitism'. These allegations were made in several high-profile investigations by *The Telegraph*, which confirmed the infiltration of the Labour Party within the borough by the Islamic Forum of Europe (IFE), as well as its covert involvement in Lutfur Rahman's successful campaign to become the borough's mayor in 2010. The newspaper's Andrew Gilligan also exposed the extremist orientations of IFE. Based in the Jama'at-i-Islami-associated East London Mosque, which has a record of hosting speakers expressing views clearly antagonistic to liberal democratic values,[46] the organisation came under the spotlight when Gilligan revealed IFE literature describing its commitment to change the 'very infrastructure of [British] society, its institutions, its culture, its political order and its creed … from ignorance to Islam'.[47] Furthermore, several IFE activists were recorded by an undercover reporter for Channel 4's *Dispatches* programme as stating that the organisation had 'a lot of influence and power in the council, councillors, politicians'.[48] Thus, it was perhaps unsurprising when, in November 2014, the government's chief inspector of schools stated that hundreds of children in six of the borough's Islamic schools were recognised by the government of being at risk of 'extremist influences and radicalisation'.[49]

In July 2015, Cameron delivered a key speech outlining the government's new counter-extremism strategy. Indicating a concern regarding non-violent extremism beyond its potential pathway to violence, Cameron emphasised the importance of combatting '[i]deas which are hostile to basic liberal values such as democracy, freedom and sexual equality … [and] which actively promote discrimination, sectarianism and segregation'.[50] Communal segregation is a theme he has touched on before; in 2008, speaking at the Community Security Trust, he identified 'the fostering of community divisions which push people into mutually antagonistic blocs' as a threat to British society, in addition to terrorism.[51] The July speech, however, consolidated the view within government policy that 'extremist ideology' posed not just the risk of terrorism but also a threat to Britain's liberal democratic culture.

This could not have been put in plainer terms than those expressed by Theresa May in the foreword to the new *Counter-Extremism Strategy*, published in October 2015. She wrote that 'the threat posed by extremists is not limited to violence'.[52] The strategy aims to address several concerns she had expressed in her March 2015 speech – namely, entryism into key British institutions, including schools, and the discrimination against women in *shari'a* courts – plus other issues alleged to stem from 'extremist ideology', such as 'isolated communities', forced marriage and female genital mutilation. A new body in the Home Office, the Extremism Analysis Unit, will play a key role in developing this strategy.

There has been a considerable backlash against the counter-extremism and counter-radicalisation strategies, particularly from revivalist individuals and groups such as MCB, the Federation of Student Islamic Societies (FOSIS), Muslim Engagement and Development (MEND), CAGE and the Islamic Human Rights Commission (IHRC). They see these strategies, particularly the government's focus on 'non-violent extremism' as a threat to their understanding of normative values as well as Islam. In July 2017, Prevent, and more specifically the Prevent duty was issued with a legal challenge, the first of its kind, by a revivalist website editor, Salman Butt. Named by the Prime Minister's Office as someone on record for 'expressing views contrary to British values', Butt claimed it impinged upon the freedom of speech. The case was rejected, but demonstrates how the government's zoning in on non-violent extremism is a highly contentious matter, particularly for Islamists. This legal challenge and the clash of narratives that underpins it will be examined in more detail later in the book.

The understanding that revivalist groups bring their own set of problems to British society independent from their potential radicalising influence has been expressed by some observers outside Whitehall. Quilliam, for instance, has warned that engagement with organisations associated with the Muslim Brotherhood and Jama'at-i-Islami, such as MCB and the Muslim Association of Britain (MAB), 'threatens integration and national cohesion by encouraging the spread of a supremacist ideology'.[53] A few others have described the problem of revivalists as one of cultural subversion. While Cameron has described 'Islamist extremism' as a 'subversive doctrine',[54] the elaboration of 'non-violent subversion' has been left for a small number of journalists and analysts.[55] Charles Moore, the former chairman of the think tank Policy Exchange, for example, in discussing the Birmingham Trojan Horse plot, asserts:

> All Islamist schools of thought are hostile to democratic processes, many explicitly so. They strive to create a global society in thrall to their version of Islamic law. As we learnt when Islamists educated in British comprehensive schools blew themselves up and killed 52 – mainly their fellow citizens – in July 2005, some use violence to try to bring this about. *Most don't, but they do work to subvert – that is the right word – the institutions that we all need.* They are organised in schools and universities. They infiltrate local government and public administration. They are expert at getting public money under false pretences. They are not 'negligible', but still we neglect the threat they pose.[56]

Shiraz Maher and Martyn Frampton, in a report published by Policy Exchange that discusses the 'challenge posed by political Islamists who ostensibly eschew violence', suggest that the British intelligence services 'need to recover some of their intellectual inheritance in relation to developing a definition of "subversion"' fit for such a challenge.[57] According to Patrick Sookhdeo, 'a careful and deliberate strategy by certain Muslim leaders' to subvert British society was presented decades ago at a conference in 1978 organised by the Islamic Council of Europe. This strategy, he writes, urged Muslims to resist assimilation and organise themselves according to Islamic principles: 'The ultimate goal of this strategy is that the Muslims should become a majority and the entire nation be governed according to Islam.'[58]

Contrary to these fears of non-violent Islamist ideology in Britain as either a disseminator of social discord or a conduit for terrorism, some observers have in recent years argued that the new leaders of some of the key organisations of concern are evolving innovative and self-critical reformulations of their religious tradition.[59] Such an analysis, as provided by Sophie Gilliat-Ray and Seán McLoughlin, supports the view that, far from being a subversive threat, the leaders of these organisations advocate a political vision inspired by Islam that is compatible with liberal democratic values. Such a vision, it is alleged, is shared by politically active Muslims across Europe.[60] Jytte Klausen, for example, states,

> Europe's Muslim leaders are not aiming to overthrow liberal democracy and to replace secular law with Islamic religious law, the shariah. Most are rather looking for ways to build institutions that will allow Muslims to practice their religion in a way that is compatible with social integration.[61]

These notions may be comforting. But although there are some Muslims, such as Dilwar Hussain, who have made a 'self-critical' journey away from revivalist groups, there is an extensive network of revivalists operating in Britain who continue to aspire for a society based on what they see as true Islamic values. Such values, which defer to classical conceptions of *shari'a*, promote Islam as a way of life that is ultimately incompatible with secular liberalism. Such values put critical thinking in the service of propagating thought that is consistent with alleged divine revelation. Such values view individual liberty as subordinate to group solidarity in deeming the protection of the Muslim *umma* – the community entrusted to spread Islam – above individual rights.[62] Social relationships are perceived and judged not in terms of individuals' free choices, but in terms of fulfilling a prescriptive ethical (and, ultimately, legal) code that condemns homosexuality and sees women's 'natural' role as subservient to men and the family unit as the preferred vehicle for an 'Islamic revival'.

The question of a 'participationist' Islamist movement in Britain

This apparent disagreement between critics of these groups and their more sympathetic observers lies at the heart of local community and national security policy conundrums. It is also the starting point for this book. Put succinctly, it concerns the nature of the politics of the organisations and individuals of concern: Do they constitute a subversive Islamist brotherhood that inculcates socially divisive values, whilst seeking the gradual imposition of *shari'a* law and ultimately an Islamic state? Or do they form a progressive Islamic movement at home in Britain's liberal democratic culture that merely seeks social justice for Muslims as equal citizens? Underlying this question, however, is the arguably more fundamental one – largely absent in the academic and think tank literature – that concerns whether and how they comprise a movement at all: do the individuals and groups in Britain that are commonly identified as non-violent 'participationist' Islamists comprise a singular phenomenon, social movement? And if so, what is distinct about this movement?

The initial objective of this study, stemming from an interest in the question of the potentially subversive nature of political Islam in Britain, was to identify and elucidate the political goals and strategies of the 'non-violent Islamist' movement in Britain. Yet preliminary research, including the conduct of a number of interviews with Muslim activists, prompted a step back to enquire as to whether such a movement exists in Britain in the first place. This step is important because the accuracy and usefulness of the term 'Islamist' in relation to individuals and groups associated with the Muslim Brotherhood and Jama'at-i-Islami in Britain – and the assumption, if not the explicit claim, that they comprise a movement – has long been something taken for granted, particularly in think tank and news media discourse.

Hence, it must be emphasised, the starting place of the book is with a cluster of individuals and the organisations they are involved in, not with 'non-violent Islamism' per se. This book is concerned with these actors precisely because they are usually considered as Islamists and because, by definition, Islamism presents interesting and serious challenges to any liberal democratic society or state. But it tries to minimise the assumptions regarding their political orientations. Rather than simply interrogate whether they aspire for an Islamic state – as all Islamists are by definition assumed to do – it more openly seeks to fathom whether and how they are bonded by a worldview and an associated set of values, regardless of its specific characteristics. It happens that they are bonded in such a way, but the Islamic state does not feature as prominently as might be expected, and thus the applicability of the moniker 'Islamist' has to be caveated.

This book is based on research conducted for a doctorate at the Department of War Studies, King's College London. It involved conducting and analysing interviews with many of the leaders of the relevant Muslim organisations. Significantly, representatives from almost all of the key participationist organisations were interviewed, including senior figures from the Muslim Council of Britain, the Muslim Association of Britain, the Islamic Forum of Europe, the Islamic Foundation, the Cordoba Foundation, the Middle East Monitor, the Islamic Sharia Council, the East London Mosque,

Muslim Aid, the International Institute of Islamic Thought UK, and Dawatul Islam UK & Eire. Supporting the data obtained from interviews, the research for this book also involved the analysis of primary source material published by the relevant individuals and organisations. Such material included books, magazines, newsletters, brochures and online articles, as well as speeches given by some of these figures that were sourced on the internet at websites such as YouTube. Some interviewees provided the book author with literature recently published by the organisations they work for.

Social movements and metapolitics

The global Muslim Brotherhood in Britain, this book argues, is a social movement. All social movements are networks. But not all networks are social movements unless they possess the following three features.

First, a social movement is a network that is *organised.* Social movements are constituted by and emerge from loose, informal social networks, but they require organisational structures through which professionals work for social change in the name of the groups they speak for. Social movements are not equivalent to organisations, including what have been described as 'social movement organisations', such as Hezbollah in Lebanon. Although they may be partly comprised of organisations – or of cross-sections of them – movements are more open-ended and lack formal integration. As Emmanuel Karagiannis notes, movements may be comprised of multiple alliances of independently working groups.[63] Social movements are not organisations, but they are organised.

This criterion distinguishes movements not just from organisations; it also distinguishes them from networks whose members may identify themselves as belonging to a distinct group, but which lack representative organisation and, thus, the potential to collectively mobilise. The movement's organisational structure – the extent to which it is centralised or hierarchical, for example – ought not to be pre-empted, since this depends upon the structural and institutional form of the power it confronts and defines itself against. The institutionalised power a movement confronts, even the state as its typical adversary, is not necessarily restricted to the political field and may be dispersed across numerous fields – for example, education, finance and law – and so its organisational structure may reflect that dispersal.

Second, a movement – an organised network – expresses *collective identity* or what the late Italian social movement theorist Alberto Melucci refers to as a 'specific solidarity'.[64] This criterion separates movements from other forms of collective action, such as coalitions. Coalitions are organised networks, but they lack the collective identity that pertains to movements, which endures beyond the specific campaigns that coalition groups come together to work on.

An example is the Stop the War Coalition comprised of the Muslim Association of Britain (MAB) and the Socialist Workers' Party (SWP), which, in 2002 and 2003 organised street protests against the allied invasion of Iraq.

While both groups campaigned together to influence British foreign policy, the interests of both groups in averting British involvement in the Middle East were related to different stakes and struggles, as well as to divergent perceptions of human rights and social justice. Put succinctly and somewhat crudely, the solidarity between the MAB and SWP was political, not cultural. It was issues-based, not identity-based. It was short-term, not long-term. A more recent example is the current 'Preventing Prevent' campaign, involving the Federation of Student Islamic Societies (FOSIS), CAGE, the National Union of Students (NUS) and the University and College Union (UCU). Whereas all groups share the view that the government's counter-radicalisation strategy risks impinging on civil liberties, FOSIS and CAGE's involvement is different from that of the NUS and UCU, since it is informed by a different worldview and carries different stakes.

Third, a movement – an organised network of individuals with cultural connections – is *conflictual*. It is engaged in a conflictual relationship with authority not just for extracting certain concessions in the name of its constituency but also over the power to determine an alternative social and political reality. Such power is both practical and symbolic – that is, it concerns the capacity to both regulate action and shape perceptions and dispositions. This criterion separates movements from collective action that seeks representation *within* existing political or social structures without fundamentally altering them. Some identity-based rights groups – for example, those concerned with gender, sexuality or race – are not conflictual in this sense, since they seek greater inclusion *within* existing systems. Others, however, that see the stakes of their struggle as bound up with a transformation *of* existing systems – those engaged in *metapolitics* – are conflictual in the sense described here.

Social movements are engaged in metapolitics since they can be seen to be challenging the basic values upon which the political system rests. Such a transformation may be conceived by its advocates as a prerequisite for a transformation in the political system. In the words of Greg Johnson, an American white ethno-nationalist writer, 'The promotion of political change through the transformation of consciousness and culture is what we call *metapolitics*. Metapolitics refers to what must come *before* the foundation of a new political order.'[65]

Thus, the global Muslim Brotherhood in Britain can be understood as a movement with the recognition of the aforementioned three elements: *organisational collaboration* between the relevant individuals and groups; shared *cultural solidarity* between them; and a *conflict of vision and values* with institutional authority. These three elements help to provide a structure for this book, as explained below.

Chapter 1 introduces the subject of the book, the network of individuals and groups associated with the Muslim Brotherhood and Jamaat-i-Islami in Britain. It describes who the key players in this network are, their historical background, and the various ways in which they have been conceived and classified by other observers. The chapter provides the platform from which the rest of the book follows, since it not only provides the global and British historical context of the emergence of the revivalist network. It also describes and analyses the key debates in which these individuals and groups have featured. Whereas some analysts view them as non-violent but subversive 'Islamists', others see them as a progressive force for Muslim activism. These debates, the chapter concludes, help to identify the key protagonists and provide some useful background information, but provide an incomplete picture of the network in Britain. It is the task of the remainder of the book to complete this picture.

The first of the three elements that comprise social movements is the focus of chapter 2, which confirms the existence of the organisational network of the individuals and groups in Britain identified in chapter 1. This analysis builds on the literature presented in chapter 1, but it incorporates additional insights gleaned from interviews with some of the Muslim leaders within the network. This enables a far more complete picture of the organisational dimensions of this network than is currently provided in any open sources.

Chapter 2 describes some of the numerous interpersonal and inter-organisational relationships comprising the network, as evident in collaborations and affiliations, but most importantly in various inter-locking leadership structures, formal and informal. These include MCB, the country's largest Muslim umbrella group, and numerous overlapping leadership clusters apparent in the multiple senior positions that key individuals have in various groups. These leadership structures also include a semi-formal group comprised of key leaders of Jama'at- and Ikhwan-associated organisations, the Coordination Committee of Islamic Organisations. This committee, which is absent from all of the academic and think tank literature on Islamism in Britain, was revealed in an interview with Abdullah Faliq, an experienced Muslim activist involved in numerous organisations, including the Islamic Forum of Europe and the Cordoba Foundation.[66]

The second element of a social movement, cultural kinship or solidarity, is the focus of chapters 3 and 4. These chapters show how the individuals comprising the network identified in chapter 2 share cultural solidarity, particularly in terms of how they classify themselves as a community, how they conceive of their relationship to the environment in which they live, and how they understand their work and its purpose.

Chapter 3 regards their conception of communal identity through specific Islamic concepts, such as the Muslim *umma*, and Islamic moral principles implicit to their work, including that of 'Enjoining the Good and Forbidding the Wrong'. Their sense of distinction as a group is expressed in their perception of non-Muslims as part of the broader community of humanity to which they have a duty to deliver Islam. It is also expressed in their perception of other Muslims as mistaken in isolating themselves from Britain's non-Muslim mainstream, or in integrating themselves seamlessly within it, or in placing the goal of an Islamic state prior to the attainment of a society infused with Islamic beliefs and values. Whilst noting some variation in the way in which these individuals understand their collective identity and certain Islamic concepts through which they understand their work, this chapter shows that there are nevertheless grounds to assert that the network embodies cultural solidarity characteristic of a social movement.

One of the key contributions of this book is a novel and nuanced understanding of what other analysts may refer to as the 'ideology' of Islamic revivalists. This includes their ideas and thinking but, underlying this, their way of perceiving and evaluating the world. Of particular significance is the concept and importance of the Islamic state in the revivalist worldview and value system. These actors are connected by their understanding of themselves as Islam's vanguard within British society but, as chapter 4 shows, their understanding of the Islamic state – contrary to their classification by critics as 'Islamists' – is not as a goal to be strived towards. It is, rather, a reward for widespread piety. Their primary aspiration is not, strictly speaking, an Islamic mode of governance, but a society in which Islam is willingly embraced. Such a society ultimately includes a government organised according to Islamic principles, however this may turn out in practice. But the application of Islamic values is sought as a matter of culture that incorporates but transcends politics, traversing all aspects of human existence, including education, economics, science and technology. This shows that what distinguishes participationists from rejectionist Islamists, such as Hizb ut-Tahrir and al-Muhajiroun, is not simply a choice of methods but an important aspect of their worldview. This finding has emerged from a number of interviews with prominent leaders of revivalist groups.

The third element of the concept of social movement, conflict with institutional authority, frames chapters 5 and 6. The key figures and groups comprising the global Muslim Brotherhood have a conflictual relationship with the British political authorities. They are engaged in a cultural and political struggle concerning perspectives, values, and a way of life, as well as the authority to determine them. As chapters 5 and 6 demonstrate, this conflict has both practical and symbolic dimensions. The practical dimension of the conflict concerns the institutional and legal structures that regulate peoples' lives. It is evident in the fields of political advocacy and local governance, the focus of chapter 5, as well as education and arbitration, the focus of chapter 6, particularly where Muslim communities are concerned. Concerns regarding Birmingham's Trojan Horse affair and *shari'a* courts, as expressed by Theresa May, point to key examples. Connected to the practical dimension of this conflict, there is also a symbolic or cognitive dimension. This is evident in competing efforts to classify – and to command the authority to classify – the 'correct' understanding of what fundamental social values are, what counts as 'extremism' and what Islam is.

The stakes of this conflict are thus twofold: on the one hand, they include the institutionalisation of competing worldviews and related values – Islamic and liberal democratic – within civil society structures, government policy and state legislation. On the other hand, they include the institutionalisation of competing worldviews and related values within the minds of people, including policymakers, British Muslims and the general public. As chapters 5 and 6 show, these two dimensions overlap, particularly in revivalist groups' efforts to undermine the government's counter-extremism strategy both *symbolically*, where concepts such as 'extremism' are contested, and *practically*, where changes in government policy are sought through protest, advocacy or testimony. In presenting this multifaceted conflict, these chapters present arguably the most comprehensive, nuanced and up-to-date analysis of the political and cultural fault lines between Islamic revivalists and the British authorities.

This book argues that the global Muslim Brotherhood in Britain is a social movement. Whether or not it is referred to as such, the three elements of the concept of social movement allows for an understanding of one strand of 'Islamist' activism in Britain that is important both academically and politically. Although there is much more to be learned about 'participationist' individuals and groups, as well as their collective nature, this book presents some valuable insights into their organisational connections, their worldview and values, and their conflict with Britain's liberal democratic culture, as well as the political authorities that have a responsibility to protect it. In identifying and elucidating some of the distinct features of participationist Islamism – what this book also refers to as Islamic revivalism – it contributes to a more nuanced understanding of what the government sees as 'non-violent Islamist extremism' in Britain. This may be helpful not only for policymakers seeking to refine an approach to what Cameron has called 'the struggle of our generation'.[67] It may also be helpful to expand and refine the academic study of Islamic activism in the West and social movements.

Notes

1 Jeffrey Bale, 'Militant Islamist Networks in the West', National Consortium for the Study of Terrorism and Responses to Terrorism website. 21 December 2009. www.start.umd.edu/research-projects/militant-islamist-networks-west.
2 Vidino (2009), pp. 165–176, and Vidino (2010), pp. 15–16. See also McRoy (2006) and Quilliam (2010).
3 Bale (2009), pp. 79, 80.
4 Jeffrey Bale, 'Militant Islamist Networks in the West'.
5 'PM's speech at Munich Security Conference', British Government website, 5 February2011.www.gov.uk/government/speeches/pms-speech-at-munich-security-conference; 'Extremism: PM speech', British Government website, 20 July 2015. www.gov.uk/government/speeches/extremism-pm-speech.
6 'PM's speech at Munich Security Conference'.
7 Home Office (2011), p. 107.
8 See Haras Rafiq, 'London has been primed for decades by Muslim Brotherhood extremists', *The Express*, 24 August 2014. www.express.co.uk/comment/expresscomment/502795/London-has-been-primed-for-decades-by-Muslim-Brotherhood-extremists. See also Sarah Ann Harris, 'As officials try to identify US journalist's killer – how do Britons become IS murderers?', *The Express*, 21

August 2014.www.express.co.uk/news/uk/501621/After-James-Wright-Foley-s-murder-how-do-Britons-becomes-IS-killers.

9 Dipesh Gadher, 'We'll fly black flag of jihad over London', *The Sunday Times*, 15 June 2014. www.thesundaytimes.co.uk/sto/news/uk_news/Defence/article1422787.ece.

10 Tom Whitehead and Steven Swinford, 'Britain facing "greatest terrorist threat" in history', *The Telegraph*, 29 August 2014. www.telegraph.co.uk/news/uknews/terrorism-in-the-uk/11065167/Britain-facing-greatest-terrorist-threat-in-history.html.

11 'Government review of the Muslim Brotherhood', British Government website, 17 April 2014. www.gov.uk/government/news/government-review-of-the-muslim-brotherhood.

12 House of Commons (2015).

13 Ibid., para. 28, p. 5.

14 Lorenzo Vidino, 'For too long, London has been a hub for the Muslim Brotherhood', *The Telegraph*, October 2014. www.telegraph.co.uk/comment/11171454/Lorenzo-Vidino-For-too-long-London-has-been-a-hub-for-the-Muslim-Brotherhood.html.

15 House of Commons (2015), paras. 36–37, pp. 6–7.

16 Ibid., para. 39, p. 8.

17 Quilliam (2010), p. 1 (note: pages references for this document refer to the page numbers of the pdf file, which includes several unnumbered pages for a covering letter, and not those as they appear on the document itself).

18 Ibid., p. 7.

19 David Shariatmadari, 'Maajid Nawaz: how a former Islamist became David Cameron's anti-extremism adviser', *The Guardian,* 2 August 2015. www.theguardian.com/politics/2015/aug/02/maajid-nawaz-how-a-former-islamist-became-david-camerons-anti-extremism-adviser.

20 'David Cameron: Speech to the Community Security Trust', Conservative website, 4 March 2008. http://conservative-speeches.sayit.mysociety.org/speech/599684.

21 Whine (2011), p. 17.

22 Samuel Westrop, 'How to Radicalize an Entire London Borough', The Gatestone Institute, 5 May 2015. www.gatestoneinstitute.org/5677/tower-hamlets.

23 Jonathan Freedland, 'Free speech: reason to hope', *The Guardian*, 6 July 2007. www.theguardian.com/commentisfree/2007/jul/06/freespeechreasontohope.

24 'David Cameron: Speech to the Community Security Trust'.

25 Shiv Malik, 'Watchdog recommends Tory U-turn on banning Hizb ut-Tahrir', *The Guardian*, 18 July 2011. www.theguardian.com/politics/2011/jul/18/watchdog-tory-uturn-hizb-ut-tahrir-ban.

26 See Raymond (2010).

27 Githens-Mazer and Lambert (2010), p. 899.

28 Ibid., pp. 894–895.

29 Kundnani (2015), p. 15.

30 Andrew Gilligan, 'Hizb ut Tahrir is not a gateway to terrorism, claims Whitehall report', *The Telegraph*, 25 July 2010. www.telegraph.co.uk/journalists/andrew-gilligan/7908262/Hizb-ut-Tahrir-is-not-a-gateway-to-terrorism-claims-Whitehall-report.html.

31 Ibid.

32 Neumann and Rogers (2007), p. 31.

33 Ibid.

34 Pantucci (2015).

35 Cabinet Office (2013), p. 1.

36 'PM statement on Tunisia and European Council', British Government website, 29 June 2015. www.gov.uk/government/speeches/pm-statement-on-tunisia-and-european-council.

37 See *Counter-Terrorism and Security Act 2015 (c. 6)*. Available online at: www.legislation.gov.uk/ukpga/2015/6/pdfs/ukpga_20150006_en.pdf. See also, 'Counter-Terrorism and Security Act', British Government website, 12 February 2015. www.gov.uk/government/collections/counter-terrorism-and-security-bill.
38 HM Government (2015b), p. 4. The 'specified authorities' are listed in Schedule 6, *Counter-Terrorism and Security Act*, pp. 63–65.
39 Department for Communities and Local Government (2011), p. 17.
40 'Guidance on promoting British values in schools published', British Government website, 27 November 2014. www.gov.uk/government/news/guidance-on-promoting-british-values-in-schools-published.
41 Jonathan Walker, 'Trojan Horse: Schools will have legal duty to fight extremism', *The Birmingham Mail*, 25 November 2014. www.birminghammail.co.uk/news/midlands-news/trojan-horse-schools-legal-duty-8166069.
42 'Direction: Tahir Alam barred from managing independent schools', Government website, September 9, 2015. www.gov.uk/government/publications/direction-tahir-alam-barred-from-managing-independent-schools.
43 'Theresa May speech A Stronger Britain, Built on our Values: A New Partnership to Defeat Extremism', Conservatives website, 23 March 2015. http://press.conservatives.com/post/115395299770/theresa-may-speech-a-stronger-britain-built-on.
44 See MacEoin (2009); Namazie, Atasheen and Waters (2010); and Cox (2015).
45 Manea (2016) and Zee (2016).
46 Hasan Afzal, 'Extremism in Abdul Bari's Mosque', *The Huffington Post*, 21 September 2011. www.huffingtonpost.co.uk/hasan-afzal/extremism-in-abdul-baris-_b_971232.html.
47 Andrew Gilligan, 'Inextricably linked to controversial mosque: the secret world of IFE', *The Telegraph*, 28 February 2010. www.telegraph.co.uk/news/newstopics/politics/labour/7333487/Inextricably-linked-to-controversial-mosque-the-secret-world-of-IFE.html.
48 Andrew Gilligan, 'Radicals with hands on the levers of power: the takeover of Tower Hamlets', *The Telegraph*, 28 February 2010. www.telegraph.co.uk/news/newstopics/politics/labour/7333537/Radicals-with-hands-on-the-levers-of-power-the-takeover-of-Tower-Hamlets.html.
49 Michael Wilshaw, 'Advice note from Her Majesty's Chief Inspector, Sir Michael Wilshaw, to the Secretary of State for Education, Rt Hon. Nicky Morgan MP, on school inspections in the London Borough of Tower Hamlets', 21 November 2014. www.gov.uk/government/uploads/system/uploads/attachment_data/file/386594/Tower_20Hamlets_20advice_20note.pdf.
50 'Extremism: PM speech'.
51 'David Cameron: Speech to the Community Security Trust'.
52 'Home Secretary Foreword', HM Government (2015a), p. 7.
53 Quilliam (2010), p. 12.
54 'Extremism: PM speech'.
55 Charle Moore, 'Why Islamist extremism perplexes our security services', *The Telegraph*, 29 November 2014. www.telegraph.co.uk/news/uknews/terrorism-in-the-uk/11260855/Why-Islamist-extremism-perplexes-our-security-services.html.
56 Charles Moore, 'A weak establishment is letting Islamists threaten British freedoms', *The Telegraph*, 18 April 2014, emphasis added. www.telegraph.co.uk/news/uknews/terrorism-in-the-uk/10775118/A-weak-establishment-is-letting-Islamists-threaten-British-freedoms.html.
57 Maher and Frampton (2009), p. 68.
58 Patrick Sookhdeo, 'The Islamization of Europe', *Virtueonline*, 11 August 2005, www.virtueonline.org/portal/modules/news/article.php?storyid=2872#.UqkiaGQW1mF.
59 McLoughlin (2005), Gilliat-Ray (2010).
60 See Mandaville (2003), Cesari (2004).

61 Klausen (2005), p. 3.
62 For example, see *Fatwas of the European Council for Fatwa and Research* (2002), p. 31.
63 Karagiannis (2009).
64 Melucci (1980), p. 202.
65 Greg Johnson, 'New Right vs. Old Right', Counter-Currents Publishing Blog, 11 May 2012. www.counter-currents.com/2012/05/new-right-vs-old-right/.
66 Interview with Abdullah Faliq, 5 September 2012.
67 'Extremism: PM speech'.

References

Bale, Jeffrey M. (2009). 'Islamism and totalitarianism'. In *Totalitarian Movements and Political Religions*, vol. 10, no. 2: 73–96.

Cabinet Office (2013). 'Tackling extremism in the UK'. www.gov.uk/government/uploads/system/uploads/attachment_data/file/263181/ETF_FINAL.pdf.

Cesari, Jocelyne (2004). *When Islam and Democracy Meet: Muslims in Europe and in the United States.* New York: Palgrave MacMillan.

Cox, Caroline (2015). *A Parallel World: Confronting the Abuse of Many Muslim Women in Britain Today.* London: Bow Group. www.bowgroup.org/sites/bowgroup.uat.pleasetest.co.uk/files/Bow%20Group%20Report%20-%20A%20Parallel%20World%20-%20Confronting%20the%20abuse%20of%20many%20Muslim%20women%20in%20Britain%20today%2024%2003%2015.pdf.

Department for Communities and Local Government (2011). 'Creating the conditions for integration'. www.gov.uk/government/uploads/system/uploads/attachment_data/file/7504/2092103.pdf.

Fatwas of the European Council for Fatwa and Research (2002). Trans. Anas Osama Altikriti and Shakir Nasif Al-Ubaydi. Cairo: Islamic INC.

Gilliat-Ray, Sophie (2010). *Muslims in Britain: An Introduction.* Cambridge: Cambridge University Press.

Githens-Mazer, Jonathan, and Robert Lambert (2010). 'Why conventional wisdom on radicalization fails: the persistence of a failed discourse'. In *International Affairs*, vol. 86, no. 4: 889–901.

HM Government (2015a). *Counter-Extremism Strategy*, Cm 9148. www.gov.uk/government/uploads/system/uploads/attachment_data/file/470088/51859_Cm9148_Accessible.pdf.

HM Government (2015b). *Revised Prevent Duty Guidance: For England and Wales.* https://assets.publishing.service.gov.uk/government/uploads/system/uploads/attachment_data/file/445977/3799_Revised_Prevent_Duty_Guidance__England_Wales_V2-Interactive.pdf.

Home Office (2011). *Prevent Strategy*, Cm 8092. www.gov.uk/government/uploads/system/uploads/attachment_data/file/97976/prevent-strategy-review.pdf.

House of Commons (2015). *Muslim Brotherhood Review: Main Findings.* HC 679. www.gov.uk/government/uploads/system/uploads/attachment_data/file/486948/53163_Muslim_Brotherhood_Review_-_PRINT.pdf.

Karagiannis, Emmanuel (2009). 'Hizballah as a social movement organization: a framing approach'. In *Mediterranean Politics*, vol. 14, no. 3: 365–383.

Klausen, Jytte (2005). *The Islamic Challenge: Politics and Religion in Western Europe.* Oxford: Oxford University Press.

Kundnani, Arun (2015). 'A decade lost: rethinking radicalisation and extremism'. Claystone, London. www.claystone.org.uk/wp-content/uploads/2015/01/Claystone-rethinking-radicalisation.pdf.

MacEoin, Denis (2009). 'Sharia Law or One Law for All?' Ed. David G. Green. Civitas, London. www.civitas.org.uk/pdf/ShariaLawOrOneLawForAll.pdf.

Maher, Shiraz, and Martyn Frampton (2009). 'Choosing our friends wisely: criteria for engagement with Muslim groups'. Policy Exchange, London. https://policyexchange.org.uk/wp-content/uploads/2016/09/choosing-our-friends-wisely-mar-09.pdf.

Mandaville, Peter (2003). 'Towards a critical Islam: European Muslims and the changing boundaries of transnational religious discourse'. In Stefano Allievi and Jørgen S. Nielsen (eds), *Muslim Networks and Transnational Communities in and across Europe*: 127–145. Leiden: Brill.

Manea, Elham (2016). *Women and Shari'a Law: The Impact of Legal Pluralism in the UK*. London: I. B. Taurus.

McLoughlin, Seán (2005). 'The state, new Muslim leaderships and Islam as a resource for public engagement in Britain'. In Jocelyne Cesari and Seán McLoughlin (eds), *European Muslims and the Secular State*: 55–69. Aldershot: Ashgate Publishing.

McRoy, Anthony (2006). *From Rushdie to 7/7: The Radicalisation of Islam in Britain*. London: Social Affairs Unit.

Melucci, Alberto (1980). 'The new social movements: a theoretical approach'. In *Social Science Information*, vol. 19, no. 2: 199–226.

Namazie, Maryam, Yassi Atasheen and Anna Waters (2010). *Sharia Law in Britain: A Threat to One Law for All and Equal Rights*. London: One Law for All. www.onelawforall.org.uk/wp-content/uploads/New-Report-Sharia-Law-in-Britain_fixed.pdf.

Neumann, Peter R., and Brooke Rogers (2007). 'Recruitment and mobilisation for the Islamist militant movement in Europe'. International Centre for the Study of Radicalisation and Political Violence (ICSR), London.

Pantucci, Raffaello (2015). *'We Love Death As You Love Life': Britain's Suburban Terrorists*. London: Hurst and Co.

Quilliam (2010). 'Preventing terrorism: where next for Britain?'. Strategic Briefing Paper. Available at: www.scribd.com/doc/34834977/Secret-Quilliam-Memo-to-government.

Raymond, Catherine Zara (2010). 'Al Muhajiroun and Islam4UK: the group behind the ban'. International Centre for the Study of Radicalisation and Political Violence (ICSR), London. http://icsr.info/wp-content/uploads/2012/10/1276697989CatherineZaraRaymondICSRPaper.pdf.

Vidino, Lorenzo (2009). 'Europe as a battlefield'. In *Totalitarian Movements and Political Religions*, vol. 10, no. 2: 165–176.

Vidino, Lorenzo (2010). *The New Muslim Brotherhood in the West*. New York: Columbia University Press.

Whine, Michael (2011). 'The radicalization of diasporas and terrorism: United Kingdom'. In Doron Zimmermann and William Rosenau (eds), *The Radicalization of Diasporas and Terrorism*: 17–39. Zurich: Center for Security Studies, ETH Zurich.

Zee, Machteld (2016). *Choosing Sharia?: Multiculturalism, Islamic Fundamentalism and Sharia Councils*. Utrecht, Netherlands: Eleven International Publishing.

1 Introducing the global Muslim Brotherhood

Subversives or reformists?

This chapter introduces the global Muslim Brotherhood network in Britain. It describes who the key players in this network are and some of the ways in which they have been conceived and classified (by themselves and other observers). The chapter provides the platform from which the rest of the book follows, since it identifies the book's main protagonists, provides the historical context of the emergence of the network that they form, and presents the key debate in which they have been framed: Whereas some analysts view these individuals and groups as non-violent but subversive 'Islamists', more sympathetic commentators see them as a progressive force for Muslim activism in the process of reforming their Islamist heritage. Most observers take either one of these stances. As the following chapters will make clear, the global Muslim Brotherhood is neither simply Islamist in striving for an Islamic state nor progressive, but it does have as its goal a society based upon values emanating from an alternative source of authority.

The global Muslim Brotherhood in the West

The 'global Muslim Brotherhood' in the title of this book refers to a transnational network of organisations and individuals associated with *al-Ikhwan al-Muslimun* (The Society of the Muslim Brothers), established in Egypt in 1928 by Hasan al-Banna, and *Jama'at-i-Islami* (The Party of Islam) established in colonial India in 1941 by Abu al-A'la Mawdudi. From the 1960s, activists linked to the Ikhwan and Jama'at began to settle in Europe and North America. Free from the particular challenges and historical contexts of their points of origin and acknowledging that their presence in the West is long-term, these individuals have since established numerous organisations dedicated to pursuing their cultural and political ambitions in the Muslim-minority West.

Revivalist visionaries: al-Banna and Mawdudi

Hasan al-Banna, a schoolteacher, established the Muslim Brotherhood in 1928 to address what he saw as the corruption of Islam in his native Egypt. Al-Banna diagnosed the poor predicament of Muslims in Egypt and elsewhere not just as a result of the abolition of the caliphate or of Western colonialism. More fundamentally, he claimed, its demise was owed to the abandonment of Islamic values, and governance based upon those values, after the period of the first four caliphs (632–661).[1] These four 'rightly guided rulers' (*al-khulafa al-rashidun*) were considered by al-Banna as guardians of the true faith.[2] This is because they were all companions of Muhammad who, due to their direct intimacy with him and his teachings, were able to implement Islamic precepts faithfully while combining both political and religious authority.[3]

Al-Banna declared the ultimate goal of the Brotherhood as the re-creation of a global Islamic order based on the *shar'ia*.[4] He also believed firmly in, and taught, the importance of *jihad*, in line with the predominant classical (and juridical) conception of warfare for the hegemony of Islam.[5] *Jihad*, asserted al-Banna, is a duty incumbent upon all Muslims for Islam to reach its zenith. He also extolled the rewards of martyrdom in the path of *jihad*, as expressed in a pamphlet he wrote in the late 1930s.[6] Al-Banna believed the basis for Islamic supremacy, and *jihad* as its means, was 'supported in Qur'anic texts, the Traditions [*hadiths*], and the four schools of [Islamic] law'.[7]

Al-Banna's exaltation of *jihad* was not an empty formula. One of the few constants in the structure of the organisation, according to Richard Mitchell, was 'the enrolment of members in various kinds of armed formations trained to perform espionage and to commit violence'.[8] The Brotherhood initiated attacks against Egypt's Jews and Copts; bombed secular cinema theatres and restaurants; and assassinated judges, businessmen, intellectuals and government officials, including the Egyptian Prime Minister, Mahmud Fahmi al-Nuqrashi.[9] Amir Taheri notes that al-Banna's 'campaign of terror was to become a model for future fundamentalist movements'.[10] These include Hamas and Palestinian Islamic Jihad in the Palestinian Territories; al-Gama'a al-Islamiyya and Islamic Jihad in Egypt; Abu Sayyaf in the Philippines; as well as the Armed Islamic Group and the Salafist Group for Call and Combat in Algeria.[11] Perhaps most importantly, Brotherhood members also played a key role in the birth of al-Qaeda.[12] Osama bin Laden was a member of the Ikhwan and his ideas were influenced by it. In his diaries, found after the American raid on his holdout in Abbottobad, Pakistan, he writes, 'I was committed with the Muslim Brotherhood'.[13]

Despite its history of violence, the most important aspect of the Brotherhood's work was, and remains, its commitment to the gradual Islamisation of society from below using non-violent means. At the organisation's fifth conference in 1939, al-Banna stated that the official focus of the Ikhwan was 'the reform of society', since before they could be ready for political power, 'there must be a period during which the principles of the Brothers are spread'.[14] The guiding thought was that 'when the people have been Islamized, a truly Muslim nation will naturally evolve'.[15] To this end, al-Banna introduced a seven-stage strategy comprised of upwardly cascading goals:

The first step is to educate and 'form' the Muslim person. From there the Muslim person would spread Islam and help 'form' a Muslim family. Muslim families would group together to form a Muslim society that would establish a Muslim government. The government would then transform the state into an Islamic one governed by *Shari'ah*, as voted by the Muslim society. This Islamic state would then work to free 'occupied' Muslim lands [from apostate Muslim regimes] and unify them together under one banner, from which Islam could be spread all over the world.[16]

Abu al-A'la Mawdudi also advocated a bottom-up approach to the achievement of an Islamic society in the Indian subcontinent. His political life, as with al-Banna's, began with a struggle against British colonial rule. He was a member of the pan-Islamic Khilafah movement, which combined support for the Ottoman caliphate with anti-colonial agitation.[17] But like al-Banna, Mawdudi's anti-colonialism was hitched to a higher purpose, the revival of Islam and its eventual global supremacy. In his early work, Mawdudi expressed his vision of an Islamic revival in strident revolutionary terms. In his first book, *Jihad Fi Sabillilah* (*Jihad in Islam*), written in the late 1920s, he wrote:

> Islam requires the earth – not just a portion, but the whole planet … because the entire mankind should benefit from … 'Islam' which is the programme of well-being for all humanity … Islam does not intend to confine this revolution to a single state or a few countries; the aim of Islam is to bring about a universal revolution.[18]

The achievement of the Islamic world system, he stated, requires Muslims to 'press into service all [the] forces which can bring about a revolution … [The] composite term for the use of all these forces,' he asserted, 'is "*Jihad*"'.[19] These forces include 'the power of the sword', physical exertion, the expenditure of one's wealth, and also the potency of speech and writing. Mawdudi viewed the 'ideological' *jihad* as the means to change people's outlooks culminating in 'a mental revolution' that would signify Islam's triumph over non-Islamic values, concepts and ideas. Such a triumph is especially pertinent given Mawdudi's concept of the Islamic state as 'an ideological state', as opposed to a nation state.[20] The ideological state, for Mawdudi, is defined by its acceptance of the *shari'a*, whose sphere of activity is not restricted to politics, or even law, but 'coexistent with the whole of human life'.[21]

In 1941, Mawdudi established Jama'at-i-Islami to realise his vision of an Islamic state on the Indian subcontinent as a prelude to an Islamic world order. Through Jama'at, he sought to produce a cadre of

> Muslim administrators, Muslim managers, Muslim scientists, Muslim philosophers, Muslim economists, Muslim bankers, and jurists … [that

> would] act as the vanguard of the movement for the reconstruction of modern thought … [leading] the struggle against the prevailing secular ideologies and power structures.[22]

As Mumtaz Ahmad observes, although Mawdudi described the goal of an Islamic world order in revolutionary terms, the bottom-up means he advocated were rather more 'evolutionary'.[23]

After the creation of Pakistan in 1947, which Mawdudi opposed, he became more pragmatic in approach and under his leadership Jama'at embraced Pakistani electoral politics. This reflected similar developments in the Ikhwan in Egypt, where some of its leaders, such as Umar al-Tilmisani, began to publicly eschew violence and adopt an accommodationist position regarding secular politics.[24] From the 1960s, thousands of party activists and sympathisers were appointed in the civil service and educational institutions, exerting a mild influence on the Pakistani government and, under General Zia ul-Haq, its programme to Islamise the state and so uslims and Zia's decree, ten years later, prohibiting the Ahmadis from describing themselves ciety.[25] This included the 1974 state declaration of the Ahmadi sect as non-M as Muslim and chanting the call to prayer.[26]

Both the Ikhwan and Jama'at-i-Islami have failed to make inroads in their respective countries as their founders had hoped for. Since President Nasser's clampdown on the Ikhwan in the mid-1950s, the group has suffered state repression for decades. After the 2011 'Arab Spring', the Ikhwan's political arm, the Freedom and Justice Party, won the country's first democratic elections with Mohammed Morsi elected as president. But, in 2013, on the back of public protests against Morsi's rule, the military ousted Morsi and the Ikhwan is once again subject to harsh state repression. Jama'at-i-Isami has periodically been repressed by the Pakistani government, but when it has participated in elections, it has failed to capture the popular vote.

Nonetheless, the success of the Ikhwan and Jama'at lies in their resilience and expansion beyond their respective home bases. The Ikhwan now has a global presence. According to Mohamed Mahdi Akef, a former supreme guide of the Egyptian Ikhwan, it is active in 70 countries.[27] Jama'at, while less expansionary, has a significant presence in South Asia. Both have played a key role in establishing Islamic networks across Europe and America comprising mosques, charities, advocacy groups and other organisations.

Contemporary classifications and conceptions

The Ikhwan and Jama'at are sometimes described as two distinct movements due to their particular historical origins and the national and ethnic composition of their original membership. But they are sometimes grouped together, by both Muslim and non-Muslim commentators alike, as one overarching movement with a global presence. The main reason for this, as a recent Pew Forum report contends, is that they share a 'political ideology … that calls for the establishment of a distinctly Islamic system of government', as well as a methodology, inspired by al-Banna and Mawdudi that emphasises institution building and active participation in politics.[28]

Some prominent Muslim activists and intellectuals, including those linked to Brotherhood- or Jama'at-related groups, refer to the 'Islamic revivalist movement' or, more simply, 'the Islamic Movement'. The defining feature of the Movement for them is the collective dedication to what they view as a restoration or revival of Islam to the forefront of social and political life. Muhammad Abdul Bari, former chairman of the East London Mosque and former secretary general of the Muslim Council of Britain, for example, describes the Islamic Movement as

> a generic term for groups that do not restrict religion to personal piety but see Islam having its own unique social and political message. Examples include the Muslim Brotherhood in Egypt and the Jamaat-e-Islami in South Asia. They are described by their detractors as 'Islamist' or 'fundamentalist'. Their off-shoot groups in Europe have been active in community work, establishing mosques and research centres, publishing houses and journals.[29]

Emphasising its 'political message', Kalim Siddiqui, the late leader of the Muslim Parliament in Britain, defined the Islamic Movement as a global phenomenon that 'consists of all those Muslims who, through individual or organized effort of whatever nature sanctioned by Islam, are trying to contribute towards the eventual establishment of one or more Islamic States under a *khalifah/imam* anywhere in the world'.[30]

Yusuf al-Qaradawi, the Egypt-born Muslim scholar and cleric best known for his popular Al Jazeera television programme *'ash-Shari'a wal-Hayat'* ('*Shari'a* and Life'), defines the Islamic Movement as

> the organised and collective work that is undertaken by the people, to restore Islam to the leadership of society and to the helm of life … The Islamic Movement has come into existence to *revive* Islam [*tajid al-Islam*] and *reinstate* it at the helm of life once again, after removing it obstacles from its path.[31]

Al-Qaradawi distinguishes the Islamic Movement from the Muslim Brotherhood. The Movement, he asserts, is more 'general and all-embracing'; the Brotherhood – i.e. the Cairo-based Ikhwan – is but one movement within 'the Movement'.[32]

Western observers of the Ikhwan, Jama'at, and their legacy groups in the West tend to refer to them not in terms of the Islamic Movement, but as *Islamists* of a certain kind. These appellations include 'non-violent Islamists' (which emphasises their eschewal of violent methods in the West), 'gradualist Islamists' (which emphasises their incremental approach through institution building) and 'participationist' Islamists (which emphasises their willingness to participate in electoral, democratic politics). In doing so, they emphasise the political aspect of al-Banna and Mawdudi's shared long-term vision of an Islamic social order.

The term 'Islamism' dates back several centuries, and was used interchangeably with Islam by some European scholars.[33] But after 9/11, the predominant usage of the term came to refer to violent, terroristic groups. So, it is perhaps unsurprising that Islamists are often characterised in terms of whether they adopt violent or non-violent methods to achieve the goal that allegedly links them all, a global Islamic state. Patrick Sookhdeo, for example, writes,

> What sets non-violent Islamists apart from the violent groups is their doctrine of gradualism, which includes a tactical willingness to work within the legal system of their countries in order to further their strategic goals. Their tactical goals include the Islamization of Muslim societies at the grass-roots level, the building of a committed vanguard of elites and the mobilisation of the masses. Gradualist movements advocate a comprehensive multi-faceted system of *jihad*, which includes struggle on all fronts – economic, cultural, political – in order to mobilise Muslims and gather Islamic strength for the final struggle, which might include the use of force.[34]

Sookhdeo refers to the Muslim Brotherhood as an example of the non-violent, 'gradualist mainstream'. How the British government views Islamism also pivots on this distinction between violent and non-violent kinds. Its counter-radicalisation strategy, Prevent, states, 'Some militant Islamists would endorse violence or terrorism to achieve their aims. Many Islamists do not'.[35] The key debate on Islamism in Britain today, as discussed later in the book, concerns the relationship between non-violent and violent extremism.

The Ihkwan and Jamaat are sometimes viewed through the prism of a taxonomy that distinguishes Islamists in terms of their participation within or rejection of democratic political systems. The willingness to use violence or not is a secondary concern, a level of classification subordinated to the primary level concerning attitudes to electoral politics. The 'rejectionist' camp is divided between violent and non-violent Islamists, and the 'participationist' camp is viewed as non-violent. Jeffrey Bale articulates such a taxonomy, referring to the Islamist groups operating in the West, as follows:

1 'Rejectionists' that openly disparage the institutions and values of Western host societies … [whose] ultimate aims [are] to destroy those societies. These rejectionist groups can be further subdivided into a) ostensibly non-violent groups (like Hizb al-Tahrir al-Islami, which is awaiting the restoration of the Caliphate before initiating 'offensive jihad'), and b) violent jihadist groups [transnational, such as al-Qaeda, or nationally

focused, such as Hamas], whether these are linked to wider networks or are so-called 'self-starter' cells; and

2 Non-violent 'participationist' groups that engage in lobbying, organizing, and publishing and at times even run for elections (such as the representatives of groups linked to the Muslim Brotherhood, South Asian Mawdudist networks, and Turkish groups linked to the AKP such as Milli Goruş).[36]

The notion of a participationist or revivalist Islamist movement in the West has been most extensively written about by Lorenzo Vidino. In his view, such a movement exists 'composed of the networks that trace their roots to the Muslim Brotherhood and other Islamist groups [including Jama'at-i-Islami] that, while publicly purporting to support democracy and the integration of Muslim communities within the European mainstream, quietly work to radicalise Europe's Muslim population'.[37] Vidino acknowledges that the 'legacy groups' of Jama'at-i-Islami have a distinct cultural and historical trajectory from those of the Muslim Brotherhood, but argues that they have been integral to the Ikhwan's transformation from a nationally focused organisation based in Cairo to 'an informal transnational movement' with a presence throughout Europe and North America.[38]

In order to distinguish this movement in the West from the original Egyptian organisation, and to identify it as 'an ideological movement that transcends formal affiliation', Vidino refers to it as the 'New Western Muslim Brotherhood'.[39] He cites the statements of various Brotherhood leaders to support his view of the global Muslim Brotherhood as an ideological movement rather than an international organisation.[40] Youssef Nada, formerly the Brotherhood's chief finance officer, for example, describes the Brotherhood as a 'common way of thinking'.[41] Mohammed Akef, a former *murshid* of the Egyptian branch of the Brotherhood, states, 'We do not have an international organization; we have an organization through our perception of things'.[42]

Vidino argues that 'there is no formal Muslim Brotherhood organization in the West … The idea of creating a global movement rather than a formally structured organisation has been present since the early days'.[43] The groups under the movement's broad umbrella, he claims, 'work according to a common vision but in complete operational independence'.[44] He elaborates his understanding of the movement as follows:

> There are consultations and constant communication, but each is free to pursue its goals as it deems appropriate. Therefore the international Muslim Brotherhood is today most properly identified not as a group or even a loose federation, but simply as an ideological movement, in which different branches choose their own tactics to achieve their short-term goals in complete independence. What binds them together is a deep belief in Islam as a comprehensive way of life that, in the long term, they

> hope to turn into a political system using different methods in different times and places.[45]

This characterisation of the Muslim Brotherhood as a global movement has been criticised by Steven Merley, founder and editor of *The Global Muslim Brotherhood Daily Watch*. Merley sees no evidence for the assertion that the Brotherhood is simply an ideological movement whose entities operate completely independently. '[T]he Brotherhood,' he counters,

> is, at it [sic] heart, *a covert organization* and their [sic] are few reasons to accept and many reasons not to accept their statements about themselves at face value. Where actual evidence exists, it points to a far more sophisticated organizational structure than admitted to by the Muslim Brotherhood itself.[46]

The evidence that Merley refers to includes documents written in Arabic released as part of the Holy Land Foundation terrorism financing trial in the United States, which ended in 2008 with the conviction of five prominent American Muslim Brotherhood leaders.[47] He argues,

> Prior to the release of the documents, it was clear that the various organizations and individuals comprising the U.S. Brotherhood were networking extensively with each other but the existence of leadership structures could only be the subject of speculation. Now however, three of the documents shed light on such structures, at least as they existed at the end of the 1980s and beginning of the 1990s.[48]

These leadership structures, Merley asserts, are composed of both covert and public entities. The covert entities include the position of a General Guide for the entire U.S. Muslim Brotherhood, a Shura Council (advisory body) and various committees.[49] These appear in a document dated December 1988, entitled *Preliminary vision for preparing future leadership*, along with a list of organisations, which Merley says includes 'almost all of the known Brotherhood organizations such as the Islamic Society of North America (ISNA), the North American Islamic Trust (NAIT) and the Muslim Student Association (MSA)'.[50] Together, these covert and public entities are listed in the document as the 'Apparatuses', which, Merley says, is 'a common word used by the Brotherhood for its organizations'.[51]

Another of the documents Merley refers to, written by Mohamed Akram and dated 22 May 1991, is entitled *An Explanatory Memorandum, On the General Strategic Goal for the Group in North America*. It contains a similar list of organisations, explicitly referred to as belonging to the Muslim Brotherhood or the Brotherhood's 'friends'. These are acknowledged in the document as part of 'the global Islamic Movement' working towards the goal of a 'global Islamic state'.[52] It also describes a strategy for the Brotherhood in

North America to attain this goal in terms of a 'Civilization-Jihadist Process' for establishing Islam as a 'civilization alternative'. It states:

> The Ikhwan [Muslim Brotherhood] must understand that their work in America is *a kind of grand Jihad in eliminating and destroying the Western civilization from within* and 'sabotaging' its miserable house by their hands and the hands of the believers so that it is eliminated and God's religion [Islam] is made victorious over all other religions.[53]

Seemingly in support of Merley's contention, this document states that the 'heart and core' of the Brotherhood's strategy for the United States is a shift from the prioritisation of ideas to that of organisations.[54] But the claim that these documents demonstrate a covert leadership structure to the Muslim Brotherhood in the United States or globally is not settled by the evidence Merley puts forward.

Akram's memorandum makes a clear distinction between, on the one hand, a desired structure of organisations, including specific roles for each organisational component, and, on the other, already existing public Brotherhood organisations – referred to as 'seeds' – which may or may not come to function within this desired structure as its components in their respective roles. The document actually concedes that 'the global Movement has not succeeded yet in "distributing roles" to its Branches' and it acknowledges that the Brotherhood organisations are *not* working 'according to one plan'. As such, the strategy outlined for non-violent *jihad* in America resembles not so much an executable programme for an established organisational entity – a 'covert organization' – than an expression of desire for the construction of *precisely* such an entity, referred to in the document as a 'Group of organizations'.

The 'westward expansion' of the Muslim Brotherhood network

Merley's claim that the global Muslim Brotherhood is a covert organisation may not be supported by the evidence he presents. But a high degree of organisation and coordination dating back to the early 1970s between cadres from the Ikhwan and Jama'at in Europe and North America, resulting in the creation of numerous institutions, supports the view of a revivalist movement in the West. This trans-ethnic networking, the plans that were produced through such networking, the consistency of the goals and methods these plans expressed, and the fruits of such plans, all testify to the emergence of the global Muslim Brotherhood as an organised movement spanning the United States and Europe, including Britain.

Ian Johnson provides the most illuminating account of this networked 'westward expansion' of the global Muslim Brotherhood, incorporating Jama'at-i-Islami, in a series of articles and a book, *A Mosque in Munich: Nazis, the CIA and the Rise of the Muslim Brotherhood in the West*.[55] The first meeting dedicated to 'forming a framework for Islamism in Europe',[56] he observes, was held in London in 1973. Present at this meeting was Ghaleb Himmat, the newly appointed head of the Munich mosque – which Johnson says was to become 'the most important Muslim Brotherhood mosque in Europe' – and Khurshid Ahmad, a senior figure in Jama'at-i-Islami Pakistan who, in the same year, established one of Britain's most prominent Islamic institutions, the Islamic Foundation.

In 1977, a follow-up meeting was held in Lugano, Switzerland, to 'set up a structure to guide the growth of political Islam in Europe and the United States'.[57] Amongst the 30 or so Islamist figures attending the meeting alongside Himmat and Ahmad, Johnson notes, were Yusuf al-Qaradawi, widely considered as the spiritual guide of the Brotherhood, Youseff Nada and Isamail al-Faruqi. To give the nascent Western Brotherhood movement some 'ideological firepower', the group quickly established a number of Islamic think tanks, the most important being the International Institute of Islamic Thought (IIIT), established by Faruqi in 1981.[58]

During the 1970s, building on the initial organisational efforts of the Mawdudists in the 1960s and early 1970s, an Islamic revivalist network transcending ethnic lines began to form across Britain and continental Europe.[59] In 1973, the same year that the Islamic Foundation was established, Europe's first '*umma*-centric' Islamist organisation was created in London, with the support of Saudi Arabia and other Muslim states: the Islamic Council of Europe (ICE). Several years later, in an early sign of collaboration between Ikhwani and Jama'ati activists, Ahmad served on the executive board of ICE alongside Hasan al-Banna's son-in-law, Said Ramadan. Further consolidating the relationship between the Ikhwan and Jama'at groups, in 1982, Ahmad and another Jama'at activist and Islamic Foundation colleague, Khurram Murad, joined the governing council of the Brotherhood-dominated Munich mosque, which Johnson says played a key role in the growth of the European Brotherhood network.[60]

Throughout the 1970s, ICE organised a number of meetings and conferences to bring Islamist thinkers and activists of various nationalities together to create, in ICE leader Salem Azzam's words, a 'theoretical basis for an *Umma*-wide political movement'.[61] But the basis of this movement did not merely consist in the theoretical justification for the global politicisation of Islam. It also included the development of practical plans for what some observers describe as the 'Islamisation' of the West, beginning with the insulation of Muslim communities. In July 1978, ICE organised a conference on Muslim minorities in non-Muslim states where, Sookhdeo says, 'a careful and deliberate strategy by certain Muslim leaders' was presented that urged Muslims to resist assimilation and organise themselves according to Islamic principles. 'The ultimate goal of this strategy,' he states, 'is that the Muslims should become a majority and the entire nation be governed according to Islam.'[62]

Some observers note a continuity of such strategies for Islam's conquest of the West, including a plan detailed in documents seized by the Swiss police in

November 2001 from the home of Nada in Lugano, where he was director of the Brotherhood-created al-Taqwa Bank.[63] Self-described as 'a global vision of a worldwide strategy for Islamic policy',[64] *The Project*, as it became known in counter-terrorism circles, dates back to 1982.[65] It amounts to a fairly comprehensive blueprint for 'civilisational' *jihad* with the long-term goal, expressed in its own words, of 'establish[ing] an Islamic power [government] on the earth'.[66] Consistent with the Brotherhood's gradualist approach, this document states that its goal of establishing an Islamic state must be worked towards 'in parallel with gradual efforts aimed at gaining control of local power centers through institutional action'.[67]

The Project's contents resonate with both the 1991 document and with al-Qaradawi's writings, particularly a treatise published in 1990 entitled *Priorities for the Islamic Movement in the Coming Phase*, which Vidino describes as 'the most recent manifesto of the Islamist revivalist movement'.[68] In this document, al-Qaradawi calls for a reinstatement of the Islamic caliphate and introduces a *modus operandi* for the movement, which includes strengthening the *umma* intellectually and politically towards this long-term goal.

Al-Qaradawi is considered by many observers as the most important intellectual figure of the global Muslim Brotherhood. Vidino describes him as 'the undisputed spiritual leader of the global and Western Brotherhood'.[69] '[C]onsistent ideological references and any organizational link to him,' he writes, 'are good indicators of an affiliation' to the movement.[70] For al-Qaradawi, Muslim settlement in the West is a religious necessity and obligation for the global 'Islamic Movement', leading to the unification of the *umma* and, ultimately, the global supremacy of the *shari'a*. An organised voice, he urges, is important to convince Western leaders that Muslims in Muslim-majority countries have a right to live by *shari'a* values and tenets.[71] But settlement in the West, for al-Qaradawi, is not just a vehicle for the 'true' Islamisation of Muslim-majority countries – it is also a vehicle for the Islamisation of the relatively new host societies.

The ultimate goal of al-Qaradawi's strategy in Muslim-minority lands, to which Vidino refers, is nothing less than Islamic conquest.[72] 'We will conquer Europe, we will conquer America,' the cleric exclaims, 'not through the sword but through Dawa. Dawa will work through Islamic groups set up by Brotherhood supporters.'[73] Al-Qaradawi does not merely advocate the 'preservation' of Muslim identity and influence upon Western governmental policy in the interests of the *umma*. He calls for a new kind of *jihad* relevant to the predicament of Muslims living as minorities in the West, making it clear that no form of *jihad*, including the non-violent type, can be detached from the overall effort to universalise the *Shari'a*.[74]

Vidino and Johnson characterise the Muslim Brotherhood in the West as pragmatically focused on its short- and medium-term goals of, in Johnson's words, 'dominat[ing] the West's Muslim communities', rather than its long-term goal of 'Islamiciz[ing] mainstream society', since the latter is simply 'too ambitious a task at this point'.[75] Its primary means to do this, they argue, has been through institution building.

Indeed, there is an uncanny continuity in aspirations and methods expressed in *The Project*, in al-Qaradawi's *Priorities* and in Akram's 1991 memorandum. There is also a recognisable correspondence between what these documents advocate and what has actually taken place on the ground in Europe and North America in recent decades. As Vidino notes, the aforementioned plans 'seem to perfectly describe what has been the *modus operandi* of the New Western Brotherhood over the last twenty to thirty years'.[76] He observes that the Brothers have 'created a sprawling network of Islamic organizations devoted to all the possible needs of the Western Muslim population, from the purely religious to the more mundane'.[77] The most important of these in Europe include the Federation of Islamic Organizations in Europe – widely considered as the Brotherhood's key institution in the West – as well as the European Council for Fatwa and Research, led by al-Qaradawi, which dispenses legal guidance for Muslims living in the Muslim-minority context of today's Europe.

The Islamic revival in Britain

Revivalist or participationist Islamism in Britain is often referred to in terms of two separate but related strands of Islamism associated with the Muslim Brotherhood and Jama'at-i-Islami. Michael Whine, for example, identifies two 'streams of Islamist ideology' related to these groups as having the most active foreign influence upon 'British Islam'.[78] In a 2009 Policy Exchange report critical of the British government's engagement with certain Muslim organisations, its authors Shiraz Maher and Martyn Frampton analyse Islamism in Britain along similar dual lines:

> Broadly speaking, Islamist groups currently operating in Britain originate from two major revivalist networks that emerged in the early twentieth century: the Muslim Brotherhood, which started in Egypt, and the Jamaat-e-Islami, whose origins lie in colonial India.[79]

Maher and Frampton identify a number of organisations in Britain as part of each movement. Under the heading of Jama'at-i-Islami, they include the Islamic Foundation, which they say was established by Jama'at activists to promote 'Islamist ideas throughout the West' and support 'the Jamaat's global political activism'.[80] They also include the Markfield Institute of Higher Education (MIHE), which they describe as operated by the Foundation to 'develop the Jamaat's political ideas'.[81] Under the heading of the Muslim Brotherhood, Maher and Frampton include the Muslim Association of Britain (MAB), established in 1997 by the former Brotherhood spokesman in Europe, Kamal al-Helbawy; the Cordoba Foundation, established in 2005 and directed by former MAB secretary general, Anas Altikriti; and the British Muslim Initiative, formed in 2006 by a group of former MAB leaders, including Altikriti.[82]

Other analysts similarly divide revivalist groups in Britain. They do so by emphasising the historical and organisational connections between certain actors in Britain and the Ikhwan or Jama'at. But the point is sometimes made – though more often implied – that these two distinct streams of Islamist activism comprise one overarching movement in Britain. For, as numerous observers recognise, individuals and organisations across Jama'at-Ikhwan lines have collaborated on various projects and, broadly speaking, share an ideological outlook.

The Mawdudists

The oldest global Muslim Brotherhood groups in Britain have their origins in Jama'at-i-Islami. Jørgen S. Nielsen identifies four British Muslim organisations as developed by Jama'at. In addition to the Islamic Foundation, these are the UK Islamic Mission (UKIM), founded in 1962; the Muslim Educational Trust (MET), created by UKIM in 1966; and Young Muslims UK (YM), an offshoot of the Foundation, established in 1984.[83] Gilles Kepel similarly describes the Islamic Foundation, UKIM and YM as 'belonging to Mawdudi's Jama'at-i Islami movement' in Britain.[84] Nielsen describes the four organisations as 'Jama'at-related' to emphasise a lack of formal ties to the Pakistani parent organisation.[85]

Ron Geaves supports this view, adding, 'These organizations have close informal links with Jamaat-i Islami in the [Indian] sub-continent but their allegiance is increasingly given to the "Islamic Movement" worldwide', which he recognises as being comprised from both Jama'at-i-Islami and the Muslim Brotherhood.[86] In addition to those listed by Nielsen, Anthony McRoy describes the 'Mawdudist network in Britain' as including the East London Mosque; the Islamic Society of Britain (ISB); Islamic Forum Europe (IFE); and the Young Muslims Organisation (YMO).[87] Each of these individual organisations has been described by political observers as Islamist or having Islamist connections.

UKIM, for example, has been described by McRoy as the 'parent Mawdudist group in Britain',[88] and by Vidino as the 'original embryo of the Mawdudist network'.[89] Kepel refers to the organisation's literature in describing its goals and methods: UKIM, he notes, defines itself as 'an ideological organization. It believes that Islam is a comprehensive way of life which must be translated into action in all sphere of life'.[90] The purpose of UKIM, according to its constitution, he observes, is 'to establish [an] Islamic social order in the United Kingdom'.[91] Geaves acknowledges the practical constraints upon the organisation to transform Britain into an Islamic state and suggests that for this reason it focuses upon education and *da'wa* within Muslim communities aimed at the preservation of Muslim identity.[92]

In order to widen its appeal, Kepel writes, UKIM established MET and the Islamic Foundation. Geaves observes that MET 'is the oldest national Muslim educational organization in Britain dealing with the concerns of

Muslims in regard to the education of their children'.[93] Kepel describes MET as engaged in the 'Islamization' of education in state schools.[94] MET has been active in providing teachers for Islamic studies in state schools, producing literature for use by teachers around the world. 'Its many publications,' Kepel writes, 'define the content and form of education designed to perpetuate a specific Islamic cultural identity and to prevent the assimilation of Muslim children into British society'.[95] MET is led by Ghulam Sarwar who, as Kepel recognises, has devoted 'his energies to the propagation of Islam throughout the world'.[96]

Kepel describes the Islamic Foundation as the 'secular arm' of 'the Islamist movement inspired by Mawdudi's Jama'at-i Islami' and as 'one of the most important centres for the propagation of militant Sunni Islamist thinking in the world'.[97] The Foundation – in addition to housing MIHE, which offers degrees and diplomas as an Associate College of the University of Gloucestershire – incorporates a think tank, the Policy Research Centre, which aims to shape government policy on matters relating to Muslims in Britain, and a publishing house, currently incorporated as Kube Publishing Ltd. Since 1976, the Foundation has also housed an Islamic Economics Unit for the promotion of Islamic economics, finance and banking as both a topic of academic study and as a commercial practice.

The Foundation's production and dissemination of pro-Mawdudi and pro-Qutb material, Kepel asserts, has exerted a significant influence on the development of Muslim identity in Britain, particularly amongst Muslim youth.[98] Following Kepel, Vidino describes the Foundation as the 'crown jewel' of the 'Mawdudist network' and 'a beacon for the spread of Islamist thought in the West'.[99] Whine writes in similar terms of the Foundation as 'the UK center' for Jama'at-i-Islami.[100] Kepel remarks that the training courses provided by the Foundation for public officials 'constitute a vital element in the [Islamist] movement's strategy aimed at achieving hegemony in the Islamic field'.[101] He notes that the first two directors – including Khurshid Ahmad – were officers of Jama'at-i-Islami. Today, Ahmad is vice president of Jama'at-i-Islami Pakistan and remains a trustee of the Foundation, after recently retiring as its long-time chair. As noted above, he is seen as a key figure in the development of the global Muslim Brotherhood in Europe.

Another key figure of the Islamic Foundation recognised as having played a significant role in the development of Islamism in Britain and Europe is the late Khurram Murad. In 1978, Murad, became the director general of the Foundation, which, he asserted, 'perpetually aims at Islamic resurgence in the world'.[102] Murad's understanding of the Foundation's mission in Britain was framed within his concept of the Islamic Movement, which he described as 'an organised struggle to change the existing society into an Islamic society based on the Qur'an and the Sunna, and make Islam, which is a code for the entire life, supreme and dominant'.[103]

Murad has been described as 'the main ideologue' of *da'wa* in Britain.[104] According to Nina Wiedl, Murad shared the Muslim Brotherhood's understanding of *da'wa* as an 'inherently political activity ... leading to the eventual establishment of an Islamic state'.[105] She observes Murad's description of *da'wa* as having two objectives. These are, she writes, firstly, to preserve Muslim identity in a secular society whose values are deemed threatening to Islam as a 'way of life', and, secondly, to spread Islam beyond Muslim communities to the West's native non-Muslim population.[106] Wiedl recognises the broad correspondence between these two objectives and al-Qaradawi's vision for the West. These objectives also align with the two-stage strategy for Muslims in Europe expressed by Muhammad Ali Kettani at the ICE conference held in 1978,[107] referred to by Patrick Sookhdeo as a plan for the Islamic control of Europe's social structures.[108]

In the words of Zahoor Qureshi, Murad established YM as the vehicle to carry out the mission of 'present[ing] Islam to the British population as an alternative way of life'.[109] Its founding committee was trained at the Islamic Foundation.[110] McRoy observes from the organisation's own literature that it supports *jihad*, seen as a war against the *kuffar,*[111] in Afghanistan, Bosnia, Kashmir and Palestine, as well as the restoration of the caliphate.[112] YM's national leader was Murad's son, Farooq, a founding member of the Muslim Council of Britain (MCB), of which he was director general between June 2010 and June 2014.

The Islamic Forum of Europe (IFE) was created in 1988, by the Bangledeshi wing of Jama'at-i-Islami.[113] Journalist Andrew Gilligan describes IFE as a 'secretive, fundamentalist political network'.[114] The blog *Harry's place* refers to IFE as the 'British section' of Jama'at-i-Islami.[115] Located at the East London Mosque, IFE is a politically active organisation and was instrumental in Respect Party George Galloway's 2005 election in the London Borough of Bethnal Green and Bow.[116] Gilligan claims to have obtained IFE documents that explicitly state its strategic objective as 'the establishment of a global society, the Khilafah [caliphate] ... comprised of individuals who live by the principles of ... the Shari'ah'. In these documents, IFE states that it is dedicated to changing the 'very infrastructure of [British] society, its institutions, its culture, its political order and its creed ... from ignorance to Islam'.[117]

IFE's 'parent organisation', the East London Mosque (ELM), is also considered by numerous analysts as a key institution within the Mawdudist stream of the global Muslim Brotherhood. It was the meeting place for the Mawdudist intellectuals who formed the first Islamist organisation in Britain, UKIM.[118] In recent years it has courted controversy over its invitation of radical preachers, including the now-deceased al-Qaeda ideologue Anwar al-Awlaki.[119] It is one of a number of mosques allegedly controlled by the Mawdudist movement, which Vidino claims to host sermons and lectures proclaiming 'the superiority of Islam and the need to turn Britain, as well as the rest of the world, into an Islamic state'.[120]

Arguably the most important Muslim organisation in Britain, the Muslim Council of Britain (MCB), was established in 1997 in the wake of the Rushdie

Affair. Designed, in founder Iqbal Sacranie's words, to present 'a united Muslim voice', the MCB was embraced by Conservative home secretary Michael Howard and, after Labour's victory in 1997, his successor Jack Straw as the key interlocutor for Muslims in Britain.[121] McRoy states that it is not accurate to designate the MCB as a 'pro-*Jama'at* front' due to the diversity of its affiliates.[122] However, its formation, he writes, should be seen as the 'means to secure the dominance of Mawdudist ideology in British Islam'.[123] Vidino concurs, noting that 'the leadership of the organization has traditionally been dominated by individuals from the Mawdudist network whose political and organizational skills have allowed them to overshadow other trends'.[124]

Other analysts agree. Journalist Martin Bright, for example, writes that the MCB leadership and some of its affiliates 'sympathise with and have links to' Jama'at-i-Islami.[125] Bright quotes Abdul-Rehman Malik, contributing editor of Muslim magazine *Q-News,* as saying that, 'Many of the affiliates of The Muslim Council of Britain are inspired by Maududi's ideology'.[126] In written evidence submitted to the Home Affairs Select Committee, The Henry Jackson Society, a London-based think tank, states that the MCB is 'closely aligned' to Jama'at-i-Islami.[127] It also refers to a Communities and Local Government document from March 2009, which asserts that Jama'at-i-Islami 'helped to create and subsequently dominate the leadership of the MCB'.[128]

But it is not just critical observers who note the Jama'ati influence on the MCB leadership. Mohammed Abdul Aziz, a former adviser to the MCB's first secretary general, Iqbal Sacranie, states, 'A large part of the influential part of the [MCB] structure consists of people who come from a Jama'ati/Ikhwani background of some sort', adding that the MCB has become more Jama'at-dominated since Sacranie's departure.[129] When asked how he makes that assessment, he refers to 'the senior echelons of the structure, the senior political structure, the secretary general, the treasurer, the chairs of the various committees'. Abdul Aziz says he relinquished the desire for an Islamic state almost a decade ago, but still describes himself as a 'Jama'ati', since he grew up in 'the Jama'ati system'.

The Ikhwanis

Similarly to how Britain's 'Mawdudist movement' is written about independently from key Arab Muslim figures and their associated organisations, the Muslim Brotherhood in Britain is sometimes written about as an Arab Islamist movement distinct from the Mawdudists, albeit connected to them, comprised of specific organisations. This is a narrower concept of the Brotherhood than that of Vidino's 'New Western Brotherhood', for it emphasises connections to the original organisation of the Ikhwan in Cairo.

The Muslim Brotherhood in Britain, according to Michael Whine, operates through 'a series of interlocking companies' of mainly Arab origin. These, he says, include the Muslim Association of Britain (MAB), the Muslim Welfare

Trust, Interpal, the Palestine Return Centre, and the Institute of Islamic Political Thought (IIPT).[130] Whine describes the MAB as the most important of these organisations. He also refers to it as 'in effect *the* MB [Muslim Brotherhood] of Britain'.[131] Vidino prefers to describe the MAB as 'a quintessentially New Western Brotherhood organization in its origins, connections and ideology', which highlights its operational independence from the original organisation while acknowledging its historical and ideological relationship with it.[132] He notes that the MAB is a 'key member' of the Federation of Islamic Organisations in Europe (FIOE), 'the Western Brothers' Brussels-based pan-European organization'.[133]

The MAB's leading figures, including its founder and first president, Kamal al-Helbawy, are commonly recognised as being related to the original Muslim Brotherhood organisation. Described by one young activist as the 'grand sheikh of the Islamic movement in the UK', al-Helbawy arrived in Britain in 1994 to establish a media and communications centre for the Cairo-based group.[134] According to John Ware, al-Helbawy came with a political vision, which he expressed in typical Islamist terms, stating, 'This religion that is Islam shall govern the whole universe, the Islamic civilisation should rule and govern and direct people in every walk of life, but not be governed by others.'[135] After a disagreement with the Ikhwani leadership in Egypt, al-Helbawy abandoned the media centre project to establish the MAB, which David Rich says 'has retained a strong Arab influence and has come to be regarded as the British branch of the MB [Muslim Brotherhood] in all but name'.[136] Rich writes that, through the MAB, al-Helbawy has done more than any other to push the Brotherhood 'into the public arena'.[137] One of the MAB's most commonly acknowledged successes was its role, as part of the Stop the War Coalition, in the organisation of public protests in 2002 and 2003 against the allied invasion of Iraq.

Another of the MAB's former leaders is Anas Altikriti, the son of Omar Altikriti, a prominent Ikhwan leader in Iraq. As Maher and Frampton observe, during Altikriti's tenure as MAB president in 2004, the MAB issued a statement that acknowledged its respect for the 'humane notions and principles of the Muslim Brotherhood, who [sic] has proven to be an inspiration to Muslims, Arab and otherwise for many decades'.[138] The statement also acknowledged the MAB's independence from the 'opinion and line of the Muslim Brotherhood' organisation. Supporting Vidino's notion of the global Muslim Brotherhood as an ideological movement, Maher and Frampton stress that while the MAB and other groups do not follow the orders of 'an Islamist equivalent of the Comintern' centred in Cairo, they may nevertheless be considered as 'in step with a broader movement, which adheres to Islamist ideology'.[139] Rich concurs with this view, writing:

> They are not yet at the state advocated by Kamal al-Helbawy of operating as an open organization under the MB [Muslim Brotherhood] name, but there is little attempt to disguise the fact that the MAB, BMI and other similar groupings are aligned with the MB *school of thought*, although not, it is often stressed, under its organizational direction.[140]

Altikriti established and currently directs the Cordoba Foundation, described by David Cameron in March 2008 as a 'front for the Muslim Brotherhood'.[141] Merley describes Altikriti as a 'UK Muslim Brotherhood leader'.[142] *The Telegraph*'s Andrew Gilligan refers to Altikriti as 'the key political lobbyist for the Muslim Brotherhood in Britain'.[143] Cameron, Merley and Gilligan's characterisations invoke a concept of the Brotherhood in the West that is more formally structured than that of the Brotherhood as ideological movement shared by Vidino and Maher and Frampton. In any case, the Cordoba Foundation is conceived as Islamist in negative, critical terms: Gilligan describes it as an 'extremist' group that seeks 'the creation of an Islamic dictatorship, or caliphate, in Europe';[144] Maher and Frampton describe the organisation less dramatically as an 'Islamist pressure group'.[145]

Journalist Innes Bowen writes that 'the Muslim Brotherhood's British story' is a 'tale of how a group of mainly Arab Islamist intellectuals attempted to win the leadership of Britain's predominantly South Asian, working-class Muslim population'.[146] Again, the Muslim Brotherhood is conceived as an organisational actor with its own historical trajectory, rooted in the politics of Arab North Africa, separate from but connected to Jama'at-i-Islami.

It is worth mentioning, as Bowen notes, that prior to the creation of the MAB, the Cordoba Foundation and other Arab-led organisations in the 1990s and 2000s, the first generally acknowledged Brotherhood organisations in Britain were established decades before. These include the Muslim Students Society, established in 1961, and the Federation of Student Islamic Societies (FOSIS), formed the year after. Both still exist today. Said Ramadan, writes Rich, was a regular visitor to FOSIS in the 1970s. The organisation, he asserts, 'has been courted constantly' by the Muslim Brotherhood.[147]

Two streams, one movement

The Brotherhood and Jama'at are usually written about as two distinct movements or 'streams' of Islamism. Ideological and organisational connections between the individuals and groups associated with them, however, are sometimes recognised, undermining the notion of their distinctness. According to Vidino, these connections, forged in the new milieus of Europe and North America, constitute the two movements into one overarching, 'multi-ethnic' movement that has become deterritorialised from the Middle East and the Indian subcontinent.[148] The Jama'at-i-Islami network, he writes, acts 'in close cooperation, if not almost complete symbiosis' with the European Brotherhood, of which, he asserts, it is a 'fully-fledged member'.[149] Vidino's contention that trans-ethnic networking is characteristic of the global Muslim Brotherhood is correct, but there are not many specific examples of such connections in Britain in the existing literature.

The singularity of the revivalist movement in Britain is more often implied with reference to the ideological connection between Ikhwani- and Jama'ati-associated groups. Maher and Frampton, after a discussion of the two strands of Islamism, imply a singular movement in their evaluation of the British government's engagement with the MCB and MAB: 'At the heart of *the* Islamist strategy,' they write, 'is a clear agenda: to mould the future direction of British Islam and the Muslim community in Britain.'[150] The Henry Jackson Society likewise clusters the MCB and MAB, since they both 'espouse a narrow form of political Islam inspired by the Islamist parties JI and MB'.[151] A similar view is expressed in the summary document of the British government's review of the Muslim Brotherhood, which clusters Ikhwani- and Jama'ati-associated groups together in what it calls '*the* UK Brotherhood movement'.[152] However, the document doesn't elaborate beyond this passing comment.

Supporting the view of an Islamist movement in Britain beyond specific associations with Mawdudi or al-Banna's original organisations, Gilles Kepel cites Manazir Ahsan, the former director general of the Islamic Foundation, as stating, 'We belong to *the international Islamic movement*, neither to Jamaat nor to Ikhwan nor to the Refah Party in Turkey – but all of them are our friends.'[153] Ahsan played a key role in the two precursor organisations to the MCB, the first of which was the United Kingdom Action Committee on Islamic Affairs (UKACIA), which lobbied Thatcher's government to ban Salman Rushdie's *The Satanic Verses.* Following UKACIA's dissolution after the Rushdie Affair, he was also involved in the group that sprang from it, the National Interim Committee on Muslim Unity (NICMU), which met in 1994 with the explicit intention of creating 'an organization that Whitehall might find appealing'.[154] Alongside Ahsan in NICMU, as a founding committee member, was a young activist, Abdullah Faliq, who today plays a leadership role in a number of allegedly Islamist organisations, including IFE and the Cordoba Foundation. Faliq's role as head of research for Altikriti's organisation, as well as his involvement in al-Helbawy's Centre for the Study of Terrorism, is an example, writes David Rich, of collaboration between the Muslim Brotherhood and Jama'at-i-Islami, whose activities, he says, 'often complement each other or *merge into one in Britain*'.[155]

Additional examples of networking between Ikhwani-Jama'ati-associated individuals in Britain are scarce in the existing literature. The following chapter aims to fill that gap. But several may be mentioned here. These include al-Helbawy's involvement in helping establish the MCB, and his status as a trustee of the Islamic Foundation.[156] From 1988 to 1994, al-Helbawy also worked as an adviser at Khurshid Ahmad's Institute of Policy Studies in Islamabad.[157] A more recent example is former MAB leader and Palestinian activist Azzam Tamimi's tenure as lecturer at the Markfield Institute of Higher Education from 2000 to 2004.[158]

Not only have certain individuals worked across ethnic divides within the network of Islamist organisations in Britain and abroad. Certain organisations have too. The Brotherhood's European body, the Federation of Islamic Organizations in Europe (FIOE), was located for some years with the Islamic Foundation at Markfield, 'the UK centre' for Jama'at-i-Islami.[159] This appears for some observers as further evidence of the blurring of the Brotherhood and Jama'at movements in the West into one. 'In this fashion,' writes Whine, 'the two organizations have advanced the ideological link made between them after the Second World War by [Brotherhood ideologue] Said Qutb and Mawlana Maududi.'[160]

Religious reform and 'post-Islamism'

Casting doubt on the notion that the Jama'ati and Ikhwani legacy groups in Britain are bonded today through an Islamist ideology, a small number of academics and other observers contend that they are experiencing a transformation in values, ideology and goals. This, they claim, is a result of exposure to the liberal democratic political and social environment in which they have developed for decades. One variant of this line of reasoning postulates a development in Muslim politics termed 'post-Islamism'. Another refers to the creation of a 'European Islam' or 'British Islam' in line with the continent's liberal democratic values.

Sara Silvestri, for example, claims that 'Europe's Islamist groups, which were once focused on their home country or region, are becoming ever more Europeanised and engaged in a process of integration'.[161] She acknowledges the existence of a Muslim Brotherhood network in Europe, but her view of this network is limited since she sees it as embodied by just one, albeit important, institution, FIOE. This body, she claims, is seriously engaged in a 'process of "Islamising" European culture, though without erasing it'.[162] Silvestri writes,

> it seems as if the original political ideology of the movement lost its significance once it had been transplanted to an alien environment, and needed to be re-elaborated in the light of the new context of Muslims being citizens of Europe.[163]

The source of her optimism that the Brotherhood's 'ideology has adapted to its context', however, is not an examination of specific activities or the network of numerous individuals and organisations that comprise the Brotherhood. It is, rather, a textual analysis of one document produced by FIOE, namely the Muslims of Europe Charter of 2008, which calls for full Muslim participation within European social and political life. Silvestri claims, 'there is no doubt that thirty years of the Muslim Brothers' presence in Europe have … modified the views and the objectives of the organisation'.[164] But this bold claim is not substantiated with a sufficiently thorough investigation of how the views and objectives of FIOE have supposedly changed. Participation in democratic politics does not necessarily imply the rejection of a long-term goal of society and state being governed by *shari'a.*

Silvestri's contention connects to a debate on the emergence of a distinctly 'European Islam', a concept originally expressed by Bassam Tibi in 1992.[165]

Tibi advocates a secularised, 'progressive' form of Islam, compatible with the West's liberal democratic culture and institutions. This idea of a European Islam relates to that of a 'British Islam', for underlying both concepts is the notion that Islam, in a Muslim-minority environment, is in the process of adapting to liberal, democratic values, as opposed to transforming or subverting them. Tibi himself does not claim that the allegedly Islamist organisations in Britain have transformed their values and strategies in line with liberal democratic values. But such a claim is sometimes made explicitly by academics and research institutions. For instance, a recent Pew report states that in Britain,

> two groups that were originally inspired by the Jama'at-i Islami – the Islamic Society of Britain and its youth wing, Young Muslims UK – are now, at least to some extent, its rivals. These newer organizations strive to promote a distinctly 'British Islam' that combines mainstream civic engagement with, as they see it, a robust and confident Muslim public identity.[166]

This notion of a 'British Islam' is supported by McRoy. He recognises that the ideologies of the Islamic Society of Britain (ISB), the Islamic Forum of Europe (IFE) and the Muslim Association of Britain (MAB) 'originally derive from the teachings of the Jama'at-i-Islami and the Ikhwan al-Muslimeen (Muslim Brotherhood)', but adds that 'their ideologies have been contextualised for the British situation'.[167] This, however, is an overly optimistic generalisation. While the ISB may have departed from its former Islamist leanings, the same cannot be said with such confidence for the MAB and IFE.

Supporting claims that the ISB has undergone a transformation away from Islamism, Dilwar Hussain, a former ISB president, describes a break with the MAB, IFE and UKIM, which were all part of a committee for revivalist groups in Britain to coordinate strategies and activities (see chapter 2 for more on this committee). In 2011, on realising that the ISB was in a 'radically different place' to that of the other groups vis-à-vis the kind of social transformation they sought and their relationship with the terms '*shari'a*' and 'Islamic state', Hussain formally withdrew the ISB from the committee.[168] Hussain is cited by some observers as an example of a 'post-Islamist' for his expressed rejection of formerly held Islamist positions on matters such as the need for an Islamic state.[169] They refer to Hussain's writings, where he calls for 'a shift towards a post-Islamist paradigm among activists in the West'.[170]

In addition to his former ISB role, Hussain was the founder and long-time director of the Policy Research Centre at the Islamic Foundation (2007–2013). Hussain's involvement with the Foundation is one of the main sources of the optimistic claim made by some academics regarding the Foundation's changing ideological outlook. In 2010, Sophie Gilliat-Ray claimed that in the past decade there has been 'a gradual transition towards a "reformist Islamism"' resulting from generational changes in the staffing of institutions such as the Foundation'.[171] To support her contention, she refers to an article of Seán McLoughlin, who asserts, 'Islamic intellectuals and activists in the West are increasingly evolving innovative, cosmopolitan and self-critical reformulations of their tradition.'[172] McLoughlin's statement is, in fact, a summary of Peter Mandaville's position, which is based upon interviews with Islamic Foundation staff members.

McLoughlin cautions that 'Mandaville perhaps overstates the widespread acceptance of such a trend in Britain, for any transformations at the IF [Islamic Foundation] are still, in my opinion, very much in transition.' Nevertheless, he argues – without qualification – that 'a critical mass hospitable to such perspectives has undoubtedly begun to emerge at the institution'.[173] McLoughlin notes that for a number of 'thirty somethings' in the Foundation's research units – presumably including Hussain – 'concepts such as "the Islamic movement" and "da'wa", are all now "up for grabs"'.[174] However, how this 'critical mass' is manifest within the organisation, strategically or operationally, is not explored in his work.

Today, the Foundation's leadership remains in the hands of its Mawdudist founders. Its trustees include Khurshid Ahmad, Manazir Ahsan, Muhammad Abdul Bari, Abdur Rashid Siddiqui and Zahid Parvez.[175] Its director general is the son of the late Khurram Murad, Farooq Murad. Expressing a typical revivalist view, Parvez, the principal of the Foundation's Markfield Institute of Higher Education, states, 'political power is essential in the eyes of Islam'; it is something to be 'brought under God, and utilised for realising His Will in society and state; for reforming and transforming society and the state for the common good'.[176] Islam is seen as the eventual solution to Britain's social and political malaise. The recent departure from the Foundation of Dilwar Hussain – a 'thirty-something' when he established its research unit – undermines Gilliat-Ray and McLoughlin's notion that generational changes are stimulating an ideological change within the organisation away from such thinking. Hussain confesses that he left the Foundation after many years, in part, because he felt his ability to effect change from within was limited.[177]

Writing optimistically of ideological change within the MAB, McRoy opines:

> Many MAB founders were connected to the *Ikhwan* [Muslim Brotherhood], but they have contextualised their beliefs and praxis for the UK situation. It is vital to recognise this to understand their policy and strategy … . MAB has a dynamic attitude to ideology that is also governed by its concern to contextualise Islam in the British sphere.[178]

McRoy supports this contention by citing a MAB statement, signed by the then chairman, Anas Altikriti, which distances itself from the thinking of the Muslim Brotherhood ideologue Said Qutb. But proximity to Qutb's strident anti-Western thought is not an appropriate measure of the extent to which a group embraces or rejects the ideal of a society or state governed by *shari'a* precepts and edicts. McRoy also cites the work of the former MAB leader and Hamas spokesman, Azzam Tamimi. He describes the 'current strategy' of the Muslim Brotherhood, in Tamimi's words, as the 'gradual reform of society and state'. It is one, Tamimi asserts, that 'considers democracy compatible with Islam, and accepts the principle of power sharing'.[179] However, McRoy omits to mention Tamimi's contention that Islam cannot be secularised and that 'Islam loses its purpose' without 'shari'ah, the body of laws and regulations'.[180]

The MAB has encouraged Muslim participation in electoral politics, but this in itself is not necessarily a departure from al-Banna and Mawdudi's bottom-up strategy to bring about an Islamic society and state, lived and governed according to the ethical and legal code of the *shari'a*. The president of MAB, Omer El-Hamdoon, states that the organisation isn't in Britain to establish an Islamic state since Islam, as a way of life, can only be realised when people embrace it willingly. El-Hamdoon says the creation of an Islamic state isn't an objective the MAB is striving for, but admits, 'As a Muslim, irrelevant of where I am living, one of my objectives is to establish an Islamic state. Islam is comprehensive and since the problems are comprehensive, the solution has to be comprehensive'.[181] Neither Tamimi nor El-Hamdoon's willingness to engage in political activism – a trait shared by IFE, but also by al-Banna and Mawdudi – ought to be taken as a sign of relinquishing aspirations for a society or state in which *shari'a* prevails.

Most sympathetic observers of Islam-inspired activism in Britain that seek to downplay the 'Islamist' character of Ikhwan- or Jama'at-associated groups focus upon a small number of specific organisations, such as the Islamic Foundation or ISB. But, aside from the misplaced optimism in some of these claims, there has not been a discussion concerning the relative strength of these allegedly reformist organisations within the larger revivalist movement and the possible effects of this upon the movement as a whole. The ISB's rejection of its Mawdudist heritage has not had a significant impact on the remainder of revivalist groups in Britain. And while there are a number of British Muslim organisations that embrace liberal democratic values and universal human rights – for example, Quilliam and British Muslims for Secular Democracy – 'post-Islamism' has not emerged as a movement from the Ikhwani-Jama'ati nexus. Although the term 'Islamist' is problematic when applied to the global Muslim Brotherhood in Britain, as subsequent chapters will show, the movement has not reformed its revivalist orientations. And the organisational connections that help comprise it, which are described in the following chapter, remain strong.

Notes

1 The first four caliphs were Abu Bakr (r. 632–634), Umar ibn al-Khattab (r. 634–644), Uthman ibn Affan (r. 644–656), and 'Ali ibn Abi Talib (r. 656–661).

2 Mitchell (1993), pp. 209–210.

3 After the fourth caliph, 'Ali, as Patricia Crone and Martin Hinds observe, 'the caliphate passed to men who had converted late and unwillingly (the Umayyads) so that the happy union of religion and politics now came to an end'. See Crone and Hinds (2003), p.2.
4 Mitchell (1993), p. 234.
5 al-Banna (1978). For a comprehensive treatment of the juridical doctrine and historical practice of *jihad*, see Cook (2005).
6 See al-Banna (1978).
7 Mitchell (1993), p. 207.
8 Ibid., p.206.
9 See Kramer (1996), p. 144; Gold (2003), pp. 55–56; and Taheri (1987), p. 52. In retaliation to the murder of Nuqrashi, al-Banna was assassinated by Egyptian government agents the following year, in 1949.
10 Taheri (1987), p. 51.
11 See Phares (2005), p. 65; and Rachel Ehrenfeld and Alyssa A. Lappen, 'The Truth About the Muslim Brotherhood', *Front Page Magazine*, 16 June 2006. www.alyssaalappen.org/2006/06/16/the-truth-about-the-muslim-brotherhood/.
12 Filiu (2009).
13 Joyce Karam, 'The Bin Laden files: Influenced by Muslim Brotherhood, offers details on Al Qaeda relation with Iran', *The National*, 1 November 2017. www.thenational.ae/world/the-bin-laden-files-influenced-by-muslim-brotherhood-offers-details-on-al-qaeda-relation-with-iran-1.672261.
14 Mitchell (1993) p. 308.
15 Ibid.
16 Investigative Project on Terrorism (2008), p. 7.
17 For an interesting study of the Khilafah movement, see Qureshi (1999).
18 Maududi (1980), p. 22, emphasis and italics added.
19 Ibid., p. 7, italics added.
20 Bukay (2008), p. 164.
21 Mawdudi, quoted in Karsh (2006), p. 208.
22 Ahmad (1991), p. 488.
23 Ahmad, ibid. See also Ahmed (1994), pp. 669–706.
24 Vidino (2010), p. 25.
25 Hussain (2007), pp. 18–19.
26 The Ahmadis are followers of Mirza Ghulam Ahmad (1835–1908) who, in 1889, founded a religious order in modern-day India. Ahmad assumed the title of *al-Mahdi,* the divinely guided one, a messiah promised in Shi'ite eschatology to restore Islam's righteous place in the world. For more on the Ahmadis, see Valentine (2008).
27 'Speech of Mr. Mohamed Mahdi Akef, Ramadan Iftar Party', *IkhwanWeb*, 6 July 2007. www.ikhwanweb.com/article.php?id=911.
28 Pew Forum (2010), p. 20.
29 Abdul Bari (2013), p. 11.
30 Geaves (1995), pp. 206–207, fn. 1.
31 al-Qaradawi (2002), pp. 1, 6, emphasis added.
32 Ibid., pp. xxii–xxiii.
33 Mozaffari (2007), pp. 18–19.
34 Sookhdeo (2012), p. 23.
35 Home Office (2011), p. 108.
36 Jeffrey Bale, 'Militant Islamist Networks in the West', National Consortium for the Study of Terrorism and Responses to Terrorism, 21 December 2009. www.start.umd.edu/research-projects/militant-islamist-networks-west. Bale's taxonomy builds upon the work of Anthony McRoy and resonates with the work of Lorenzo Vidino as well as with that of the London-based counter-extremism think

tank, Quilliam. See McRoy (2006), pp. 194–196, 198; Vidino (2009), pp. 165–176, and Vidino (2010), pp. 15–16; Quilliam (2010).

37 Vidino (2009), p. 165.
38 Vidino (2010), pp. 41–53, emphasis added.
39 Ibid. p. 41. See also Vidino (2011).
40 Vidino (2010), p. 52.
41 Ibid., p. 42.
42 Ibid.
43 Ibid., pp. 38–39.
44 Ibid., p. 40.
45 Ibid.
46 *The Global Muslim Brotherhood Daily Watch*, 'ANALYSIS; The Global Muslim Brotherhood Is No 'Myth", 6 March 2011, emphasis added. www.globalmbwatch.com/2011/03/06/analysis-global-muslim-brotherhood-myth/.
47 *The Investigative Project on Terrorism*, 'HLF Founders Sentenced to Long Prison Terms,' 27 May 2009. www.investigativeproject.org/1046/hlf-founders-sentenced-to-long-prison-terms.
48 *The Global Muslim Brotherhood Daily Watch*, 'ANALYSIS: Holy Land Documents Point to Covert Muslim Brotherhood Structure In The U.S.', 29 August 2007. www.globalmbwatch.com/2007/08/29/analysis-holy-land-documents-point-covert-muslim-brotherhood-structure/.
49 *The Global Muslim Brotherhood Daily Watch*, 'ANALYSIS; The Global Muslim Brotherhood Is No "Myth"'.
50 *The Global Muslim Brotherhood Daily Watch*, 'ANALYSIS: Holy Land Documents Point to Covert Muslim Brotherhood Structure In The U.S.'.
51 Ibid.
52 Akram (1991), pp.7, 5, emphasis added.
53 Akram (1991), p. 7, emphasis added.
54 Ibid., pp. 6, 11–12.
55 See Ian Johnson, 'How Islamic Group's Ties Reveal Europe's Challenge', *The Wall Street Journal*, December 29, 2005. www.wsj.com/articles/SB113582317237133576; Ian Johnson, 'Big Brotherhood is Watching', *Foreign Policy*, 26 May 2010. www.foreignpolicy.com/articles/2010/05/26/big_brotherhood_is_watching; Johnson (2008); and Johnson (2010).
56 Johnson (2010), p. 41.
57 Johnson (2008), p. 77. See also Johnson (2010), pp. 195–196, and Vidino (2010), pp. 34–35.
58 Johnson (2008), p. 78.
59 Vidino (2010), pp. 32–34.
60 Johnson (2008), pp. 72, 76; Johnson (2010), p. 197; and Vidino, ibid., p. 34.
61 'Salem Azzam (1924–2008)', *The Muslim Weekly*, 22 February 2008, p.15, cited in Rich (2010), p. 118, emphasis added.
62 Patrick Sookhdeo, 'The Islamization of Europe', *Virtueonline*, 1 August 2005, www.virtueonline.org/portal/modules/news/article.php?storyid=2872#.UqkiaGQW1mF.
63 See Lappen (2010), for example.
64 Patrick Poole, 'The Muslim Brotherhood "Project"', *FrontPageMagazine.com*, May 11, 2006. http://archive.frontpagemag.com/readarticle.aspx?ARTID=4476.
65 It wasn't until October 2005, with the publication of Sylvain Besson's *La conquête de l'Occident: Le projet secret des Islamistes* (*The Conquest of the West: The Islamists' Secret Project*), that *The Project* was finally made public. The first English translation appeared a year later in 2006.
66 Quoted from *The Project* in Patrick Poole, 'The Muslim Brotherhood "Project" (continued)', Scott Burgess (trans.), *FrontPageMagazine.com*, 11 May 2006. http://archive.frontpagemag.com/readArticle.aspx?ARTID=4475.

67 Ibid.
68 Vidino (2006), p. 22. This is indeed an important treatise, but a more recent manifesto for Islamic revivalism, and one that is more relevant to Britain, is Zahid Parvez's '*Building a New Society: An Islamic Approach to Social Change*', published in 2007 by the Islamic Foundation. For more on this, see chapters 3 and 4.
69 Vidino (2011), p. 11.
70 Vidino (2010), p. 50.
71 al-Qaradawi (2002), p. 159.
72 Vidino (2010), p. 92. See also Vidino (2009), p. 165.
73 Yusuf al-Qaradawi, MAYA Conference, 1995, Toledo, Ohio, US, cited in Emerson Vermaat, 'Dutch Security Service warns against Muslim Brotherhood's clandestine infiltration tactics,' *Militant Islam Monitor*, 19 December 2007. www.militantislammonitor.org/article/id/3293.
74 '*Jihad*,' proclaims al-Qaradawi, 'may be educational, journalistic, social, economic, or political *jihad* as much as military *jihad*. We must remember that in all kinds of *jihad*, the essential condition is that *the action helps make God's word supreme on earth* … The most important form of *jihad* today is serious, purposive organized work to re-build the Islamic *society and state* and to implement the Islamic way of life in the political, cultural, and economic areas … .' See al-Qaradawi (1999), pp. 76, 70, emphasis added.
75 Johnson (2010), p. 200.
76 Vidino (2010), p. 80.
77 Ibid.
78 Whine (2005), p. 52.
79 Maher and Frampton (2009), p. 19.
80 Ibid., p. 22.
81 Ibid., p. 23.
82 Ibid., pp. 20–21.
83 Nielsen (1989), p. 232, cited in Geaves (1995), p. 195.
84 Kepel (1997), p. 131.
85 Nielsen (1992), p. 136, cited in Geaves (1995), p. 187.
86 Geaves (1995), p. 195.
87 McRoy (2006), p. 166.
88 Ibid., p. 167.
89 Vidino (2010), p. 116.
90 Kepel (1997), p. 131.
91 Ibid.
92 Geaves (1995), p. 197.
93 Ibid., p. 205.
94 Kepel (1997), p. 122.
95 Ibid., p. 110.
96 Ibid.
97 Ibid., pp. 130, 132–133.
98 Ibid., pp. 122, 132–133
99 Vidino (2010), p. 117.
100 Whine (2006), p. 34.
101 Kepel (1997), p. 133.
102 Interview with Khurram Murad, cited in Ali (1996), p. 84.
103 Murad (1981), p. 3, cited in Cox and Marks (2006), p. 73.
104 McRoy (2006), p. 118.
105 Wiedl (2009), p. 120.
106 Ibid. pp. 124–125.
107 Kettani (1980), pp. 96–105.

108 Patrick Sookhdeo, 'The Islamization of Europe'.
109 Qureshi, 'Building Foundations in the West', *Q-News*, no. 251–254, February 1997, p. 21, cited in McRoy (2006), p. 119.
110 McRoy (2006), pp. 119–120.
111 *Kuffar* (singular: *kafir*) is the most common word in Arabic used for non-Muslims within the Quran. Mawdudi explains the significance of the root word, *kufr*, as follows: '*Kufr* literally means "to cover" or "to conceal." The man who denies God is called *Kafir* (concealer) because he conceals *by his disbelief* what is inherent in his nature … [O]ne who disobeys God and resorts to *Kufr* is the person who perpetrates the greatest injustice.' See Abul Ala Mawdudi (1980), quoted in Bat Ye'or (2002), p. 197.
112 McRoy (2006), p. 168.
113 Bowen (2012), p. 112.
114 Andrew Gilligan, 'Inextricably linked to controversial mosque: the secret world of IFE', *The Telegraph*, 28 February 2010. www.telegraph.co.uk/news/newstopics/politics/labour/7333487/Inextricably-linked-to-controversial-mosque-the-secret-world-of-IFE.html.
115 Lucy Lips (pseud.), 'Islamic Forum Europe Calls for the Eradication of Israel', *Harry's Place*, 16 November 2012. http://hurryupharry.org/2012/11/16/islamic-forum-europe-calls-for-the-eradication-of-israel/.
116 Andrew Gilligan, 'The infiltration of Labour', *The Telegraph*, 28 February 2010. www.telegraph.co.uk/news/newstopics/politics/labour/7333470/The-infiltration-of-Labour.html.
117 Gilligan, 'Inextricably linked to controversial mosque: the secret world of IFE'. For more on this, see chapter 5.
118 'The Founding Mission', *emel*, issue 99, December 2011, http://emel.com/article?id=108&a_id=2894.
119 Hasan Afzal, 'Extremism in Abdul Bari's Mosque', *The Huffington Post*, 21 September 2011. www.huffingtonpost.co.uk/hasan-afzal/extremism-in-abdul-baris-_b_971232.html.
120 Vidino (2010), p. 118.
121 Iqbal Sacranie, quoted in Vidino, ibid., p. 122.
122 McRoy (2006), p. 173.
123 Ibid., p. 121.
124 Vidino (2010), p. 122.
125 Martin Bright, 'Radical links of UK's "moderate" Muslim group', *The Observer*, 14 August 2005. www.theguardian.com/uk/2005/aug/14/religion.immigrationpolicy.
126 Ibid.
127 Henry Jackson Society (2012), p. Ev108.
128 Department for Communities and Local Government (2009), p. 40.
129 Interview with Mohammed Abdul Aziz, 3 September 2012.
130 Whine (2006), p. 38.
131 Ibid., p. 35, emphasis added.
132 Vidino (2010), p. 140.
133 Ibid., p. 141.
134 Bowen (2012), p. 115.
135 John Ware, 'Time to Wise Up to the Muslim Brotherhood', *Standpoint Magazine*, July/August 2013. http://standpointmag.co.uk/node/5082/full.
136 Rich (2010), p. 121.
137 Ibid.
138 'MAB Responds To Vile Attack', Islamic Human Rights Commission website, 13 August 2004. www.ihrc.org.uk/show.php?id=1216.
139 Maher and Frampton (2009), p. 21, emphasis added.

140 Rich (2010), p. 131, emphasis added.
141 'David Cameron: Speech to the Community Security Trust', Conservative website, 4 March 2008. http://conservative-speeches.sayit.mysociety.org/speech/599684.
142 *The Global Muslim Brotherhood Daily Watch*, 'UK Human Rights Center Tied To UK Muslim Brotherhood Holds Meetings At Parliament', 25 November 2013. www.globalmbwatch.com/2013/11/25/uk-human-rights-center-tied-uk-muslim-brotherhood-holds-meetings-parliament/.
143 Andrew Gilligan, 'Terror-link group met in parliament', *The Telegraph*, 23 November 2013. www.telegraph.co.uk/news/uknews/terrorism-in-the-uk/10470307/Terror-link-group-met-in-parliament.html.
144 Andrew Gilligan, 'Terror-link group met in parliament'.
145 Maher and Frampton (2009), p. 6.
146 Bowen (2012), p. 111.
147 Rich (2010), p. 118.
148 Vidino (2012), p. 63
149 Ibid., p. 64
150 Maher and Frampton (2009), pp. 24–25, emphasis added.
151 Henry Jackson Society (2012), p. Ev108.
152 House of Commons (2015), para. 28, p. 5, emphasis added.
153 Kepel (1997), p. 133, emphasis added.
154 Malik (2009), p. 127.
155 Rich (2010), p. 132, emphasis added.
156 Vidino (2010), p. 140.
157 'Kamal Helbawy, Centre for the Study of Terrorism, London, UK', Centre for the Study of Islam and Democracy website, 3 April 2009. www.csidonline.org/kamal-helbawy-centre-for-the-study-of-terrorism-london-uk/.
158 Azzam Tamimi biography, Institute of Islamic Political Thought website. https://web.archive.org/web/20091229015058/http://www.ii-pt.com:80/reviews/r20Azam%20Tamimi.pdf.
159 Whine (2006), p. 34.
160 Ibid.
161 Silvestri (2010), p. 267.
162 Ibid., p. 278.
163 Ibid., p. 284
164 Ibid., p. 285.
165 Tibi (1995).
166 Pew Forum (2010), p. 24.
167 McRoy (2006), p. 3.
168 Interview with Dilwar Hussain, 15 January 2015.
169 For example, see Bowen (2012) and Brandon and Pantucci (2012).
170 Dilwar Hussain, 'Beyond Islamism', *emel*, issue 88, January 2012. www.emel.com/article?id=94&a_id=2569. Cited in Brandon and Pantucci (2012), p. 38.
171 Gilliat-Ray (2010), p. 102.
172 McLoughlin (2005), p. 64; this quotation is partially cited in Gilliat-Ray (2010).
173 Ibid.
174 Ibid.
175 'The Islamic Foundation, Data for financial year ending 31 December 2016', undated, Charity Commission website. http://beta.charitycommission.gov.uk/charity-details/?regid=263371&subid=0.
176 Parvez (2007), p. 39.
177 Interview with Dilwar Hussain, 15 January 2015.
178 McRoy (2006), pp. 160, 161.

179 Azzam Tamimi, 'Fundamentalism & violence: An Islamic viewpoint', Institute of Islamic Political Thought website, 2001. https://web.archive.org/web/20060621094429/http://www.ii-pt.com/web/papers/view.htm.

180 Azzam Tamimi, 'Can Islam be Secularized?', Institute of Islamic Political Thought website, November 2002. https://web.archive.org/web/20060626002606/http://www.ii-pt.com/web/articles/Can%20Islam%20be%20Secularized.htm.

181 Interview with Omer El-Hamdoon, 14 February 2012.

References

Abdul Bari, Muhammad (2013). 'Meet the challenge, make the change: a call to action for Muslim civil society in Britain'. *Cordoba Papers*, vol. 2, no. 1. Cordoba Foundation, London. www.thecordobafoundation.com/attach/A5_TCF_CS_BARI_FINAL.pdf.

Ahmad, Mumtaz (1991). 'Islamic fundamentalism in South Asia: the Jamaat-i-Islami and the Tablighi Jamaat'. In Martin E. Marty and R. Scott Appleby (eds), *Fundamentalisms Observed*, Chicago, IL: Chicago University Press.

Ahmed, Rafiuddin (1994). 'Redefining Muslim identity in South Asia: the transformation of the Jama'at-i-Islami'. In Martin E. Marty, and R. Scott Appleby (eds), *Accounting for Fundamentalisms: the Dynamic Character of Movements*, Chicago, IL: Chicago University Press.

Akram, Mohammed (1991). 'An explanatory memorandum on the general strategic goal for the Brotherhood in North America – May 22, 1991'. Government Exhibit Elbarasse Search – 3 3:04-CR-2. 40-G U.S. v. Holy Land Foundation et al. Available at: www.investigativeproject.org/documents/misc/20.pdf.

Ali, Muhammad Mumtaz (1996). *The Muslim Community in Britain*. Subang Jaya, Malaysia: Pelanduk Publications.

al-Banna, Hasan (1978). *On Jihad*, in Charles Wendell (trans. and annot.), *Five Tracts of Hasan al-Banna (1906–1949): A Selection from the Majmu'at Rasa'il al-Imam al-Shahid*: 133–161. Berkeley: University of California Press.

Bat Ye'or (2002). *Islam and Dhimmitude: Where Civilizations Collide*. Cranbury, NJ: Farleigh Dickinson University Press.

Bowen, Innes (2012). 'The Muslim Brotherhood in Britain'. In Roel Meijer and Edwin Bakker (eds), *The Muslim Brotherhood in Europe*: 111–126. London: Hurst and Co.

Bowen, Innes (2014). *Medina in Birmingham, Najaf in Brent*. London: Hurst & Co.

Brandon, James, and Rafaello Pantucci (2012). 'UK Islamists and the Arab uprisings'. In *Current Trends in Islamist Ideology*, vol. 13: 18–46. The Hudson Institute Center on Islam, Democracy, and the Future of the Muslim World. www.hudson.org/research/9902-uk-islamists-and-the-arab-uprisings.

Bukay, David (2008). *From Muhammad to Bin Laden: Religious and Ideological Sources of the Homicide Bombers Phenomenon*. New Brunswick, NJ: Transaction Publishers.

Cook, David (2005). *Understanding Jihad*. Berkeley and Los Angeles: California University Press.

Cox, Caroline, and John Marks (2006). *The West, Islam and Islamism: Is Ideological Islam Compatible with Liberal Democracy?* 2nd edition. London: Civitas.

Crone, Patricia and Martin Hinds (2003). *God's Caliph: Religious Authority in the First Centuries of Islam*. Cambridge: Cambridge University Press.

Department for Communities and Local Government (2009). *The Pakistani Muslim Community in England: Understanding Muslim Ethnic Communities in England.* http://webarchive.nationalarchives.gov.uk/20120919132719/http://www.communities.gov.uk/publications/communities/pakistanimuslimcommunity.

Filiu, Jean-Pierre (2009). 'The Brotherhood vs. Al-Qaeda: a moment of truth?'. In *Current Trends in Islamist Ideology*, vol. 9: 18–25. Hudson Institute Center on Islam, Democracy, and the Future of the Muslim World. www.hudson.org/research/9852-the-brotherhood-vs-al-qaeda-a-moment-of-truth.

Geaves, Ron (1995). 'The reproduction of Jamaat-i Islami in Britain'. In *Islam and Christian-Muslim Relations*, vol. 6, no. 2: 187–210. Note: This publication states the author's name incorrectly as 'Ron Greaves'.

Gilliat-Ray, Sophie (2010). *Muslims in Britain: An Introduction*. Cambridge: Cambridge University Press.

Gold, Dore (2003). *Hatred's Kingdom: How Saudi Arabia Supports the New Global Terrorism*. Washington, DC: Regnery Publishing.

Henry Jackson Society (2012). 'Written evidence submitted by The Henry Jackson Society'. In 'Roots of violent radicalisation: Nineteenth Report of Session 2010–12, volume 1'. Home Affairs Committee, House of Commons. www.publications.parliament.uk/pa/cm201012/cmselect/cmhaff/1446/1446.pdf.

Home Office (2011). *Prevent Strategy*, Cm8092. https://assets.publishing.service.gov.uk/government/uploads/system/uploads/attachment_data/file/97976/prevent-strategy-review.pdf.

House of Commons (2015). *Muslim Brotherhood Review: Main Findings.* HC 679. www.gov.uk/government/uploads/system/uploads/attachment_data/file/486948/53163Muslim_Brotherhood_Review_-_PRINT.pdf.

Hussain, Zahid (2007). *Frontline Pakistan: The Struggle With Militant Islam*. New York: Columbia University Press.

Investigative Project on Terrorism (2008). *Report on the Roots of Violent Islamist Extremism and Efforts to Counter It: The Muslim Brotherhood.* www.investigativeproject.org/documents/testimony/353.pdf.

Johnson, Ian (2008). 'The Brotherhood's westward expansion'. In *Current Trends in Islamist Ideology*, vol. 6: 71–84. The Hudson Institute Center on Islam, Democracy, and the Future of the Muslim World. www.hudson.org/research/9853-the-brotherhood-s-westward-expansion.

Johnson, Ian (2010). *A Mosque in Munich: Nazis, the CIA and the Rise of the Muslim Brotherhood in the West*. New York: Houghton Mifflin Harcourt.

Karsh, Efraim (2006). *Islamic Imperialism: a History*. New Haven and London: Yale University Press.

Kepel, Gilles (1997). *Allah in the West: Islamic Movements in America and Europe.* Trans. Susan Milner. Cambridge: Polity Press.

Kettani, M.Ali (1980). 'The problems of Muslim minorities and their solutions'. In *Muslim Communities in Non-Muslim States*: 91–107. London: Islamic Council of Europe.

Kramer, Martin (1996). *Arab Awakening and Islamic Revival: The Politics of Ideas in the Middle East*. New Brunswick, NJ: Transaction Publishers.

Lappen, Alyssa A. (2010). 'The Muslim Brotherhood in North America'. In Barry Rubin (ed.), *The Muslim Brotherhood: the Organization and Policies of a Global Islamist Movement*: 161–179. New York: Palgrave Macmillan.

Maher, Shiraz, and Martyn Frampton (2009). 'Choosing our friends wisely: Criteria for engagement with Muslim groups'. Policy Exchange, London. https://policyexchange.org.uk/wp-content/uploads/2016/09/choosing-our-friends-wisely-mar-09.pdf.

Malik, Kenan (2009). *From Fatwa to Jihad: The Rushdie Affair and its Aftermath*. London: Atlantic.

Maududi, Abul A'la (1980 [1929]). *Jihad in Islam* (*Jihad Fi Sabillilah*). Beirut: Holy Koran Publishing House.

Mawdudi, Abul Ala (1980). *Towards Understanding Islam*. Trans. Khurram Murad. Leicester: Islamic Foundation.

McLoughlin, Seán (2005). 'The state, new Muslim leaderships and Islam as a resource for public engagement in Britain'. In Jocelyne Cesari and Seán McLoughlin (eds), *European Muslims and the Secular State*: 55–69. Aldershot: Ashgate Publishing.

McRoy, Anthony (2006). *From Rushdie to 7/7: The Radicalisation of Islam in Britain*. London: Social Affairs Unit.

Mitchell, Richard P. (1993 [1969]). *The Society of the Muslim Brothers*. Oxford: Oxford University Press.

Mozaffari, Mehdi (2007). 'What is Islamism? History and definition of a concept'. In *Totalitarian Movements and Political Religions*, vol. 8, no. 1: 17–33.

Murad, Khurram (1981). *The Islamic Movement in the West: Reflections on Some Issues*. Leicester: The Islamic Foundation.

Nielsen, Jørgen (1989). 'Islamic communities in Britain'. In Paul Badham (ed.), *Religion, State and Society in Modern Britain*: 225–241. Lampeter: Edwin Mellin Press.

Nielsen, Jørgen (1992). *Muslims in Western Europe*. Edinburgh: Edinburgh University Press.

Parvez, Zahid (2007). *Building a New Society: An Islamic Approach to Social Change*. Markfield: Revival Publications.

Pew Forum on Religion and Public Life (2010). 'Muslim networks and movements in Western Europe'. Pew Research Center, Washington, DC. www.pewforum.org/2010/09/15/muslim-networks-and-movements-in-western-europe/.

Phares, Walid (2005). *Future Jihad: Terrorist Strategies Against America*. New York: Palgrave MacMillan.

al-Qaradawi, Yusuf (1999). *Fiqh Al Zakah (Volume II): A Comparative Study of Zakah, Regulations and Philosophy in the Light of Qur'an and Sunnah*. Trans. Monzer Kahf. Jeddah. Saudi Arabia: Scientific Publishing Centre, King Abdulaziz University.

al-Qaradawi, Yusuf (2002). *Priorities of the Islamic Movement in the Coming Phase*. Swansea: Awakening Publications.

Quilliam (2010). 'Strategic briefing paper, preventing terrorism: where next for Britain?' Available at: www.scribd.com/doc/34834977/Secret-Quilliam-Memo-to-government.

Qureshi, M.Naeem (1999). *Pan-Islam in British Indian Politics: A Study of the Khilafat Movement, 1918–1924*. Leiden: Brill.

Rich, David (2010). 'The very model of a British Muslim Brotherhood'. In Barry Rubin (ed.), *The Muslim Brotherhood: the Organization and Policies of a Global Islamist Movement*: 117–136. New York: Palgrave Macmillan.

Silvestri, Sara (2010). 'Moderate Islamist groups in Europe: The Muslim Brothers'. In Khaled Hroub (ed.), *Political Islam: Context versus Ideology*: 265–285. London: Al Saqi.

Sookhdeo, Patrick (2012). 'The West, Islam and the counter-ideological war'. In Katharine C. Gorka and Patrick Sookhdeo (eds), *Fighting the Ideological War: Winning Strategies from Communism to Islamism*: 15–44. McClean, VA: Isaac.

Taheri, Amir (1987). *Holy Terror: Inside the World of Islamic Terrorism*. Bethesda, Maryland: Adler & Adler.

Tibi, Bassam (1995). 'Les conditions d'un "euro-Islam"'. In Robert Bistolfi and François Zabbal (eds), *In Islams d'Europe: intégration ou insertion communautaire?* Paris: L'Aube.

Valentine, Simon Ross (2008). *Islam and the Ahmadiyya Jama'at: History, Belief, Practice*. New York: Columbia University Press.

Vidino, Lorenzo (2006). 'Aims and methods of Europe's Muslim Brotherhood'. In *Current Trends in Islamist Ideology*, vol. 4: 22–44. The Hudson Institute Center on Islam, Democracy, and the Future of the Muslim World. www.hudson.org/research/9776-aims-and-methods-of-europe-s-muslim-brotherhood.

Vidino, Lorenzo (2009). 'Europe as a battlefield'. In *Totalitarian Movements and Political Religions*, vol. 10, no. 2: 165–176.

Vidino, Lorenzo (2010). *The New Muslim Brotherhood in the West*. New York: Columbia University Press.

Vidino, Lorenzo (2011). 'The Muslim Brotherhood in the West: evolution and Western policies'. International Centre for the Study of Radicalisation and Political Violence (ICSR), London. http://icsr.info/wp-content/uploads/2012/10/1300106834ICSRTheNewMBintheWest.pdf.

Vidino, Lorenzo (2012). 'The European organisation of the European Muslim Brotherhood: myth or reality?'. In Roel Meijer and Edwin Bakker (eds), *The Muslim Brotherhood in Europe*: 51–69. London: Hurst & Co.

Whine, Michael (2005). 'The penetration of Islamist ideology in Britain'. In *Current Trends in Islamist Ideology*, vol. 1: 50–67. The Hudson Institute Center on Islam, Democracy, and the Future of the Muslim World. www.hudson.org/research/9886-the-penetration-of-islamist-ideology-in-britain.

Whine, Michael (2006). 'The advance of the Muslim Brotherhood in the UK'. In *Current Trends in Islamist Ideology*, vol. 2: 30–40. The Hudson Institute Center on Islam, Democracy, and the Future of the Muslim World. www.hudson.org/content/researchattachments/attachment/1363/whine_vol2.pdf.

Wiedl, Nina (2009). 'Dawa and the Islamist revival in the West'. In *Current Trends in Islamist Ideology*, vol. 9: 120–150. The Hudson Institute Center on Islam, Democracy, and the Future of the Muslim World. www.hudson.org/research/9789-dawa-and-the-islamist-revival-in-the-west.

2 Organisation and leadership

Informal networks and formal bodies

Social movements typically combine three interrelated characteristics, namely, organisational networking, shared cultural solidarity, and a conflict of vision and values with institutional authority. The current chapter examines whether or not the key individuals and groups often considered as comprising a participationist Islamist movement in Britain possess the first characteristic. That is, it examines the way in which, and the extent to which, these individuals and groups are networked organisationally. This chapter builds on chapter 1, which illustrated some of these organisational relationships as observed by others. But it incorporates additional insights gleaned from original interviews with some of the leading Muslim activists within the network, as well as some more recent primary sources, to present a more complete picture of the organisational dimensions of this network. This chapter – novel in its explicit and detailed attention to the question of organisational links between two 'streams' of Islamist activism in Britain – concludes that there is a dynamic and enduring network made up of several interrelated levels

This chapter observes the working relationships between the relevant individuals and organisations in terms of collaborative activities and intermeshing leadership structures, formal and informal. As this chapter will show, in addition to instances of inter-organisational collaboration are the complex webs of interpersonal relationships between an elite cadre of individuals. Even when these interpersonal relationships appear indistinguishable from inter-organisational relationships – as is most apparent when a given individual or group exercises clear control over a specific organisation – it is most useful to view them as forming an organised network that cuts *across* the formalised structures of named organisations. These interpersonal relationships form what may be called a *meta-organisational network*: an informal and decentralised network of individuals nested within and inseparable from the organisations that form a broader network viewable in more formal terms.

The elements of this network are not synonymous with organisations, but neither are they simply individuals: they are individuals that have authoritative roles within organisations or influence upon them, but they do not simply communicate and collaborate as representatives of specific organisations. In numerous instances these individuals have roles in multiple organisations, so even when they are officially representing one organisation in a given meeting or communicative exchange, the others for which they also play a key role have a direct, albeit invisible and only latent, involvement. Their connections, even public collaborations, are inseparable from – and fundamentally based upon – informal associations and shared histories. It is these associations and histories that enable the visible, formal structure of an overall network in the shape of organisations, but they are also what guarantee its fluidity. It is these associations and histories that enable the creation of new organisations and campaigns.

The interpersonal relationships of these individuals may be observed not just at the level of co-involvement in activities and events, but also at the level of planning and coordination beyond visible, public collaboration. This might suggest the existence of a vanguard, an elite or core group, driving the overall network, although if there is, its influence within this network is questionable. The core group within the broader network does not comprise a central command structure but, rather, multiple leadership clusters.

Networking and collaboration

Networking through collaboration may be observed between individuals and organisations in Britain associated with Jama'at-i-Islami, between those associated with the Ikhwan, and – most importantly for the recognition of a singular Islamic revivalist network – between individuals and organisations *across* the Jama'at-Ikhwan divide.

As discussed in the previous chapter, the emergence of a trans-ethnic network in Europe, including Britain, has been recognised by a number of observers. But there is plenty of room to further illuminate the working relationships that traverse Jama'at-Ikhwan lines in Britain.[1] There are, in fact, very few references in the academic and think tank literature to trans-ethnic networking in Britain where specific examples are provided. One exception is in an article, as noted in chapter 1, by David Rich that refers to the work of Abdullah Faliq, who is involved in both Ikhwan-associated organisations, such as the Cordoba Foundation, and Jama'at-associated organisations, including the East London Mosque and the Islamic Forum of Europe (IFE). Faliq's portfolio, Rich asserts, demonstrates how the activities of the Muslim Brotherhood and Jama'at-i-Islami 'often complement each other or merge into one in Britain'.[2]

This chapter provides additional examples of such trans-ethnic networking with reference to campaign work, speaking events and publications. Although this does not undermine the importance and strength of ethnic- and linguistic-related networking amongst revivalist individuals and groups, it does, at the very least, question the notion of two distinct movements and suggests a singular network whose present concerns and future orientations are at least as important as its multiple historical lineages.

Campaigns and other events

Collaborative working relationships between individuals and groups associated with the Ikhwan and Jama'at may be seen in a number of campaigns and other events concerned with the perception and treatment of Muslims as a community – expressed in Quranic terms as the Muslim *umma* – or the perception of Islam itself. These campaigns involving the various revivalist individuals and groups have been spearheaded to raise awareness of social or political issues affecting Muslims or to raise funds to support Muslims suffering from hardship or persecution. Key themes include the predicament of the *umma* and Islamophobia in Britain and Palestine and the plight of the Rohingya Muslims of Myanmar. These working relationships may also be seen in other events, such as speaking engagements and skills development workshops, and in the sharing of resources, such as venues for events.

Islamophobia is an issue that has for some years brought Muslim groups together in awareness-raising initiatives, sometimes with the purpose of lobbying government for changes in law to protect Muslims from religious discrimination and hatred.[3] As chapter 5 will show, Islamophobia also features strongly in their symbolic struggle with the British government over the authority to establish a way of seeing and evaluating social and political reality: Islamophobia blurs the line between anti-Muslim bigotry and the legitimate criticism of what the government refers to as Islamist 'non-violent extremism'.

In November 2012, the now-annual 'Islamophobia Awareness Month' was launched at the London Muslim Centre, housed in the East London Mosque.[4] The event was co-founded by the Muslim Council of Britain (MCB), iEngage, and the Enough Coalition Against Islamophobia. The Enough Coalition was formed in May 2011 by a number of Muslim and non-Muslim groups. The Muslim groups included those with revivalist associations, including the British Muslim Initiative (BMI), the Islamic Forum of Europe (IFE), the Federation of Student Islamic Societies (FOSIS) and the Islam Channel.[5] Unsurprisingly, speakers at the inaugural Islamophobia Awareness Month event also came from revivalist groups, including the Muslim Association of Britain (MAB), IFE and FOSIS. In November 2012, the MCB organised an event called 'Islamophobia Analysed'. Among the participants were Azad Ali and Shenaz Bunglawala from iEngage.[6] Both still work for iEngage, which was rebranded as Muslim Engagement and Development (MEND) in 2014 after the group was removed from its position on the All-Party Parliamentary Group on Islamophobia.[7] In recent years, MEND has become the lead campaigning force against Islamophobia in Britain, and is the main co-ordinator for Islamophobia Awareness Month.

The MCB, MAB and MEND were all official supporters of an event held in London in December 2014 organised by the Islamic Human Rights Commission (IHRC) entitled, 'Institutional Islamophobia: A conference to examine state racism and social engineering of the Muslim community'.[8] This event was also supported by a relatively new Muslim activist group, CAGE (formerly Cageprisoners) which, in partnership with MEND and FOSIS, campaigns against the government's counter-radicalisation strategy, Prevent.[9] Just a month earlier, representatives from the MCB and MAB, as well as MEND, attended a meeting together in Parliament dedicated to tackling Islamophobia.[10]

Although MEND is now the most active organisation targeting Islamophobia, the MCB and MAB – the two key organisations respectively associated with the Jama'at and Ikhwan streams of the global Muslim Brotherhood in Britain – have both campaigned against Islamophobia for many years. Both organisations were official supporters of a national rally organised in November 2006 by the Ikhwan-associated British Muslim Initiative and the human rights group Liberty to combat the 'demonisation' of Muslims and 'defend freedom of thought, conscience and religion'. Other supporters included IFE, the Cordoba Foundation, IHRC, the Islam Channel, and Dawatul Islam UK and Eire.[11] The rally marked the beginning of the thirteenth annual Islam Awareness Week, a programme initiated by the Islamic Society of Britain (ISB). In February of the same year, a 'who's who' of British revivalist groups spanning the divide between Jama'at-i-Islami and the Ikhwan organised a public rally to demonstrate against Islamophobia in the wake of the publication in Denmark of cartoons depicting the prophet Muhammad. The organisers included the MAB, IFE, the UK Islamic Mission (UKIM), Dawatul Islam, FOSIS and the ISB. Coordinating partners included the East London Mosque's London Muslim Centre, Young Muslims UK (an offshoot of UKIM), Young Muslims Organisation UK (an offshoot of IFE), Muslim Welfare House, and the Institute of Islamic Political Thought (headed by Azzam Tamimi). The event was supported by the MCB and sponsored by the Islam Channel.[12]

Islamophobia is one of the most important themes for the MCB and MAB, as well as for other organisations in the revivalist network in Britain. However, the two organisations haven't often worked jointly to address to it. This is partly due to the different organisational environments they inhabit and their different everyday roles and working partners. The MCB, as Britain's 'national representative Muslim umbrella body', has understandably taken a more proactive advocacy role in relation to the British government. The MAB, on the other hand, is primarily concerned with providing services to its members and spreading what it deems as the 'correct' understanding of Islam.[13] The MCB and MAB most certainly share close links, but this is less in the form of collaborative activities or campaigns and more in the form of personal connections and shared leadership roles within other structures.

The MAB's president, Omer El-Hamdoon, for example, is the MCB's current deputy secretary general (2016–2018).[14] In this capacity, he works alongside MCB National Council members including former secretary generals Muhammad Abdul Bari and Farooq Murad; the Islamic Foundation's chairman, Manazir Ahsan; and the former president of UKIM, Zahid

Parvez. Mohammed Kozbar, MAB's vice-president is also a council member, further dissolving the boundaries between the Ikhwan-associated MAB and the Jama'at-associated MCB. The two organisations are also two of the four founding groups of the Mosques and Imams National Advisory Board (MINAB), established in 2006 to set standards and establish a system of self-regulation for mosques. As the MAB's founding representative in the organisation, El-Hamdoon is a trustee of MINAB alongside Shaykh Ibrahim Mogra, a national council member and former assistant secretary general of the MCB.[15] El-Hamdoon was until recently MINAB's vice-chair, working with Shuja Shafi, then MCB secretary general.[16]

These associations have occasionally resulted in collaborations on events. In December 2011, for example, the MAB organised an event in Birmingham with the MCB's official support, entitled, 'Creating Hope', aimed at a British Muslim audience.[17] The event featured a number of key speakers from across the Jama'at-Ikhwan divide. These included Rashid al-Ghannushi, co-founder of Tunisia's al-Nahda party; Anas Altikriti, director of the Cordoba Foundation; Zahid Parvez, then director of the UKIM; and Farooq Murad, then secretary general of the MCB. Others included Faisal Hanjara of the MCB; Mohamed Ali Harrath, director of the Islam Channel; Batool Al-Toma of ISB; and Nabil Ahmed, then president of FOSIS. According to El-Hamdoon, the event aimed to galvanise British Muslims' greater participation in society at all levels, including politics, education and the media.[18]

Several other examples of Jama'at-Ikhwan collaboration addressing the issue of Islamophobia and the perception of Muslims may be provided. In January 2012, Harrath's Islam Channel initiated an 'alternative Leveson inquiry' to investigate 'widespread and systematic discriminatory practices in reporting on Muslims and Islam in the British media'.[19] Based on a public opinion poll that found that people believe the media are responsible for 'whipping up a climate of fear of Islam in the UK', the inquiry set out to examine the possible causal effect between media coverage and social attitudes towards Muslims. In addition to Harrath, a number of key individuals associated with Jama'at and Ikhwan legacy groups signed an open letter published in *The Guardian*, identifying themselves as 'supporters of the alternative Leveson inquiry'.[20] These included Murad, on behalf of the MCB; El-Hamdoon, for the MAB; Massoud Shadjareh, the director of IHRC; Altikriti, representing the Cordoba Foundation; Faliq, representing IFE; Ahmed, for FOSIS; and Daud Abdullah, on behalf of the Middle East Monitor (MEMO).

Several months earlier, in October 2011, the Cordoba Foundation and MEMO headed by Abdullah, a former deputy secretary general of the MCB, jointly hosted the launch of a SpinWatch-authored report on the spread of Islamophobia in Britain entitled, *The Cold War on British Muslims: The Instigators and Funders*.[21] The event, held in the House of Commons, presented the main findings of the report, which amounted to an attack on the two London-based think tanks that have been most critical of Islamism in Britain, Policy Exchange and the Centre for Social Cohesion.

In addition to protests against Islamophobia, revivalist groups have sometimes collaborated on workshops to develop Muslims' engagement with the media. While MCB deputy secretary general in 2009, Abdullah and the Cordoba Foundation's Altikriti jointly hosted a workshop entitled 'Muslims and the Media: Positive Engagement from the Whole Community'. The event included a panel discussion 'on how individuals, organisations and Mosques can better engage with the media, to promote positive stories'.[22] This built upon an earlier workshop, held in December 2007, jointly run by the Cordoba Foundation and MCB that aimed to improve the media and communication skills of 'young Muslims involved in faith and BME groups, including charities, Mosques, local campaigns, voluntary and social-welfare organisations'.[23] The event was part of the Muslim Media Empowerment Project, initiated by the Cordoba Foundation and the London Borough of Tower Hamlets. The MCB was one of the partners and publicised it on its website.[24]

These examples demonstrate active collaborative relationships between individuals and groups linked with the Jama'at and Ikhwan-associated streams of Muslim activism in Britain centred on the shared concern over the public perception of Muslims and Islam. It may be argued that, taken collectively, these events comprise an ongoing campaign to assert control over how Muslims and Islam are generally perceived. A related and equally important concern for them is how Muslims view themselves. Although this may be more apparent when looking at the work of individual organisations, as subsequent chapters will show, representatives of Jama'at and Ikhwan-associated groups have sometimes collaborated in events targeting Muslims that address issues of Muslim identity.

In August 2013, for example, the then secretary general of the MCB, Farooq Murad, and the Cordoba Foundation's Anas Altikriti were both key speakers at an event at the Muslim Cultural Heritage Centre entitled, 'Rethinking the Muslim Community'. The event sought to address 'the challenges of inspiring and instituting a communal spirit' within Muslims in Britain.[25] Contention over the public perception of Muslims and Islam, and over Muslim collective identity, are an important bonding factor for the global Muslim Brotherhood in Britain and will be explored in greater depth in the following chapters. Here it suffices to note specific instances of organisational collaboration that touch on those themes.

In addition to protesting against certain perceptions of Muslims and Islam, and galvanising a particular self-perception of Muslim identity, Jama'at- and Ikhwan-associated groups have occasionally collaborated to directly influence the public perception of Muslims and Islam. In September 2014, for example, the MCB officially supported two related events organised by the Cordoba Foundation. One was a conference entitled 'Peace-Building in the 21st Century: Celebrating Achievements and Hopes, Confronting Real Issues'.[26] The second event, to commemorate the UN International Day of Peace, included discussions between different religious and community leaders, and an 'open door' day for the general public at mosques around the country.[27] This opportunity to present Muslims and Islam to the broader society was coordinated through a network of Islamic centres and organisations including the MCB, the Jama'at-associated East London Mosque, and MINAB, represented on the official promotional material by its then chairman, Maulana Muhammad Sarfraz Madni, a former president of UKIM. This endeavour to build a bridge to Islam for the general public was collectively organised across ethnic lines. The first of these events was held in 2012. The idea of providing the wider public with access to British mosques was taken up by the MCB and turned into an annual event in February 2015 called 'Visit My Mosque'.[28]

Trans-ethnic collaboration that fuzzes the Jama'at-Ikhwan division is also evident in recent campaigns focusing on the plight of Muslims outside Britain. An issue that for many years has been an effective rallying point for British Muslims is that of Palestine. In May 2013, the London Muslim Centre at the Jama'at-associated East London Mosque hosted a fundraising event for the Palestinian Solidarity Campaign (PSC), entitled 'An Evening for Palestinian Solidarity'.[29] The event was supported by Jama'at- and Ikhwan-associated groups, including IFE, the MAB, the Cordoba Foundation and FOSIS. In July 2015, the Centre hosted another fundraising event for PSC with the same name, which was publicised by the MCB and supported by FOSIS, BMI and IFE.[30]

Some years earlier, in February 2009, a number of British revivalist groups sent representatives to the Turkish ambassador in London in gratitude of Turkish prime minister Erdogan's remarks lambasting Israeli actions in Gaza. These representatives included Abdullah, then MCB deputy secretary general; Said Ferjani, then head of policy and public relations for MAB; Dilwar Hussain Khan, then IFE secretary general; Faisal Hanjra, then FOSIS president; Harrath, Islam Channel's CEO; and Mohammed Sawalha, the British Muslim Initiative's president. Other groups represented included Dawatul Islam, the Palestinian Return Centre, and the Palestinian Forum in Britain.[31] In Steven Merley's words, all of these individuals and/or organisations 'are known to have ties to the U.K. Brotherhood'.[32]

Another recent fundraising event for Muslims in need abroad focused on the plight of the Rohingya in Myanmar. Involving speakers from IFE, the Cordoba Foundation and the East London Mosque, a 'Charity Dinner in Aid of Muslims of Burma' was held in September 2012 in collaboration with the charity Muslim Aid, an organisation that, as this chapter will show, serves as a nexus for numerous individuals involved in other revivalist groups.[33]

A final example of Jama'at and Ikhwan-associated groups collaborating may be provided on the theme of their characterisation as 'participationists'. According to Abdullah Faliq, IFE, the MAB and UKIM worked together over a decade ago on a campaign to encourage civic engagement and voting. This was in conflict with the rhetoric of Hizb-ut Tahir, which had labelled participation in the democratic system as *haram*, Islamically forbidden. 'We brought in a lot of literature supporting participation published by IFE,' remarks Faliq. 'I produced that. Scholars included al-Qaradawi, al-Ghannushi, Khurshid Ahmad, as well as Salafis and Tablighis. ISB produced similar literature. This provided Muslims with the argument as to why they ought to be politically engaged.'[34] This campaign to encourage voting was not only designed to promote participation per se. It was also put behind George Galloway's Respect Party in the 2005 general election and, it may be argued, was a significant factor in the election of Galloway as MP for Bethnal Green and Bow in East London.[35] Galloway's appeal for these groups was his active role in the Stop the War Coalition, in which the MAB was a key partner, as well as his ongoing support for the Palestinians, which includes funding Hamas, in its conflict with Israel.[36]

The MCB publicly lauded the efforts of IFE and the MAB in promoting Muslim political participation. And in the run-up to the 2005 general election, it launched its own strategy aimed at urging British Muslims 'to participate more actively in mainstream politics'.[37] It published a brochure, 'Electing to Deliver', and a 'Voter Card' that highlighted 'the ten key questions that Muslims had to ask of all prospective parliamentary candidates'. It promoted this campaign on the Islam Channel and through other media outlets. Although not endorsing a particular political party, the MCB has continued to encourage Muslims to vote in British elections. In the run-up to the 2010 general election, it launched a new campaign with the publication of a statement signed by numerous imams and Islamic scholars encouraging Muslim political participation. Signatories included Musleh Uddin Faradi, IFE president; Maulana Muhammad Sarfraz Madni, UKIM president; Shaykh Ibrahim Mogra, a senior MCB official and the organisation's imam; and Hafiz Shafiqur Rahamn representing Dawatul Islam.[38] Ahead of the 2015 general election, the MCB launched a platform, 'Muslim Vote', 'to engage Muslims to participate in politics', and published a report, *Fairness, Not Favours*, that identified a number of issues that it considered as important for Muslims in Britain.[39] In 2017, anticipating Britain's next general election, the MCB produced a guide for Muslims that compared the three main parties' manifesto positions on a number of issues, including security, education and the recognition of Palestine as an independent state.[40]

In 2015, in parallel with the MCB's new platform, MEND launched its first 'Muslim Manifesto' to mobilise Muslims' participation in British politics.[41] It launched its second such document for the 2017 election.[42] Commenting on the two organisations' 2017 campaigns, Azad Ali, MEND's head of head of community development and a former MCB official, noted, 'We [MEND and the MCB] have similar interests in the areas of Islamophobia, concerns with the counter-terrorism legislation and the protection of human rights … that kind of stuff we share similar asks.'[43]

Publications

Collaborative networking between participationist or revivalist groups is also evident, albeit to a limited extent, in the publication of books and reports.

The Islamic Foundation is one of Britain's most established and prolific publishers of Islamic books. As many observers have noted, in the first few decades after its founding in 1973, the Islamic Foundation published numerous works of both Jama'at-i-Islami and Muslim Brotherhood ideologues, including al-Banna and Mawdudi. Some of Mawdudi's books were edited by the Islamic Foundation's chairman, Khurshid Ahmad and its then director general, Khurram Murad. In recent years, the Foundation has broadened the scope of its publications, including works on matters of greater contemporary significance, but despite its increasingly diverse catalogue it still publishes a significant number of books by Mawdudi, in addition to Mawdudi-inspired authors and activists including Ahmad, Murad and vice-chairman Abdur Rashid Siddiqui.

In 2003, the Foundation edited and published a two-part series, *Islam: The Way of Revival*, which collated the works of al-Banna, Mawdudi, Said Qutb, Khurshid Ahmad, Khurram Murad, Yusuf al-Qaradawi, Said Ramadan and others widely considered as revivalist or participationist Islamist writers. In a clear endorsement of the presentation of Islam as 'an integrated, comprehensive way of life', the editors, Riza Muhammad and Dilwar Hussain, write that although Islam is essentially concerned with a relationship with Allah, it is through organised activism in line with an Islamic socio-political vision that this relationship is given its 'deepest meaning'.[44] The production of the series involved collaboration with FOSIS, established in 1962 by members of the Muslim Brotherhood and Jama'at-i-Islami,[45] which provided many of the selected texts that originally appeared in its magazine, *The Muslim*. [46]

More will be said in subsequent chapters about the shared ideas and beliefs of the above-mentioned figures and other key individuals within the Jama'at-Ikhwan network in Britain. Here it suffices to note some of the working collaborations involved in publishing. In addition to working with individual authors for the publication of their works, such as former UKIM president Zahid Parvez, the Islamic Foundation has institutional partnerships with other publishers whose works it distributes. These include the Muslim Educational Trust (MET), established by UKIM in 1966 to 'Islamise knowledge' in Britain, and the Muslim Brotherhood-associated International Institute of Islamic Thought (IIIT), which, while based in the United States, has an office in London. The Foundation is the only distributor for IIIT's publications other than IIIT itself.

These relationships, however, appear rather limited. MET is a small and rather inactive publishing house, although, as discussed later, it has played a significant advocacy role in Britain for the education of Muslims in line with Islamic principles. It has published less than ten books, mostly written by its director, Ghulam Sarwar. In contrast, IIIT's London office, headed by Anas al-Shaikh-Ali, has been very actively engaged in publishing, as well as organising conferences across Europe, working closely with the Association of Muslim Social Scientists (AMSS) UK, of which al-Shaikh-Ali is also chairman. But despite what might appear to be a potentially fruitful overlap of thematic concerns between IIIT and the Islamic Foundation – for example, the impact of globalisation upon Muslims in Europe – the two organisations have not collaborated over joint publications or co-organised events. The reason for this, suggests Dilwar Hussain, former head of research at the Foundation and former ISB president, is that although there was a 'reasonable relationship' between IIIT and the Foundation, 'there were also personality conflicts' and 'differences of view' between the leadership of the two organisations.[47]

Nonetheless, there have been some noteworthy organisational connections between the Islamic Foundation and IIIT/AMSS. Such connections are the topic of the next section of this chapter, but links between these particular organisations can be mentioned briefly here. Khurshid Ahmad, the Islamic Foundation's former chairman, is a member of the advisory board for AMSS-UK and IIIT's American Journal of Islamic Social Sciences.[48] Mohammad Siddique Seddon, a former research fellow at the Islamic Foundation, which publishes his books, is an executive committee member of AMSS-UK.[49] Until his death in April 2016, Zafar Ishaq Ansari, who translated Mawdudi's work into English for the Islamic Foundation, was member of the Foundation's Board of Advisers and a fellow at the American branch of AMSS.[50] Another former researcher at the Islamic Foundation, Mohammed Abdul Aziz, was also an executive committee member of AMSS-UK.[51] Noteworthy too, but perhaps less importantly, Islamic Foundation staff have appeared as speakers at IIIT/AMSS events. Former Islamic Foundation research fellow and former ISB president, Sughra Ahmed, was one of numerous speakers at a 2009 conference entitled 'Muslim Youth: Challenges, Opportunities and Expectations', co-organised by AMSS-UK.[52] Hussain, then also representing the Foundation as a research fellow, was a speaker at a joint IIIT/AMSS-UK conference held at the University of Westminster in 2004, which sought to address the issue of the practice of Islamic law within a Muslim minority context.[53]

Aside from the Islamic Foundation and IIIT, the most active publisher within the network of Jama'at- and Ikhwan-associated organisations is the Cordoba Foundation. The organisation produces a quarterly magazine called 'Arches'; toolkits, including guides to conducting effective lobbying and media; policy papers; and reports. These materials feature the work of Muslim and non-Muslim contributors on a range of topics most of whom, while broadly sympathetic to the organisation's ethos, are not associated with the global Muslim Brotherhood. One significant collaboration, however, that cuts across Jama'at-Ikhwan lines is the report, *Meet the Challenge, Make the Change: A Call to Action for Muslim Civil Society in Britain*, authored by the former chairman of the East London Mosque and former MCB general secretary, Muhammad Abdul Bari. In this report, Bari decries what he sees as the 'collective under-achievement' and a lack of effective leadership of Britain's Muslim community, and calls for Muslims to become more engaged 'in neighbourhood and community works, social activities, economic exchanges, culture and politics'.[54]

Leadership structures

The collaborations observed above provide a glimpse of active networking between individuals and groups associated with the global Muslim Brotherhood in Britain. The overriding theme of these partnerships, reflected most clearly in events such as the MAB-organised conference, 'Creating Hope', and Bari's report, *Meet the Challenge, Make the Change*, is Muslim identity and unity. But such collaborations do not adequately capture the extent to which these individuals and groups are networked, since they are typically engaged in work within different fields and with stakes that are different, at least in the short term. The potential for practical partnerships between organisations is limited somewhat by their respective official missions and areas of interest, as well as their practical expertise and organisational ability. But between the individuals working for these organisations is a fluid network of relationships.

The Islamic Foundation, for example, has not collaborated publicly with the Cordoba Foundation. The two organisations operate in two different fields, the former in publishing and academia, with a focus on higher education and economics, the latter mainly in advocacy and public policy with an eye to international affairs. However, they are connected in terms of personal networks. The Islamic Foundation's long-time trustee and current chairman, Manazir Ahsan, is a former colleague of the Cordoba Foundation's Abdullah Faliq. Along with Iqbal Sacranie, Ahsan and Faliq were key players in the establishment of the MCB and its precursor, the National Interim Committee on Muslim Unity. Ahsan and Faliq remain linked through the MCB. Ahsan is a member of the MCB's National Council and Faliq is a directly nominated affiliate, as well as a former member of the MCB's Europe and International Affairs Committee.[55] Through the MCB, Faliq is also linked to the Islamic Foundation by his relationship with Foundation director general and former MCB secretary general, Farooq Murad. Another example is with Muslim Aid. While it has collaborated on some charity-related events in Britain, its public collaborations with other Jama'at- and Ikhwan-associated Muslim organisations are scarce. Yet, Muslim Aid, as detailed below, informally connects numerous organisations through its board of trustees. Despite a lack of official partnerships between certain organisations, there are a multitude of personal connections that link them.

To more fully appreciate the network of relationships between Jama'at- and Ikhwan-associated individuals and groups it is important to look beyond public collaborations and regard the personal connections between the key figures, as well as the leadership structures of these groups, both formal and informal. The personal connections between the key players in the network, it is argued, are inseparable from organisational roles, but these roles are fluid and often overlapping.

In an interview with the book author, Abdullah Faliq provides an invaluable insight into the ways in which Muslim activists and groups of Ikhwani and Jama'ati heritage are networked in Britain.[56] He identifies three ways: first, there is the formal body of the MCB. Second, there is a coordination committee made up from the leaders of key organisations, called the Coordination Committee of Islamic Organisations. And, third, there are loose, informal social connections comprised of working friendships. These three ways or modes of networking are each explored and elaborated below. In addition to these, it is important to look more holistically at the overall network, for there are numerous other connections beyond Faliq's involvement in the network in the three ways he describes. In some cases, for example, the trustees of a given organisation are directly involved in the work of other organisations that are Jama'at- or Ikhwan-associated. In other cases, the founding organisations of a certain organisation are Jama'at- and Ikhwan-associated.

The Muslim Council of Britain

The Muslim Council of Britain (MCB) was founded in November 1997, according to its first secretary general, Iqbal Sacranie, to present 'a united Muslim voice'.[57] The event that galvanised its founding was the Rushdie Affair in 1988. The publication of Salman Rushdie's novel, *The Satanic Verses*, was deemed offensive to many Muslims in Britain for its scandalous portrayal of the prophet Muhammad. The United Kingdom Action Committee on Islamic Affairs (UKACIA) was hastily set up to express Muslim discontent and protest the government to ban the book and to extend the existing blasphemy laws to include Islam. UKACIA was dissolved shortly after the Rushdie affair, but a small number of activists involved in UKACIA, including Manazir Ahsan and Islamic Foundation trustee Hashir Faruqi, saw a longer-term need for national Muslim representation. In consultation with the then home secretary, Michael Howard, who recommended that Muslim leaders form a 'representative body' that he could 'support and recognise',[58] they established the National Interim Committee on Muslim Unity (NICMU). The blueprint for the MCB was sketched at a NICMU meeting in 1994.

Anthony McRoy suggests that the formation of UKACIA 'was an attempt not only to unite British Muslims on a specific issue of concern, but also to unite them behind the pro-Jama'at element'.[59] He acknowledges Gilles Kepel's argument that by being the first to launch the campaign, 'the Mawdudites had a real chance of taking over the leadership of a movement which promised to mobilise large numbers and this considerably extend their influence over British Islam'.[60] According to McRoy, the MCB is 'the result of longstanding plans by pro-Jama'at forces to take over the leadership of British Muslims'. McRoy acknowledges the Rushdie Affair as the watershed moment for the emergence of an *umma*-centric, Muslim political identity in Britain, consolidated by the first Iraq war (1990–1991) and the Bosnian war (1992–1995).[61] These fed the perception, commonly preached in radical mosques throughout Britain in the 1990s, of an attack on Islam. Yet, he notes, calls for the formation of a federation of Muslim organisations in Britain were made as far back as 1980 by the late Jama'at-i-Islami activist and Islamic Foundation director, Khurram Murad, and others.[62]

The MCB is, in its own words, 'a national representative Muslim umbrella body'. Shaykh Ibrahim Mogra, former assistant secretary general of the MCB, describes the organisation as 'the most representative Muslim umbrella organisation in Britain'. But he concedes that it 'has failed to attract some groupings'.[63] A number of polls suggest a bigger failing. As Kenan Malik observes, 'An NOP/Channel 4 poll of Muslims in 2006 found that less than 4 per cent thought that the MCB represented British Muslims, and just 12 per cent felt it represented their political views. This is in line with many other surveys. An NOP poll for the conservative think tank Policy Exchange found only 6 per cent of Muslims thought the MCB represented their views.'[64]

Nevertheless, from its inception until around 2005, the MCB served as the British government's primary interlocutor for Britain's diverse Muslim communities. Its well-documented fall from government favour is usually linked to two events. The first was its boycotting of the Holocaust Memorial Day, first in 2005. The second, more decisive event was the signing of the Istanbul Declaration by its deputy secretary general, Daud Abdullah, in 2009. Exhorting the Muslim *umma* to wage *jihad* against Israel 'until the liberation of all of Palestine', this document defined as a 'declaration of war' any country's support for Israel or deployment of forces in the 'Muslim waters' facing Gaza preventing the smuggling of arms and supplies.[65] Since the British government was considering deploying naval forces to the Gaza coastline, it viewed this as an unwarranted provocation and suspended ties with the MCB. Although this decision was reversed in January 2010, subsequent governments, led by David Cameron and Theresa May, have not granted the MCB any special partnership status.[66]

The loss of the MCB's monopoly of engagement, lamented by Mogra as a denial of Muslim political representation,[67] was consolidated by 'the growing array of different claims from groups such as the British Muslim Forum, the Al-Khoei Foundation, Progressive British Muslims, British Muslims for Secular Democracy and others', including the Sufi Muslim Council and Quilliam.[68] But despite the growing multiplicity of Muslim voices in British civil society, according to Mohammed Abdul Aziz, a former adviser to Sacranie during his time as secretary general, the MCB has become more Jama'at-dominated since Sacranie's departure in 2005. 'A large part of the influential part of the organisational structure,' he notes, 'consists of people who come from a Jama'ati-Ikhwani background of some sort.'[69] Regardless of how representative or influential upon government it may or may not be, the MCB remains an important body within the broader network of Jama'at-Ikhwan-associated individuals and groups.

Daud Abdullah describes the MCB as a concerted effort to connect and unite British-based Muslims organisations. The mosques and other institutions that make up MCB's affiliates each pursue their own agendas, he explains, but work through the MCB on national issues. 'The parameters,' he says, 'are clearly defined.'[70] Yet, it would be a mistake to think of the MCB as the sole body within the global Muslim Brotherhood network in Britain advocating for Muslims' interests at the national level. Some of its affiliates, connected by association with a Jama'at-Ikhwan heritage, also have an interlocutionary role and advocate for changes in government policy.

The Muslim Educational Trust, for example, set up by the Mawdudi-inspired UKIM in 1966, has a long track record of working with government. In 1993 it was instrumental in obtaining government approval for an Islamic studies syllabus in secondary schools, for which it has provided teachers and teaching materials.[71] It states it has also persuaded local educational authorities to recognise and accept the 'special needs' of Muslim pupils in schools. For some years it was one of the main interlocutors between Muslim communities and the government with regard to educational matters. Today, this role has been taken over by the Association of Muslim Schools UK (AMS-UK), established in 1992. One of its core roles, AMS-UK asserts, is to represent the views and interests of 150 or so Muslim schools in Britain to the Department for Education (DfE), statutory bodies and the private sector. DfE officially recognises its interlocutionary function and contracts AMS-UK to conduct inspections of state-funded Muslim schools regarding their religious designation.[72]

Whether or not the MCB is understood as the main institutional interlocutor for Muslims on national matters, its greatest importance perhaps lies beyond its interlocutional function. The MCB is a central hub within the network of Jama'at- and Ikhwan-associated individuals and groups. While a hierarchical organisation with a formal leadership structure and clear mandate to advocate on behalf of its listed affiliates, the MCB also functions as a meshwork of interaction through which numerous individuals, and hence organisations, are informally connected. Nested within the formal structure of the MCB, but not restricted to it, is a network of related individuals that can only be observed with regard to their multiple associations and shared histories both within and outside the MCB. Most observers note MCB's declining influence as a government partner. But the MCB's far greater significance, it may be argued, even at the height of its popularity with the government, is its facilitation of numerous connections that traverse various fields of social activism, including public policy, education, law and finance. Some of these connections are explored in the last section of this chapter.

The Coordination Committee of Islamic Organisations

In addition to the MCB, states Faliq, there is a less hierarchical, semi-formal committee through which some of the key organisations associated with Jama'at-i-Islami and the Muslim Brotherhood meet. 'Within the mainstream Islamic groups,' he discloses, 'there is a coordination committee, where the leaders of these groups meet every now and then to discuss strategies, their achievements and what to focus on. It is called "the Coordination Committee of Islamic Organisations".'[73]

Faliq identifies the organisations that comprise this committee as the Islamic Foundation, IFE, the MAB, UKIM and Dawatul Islam UK & Ireland. It is significant that in the academic and think tank literature with a focus on Muslim activism, all of these groups are associated with Jama'at-i-Islami or the Ikhwan. The individual committee members, Faliq explains, are from the *shuras* – the management – of the organisations represented on the committee, which meet occasionally, sometimes on camps and 'residentials'. Attendees include the leadership of the member organisations, plus other colleagues. Usually, around four or five people attend from each organisation. Along with Dilwar Hussain Khan – not to be mistaken for Dilwar Hussain formerly of the Islamic Foundation and ISB – Faliq represents IFE at these meetings. MAB, he notes, is represented by Omer El-Hamdoon. UKIM is represented by Maulana Muhammad Sarfraz Madni. Committee members have to be a representative of an organisation, informs Faliq, but, 'beyond the leaders of the organisations, you have some other key leaders, including Khurshid Ahmad and Muhammad Abdul Bari'. The Cordoba Foundation and IIIT are not involved in this committee, explains Faliq, because they are not community-oriented groups. The committee is mainly comprised of community-focused membership organisations.

The Coordination Committee of Islamic Organisations is a discreet and hitherto unreported mechanism for the networking of Jama'at and Ikhwan-associated individuals and groups in Britain. In an interview with Innes Bowen, the former spokesperson for the Muslim Brotherhood in the West, Kemal al-Helbawy, says he led a group in the 1980s and 1990s almost identically named, the 'Coordination Committee between Islamic Movements', and worked closely with the Islamic Foundation's Khurshid Ahmad 'to bring together leading representatives of the Islamic Movement from around the world'.[74] It is unclear if this is the same committee. But, if so, it is likely to have undergone some changes, since the committee Faliq describes is composed mostly of British citizens and focused on Britain. In any case, this coordination committee, as it functions today, is absent from the available literature on Islamism in Britain.

Despite being involved in the MCB and the coordination committee, Faliq is candidly critical of both, referring to them as overly bureaucratic. He describes the MCB as 'too statesmanlike' and the committee's leadership as mostly aged and inflexible.[75] A different line of criticism directed at the committee is voiced by Dilwar Hussain, former ISB president. According to Hussain, the ISB was a member of the coordination committee, but under his leadership formally withdrew in 2011, participating with a gradually increasing sense of detachment from the other committee members' ideas and values from around 2003 to 2004.

Questions that were raised by Hussain and his colleagues in ISB at this time, he says, included the following: 'What sort of social transformation do we want? Are we advocating social transformation in the name of Islam? What is our relationship with terms like "*shari'a*" and "Islamic state"?'[76] Their answers to these questions, he notes, made them realise that they were at a 'radically different place' to that of other committee members such as the MAB, UKIM and IFE. Hussain's description of the coordination committee underplays its function as a forum for effective strategic planning and coordination. 'If these meetings were effective, 'he says, 'you'd see many more programs and activities with these organisations doing things together – and you don't. You hardly see any activities where you've got UKIM, MAB, IFE and ISB working on the same platform.'

Regardless of how effective the coordination committee was in the past and is today, the connections facilitated by it, as with those facilitated by the MCB, help comprise a network of dedicated activists inspired by Islamic principles working, in their eyes, for the betterment of Britain's Muslim communities and the society at large. The coordination committee member organisations are linked to numerous other Islamic organisations, including Jama'at- or Ikhwan-associated ones, by virtue of the committee member representatives' authoritative roles in other organisations.

The coordination committee, for example, is linked to the Mosques and Imams National Advisory Board (MINAB), whose membership, like the committee, is composed of organisations. El-Hamdoon, representing MAB in the committee, as mentioned, is a trustee of MINAB and represented MAB on MINAB's board as vice-chair.[77] Madni, representing UKIM on the committee, formerly represented the MCB on MINAB's board in the position of chairman until October 2015.[78] The committee is linked to the MCB through Faliq and Abdul Bari's long-time involvement in the umbrella group and through El-Hamdoon's current position as deputy secretary general. Khan's position as executive director of the East London Mosque (ELM), where Abdul Bari was for many years its chairman and is currently a trustee, links the mosque and the associated London Muslim Centre to the committee.[79] A final example of how the coordination committee is linked to Islamic organisations external to it is with Dawatul Islam's connection to Britain's national Islamic Sharia Council network: The current chairman and former president of Dawatul Islam, Maulana Abu Sayeed, is also the chairman of the Islamic Sharia Council and was involved in the creation of a national federation of *shari'a* councils, the UK Board of Sharia Councils.[80]

This glimpse of connections between the coordination committee and other Islamic organisations provided above is limited to some of the main organisations associated with the global Muslim Brotherhood in Britain. But most of the individuals on the committee are also involved in smaller, more local organisations, including mosques and schools. The revivalist network of the Brotherhood in Britain extends to local communities via these organisations and grassroots initiatives, although these connections are rarely discussed or explored in the academic and think tank literature or news media that is concerned with Islamism in Britain. It is through these local groups that the leadership network of most concern to observers in academic and think tank circles extends to what the sociologist Alberto Melucci refers to as 'submerged networks'.[81]

For example, in addition to his role in IFE, Dilwar Hussain Khan, is vice-chair of the Faiths Forum for London. According to his biography, he has been director of Islamic community centre, finance manager of a housing association, and manager of a special educational needs organisation in East London, the Asian Parents Association for Special Educational Needs in Tower Hamlets.[82] Madni is actively involved in the Blackheath Mosque in Birmingham. He represented the mosque as a signatory on an open letter, signed in July 2014 by over 100 imams, urging Muslims not to go to Syria and Iraq to fight in the conflict there.[83] A teacher by profession, Madni was the interim headteacher at Al-Hijrah School in Birmingham after it was placed in special measures in 2013 and is the school's current assistant headteacher.[84] Muhammad Abdul Bari's involvement in community work is extensive. He is the founder director of Amana Parenting, which publishes books and provides workshops, as well as consulting services, on parenting. He is a founding member of the East London Communities Organisation, part of the Citizens UK. Abdul Bari is also a patron of Anchor House, a homeless charity, the Ramphal Institute, and the educational charity, the Nida Trust.

Informal personal connections

In addition to the MCB and the Coordination Committee of Islamic Organisations, Faliq identifies an informal network of friendships as the 'third front' in which he and his associates collaborate.[85] Within his personal network, he says, is Anas Altikriti, Dilwar Hussain Khan, Daud Abdullah, Muhammad Abdul Bari, and Mohammad Kozbar. He describes this group as more informal and 'advanced', since it is less burdened with formalities and more actively involved with the organisation of various campaigns. This network of friends meets more regularly and communication is frequent. This group partially overlaps with the coordination committee and has strong connections with the MCB.

All of the individuals in Faliq's personal network named above are or have been involved in organisations with Jama'at-i-Islami or Muslim Brotherhood associations, and all are actively involved in Islamic activism or advocacy work today. Altikriti, whose father was the leader of the Muslim Brotherhood's political wing in Iraq, was a founding member of MAB prior to establishing the Cordoba Foundation. He set up the MAB alongside Kemal al-Helbawy; Azzam Tamimi, a former activist in the Brotherhood's political party in Jordan; and Mohammed Sawalha, recently reported to be a member of the political bureau of Hamas.[86] After a stint as MAB president, Altikriti left the MAB, along with Tamimi and Sawalha in 2006 to form the British

Muslim Initiative (BMI), which government records state was dissolved in September 2014.[87]

Kozbar is the vice-president of the MAB,[88] a national council member of the MCB,[89] and was a listed director and spokesperson for BMI.[90] Steven Merley identifies him as 'a well-known leader in the U.K Muslim Brotherhood' who 'has been an officer in numerous U.K. Brotherhood organizations including BMI and the MAB, the Finsbury Park Mosque, the Muslim Council of Britain (MCB), and the Muslim Welfare House'.[91] Kozbar is also a project director for IslamExpo, an Islamic cultural festival and political conference established by Sawalha in 2004. Khan, as mentioned above, is a key figure in both IFE and the East London Mosque, as well as the London Muslim Centre, where Abdul Bari has held senior leadership positions. Daud Abdullah, in addition to his former role in the MCB worked as a senior researcher for the Palestinian Return Centre and currently directs the Middle Eastern Monitor, a pro-Palestinian media research organisation.[92]

This informal network is inseparable from the multiple formal roles that each of these individuals has in their respective organisations. This is not just a circle of friends. The friendships between these individuals are shaped in part by shared, religiously conceived values and perspectives, and shared histories of association, but, equally importantly, they are also shaped by a shared commitment to social activism enabled by their positions of authority. Collectively, they comprise a web of latent working partnerships that may be actualised in response to specific emerging issues. This network extends to other contacts, including similarly minded Muslim colleagues and friends – some of whom are not in equivalent leadership positions, but active as volunteers and interns – and non-Muslim partners who share concerns on particular issues.

The informal network that Faliq describes as the third way in which he and others collaborate is not really a distinct alternative to the organisation-to-organisation approach of the coordination committee, or to their everyday official work within these organisations. It is not an informal as opposed to a formal way of working. It is, rather, an informal mode of organisation that is in a sense dependent on these formal structures – particularly for the recognition and contacts that they provide – while being unconstrained by them. The formal roles of Faliq and his close associates within his informal network facilitate collaboration on projects, campaigns, and other events, but the organisations for which they officially work are not always formally recognised in these activities as coordinators or hosts. Their formal roles have endowed them with contacts, reputation amongst these contacts and, thus, their ability to organise new initiatives and establish new coalitions or organisations through informal channels.

Faliq's role in the formation of the Rohingya Minority Crisis Group (RMCG) in August 2012 exemplifies this blurring of formal and informal networking. Faliq was the key instigator of RMCG, but did not play this central role on behalf of the Cordoba Foundation or IFE where he holds senior positions. 'I've got most of the people together, most of them are my contacts,' he says. 'This is what I'll do. I'll just bring them to the table and let them run with it. I did the same thing with Syria and Palestine.'[93] In convening this group and coordinating a series of related events, Faliq drew upon his close, informal connections: the charity dinner mentioned earlier was co-hosted by IFE, where he and Khan have official leadership roles, and a related conference was held at the London Muslim Centre at the East London Mosque, where Khan is the executive director; Altikriti was one of the key speakers. Yet, although the Cordoba Foundation is listed as a founding partner of RMCG, Faliq didn't convene RMCG on behalf of the Cordoba Foundation. 'I don't do it with a certain organisational hat on,' explains Faliq, 'but the people involved know where I'm from.'[94]

Faliq's personal network ought not to be seen in isolation from the connections each one of his close associates has outside it, particularly those to other Jama'at- or Ikhwan-associated individuals. Each individual within Faliq's close network has his own network with expected overlaps but also new nodes. As with any politically active social network, global Muslim Brotherhood figures in Britain and abroad are not all directly connected by personal acquaintance or organisational collaboration. But their overlapping connections provide a fuller picture of their organisational network as a whole. The following section seeks to provide such a picture – although not an exhaustive one – with regard to connections between individuals, between individuals and organisations, and between organisations.

Overlapping organisational structures

The connections between revivalist individuals and groups are both extensive and complex. In addition to collaborative links (some of which have been described in this chapter), the coordination committee, and informal personal links (of which Faliq's are but one example), there are numerous other connections between individuals and organisations that help collectively comprise an organised network. This section of the chapter maps out some of these other connections. There is no ideal starting place to do this, so it will focus on several hubs or clusters.

A significant hub that connects a number of key individuals within the revivalist network is Muslim Aid, a charity established by Yusuf Islam in 1985. Muslim Aid is located alongside IFE and the East London Mosque within the London Islamic Centre. The individuals involved in its strategic management include leaders associated with Jama'at-linked groups. It has also been linked with the Union of Good (UG), an umbrella group of charities led by al-Qaradawi that is dedicated to serving Hamas, which places it within the ambit of the Ikhwan.[95] Muslim Aid denies claims that it was ever a member of UG, and the British Charity Commission has cleared the group of any connection with terrorist groups. Allegations persist, however, of involvement in UG and of funding Palestinian terrorist groups, based on evidence from a range of sources.[96] In any case, Muslim Aid's senior management, by virtue of sharing an active role in the charity as well as other organisations, informally link the MCB, the Islamic Foundation, UKIM, the Muslim Educational Trust (MET), the MAB, the Cordoba Foundation, IFE, the East London Mosque, the Islamic Sharia Council, Muslim Welfare House, and two other organisations headed by al-Qaradawi, the European Council for Fatwa and Research (ECFR) and the International Union of Muslim Scholars (IUMS).

Manazir Ahsan was until recently the chairman of Muslim Aid's board of trustees, but remains a member of the board.[97] He retired as director general of the Islamic Foundation in June 2014 to replace Khurshid Ahmad as its chairman.[98] Ahmad remains a trustee of the Foundation.[99] In addition to Ahsan, two others hold trustee positions in both the Islamic Foundation and Muslim Aid, namely Muhammad Abdul Bari and Zahid Parvez.[100] Abdul Bari, a former MCB secretary general and former president of IFE, was until recently Muslim Aid's secretary but is still a member of its board. Parvez is the director of the Islamic Foundation's Markfield Institute of Higher Education (MIHE).[101] He is also a trustee of UKIM.[102] Further linking Muslim Aid with the Islamic Foundation are the positions held by Farooq Murad. In addition to being a trustee of Muslim Aid,[103] Murad has been the director general of the Islamic Foundation since completing his term as MCB secretary general in June 2014. He is also a trustee of MIHE, alongside Ahsan and Ahmad.[104]

Accompanying Ahsan, Abdul Bari, Parvez, and Murad on Muslim Aid's board is Suhaib Hasan, who is its acting chairman.[105] Hasan is also the secretary of the Islamic Sharia Council, an active member of ECFR and IUMS, and the presenter of the show 'Journey Through the Qur'an' on the Islam Channnel.[106] Riyadh al-Rawi, yet another trustee of Muslim Aid, is also the director and a trustee of Muslim Welfare House, a founding organisation of the Islamic Sharia Council.[107] Other Muslim Aid trustees include Iqbal Sacranie, the MCB's founding secretary general; Ghulam Sarwar, a former Muslim Aid treasurer and the longtime director of the MET; and Syed Tanzim Wasti, a former Muslim Aid secretary and a founding member of UKIM.[108]

Each of these individuals, in addition to being involved in multiple organisations, has his own trajectory through various other connected organisations. Ahsan's role in NICMU and the founding of the MCB has been noted. Sacranie and Murad were also founding MCB members alongside Ahsan. All three remain involved in the MCB in some capacity.[109] The involvement of Abdul Bari in other organisations has been described above. Additionally, Parvez is a former president of Young Muslims UK (YMUK), the Islamic Society of Britain (ISB), and UKIM; Murad, who was the chair of Muslim Aid, is also a former president of both YMUK and ISB; al-Rawi is a former president of FOSIS; and Wasti is a former MCB central working committee member. Besides these senior figures, other Muslim Aid staff members have historical connections with other Brotherhood- or Jama'at-associated organisations. The former Muslim Aid country director for Sri Lanka, Amjad Saleem,[110] for instance, was the head of communications for the Cordoba Foundation as well as a member of the MCB's central working committee.[111]

Muslim Aid is a key hub within the overall network of revivalist organisations in Britain, although perhaps it is more accurate to describe it as a network nested within the overall network. But the most significant node or nested network is undoubtedly the MCB. As noted earlier, the MCB acts as a web of communication and interaction through which numerous individuals and organisations are informally connected. It has been noted by numerous observers that many of its affiliate organisations have their origins in Jama'at-i-Islami or the Ikhwan. These include the Islamic Foundation, UKIM, MET, the East London Mosque, IFE, Young Muslim Organisation-UK (YMO-UK), Dawatul Islam, YMUK, the Islamic Sharia Council, Muslim Aid, the MAB, FOSIS and Muslim Welfare House. They also include some other smaller organisations, such as the Association of Muslim Schools UK and the Association of Muslim Lawyers. But for the purposes for ascertaining the existence of an organised network and understanding how it is composed, more interesting than these organisational affiliations are the numerous overlapping roles that the key leadership of the MCB share in these organisations as well as others.

Many of the senior figures actively involved in the MCB today are also involved in other organisations associated with Jama'at-i-Islami or the Ikhwan. Some of these have been mentioned above in relation to Muslim Aid. For example, in addition to being a Muslim Aid board member and the chairman of the Islamic Foundation, Ahsan is a member of the MCB's National Council.[112] He was also the chair of MINAB's Membership Committee.[113] Abdul Bari is still involved in the MCB. He is a member of both the Executive Committee and the National Council.[114] Between 2014 and 2016 he was the council's chair.[115] Alongside Ahsan and Abdul Bari, Murad and Parvez are members of the MCB's National Council, and Sacranie is an advisor to the MCB as well as an executive committee member.[116]

Other MCB figures similarly have multiple roles within other revivalist organisations. Faliq was involved in the creation of the MCB and, as noted earlier, is currently a member of its National Council. He is also the head of research for the Cordoba Foundation, the director of media and public relations for IFE, a trustee of IFE and the East London Mosque, the director of training at the Centre for the Study of Terrorism, which was founded by Kemal al-Helbawy, and a former president of YMO-UK.[117] As mentioned, both El-Hamdoon and Kozbar have senior roles within the MCB and MAB. Kozbar was also a director for BMI alongside Mohammed Sawalha, a former member of the MCB's Central Working Committee. Kozbar, Sawalha, El-Hamdoon and al-Rawi are all connected through their involvement in Muslim Welfare House. Kozbar, Sawalha and El-Hamdoon are all former directors of the organisation.[118]

Other active MCB figures include Iqbal Asaria, Maulana Muhammad Abu Sayeed, and Ibrahim Mogra. Asaria has been a special adviser to the secretary general on business and economic affairs since 2005.[119] He is also a lecturer at MIHE and is a member of the Islamic Foundation's advisory board alongside Mogra.[120] According to some reports, Asaria was the webmaster for the websites of Muslim Aid, IHRC and Tamimi's Institute of Islamic Political Thought.[121] Alongside Sacranie he is a guest speaker for the Ramphal Institute, where Abdul Bari is a patron.[122] Abu Sayeed, a former member of the MCB's National Council, is an executive council member and former president of Dawatul Islam.[123] He is also the chair of the Islamic Sharia Council, where he works closely with Suhaib Hasan. Both Abu Sayeed and Hasan are members of ECFR and IUMS, strengthening the connection between al-Qaradawi and the Islamic revivalist network in Britain.[124] Mogra, a former assistant secretary general of the MCB, is a member of its National Council. He is also a trustee MINAB, a trustee of the Al-Aqsa School Trust, alongside Ibrahim Hewitt.[125]

Former MCB senior figures such as Hewitt also help comprise the network of individuals and organisations in Britain associated with Jama'at-i-Islami and the Muslim Brotherhood. Hewitt, MCB assistant secretary general between 2004 and 2006, is the chairman of Interpal, the Palestinian Relief and Development Fund, which the US government classified as a Specially Designated Global Terrorist organization in 2003 due to allegations of funding Hamas in the Gaza Strip.[126] He is also a senior editor at MEMO, where he works alongside former MCB assistant secretary general Daud Abdullah. He is a founder and former executive committee member of the Association of Muslim Schools UK (AMS-UK), the former assistant director of MET, where he worked alongside Ghulam Sarwar, and a former public affairs committee member at MINAB.[127] Additionally, Hewitt is a trustee of the International Board of Educational Research and Resources (IBERR), founded by Yusuf Islam in 1996, in its own words, 'to "Islamise" the provision of educational services'.[128]

IBERR, although based in South Africa, is linked to several British organisations that connect a number of individuals and groups in Britain's Muslim Brotherhood network. IBERR and the Nida Trust have worked together on events and educational training. IBERR's CEO, Mohammed Akram Khan-Cheema was a keynote speaker at the Nida Trust's Education Fair in March 2012.[129] Together with the Islamic Shakhsiyah Foundation, IBERR and the Nida Trust have collaborated in the design and provision of teacher training for Muslim teachers in Britain.[130] The venue they have regularly used, the Regent's Park Mosque, is a founding organisation of the Islamic Sharia Council. Amongst the listed advisers of the Islamic Shakhsiyah Foundation is Edris Khamissa of IBERR and Ibrahim Hewitt.[131] The Nida Trust also has working relationships with MAB and the Islamic Foundation. The Nida Trust was invited to run MAB's annual leaders training camp in May 2012. It has also worked with the Islamic Foundation's Markfield Institute of Higher Education (MIHE) for the provision of courses delivered by MIHE senior lecturer Abdullah Sahin on 'Qur'anic pedagogy' and Islamic education, the latter of which was sponsored by Muslim Aid.[132]

In addition to Hewitt, other former MCB figures with overlapping roles in the revivalist network include Azad Ali, Tahir Alam and Mohammed Abdul Aziz. Azad Ali was a member of the MCB's Central Working Committee and the chair of its Membership Committee.[133] He is the community affairs co-ordinator for IFE, a member of the East London Mosque, a presenter on the Islam Channel, and the founding chairman of the Muslim Safety Forum. But his most prominent role today is as the head of community development and engagement for Muslim Engagement and Development (MEND), the current incarnation of iEngage. Before iEngage was rebranded at MEND, its CEO was Inayat Bunglawala, the long-time media secretary for the MCB who now heads Muslims4UK.

Tahir Alam was assistant secretary general in 2006–2008, as well as the chair of the MCB's Education Committee during the same period, and was also involved in AMS-UK as an executive committee member.[134] Until his resignation in July 2014, Alam was the director and chair of the Parkview Educational Trust, responsible for the management of three schools at the centre of the Trojan Horse affair.[135]

Mohammed Abdul Aziz was also involved in the MCB as its representative on the Department of Trade's Equality and Diversity Forum in 2006 and as the former adviser to MCB secretary general Sacranie. He was, as mentioned, a former researcher at the Islamic Foundation and an executive committee member of AMSS-UK, as well as an honorary trustee of the East London Mosque and a former executive committee member at YMO-UK.

The networked individuals identified above all share a connection to the MCB or Muslim Aid. Yet, there are other connections that also form part of this network that are worth noting. The Islamic Sharia Council, for example, is linked to the Association of Muslim Lawyers (AML) through Ahmad Thomson. The AML was co-founded in 1993 by Thomson, a former deputy chair. He is also a member of the Islamic Sharia Council committee.[136] The Islamic Sharia Council also has a connection with the MCB, in addition to its affiliation to the MCB. Although the MCB has no formal role with *shari'a*, since it abstains from being associated with any particular school of Islamic law, informally it does: Ibrahim Mogra explains that although the MCB does not issue *fatwas* (religious rulings), it does 'signpost people to *shari'a* councils and to *shari'a* bodies and the like'.[137]

The numerous overlapping positions in organisations associated with Jama'at-i-Islami, the Muslim Brotherhood, and newer ones described above, in addition to the collaborative relationships between them described earlier, form a complex network, referred to in this book as the 'revivalist network'. This network may be termed *meta-organisational*, since it cuts *across* the formal structures of named organisations. Certainly, it encompasses collaborative partnerships and official affiliations between registered companies and charities. But it also includes *informal* relationships between numerous organisations that are inseparable from the personal relationships between the leaders of these organisations. Informal organisational links are furthermore implied in the multiple and overlapping leadership roles that numerous individuals within certain organisations have in various other organisations. Thus, the network described in this chapter is not, strictly speaking, a network *of* organisations, since it is the individuals within organisations that drive them and make connections. In some organisations, it is only certain individuals within them that are part of the network. Yet, it may be described as *organised*: all of the individuals within the network are related to at least one organisation. They are all engaged in what al-Qaradawi terms as 'serious, purposive organized work' for the sake of Islam.[138]

The global Muslim Brotherhood groups in Britain are typically written about as two distinct constellations of personalities and groups, those with their roots in the Indian subcontinent and those with Arab origins. Innes Bowen's 2014 book, *Medina in Birmingham, Najaf in Brent*, exemplifies this approach by dedicating separate chapters to Jama'at-i-Islami-related groups and those connected to the Ikhwan. But, while there are close relationships between individuals and groups with Arab connections that cluster on the issue of Palestine, and while there are tight relationships between those with connections to Pakistan and Bangladesh, these two strands within the network are thoroughly interlinked. Even clusters of individuals and organisations at the outer edge of the network, such as the Palestine Return Centre, are just several connections away from the central region of the network where the MCB is situated. The four most important hubs in this trans-ethnic network, as described in this chapter, are the MCB, Muslim Aid, the Islamic Foundation and the MAB. They each play an important role in connecting the various other smaller groups and associated individuals, as well as fostering trans-ethnic Muslim solidarity.

The individuals that feature prominently in the network are involved in organised work, but do not constitute a clear vanguard in the sense of a unified front with control over the strategic direction of the network. There are multiple leadership clusters but, while these overlap somewhat, they do not amount to (or enable) a central command structure. Nevertheless, it is clear that the groups and individuals of concern collectively comprise an organised network. It remains to be seen to what extent this network is bonded in terms of cultural solidarity, including shared ways of seeing and evaluating the world, the subject of chapters 3 and 4, and in terms of a shared conflictual relation with social norms and political authority, the subject of chapters 5 and 6.

Notes

1 Lorenzo Vidino's work is arguably the most insightful on the subject of revivalist Islamist groups in the West. This includes British Jama'at-related organisations within what he sees as a broad ideological Brotherhood movement spread across Europe and the United States. But it does not extensively explore this

movement in Britain beyond one chapter in his book on the subject. See Vidino (2010).

2 Rich (2010), p. 132.

3 For example, see 'Secretary General's Report', report from MCB Eighth Annual General Meeting, 14 May 2005, pp. 10–11. Available at http://web.archive.org/web/20111105153148/http://www.mcb.org.uk/downloads/Secretary_General_2005.pdf.

4 Islamophobia Awareness Month, Facebook home page. www.facebook.com/pg/IAMonth/about/?ref=page_internal.

5 'UK Islamophobia Awareness Month Controlled By UK Muslim Brotherhood', *The Global Muslim Brotherhood Daily Watch*, 18 November 2013, www.globalmbwatch.com/2013/11/18/uk-islamophobia-awareness-month-controlled-by-uk-muslim-brotherhood/; 'Confronting Anti-Muslim Hatred in Britain and Europe', event poster, Cordoba Foundation website, undated, www.thecordobafoundation.com/attach/enough%20event.PDF.

6 'Islamophobia Analysed', MCB website, 26 November 2012. www.mcb.org.uk/islamophobia-analysed/.

7 Paul Goodman, 'The All-Party Group on Islamophobia has dispensed with the services of IEngage', *Conservative Home*, 19 July 2011. www.conservativehome.com/thetorydiary/2011/07/the-all-party-group-on-islamophobia-has-dispensed-with-the-services-of-iengage.html.

8 'Institutional Islamophobia: A conference to examine state racism and social engineering of the Muslim community', IHRC website, 8 December 2014. www.ihrc.org.uk/events/11207-institutional-islamophobia-a-conference-to-examine-state-racism-and-social-engineering-of-the-muslim-community.

9 Stuart (2015); Wilson (2017).

10 'Tackling Islamophobia – UAF Roundtable event at Parliament', MCB website, 24 November 2014.www.mcb.org.uk/tackling-islamophobia-uaf-roundtable-event-parliament/.

11 'Mayor of London to speak at cross party rally to defend religious freedom', Mayor of London's website, 17 November 2006. Original link inactive, but available at: www.ikhwanweb.com/article.php/article.php?id=3036.

12 'Rally against incitement & Islamophobia', IFE website, 7 February 2006. https://web.archive.org/web/20120114214844/http://www.islamicforumeurope.com/live/ife.php?doc=eventitem&itemId=69.

13 Interview with Omer El-Hamdoon, 14 February 2012.

14 'Governance', MCB website, undated. www.mcb.org.uk/about-mcb/leadership/.

15 'Mosques and Imams National Advisory Board, Data for financial year ending 31 December 2016', undated, Charity Commission website, http://beta.charitycommission.gov.uk/charity-details/?regid=1135814&subid=0;'Governance', MCB website, ibid.

16 'The Executive Board', MINAB website, web capture from 5 June 2014. http://web.archive.org/web/20140605083636/http://minab.org.uk/about-us/executive-board.

17 'MAB Conference: Creating Hope', event listing on Eventbrite website, undated. www.eventbrite.co.uk/e/mab-conference-creating-hope-tickets-2364646722?aff=event#.

18 Interview with Omer El-Hamdoon, 14 February 2012.

19 'Background', Alternative Leveson Inquiry website, captured on 24 March 2012. http://web.archive.org/web/20120324163906/http://www.alternativeleveson.org.uk/?page_id=13.

20 'We need an inquiry into anti-Islam press', *The Guardian*, 23 January 2012. www.theguardian.com/media/2012/jan/23/inquiry-into-anti-islam-press.

21 Samira Quraishy, 'Event Review: The Cold War on British Muslims – The Instigators and Funders', MEMO website, 12 October 2011. www.middleeastmonitor.com/20140515-event-review-the-cold-war-on-british-muslims-the-instigators-and-funders/.
22 'Muslims and the Media: Positive Engagement from the Whole Community', event listing on Cordoba Foundation website, 4 June 2009. www.thecordobafoundation.com/events.php?id=1&art=22
23 'FREE TRAINING: Introduction to Media', event poster on Cordoba Foundation website, December 12, 2007. https://web.archive.org/web/20071222172721/http://www.thecordobafoundation.com.
24 'FREE Media & Public Relations Training for Young Muslims', MCB website, 3 January 2008. http://web.archive.org/web/20080113205413/http://www.mcb.org.uk/features/features.php?ann_id=1671.
25 'Rethinking the Muslim Community', event listing on FRF website, 5 August 2013. www.thefrf.org/component/zoo/item/rethinking-the-muslim-community-2.
26 'Peace Conference: Peace-Building in the 21st Century', event listing on MCB website, 4 September 2014. www.mcb.org.uk/peace-conference-peace-building-in-the-21st-century/.
27 'International Day of Peace' event leaflet, Cordoba Foundation website, undated. www.thecordobafoundation.com/attach/peace_leaflet_muslim_final.pdf.
28 See MCB's 'Visit My Mosque' website, www.visitmymosque.org/.
29 'An Evening for Palestine Solidarity', event promotional poster, IFE website, March 2013. https://web.archive.org/web/20131121073551/http://islamicforumeurope.com/images_uploaded/2013/03/img3542.jpg.
30 'EVENT: An Evening For Palestine Solidarity', MCB website, undated. www.mcb.org.uk/an-evening-for-palestine-solidarity-event/.
31 'British Muslims to deliver letter of thanks to Turkish Government', MCB website, 6 February 2009. https://web.archive.org/web/20090217023540/http://www.mcb.org.uk/article_detail.php?article=announcement-774.
32 'Global Muslim Brotherhood Thanks Turkish Prime Minister Over Gaza Remarks', *Global Muslim Brotherhood Daily Watch*, 8 February 2009. www.globalmbwatch.com/2009/02/08/global-muslim-brotherhood-thanks-turkish-prime-minister-over-gaza-remarks/.
33 'Charity Dinner in Aid of Muslims of Burma', event promotional poster, undated, available at: http://tiny.cc/charitydinnerburma2012.
34 Interview with Abdullah Faliq, 5 September 2012. See also 'Voting in Islam: Guidance to Muslims in Britain from the Scholars of Islam', leaflet on IFE website, April 2010. https://web.archive.org/web/20131108062513/http://www.islamicforumeurope.com/images_uploaded/2010/04/img3205.pdf.
35 Peace (2013), p. 313.
36 Shiraz Maher, 'UK: George Galloway Funds– Surprise! – Hamas', Gatestone Institute, 29 April 2010. www.gatestoneinstitute.org/1175/uk-george-galloway-funds—surprise——hamas.
37 'Secretary General's Report', report from MCB Eighth Annual General Meeting, pp. 8–9. http://archive.mcb.org.uk/wp-content/uploads/2015/12/SG_MCB_AGM_Speech_2005.pdf.
38 'Vote 2010 Ulema Statement', Muslim Vote website, undated. https://web.archive.org/web/20100816062831/http://www.muslimvote.org.uk:80/index.php?option=com_content&view=article&id=128&Itemid=158.
39 MCB (2015).
40 'General Election 2017 and Muslims: Comparing Manifesto Commitments' flyer, MCB website, undated. www.mcb.org.uk/wp-content/uploads/2015/03/manifestocomparison-mcb-a3.pdf/.
41 MEND (2015).

42 MEND (2017).
43 'Muslim campaign groups publish key demands ahead of UK election', Arwa Ibrahim, *The Middle East Eye*, 17 May 2017. www.middleeasteye.net/news/uk-muslim-advocacy-groups-publish-key-demands-ahead-june-elections-1352453825.
44 Mohammed and Hussain (2003), p. xiv. Since the publication of this book, Hussain's understanding of Islam, its meaning as a 'way of life' and its role in relation to the state has undergone quite a transformation. For more on this, see chapter 4.
45 Bowen (2014), p. 103
46 Mohammed and Hussain (2003), p. xxi.
47 Interview with Dilwar Hussain, 15 January 2015.
48 'About us', AMSS-UK website, webpage captured on 11 September 2011, http://web.archive.org/web/20110911192237/http://www.amssuk.com/aboutus.html; 'American Journal of Islamic Social Sciences (AJISS)', IIIT website, undated, www.iiit.org/ajiss.html.
49 Ahmad and Seddon (eds) (2012).
50 'MEF Advisory Board', Muslim Education Foundation website, undated. www.mef-ca.org/mef-ad-board.html.
51 Conference booklet for 'Muslim Education In Europe Conference', p. 3, available on AMSS-UK website, October 2002. www.amssuk.com/docs/pdf/AMSSUK%20MEiE%20Conf%20Sep2002%20-%20booklet.pdf.
52 Conference programme for 'Muslim Youth: Challenges, Opportunities and Expectations' event, p. 11, available on AMSS-UK website, February 2009. www.amssuk.com/docs/pdf/AMSSUK%20Chester%202009%20Conference%20Briefing.pdf.
53 AMSS-UK Newsletter no. 7, 2006, p. 5. http://web.archive.org/web/20111027062825/http://www.amssuk.com/docs/pdf/AMSSUK%20-%20NewsLetter7.pdf.
54 Abdul Bari, Muhammad (2013), p. 38.
55 'Governance', MCB website, ibid.
56 Interview with Abdullah Faliq, 5 September 2012.
57 Iqbal Sacranie , quoted in Vidino (2010), p. 122.
58 Kenan Malik, 'take me to your leader', 23 April 2009. www.kenanmalik.com/essays/hp_fatwa_extract.html.
59 McRoy (2006), p. 12.
60 Kepel, (1997), p. 133.
61 McRoy (2006), pp. 7–79.
62 Ibid., p. 12.
63 Interview with Ibrahim Mogra, 29 August 2012.
64 Kenan Malik, 'take me to your leader'.
65 For the text of the Istanbul Declaration, see 'A statement by the religious scholars and proselytisers (*du'a*) of the Islamic Nation (*ummah*) to all rulers and peoples concerning events in Gaza', available at: http://hurryupharry.org/wp-content/uploads/2009/03/istpdf.pdf.
66 See Alan Travis, 'Hazel Blears' standoff with Muslim Council overshadows new anti-terror launch', 25 March 2009, *The Guardian*. www.guardian.co.uk/politics/2009/mar/25/muslim-council-britain-hazel-blears; and Nicholas Watt, Government restores links with biggest Muslim group', *The Guardian*, 15 January 2010. www.guardian.co.uk/politics/2010/jan/15/government-relations-muslim-council-britain-mcb.
67 Interview with Ibrahim Mogra, 29 August 2012.
68 Stephen H. Jones, Therese O'Toole, Daniel Nilsson DeHanas, Tariq Modood and Nasar Meer, A 'system of self-appointed leaders'?, *Public Spirit*, 20 August 2013. www.publicspirit.org.uk/a-system-of-self-appointed-leaders/.
69 Interview with Mohammed Abdul Aziz, 3 September 2012.

70 Interview with Daud Abdullah, 10 February 2012.
71 'About Us', MET website, webpage captured on 8 March 2005. https://web.archive.org/web/20050308130740/http://www.muslim-ed-trust.org.uk:80/about.html.
72 AMS-UK brochure, December 2013. http://ams-uk.org/wp-content/uploads/2013/12/AMS-Brochure.pdf.
73 Interview with Abdullah Faliq, 5 September 2012.
74 Bowen (2012), p. 115.
75 Interview with Abdullah Faliq, 5 September 2012.
76 Interview with Dilwar Hussain, 15 January 2015.
77 'Board of Trustees', MINAB website, undated. www.minab.org.uk/news/press-releases/49-about-us-sp-546/trustees-a-advisors.html.
78 Ibid; 'Revival of MINAB', MINAB website, 28 December 2017, www.minab.org.uk/news/258-madaris-consultation.html.
79 'East London Mosque Trust, Data for financial year ending 31 March 2016', undated, Charity Commission website, http://beta.charitycommission.gov.uk/charity-details/?regid=1122613&subid=0; 'East London Mosque & London Muslim Centre Annual Review 2016', East London Mosque website, undated. www.eastlondonmosque.org.uk/sites/default/files/documents/ELM%20Annual%20Report%202016-2017%20web.pdf.
80 'Dawatul Islam Uk And Eire, Data for financial year ending 30 June 2016', undated, Charity Commission website, http://beta.charitycommission.gov.uk/charity-details/?regid=289202&subid=0; Interview with Maulana Abu Sayeed, February 15, 2012.
81 Melucci (1989).
82 'Management', East London Mosque website, undated. www.eastlondonmosque.org.uk/content/management.
83 'Over 100 UK imams unite to sign open letter urging British Muslims not to travel to Syria and Iraq', Imams Online website, 4 July 2014. https://web.archive.org/web/20160821141542/http://imamsonline.com:80/blog/over-100-uk-imams-unite-to-sign-open-letter-urging-british-muslims-not-to-travel-to-syria-and-iraq/.
84 'Al-Isra' wal Miraj – "The Night Journey"', letter to parents, Al-Hijra School website, April 27, 2017. http://alhijrahschool.co.uk/wp-content/uploads/2017/04/Al-Isra-Wal-Miraj-Th27Apr2017.pdf.
85 Interview with Abdullah Faliq, 5 September 2012.
86 David Brown, 'Finsbury mosque leader Mohammed Sawalha part of Hamas politburo', *The Times*, 7 November 2017. www.thetimes.co.uk/article/finsbury-mosque-leader-mohammed-sawalha-part-of-hamas-politburo-0cdn3gs80.
87 Companies House website. http://wck2.companieshouse.gov.uk.
88 'PR – The Muslim Council of Britain elects its new leadership, MAB website, 20 July 2016. https://www.mabonline.net/pr-the-muslim-council-of-britain-elects-its-new-leadership/.
89 'Governance', MCB website, ibid.
90 British Muslim Initiative listing on Company Check website. http://companycheck.co.uk/company/05703363/BRITISH-MUSLIM-INITIATIVE-LIMITED/directors-secretaries.
91 'U.K. Muslim Brotherhood Leaders Threatens Israel With Destruction', *The Global Muslim Brotherhood Daily Watch*, 15 March 2012. www.globalmbwatch.com/2012/03/15/u-k-muslim-brotherhood-leaders-threatens-israel-with-destruction/.
92 Daud Abdullah, speaker profile, Islam and Democracy conference, Cordoba Foundation website, 12 February 2015. https://webcache.googleusercontent.com/search?q=cache:LE-TFyINKkUJ:https://www.thecordobafoundation.com/attach/Profiles_Final.pdf+&cd=16&hl=en&ct=clnk&gl=in.

93 Interview with Abdullah Faliq, 5 September 2012.
94 Ibid.
95 Merley (2009).
96 See Andrew Gilligan, 'Muslim Aid: Hopeless Charity Commission whitewashes yet another Islamist group', Andrew Gilligan's blog (originally on *The Telegraph* website), 17 December 2010, https://andrewgilliganblog.wordpress.com/2010/12/17/muslim-aid-hopeless-charity-commission-whitewashes-yet-another-islamist-group/; and 'U.K. Charity Denies Being Member of Union Of Good', *The Global Muslim Brotherhood Daily Watch*, 2 August 2011, www.globalmbwatch.com/2011/08/02/u-k-denies-being-member-of-union-of-good/.
97 'Governance', Muslim Aid website, webpage captured on 16 April 2016. https://web.archive.org/web/20160416144844/https://www.muslimaid.org/about-us/governance.
98 'Appointment of new Chairman and Director General', *Islamic Foundation Newsletter*, November 2014, p. 2. Available at: https://issuu.com/islamicfoundation/docs/issue_44-newsletter.
99 'Board of Trustees', Islamic Foundation website, undated. www.islamicfoundation.org.uk/User/BoardofTrustees.aspx.
100 'Governance', Muslim Aid website, ibid.; 'The Islamic Foundation, Data for financial year ending 31 December 2016', undated, Charity Commission website. http://beta.charitycommission.gov.uk/charity-details/?regid=263371&subid=0.
101 'Staff', MIHE website, undated. http://www.mihe.org.uk/staff.
102 'The United Kingdom Islamic Mission, Data for financial year ending 31 March 2016', undated, Charity Commission website. http://beta.charitycommission.gov.uk/charity-details/?regid=250275&subid=0.
103 'Governance', Muslim Aid website, ibid.
104 'Markfield Institute of Higher Education, Data for financial year ending 31 December 2016', undated, Charity Commission website. http://beta.charitycommission.gov.uk/charity-details/?regid=1125851&subid=0.
105 'Governance', Muslim Aid website, ibid.
106 Programme details for 'Journey Through the Quran', Islam Channel website. www.islamchannel.tv/video-category/journey-through-the-quran/.
107 'Muslim Welfare House, Data for financial year ending 31 March 2016', Charity Commission website, undated, http://beta.charitycommission.gov.uk/charity-details/?regid=271680&subid=0; 'About Us', Islamic Sharia Council website, http://www.islamic-sharia.org/aboutus/.
108 'Governance', Muslim Aid website, ibid; 'MUSLIM AID Trustees' report and financial statements For the year ended 31 December 2008', 25 June 2009, Muslim Aid website, www.muslimaid.org/download/1033/.
109 'Governance', Muslim Aid website, ibid.
110 Amjad Saleem, 'Going beyond the Rhetoric: The Muslim Aid/UMCOR Partnership in Sri Lanka', Inter-Religious Studies website, December 2010. http://irdialogue.org/wp-content/uploads/2010/12/Going-beyond-the-Rhetoric-The-Muslim-Aid_UMCOR-Partnership-in-Sri-Lanka-by-Amjad-Saleem-.pdf.
111 'Central Working Committee 2004', MCB website, webpage captured on 14 February 2005. http://web.archive.org/web/20050214094055/http://www.mcb.org.uk/cwc.html.
112 'Governance', MCB website, ibid.
113 'Membership Committee', April 26, 2001, MINAB website. www.minab.org.uk/news/52-about-us-sp-546/committees/144-membership-committee.html.
114 'Governance', MCB website, ibid.

115 'Governance [2014–2016]', MCB website, webpage captured 19 September 2015. https://web.archive.org/web/20150919015752/http://www.mcb.org.uk:80/about-mcb/leadership.
116 'Governance', MCB website, ibid.
117 https://www.soas.ac.uk/politics/events/muslimgovtconf/participants/#AbdullahFaliq.
118 'Muslim Welfare House, Data for financial year ending 31 March 2016', Charity Commission website, ibid.; 'Muslim Welfare House', Companies House website, undated, https://beta.companieshouse.gov.uk/company/04041294/officers; 'Dr Omer El-Hamdoon', speaker profile, Best of British Muslims website, undated, http://bestofbritishmuslims.com/speaker/omer-el-hamdoon-2/.
119 Aqbal Isara speaker profile, 2017 International Takaful Summit website, undated. www.takafulsummit.com/2017/speakers/m-iqbal-asaria/.
120 'Honorary Visiting Fellows', MIHE website, undated, www.mihe.ac.uk/personnel/honorary-visiting-fellows; 'First meeting of the Islamic Foundation Advisory Board', Islamic Foundation website, June 23, 2011, www.islamic-foundation.org.uk/user/NewsDetails.aspx?Id=47.
121 'Iqbal Asaria: Al Qaeda webmaster of Jihad and Ummah.org heads Muslim Council of Britain business and finance committee', Militant Islam Monitor website, 18 August 2004, www.militantislammonitor.org/article/id/293; 'Yusuf Islam & The Muslim Council of Britain's terrorism ties – Muslim Aid 'charity' funds Al Qaeda & sent Mujahideen to Bosnia', Militant Islam Monitor website, 24 September 2004, www.militantislammonitor.org/article/id/248.
122 'Islamic Finance for Development', Ramphal Institute website, undated. www.ramphalinstitute.org/islamic-finance-for-development.html.
123 'Governance [2014–2016]', MCB website, ibid.; *East London News*, 'Da'watul Islam elects new President and Executive Council', 19 July 2017, http://eastlondonnews.co.uk/dawatul-islam-elects-new-president-and-executive-council.
124 'Team', The European Council for Fatwa and Research in UK website, undated. http://fatwacommitteeuk.com/team; Interview with Suhaib Hasan, 9 February 2012; Interview with Maulana Abu Sayeed, 15 February 2012.
125 'Al-Aqsa Schools Trust, Data for financial year ending 31 August 2016', undated, Charity Commission website. http://beta.charitycommission.gov.uk/charity-details/?regid=1072676&subid=0.
126 'U.S. Designates Five Charities Funding Hamas and Six Senior Hamas Leaders as Terrorist Entities', U.S. Department of Treasury website, August 22, 2003. www.treasury.gov/press-center/press-releases/Pages/js672.aspx.
127 'Public Affairs Committee', MINAB website, undated. www.minab.org.uk/news/press-releases/52-about-us-sp-546/committees/143-public-affairs-committee.html.
128 'Aims & Objectives', IBERR website, webpage captured on 8 April 2013. http://web.archive.org/web/20130408051924/http://www.iberr.net/aims-objectives.
129 *Nida News,* Nida Trust newsletter, Summer 2012 issue. Available at: https://issuu.com/nidatrust/docs/newsletter_summer_2012.
130 'Teacher Education and Consultancy', Islamic Shakhsiyah Foundation website, webpage captured on 17 February 2014. http://web.archive.org/web/20140217063046/http://www.isfnet.org.uk/index.php/teacher-education-and-cpd.html.
131 'Advisors', Islamic Shakhsiyah Foundation website, webpage captured on 19 February 2014. http://web.archive.org/web/20140219084045/http://www.isfnet.org.uk/index.php/advisors.html.
132 'Qur'anic Pedagogy' course outline, Nida Trust website, http://nidatrust.org.uk/content/booking; Conference programme for 'Islamic Education in the Western

Context: Challenges & Opportunities', Nida Trust website, http://nidatrust.org.uk/uploads/docs/conference_programme3.pdf.

133 'MCB Annual Report 2009–2010', MCB web archive, November 2015.

134 'Central Working Committee 2006–2008', MCB website, webpage captured on 20 June 2008, https://web.archive.org/web/20080620031755/http://www.mcb.org.uk.:80/committee/21.php; AMS-UK Annual Report, 17 July 2010, available at: www.ams-uk.org/general/AMS%20UK%20Annual%20Report%202009-10.pdf.

135 BBC News, 'Trojan Horse: Park View Educational Trust board resigns', 15 July 2014. www.bbc.com/news/uk-england-28317920.

136 Interview with Maulana Abu Sayeed, 15 February 2012.

137 Interview with Ibrahim Mogra, 29 August 2012.

138 al-Qaradawi (1999), p. 70.

References

Abdul Bari, Muhammad (2013). 'Meet the challenge, make the change: A call to action for Muslim civil society in Britain'. *Cordoba Papers*, vol. 2, no. 1. Cordoba Foundation, London. www.thecordobafoundation.com/attach/A5_TCF_CS_BARI_FINAL.pdf.

Ahmad, Fauzia and Mohammad Siddique Seddon (eds) (2012). *Muslim Youth: Challenges, Opportunities and Expectations*. London: Bloomsbury.

Bowen, Innes (2012). 'The Muslim Brotherhood in Britain'. In Roel Meijer and Edwin Bakker (eds), *The Muslim Brotherhood in Europe*: 111–126. London: Hurst and Co.

Bowen, Innes (2014). *Medina in Birmingham, Najaf in Brent*. London: Hurst and Co.

Kepel, Gilles (1997). *Allah in the West: Islamic Movements in America and Europe*. Trans. Susan Milner. Cambridge: Polity Press.

MCB (2015). *Fairness, Not Favours*, Muslim Council of Britain. www.mcb.org.uk/wp-content/uploads/2015/03/fairnessnotfavours-MCB.pdf.

McRoy, Anthony (2006). *From Rushdie to 7/7: The Radicalisation of Islam in Britain*. London: Social Affairs Unit.

Melucci, Alberto (1989). *Nomads of the Present: Social Movements and Individual Needs in Contemporary Society*. Philadelphia, PA: Temple University Press.

MEND (2015). 'Muslim Manifesto 2015', *Muslim Engagement and Development*. https://mend.org.uk/wp-content/uploads/2017/03/MEND-Muslim-Manifesto-GE2015_LowRes.pdf.

MEND (2017). 'Muslim Manifesto 2017', *Muslim Engagement and Development*. https://mend.org.uk/wp-content/uploads/2017/05/MEND-Muslim-Manifesto-2017_FINAL_lowres-1.pdf.

Merley, Steve (2009). 'The Union of Good: INTERPAL and the U.K. member organizations'. NEFA Foundation. https://globalmbwatch.com/wp-content/uploads/2013/04/27722268-The-Union-of-Good-Interpal-and-the-UK-Member-Organizations-NEFA-Foundation.pdf.

Mohammed, Riza, and Dilwar Hussain (eds) (2003). *Islam: The Way of Revival*. Markfield: Revival Publications.

Peace, Timothy (2013). 'Muslims and electoral politics in Britain: the case of the Respect Party'. In Jørgen Nielsen (ed.), *Muslim Political Participation in Europe*: 299–321. Edinburgh: Edinburgh University Press.

al-Qaradawi, Yusuf (1999). *Fiqh Al Zakah (Volume II): A Comparative Study of Zakah, Regulations and Philosophy in the Light of Qur'an and Sunnah*. Trans.

Monzer Kahf. Jeddah, Saudi Arabia: Scientific Publishing Centre, King Abdulaziz University.

Rich, David (2010). 'The very model of a British Muslim Brotherhood'. In Barry Rubin (ed.), *The Muslim Brotherhood: the Organization and Policies of a Global Islamist Movement*: 117–136. New York: Palgrave Macmillan.

Stuart, Hannah (2015). 'Understanding CAGE: a public information dossier'. Centre for the Response to Radicalisation and Terrorism, Policy Paper No. 5. Henry Jackson Society, London.

Wilson, Tom (2017). *Mend: Islamists Masquerading as Civil Libertarians.* Henry Jackson Society. http://henryjacksonsociety.org/wp-content/uploads/2017/10/HJS-Mend-Report-2.pdf.

Vidino, Lorenzo (2010). *The New Muslim Brotherhood in the West*. New York: Columbia University Press.

3 Cultural solidarity

Communal classifications and missionary concepts

In addition to being organisationally networked, the groups and individuals comprising the global Muslim Brotherhood in Britain are connected in how they see and evaluate the world, and their role within it as advocates of societal renewal. In much of the academic, think tank and news media literature, the individuals and groups of concern are characterised as sharing a 'political ideology … that calls for the establishment of a distinctly Islamic system of government'.[1] However, the key factor bonding the network is not ideology as such. They are linked most fundamentally not by a conscious commitment to an explicitly formulated doctrine but, rather, by an identifiably similar set of classifications, concepts and dispositions. This relates to the individuals' sense of themselves as members of a group and their concern with the social world they inhabit, including but by no means restricted to matters of politics and governance. Accordingly, this chapter shows how the individuals comprising the network identified in chapter 2 share cultural solidarity in terms of how they classify themselves as a community and the environment or territory within which they live. It regards their conception of communal identity and solidarity through certain Islamic concepts, such as the Muslim *umma*, and Islamic principles implicit to their work, including that of 'Enjoining the Good and Forbidding the Wrong'. Although there is some variation in the way in which these individuals understand their collective identity and certain key Islamic concepts and principles, to a large extent they share a common understanding of themselves as a community, of their place in the world, and of their work and its purpose.

Communal and territorial classifications

Individuals and groups in the revivalist network share a way of seeing themselves as part of a religious community, the *umma*, and as part of humanity, within which the *umma* is nested. Although these forms of identification are not mutually exclusive, the Muslim *umma* takes precedence because of its perceived possession of divine knowledge and its duty to share Islam. Also common within the network is a perception of the territory in which they reside, understood in terms of reformed Islamic concepts.

Community: the Muslim umma *and humanity*

The *umma* is an Islamic concept that derives from the Qur'an. As Frederick Denny observes, 'in the Qur'an the *ummah* concept itself develops from a general one, applying to non-Arab groups, too, toward a more exclusive one which is limited to the Muslim community'.[2] By regarding the appearance of the term *umma* as it appears in the Qur'an according to the order in which the verses were allegedly revealed, Denny notes that the meaning of the term changes from religious communities, including Christians and Jews, to Muslims as the ideal religious community. He writes that in the latter part of the Qur'an, the term seems to apply exclusively to Muslims 'as the *Ummah* par excellence, a concept and reality which possess an ontological status'.[3]

This concept of the *umma* as the community or nation of Muslim believers is a basic feature of the perceptual schemata, and thus the cultural solidarity, shared by members of the revivalist network in Britain. A sense of religious fraternity is certainly not exclusive to these individuals, or Muslims more generally, but a specific sense of the *umma*, along with other ways of seeing and evaluating their position in the world, connects them to a distinct social and politically oriented habitus. The notion of belonging to the *umma* as a singular community involves a bonding in terms of shared beliefs and a collective Islamic identity. This may be compatible with other forms of identification, such as 'Britishness', but may not be subordinate to them. Yet, importantly, it also involves an obligation to share Islam, principally its ethical code, beyond this community within the broader society.

Such a concept is clearly expressed, explicitly or implicitly, by prominent leaders within Jama'at- and Ikhwan-associated organisations in Britain. For example, Muhammad Abdul Bari, former MCB secretary general, writes in a report for the Cordoba Foundation that the term *umma* 'is commonly used to mean the collective community of Islamic peoples. It can be used to mean the concept of a commonwealth of the Believers.'[4] Elsewhere he writes, 'Muslims are one *ummah*', a 'community of people bonded by their desire to surrender to the will of God'.[5] Ibrahim Hewitt, senior editor at the Middle Eastern Monitor and the former assistant director of the Muslim Educational Trust, defines *umma* as 'Community; in particular, the global Muslim community.'[6] Zahid Parvez, the director of the Islamic Foundation's Markfield Institute of Higher Education (MIHE) and a former president of UKIM, similarly defines *umma* as 'the Muslim world community', which is 'connected into one brotherhood and sisterhood by the Islamic faith and vision'.[7]

Acknowledgement of the *umma* as the Muslim community or nation, and of the importance of the solidarity of the *umma*, has been expressed at numerous events in Britain or involving Muslim activists based in Britain. Such an acknowledgement was expressed by numerous figures in the revivalist network in Britain at the 'Muslims in Europe Conference', held in Istanbul in July 2006. These included Khurshid Ahmad, chairman of the Islamic Foundation; Manazir Ahsan, the Foundation's director general; Iqbal Sacranie, secretary general of the MCB; Mohammed Abdul Aziz, Sacranie's adviser; Iqbal Asaria, MCB finance director; Said Ferjani, head of public relations for the Muslim Association of Britain (MAB); Wakkas Khan, president of the Federation of Student Islamic Societies (FOSIS); Mohamed Mukadam, chairman of the Association of Muslim Schools UK; Anas al-Shaikh-Ali, director of the London branch of the International Institute of Islamic Thought (IIIT-UK); and Ahmed al-Rawi, president of the Federation of Islamic Organisations in Europe. Assuming a fundamental social reality designated by the term *umma*, but concerned with its manifest cohesiveness, the conference delegates declared,

> We recognise that [the] solidarity of the Ummah is a key priority for all Muslims – both in Europe and throughout the world … . We call for solidarity between us and the upholding of Islam's universal vision of peace, fraternity, tolerance and social harmony.[8]

A similar invocation of the *umma* as a unitary Muslim community was made in June 2011 at the MCB's fourteenth Annual General Meeting by Maulana Shahid Raza, then the chairman of the Mosques and Imams National Advisory Board (MINAB). He stated, 'despite our diversity, we are one Muslim ummah (nation) and there are fundamental beliefs and practices that make us one'.[9] He added, the 'MCB is one of the strongest expressions of that unity in this country'. The same sense of the term *umma* was expressed in the Cordoba Foundation-supported event held in 2012 entitled, 'Staging the Ummah', which addressed the issue of a 'culturally relevant Islam'.[10] Other, earlier events focused on the concept of the *umma* as a singular Muslim community, and upon rousing Muslim solidarity based upon this concept, include those held by FOSIS. In 2003, for example, Zahid Parvez and Azzam Tamimi both gave presentations on the topic of the Muslim *umma* at the organisation's annual summer conference.[11]

For revivalists, a sense of brotherhood amongst Muslims is central to being a Muslim. Daud Abdullah, the former assistant secretary general of the MCB, expresses this as follows: 'The Qur'an says, "All of the believers are brothers," and there are so many traditions [*hadiths*] on this subject of brotherhood that you cannot be a sincere Muslim and not take these teachings seriously.'[12] Citing from the *hadith* collection of al-Bukhari, the director of the Muslim Educational Trust, Ghulam Sarwar, writes, 'Believers are like parts of a building to one another – each part supporting the others.'[13] He cites another *hadith*, adding, 'None of you can be a believer unless he loves for his brother what he loves for himself.'[14]

However, the Muslim *umma* is perceived by members of the revivalist network not simply as a source of identity or solidarity, but more specifically as a vanguard for ushering in Allah's divine will within the entirety of human society. Zahid Parvez describes the *umma*'s responsibility as 'uphold[ing] morality, truth and justice' and 'lead[ing] Mankind [*sic*] from the depths of ignorance to the true knowledge: Islam'.[15] IIIT-UK declares it is 'dedicated to the revival and reform of Islamic thought and its methodology in order to enable the Ummah to deal effectively with present challenges' and bestow divine 'guidance' upon human civilisation.[16] This duty of guiding humanity out of ignorance is similarly expressed by al-Qaradawi's International Union of Muslim Scholars (IUMS), which is connected to the Islamic Sharia Council and the UK Board of Sharia Councils by the overlapping roles of Suhaib Hasan and Maulana Muhammad Abu Sayeed in these organisations. 'IUMS does not follow a certain country, group, or sect,' it asserts, 'it is only proud of belonging to Islam and its transnational community – Ummah'.[17] It adds:

> We have been taught by the Quran as well as by the Sunnah that this Muslim Ummah will never agree to commit an error, whereas the Quran says: 'And of those whom We have created, *there is a community who guides (others) with the truth, and establishes justice therewith*'.[18]

Numerous individuals in the revivalist network, particularly those active in the field of inter-faith work, articulate a notion of the *umma* as embracing all humanity, including Muslims and non-Muslims alike. For example, expressing this view as the executive director of the Islamic Foundation, Irshad Bacqui states, 'The whole world is *umma* because it's the *umma* of humanity.'[19] This is, however, by no means an alternative notion to that of the Muslim *umma*. The *umma* as humanity and the *umma* as the nation of Muslim believers may, in fact, be viewed as inter-related social classifications within a distinct perceptual schemata shared by individuals within the network. Importantly, what connects them is a perception of Islam's universal mission to embrace the whole of human society.

Anas al-Shaikh Ali, the director of IIIT-UK, Ibrahim Mogra, the former assistant secretary general for the MCB, and Anas Altikriti, director of the Cordoba Foundation, all support this view. 'The *umma*,' says al-Shaikh Ali, 'is both Muslim society and humanity, since Muslims are part of humanity. Whatever we do, it's not only for the betterment of Muslims, it's also for the betterment of humanity in general'.[20] Mogra similarly explains: 'The *umma* is the global *umma*,' he states. 'It is not just about Muslims. If we say Muhammad was a universal messenger and then exclude non-Muslims, where's the universality?'[21] Altikriti echoes this, asserting that because of the universality of Islam, the *umma* includes both Muslims as a community and, more widely, non-Muslims.[22] 'The message of Islam,' he states, 'does not resonate to the borders of the Muslim community. It resonates far beyond … and that is why people are turning to Islam.'[23] For these prominent individuals, the term *umma* denotes different but related communities, with the Muslim *umma* nested within the more general *umma* of humanity. In Mogra's words:

> When we talk of the *umma* we should be thinking globally. But sometimes you have to bring it closer to home. When you have Muslims in

> Burma being persecuted, then I would say, yes, this is part of our *umma*, these are brothers and sisters in Islam, that is our *umma*, and when one part of the body aches, every part of the body is restless.[24]

The metaphor Mogra uses is derived from canonical *hadiths.* [25] It is one that is commonly referred to by other revivalist Muslims. Abdul Bari, for example, writes, 'According to the traditions [*hadiths*] from Prophet Muhammad, "You see the believers … as if they were a single body; when one of its members is ailing, the rest of the body joins it in sleeplessness and fever".'[26] Manazir Ahsan, the director general of the Islamic Foundation and elected council member of the MCB, similarly observes, 'In a Prophetic Hadith (Traditional saying) Muslims have been compared to the body – if one part of it aches, the whole body feels its effect and rushes to its relief.'[27] It seems that despite expressions of humanity as one *umma*, the notion of the Muslim *umma* takes precedence when Muslims are enduring hardship, and that this is inextricable from a scripturally informed religious perspective.

This conceptual precedence – to see Muslims as part of the Muslim *umma* prior to seeing them as part of the broader *umma* of humanity – sometimes expresses an unconscious bias towards Muslims over non-Muslims. Such a bias was expressed by MCB secretary general Iqbal Sacranie in his explanation of the MCB boycott of Holocaust Memorial Day in 2005 and its campaign to have it replaced with a more 'inclusive' event. Sacranie claimed that a new, 'EU genocide memorial day' would be able to commemorate 'other ongoing genocide and human right abuses around the world'. The examples he gave in his letter to the Home Office were all concerned with Muslims (and questionable as genocides): 'the occupied Palestinian territories, Chechnya, Kashmir'.[28] Only when the story broke in the news media did he add Rwanda and Vietnam as examples.[29]

This bias is inseparable from a distinctive religious habitus in which the Muslim *umma* is perceived – and indeed referred to in the Qur'an, verse 3:110 – as the '*best* community'. Its special value, indeed superiority, lies in its piety. In Abdul Bari's words, within humanity, the Muslim *umma* is 'blessed' because of its wilful submission to 'the will of God'.[30] His view that only the possession of 'God-consciousness' distinguishes some people as superior to others implicitly portrays the Muslim *umma* as a superior community over others.[31] The Muslim *umma* is also deemed special because of its responsibility towards humanity of sharing the message and way of life of Islam. This sense of responsibility is what connects the concept of the *umma* as humanity with that of the Muslim *umma*. The latter, gifted for its possession of divine revelation and right guidance, is seen to be the vanguard community at the cutting edge of a social transformation for the benefit of all towards Islam: The *umma* as humanity forms the broader, global community within which Islam's universal mission is yet to be realised. Sacranie expresses this view in suggesting that although the concept of the *umma* marks a communal Muslim identity, this does not entail an isolated community, since 'Islam is a universal religion' and 'engagement and exchange' is necessary for Islam to benefit humanity as a whole.[32]

Sacranie's claim that Muslim identity does not engender a mentality of separatism was voiced in a political environment where a perceived 'hardening of attitudes' towards Muslims after the July 2005 London bombings put the MCB on defensive footing. But it may also be seen in relation to an Islamic point of view in which non-Muslims are yet to be 'awakened' to the reality of their 'forgotten' Muslim identity. According to an orthodox Islamic belief based upon Muhammad's *sunna*, each child is born a Muslim, but many are raised in ignorance of this status. Ahsan expresses this view clearly. Islam, he declares, 'teaches that every man is born naturally a Muslim'.[33] This view is explicitly supported by other leading figures in the network, including Adbul Bari.[34] In acknowledgement of this original status, Muslim converts are sometimes referred to as 'reverts' because they are seen to be 'reverting' to their original and true nature as believers. This perspective, popularised in the works of the late Khurram Murad, is reflected in some of the initiatives for new converts established by revivalist organisations, such as UKIM's Revert Support Programme.[35] In Glasgow, UKIM also has a 'revert coordinator'.[36]

The notion of individuals reverting to a 'true' Muslim nature, indeed the desire for a mass reversion of non-Muslims to their alleged original state as Muslims, is closely linked to the notion of the Islamic revival: whereas individuals are seen to be in need of returning to the faith that they have lost, society at large, including its political structures, is seen to be in need of returning to the former greatness and glory of Islam. In both cases, a return to a lost but superior state of affairs is sought.

Other leading figures in the revivalist network similarly express a broad concept of community in which Muslims and non-Muslims, distinguished only by their embrace of their 'true' Muslim identity, are connected as one family. Farooq Murad, the current director of the Islamic Foundation and former MCB secretary general, asserts, 'In the Qur'an it is said that all of mankind is one *umma* – one people. Some recognise that they are members of this family. Some may not.'[37] Muslims are viewed as those who readily acknowledge themselves as part of God's family and non-Muslims are viewed as those who are yet to do so. Non-Muslims, Murad believes, need to be drawn 'back into the family' of God. The method of doing this – and a duty incumbent upon Muslims – is, Murad says, *da'wa*. Non-Muslims are thus seen as part of God's family that, by virtue of failing to recognise this, have gone astray. And *da'wa* is seen as the dutiful means by which Muslims are to bring them *back* into the fold of Islam, a return to their original, 'natural' status. Such a return ultimately dissolves the barrier between the Muslim *umma* and the *umma* of humanity which it lies within. Framing this view of the relationship between Muslims and the rest of humanity, and the importance of *da'wa*, is the perception of Islam, expressed in Ahsan's words, as 'the universal religion meant for mankind of all races, colours and times'.[38]

Abdul Bari likewise sees Islam as a 'universal religion' and *da'wa* as 'the most important duty of Muslims'.[39] He asserts that although serving 'the Muslim community' is the core of the MCB's work, this 'community focus' does not absolve it of its 'greater societal responsibilities'.[40] Abdul Bari invokes the idea of *qawm* as equivalent to the British nation which includes all British citizens, Muslim and non-Muslim alike. Addressing a Muslim audience, he says non-Muslim British citizens 'may not be part of the "Muslim Ummah", but they are our "Qawm"'.[41] Drawing attention to the social challenges that affect all people regardless of religious identity, Abdul Bari takes a practical view of 'working for the common good'.[42] Yet, the notion of *qawm* also delineates the broader community within which the Muslim *umma* in Britain is part and with which it is obliged to share the message of Muhammad for the benefit of all. Thus, there are both practical and religious motivations underlying Abdul Bari's concern for the 'common good'.

The Muslim *umma*, in one sense, is not perceived as a community apart from the more inclusive community of the British *qawm* or even humanity. There are several factors that have prompted MCB leaders and other prominent Muslim figures to articulate this publicly. Their expressions of Muslims' willingness to be an integral part of Britain are inseparable from public concerns and fears relating to Muslim radicalisation and terrorism. They are also inseparable from a perceived need to distinguish themselves and their organisations from 'quietist' groups, such as Tablighi Jama'at, which advocate a withdrawal from politics and the mainstream non-Muslim culture, and 'rejectionist' groups, such as Hizb ut-Tahrir, which consider political participation *haram*, Islamically forbidden. Public announcements regarding the inclusive character of the *umma* and the pro-integration attitude of British Muslims, such as Sacranie and Abdul Bari's, no doubt occur in a field of contention in which the public perception of Muslims and Islam is a key stake.

But it is important to note that this is not purely defensive, since what is at stake are distinctive perceptions and positively conceived notions of the Muslim *umma* in relation to non-Muslims and Muslim-minority culture: The Muslim *umma* is perceived as a distinct brotherhood united by its possession of an ethics and a mode of knowledge rooted in the divine and, importantly, its obligation to share these universally. As Adbul Bari writes, 'Muslims belong to a global family and they are commanded to remain united in the pursuit of Islam, as "all believers are brethren".'[43] And as Zahid Parvez articulates it, 'The purpose and mission of the Muslim world-community (Ummah) … is no other than to align individuals and society to the natural way shown by Allah through the glorious Quran.'[44] This sense of the *umma*'s 'purpose and mission' was similarly articulated by the late Khurram Murad, the former vice president of Jama'at-i-Islami and secretary general of the Islamic Foundation. A hugely influential figure for his son, Farooq Murad, and others including Parvez, he wrote:

> [T]he Muslim Ummah has not been constituted to become just another nation among nations, to compete with others to advance its interests. No, it has been 'raised for all mankind'. It is the 'best community' [a reference to the Qur'an, verse 3:110] only if it serves their [i.e. mankind's] interests, their foremost interest being that they should *find guidance to the right path* [i.e. to Islam].[45]

Territory: dar al-Islam and dar al-harb

Individuals of the revivalist network express a similar sense of the terrain in which they live and practise their faith. Traditionally, Islamic legal thought classified territory into *dar al-Islam* (the abode of peace or submission to Allah) and *dar al-harb* (the abode of war).[46] Contemporary revivalist thinkers, including Yusuf al-Qaradawi and Khurram Murad, began to question the applicability of this classification when it became clear, from the late 1970s, that Muslims in Europe were not temporary residents but permanent citizens. Europe could not be considered *dar al-harb,* since it was now the home of some millions of Muslims who were more or less free to practise Islam, though it could not be considered *dar al-Islam,* since *shari'a* was not fully applied. Thus, a new legal category was devised for it, *dar al-da'wa* (the abode of the call to Islam). Al-Qaradawi also speaks of Europe as *dar al-ahd* (the abode of contact), while Tariq Ramadan describes it as *dar al-shahada* (the abode of testimony).[47] These alternative conceptual categories are explicitly or implicitly endorsed by some members of the revivalist network, indicating a shared perspective of their relationship with their social and political environment.

Abdullah Faliq, for example, notes that from the early 1980s, organisations such as the Islamic Forum of Europe (IFE) and the MAB, continued the trend established by other organisations, including the UK Islamic Mission (UKIM) and FOSIS, to serve Muslims' interests and protect Muslim identity, but also began to view Britain as home. Their activities began to be directed to Muslims as British citizens. He contends that events such as the Rushdie Affair not only helped galvanise a trans-ethnic sense of Muslim solidarity amongst British Muslims, but also made clear that the classical Islamic definitions of territory were irrelevant to Muslims' contemporary situation in Britain. 'This is a place where Islam can be practiced,' asserts Faliq, 'so it is not *dar al-harb.* Britain is home to me, so I consider it "land of peace".'[48] Other leading figures in the network seem to agree. Citing the influence of his late father upon his thinking, Farooq Murad rejects the relevance of the idea of *dar al-Islam* versus *dar al-harb.* 'Islam is not a geographical idea,' he states, 'it is a universal message.'[49] Muslims, he believes, should integrate and participate in Britain though democratic means. 'There is no idea of isolation, withdrawal or rejection.' This is not merely his father's teachings, he insists, since 'it comes from the Islamic concept of *da'wa*. This is invitation, interaction. We have a message and we should share it.'

The rejection of traditional, dichotomous Islamic notions of space was similarly articulated in a report, *Contextualising Islam*, published by the

University of Cambridge. Authored by a group including some individuals identified as playing key roles in the revivalist network, such as Mohammed Abdul Aziz, Anas al-Shaikh Ali, Ibrahim Mogra and Mohamed Mukadam, the report states that it is 'important to move away from the terminology of the "dar al-Islam" and "dar al-harb" dichotomy,' which, it says, is not found in the Qur'an, but 'developed by classical jurists in an era before globalisation'.[50] The report claims that the concept of *dar al-Islam* was equivalent to *dar al-amn* – 'land of security' – as opposed to a 'land of insecurity'. It also states that security means the 'freedom to perform public acts of worship, including the five prayers, giving alms (*zakah*), performing pilgrimage to Makkah, performing the fast of Ramadan, slaughter of animals for halal food, building mosques, giving the call to prayer (*adhan*), wearing appropriate dress and avoiding the cardinal sins'.[51] In Britain, the report notes, there is freedom to do all of these things, the implication being that Britain may be considered in this sense as *dar al-Islam* or, at the very least, *not* as *dar al-harb.* Mogra concurs with this view. 'Britain for me is the best place in Europe for Muslims,' says. 'We have everything we would wish for in this country. I can dress as I like, we have *halal* shops, you can call out the call to prayer from the minarets, we have every freedom within the parameters of the law.'[52]

The perception of Britain beyond the dichotomous terms of *dar al-Islam* and *dar al-harb* is not unique to revivalists who seek a transformation of society towards the universalisation of Islam. Whilst revivalists who perceive Islam's rightful place as comprehensively embedded throughout the entire social fabric reject an attitude of hostility towards Britain and non-Muslim fellow citizens, there are others who likewise view Britain in non-confrontational terms but see Islam as needing to find a home within a mostly secular society and a liberal democratic political system. Both groups of individuals view Islam and the Muslim-minority environment of Britain in compatible rather than antagonistic terms. But what distinguishes these two groups is how Islam is viewed as best at home in Britain. Whereas revivalists see no limit to the applicability of Islam within Britain's social and political structures – and in fact sees such change in the long term as the will of God – Muslim secularists see a need for a clear separation of religion and the state, and a need to re-interpret the fundamentals of the religion within the contemporary context of today's liberal democratic, human rights framework.

Classifications of Britain or Europe more broadly as *dar al-da'wa, dar al-ahd* or *dar al-shahada* certainly separate their proponents from the 'rejectionist' groups such as Hizb ut-Tahrir, who eschew any third possible classification of territory beyond *dar al-Islam* and *dar al-harb.* But what separates them internally is whether or not Islam is viewed as a universal religion and whether or not the *umma* is seen as having a 'purpose and mission' to guide humanity through *da'wa* to a comprehensive social transformation in the name of Islam. What distinguishes Islamic revivalists is not just a non-confrontational sense of the territory in which they live, but – as the next section aims to show – a certain sense of the nature, purpose and meaning of their work, as well as a certain orientation to the future.

Missionary concepts and perceptions

In addition to a shared sense of themselves as part of a religious community, the *umma*, and a sense of the terrain upon which they live, individuals and groups in the revivalist network share a sense of their work and its purpose. This section of the chapter identifies three ways in which this manifests. First, in terms of an effort to educate Muslims on their faith; second, as a call to non-Muslims to Islam, understood through the Islamic concept of *da'wa*; and third, in terms of a proactive moral duty to 'enjoin good and forbid wrong'. These are all interrelated, and together amount to a collective tendency to define and classify Islam, but for the purposes of elucidation are introduced separately.

Speaking for Muslims and Islam

Many of the individuals and groups of the revivalist network are involved in classificatory work that acts to influence Muslims' own understanding of their faith. They are connected by a similar approach, adopted consciously or unconsciously, to shape the perceptions and realities of Muslims in line with a particular way of seeing and appreciating the world – a particular Islamic habitus. There is some variation between individuals' practical or reflexive understanding of Islam, including certain key religious concepts, but this does not undermine the basic observation that there is a shared concern to represent what is deemed to be the true understanding of Islam. There is a collective effort, albeit largely uncoordinated and distributed, to classify the 'correct' and, thus, the 'incorrect' practice of the religion.

At the nexus of the revivalist network, the MCB's official aims include working 'for a more enlightened appreciation of Islam and Muslim in the wider society' and promoting 'cooperation, consensus and unity on Muslim affairs in the UK'.[53] However, as the former advisor to Iqbal Sacranie, Mohammed Abdul Aziz, admits, the constitution of its leadership and organisational affiliates is dominated by Jama'at or Ikhwan-associated individuals and groups.[54] Ostensibly, the MCB seeks to build consensus and represent the broad range of Islamic viewpoints on policy matters, though in practice the views it expresses belie a certain outlook that is difficult to separate from the specific background of its leadership. The distinctiveness of this outlook is marked by not just certain views or concepts – for example, the *umma* as a community with a universal mission to share Islam – but also the perception of its own mission to speak on behalf of Islam. In speaking for Muslims, the MCB adopts a significant role in presenting a specific understanding of Islam to the government and the wider public, as well as to Muslims themselves.

Former secretary general Farooq Murad states, 'On many issues we have tried to build consensus. It is not easy, I accept, but we feel that there are issues that we need to make provision for. This includes the *education of our faith*.'[55] While presenting itself as an interlocutionary agent for the diversity of Muslim views – a conduit for different Islamic perspectives – the MCB no doubt sees as part of its mission the education of Muslims and non-Muslims on what Islam is. Murad states, 'We try to build consensus within the [Muslim] community, try *to articulate what Islam is* for the majority of the community.' Murad's assertion that the MCB seeks to express the understanding of Islam held by the majority of Muslims is highly contentious. It is possibly based upon a belief that most British Muslims adhere to what he and his associates deem to be orthodox Islam, rather than any systematic study of what British Muslims perceive their faith to consist of. It certainly appears more aspirational or prescriptive than descriptive.

This is supported by some of the events the MCB has organised. For example, in September 2004, the MCB held a seminar at the East London Mosque's London Muslim Centre, which marked the launch of the publication of the MCB's 'Guide to the British Media'. The media guide and the seminar aimed 'to develop the skills needed by British Muslims to ensure *a better and more accurate representation of their faith and values* in the print and broadcast media'.[56] The MCB is not the only organisation that sees itself as speaking on behalf of Islam. Manazir Ahsan, the director general of the Islamic Foundation, acknowledges that the organisation, particularly its publication arm, is dedicated to portraying Islam in authentic terms. 'Since its inception,' he notes, 'the Islamic Foundation has been engaged in bringing out works which may enable readers to gain a better, sharper understanding of things Islamic.'[57]

Irshad Bacqui, speaking as the Foundation's executive director, supports this view. When the Foundation was established, he says, 'it was about how to present Islam to society'.[58] In the 1970s, there was hardly any literature from the perspective of Muslims living in a Muslim-minority country. The Foundation tried to fill this gap, he says, by providing guidance on 'the roles and responsibilities' of Muslims in this different context. Initially focusing on children's literature, Bacqui states, it was important to help create a new mindset, of 'how to live according to Islamic values' in a new environment. The authoritative presentation of Islam continues to be important to the Foundation's work today. 'We want to present Islam to the Muslim community and the wider society,' says Bacqui, 'to create awareness, so that people become aware.' He adds that this is important in order to combat 'misunderstandings that occur from ignorance about each other. The Muslim community is as guilty of that as any other community. We try to explain, interpret and raise awareness about each other so we can live better together.'[59]

Other individuals and groups in the network similarly see themselves as working to increase the understanding of Islam. In October 2017, in an address to Muslim students of Islam, Zahid Parvez, the director of MIHE and a member of the MCB's National Council, urged them to 'work hard to articulate the Islamic thought and the spiritual and moral values of Islam'. This, he urged, 'will help to bring forward correct interpretations of the Quran and Sunnah and thereby remove misunderstandings and fears about Islam and the Muslim community'.[60] The task of presenting the correct, as opposed to incorrect, understanding of Islam is also shouldered by Omer El-Hamdoon, MAB president and deputy secretary general of the MCB. He explains the MAB's work as targeting three distinct groups, namely, Muslim members, Muslim non-members and non-Muslims. Amongst members, El-Hamdoon describes the MAB's work as promoting a 'better understanding of Islam, better knowledge', as well as developing greater awareness of local and global issues affecting Muslims. Amongst Muslim non-members, he states, 'We try to promote *the correct* understanding of Islam.' Explaining what he means by this, he says:

> The people who have deviated in Islam are the people who have deviated from *the texts*. If you really want to understand Islam you have to go back to the texts of Islam, the Qur'an and the *sunna*, the teaching of the Prophet Muhammad.

El-Hamdoon summarises MAB's aspirations as follows:

> We hope that the Muslim Association of Britain tries to *correct* Muslims' understanding of Islam, so they are not narrow minded … . At the same time we try to reach out to non-Muslims and say to them, 'This is Islam, these are the ideals of Islam, this is what Islam talks about.'[61]

UKIM and IFE – described by IFE's press secretary, Abdullah Faliq, as the two 'strongest' Muslim organisations in Britain – also view themselves as working to enhance Muslims' understanding of Islam, as well as educating non-Muslims about Islam through *da'wa*, or outreach work. More will be said shortly on *da'wa*, since it is a key element of their *modus operandi* to attain an Islamic society. Here it suffices to observe that both organisations regard their work as beginning with disseminating the right understanding of Islam amongst Muslims. This is at least partly because only Muslims with the right understanding of Islam may engage in *da'wa*.

Like the Islamic Foundation, IFE sees itself as speaking for Islam through the facilitation of 'an enlightened appreciation of Islam that is relevant to the context and realities of our time'.[62] Such an appreciation is fostered by a range of activities, including formal and informal courses, retreats, workshops and seminars, including training programmes in leadership development for imams. UKIM likewise has a grassroots connection with over 40 branches and around 30 mosques. It similarly targets local communities with a range of social programmes, including youth clubs and cultural events. According to its website, around 5,000 children annually receive an Islamic education through its *madari* system.[63] UKIM states that it is important for its members to acquire a 'basic knowledge and understanding of the Islamic faith and values'. This includes 'knowing what is obligatory (*fard* and *wajib*) and prohibited (*haram*)'.[64] UKIM has a very clear concept of Islam that it deems authentic and for which it sees itself as struggling to comprehensively *revive* throughout British society.

Both UKIM and IFE, as with the Islamic Foundation, the MCB and others, are involved in an effort to define and classify Islam. This can take the form of educating Muslims on their faith in the context of competing Islamic interpretations, particularly secular liberal ones, or challenging mainstream public perceptions of Islam, particularly those critical (or perceived to be critical) of Islamic beliefs and practices. Some groups speaking on behalf of Muslims and Islam in recent years have taken a strident tone against what they see as government-led 'Islamophobia'. Implicit to this is a certain understanding of Islam that requires protection. Muslim Engagement and Development (MEND), for example, states, 'The desperate need to challenge the status quo, to present Islam and Muslims in a more balanced light and to defend civil liberties has never been more acute.'[65]

These groups appear united in having a vision of their work as providing the 'right' understanding of the religion, even though they may differ upon some of the details. What this understanding consists in may be elaborated through several concepts, including *da'wa*, and doctrines, such as Enjoining the Good and Forbidding the Wrong, that characterise their work.

Da'wa*: the call to Islam*

Related to the efforts to present an authentic vision of Islam to Muslims are the efforts to present Islam to non-Muslims. These efforts are entwined within a tendency to control the legitimate classification of Muslim identity and the Islamic faith. Indeed, for Islamic revivalists, what it is to be a Muslim is in part comprised of a commitment to conduct *da'wa,* to present Islam to non-believers.

The special significance of *da'wa* is related to the importance placed upon a genuine embrace of Islam – a willing rather than a coerced submission to God – for the universalisation of the religion. The propagation of Islam, it is believed, cannot be done effectively through the isolation of Muslims from the surrounding Muslim-minority culture, nor through violent means. The importance of *da'wa* underlies revivalists' active participation in democratic politics and their condemnation of violent jihadists, such as the Islamic State in Iraq and Syria. This is exemplified by the MCB's campaign to encourage Muslims to vote[66] and its condemnation of the Islamic State as *un*Islamic.[67] Thus, revivalists may be distinguished from militants who seek an Islamic world order through military-driven territorial expansion and from 'quietists' who wish to isolate themselves in communities of putative spiritual purity.

The characterisation of groups such as the Islamic Foundation and the MCB as 'participationist' accurately highlights the importance they place upon Muslims' active involvement in Western social and political structures. However, it obscures a more fundamental conviction underlying their willingness to participate in politics, which concerns the importance of sharing Islam, or from their perspective *reviving* it, through willing submission. For this reason, the term '*dawa*-ist' might be more accurate, though 'revivalist' is maintained throughout this book due to its relative ease of use. The term 'participationist' also assumes that the groups and individuals in question share the same fundamental goal as 'rejectionists', such as Hizb ut-Tahrir, and are just best distinguished from them on the basis of their chosen methods. Yet, the notion of an Islamic state as something that evolves organically within society is arguably quite different from one that is imposed from above; it is different enough to raise the question as to whether 'participationists' and 'rejectionists' in fact seek the same thing.

Prominent individuals and groups in the revivalist network of the global Muslim Brotherhood consistently characterise *da'wa* as a religious duty. IFE's website states, 'Islam obligates Muslims to share and discuss their faith with those around them, as directed by the Qur'an: "Invite people to the way of your Lord, with wisdom and beautiful speech". [Qur'an, 16:125].'[68] It adds, 'This principle, known as Da'wa, requires Muslims to undertake dialogue and discourse about our faith in a manner that resonates with the people around us.' Through the principle of 'Islamic Dawah,' states IFE's website, the 'responsibility of promoting Islam is a duty placed on us all'.[69] IFE meets this perceived duty by organising 'Islam awareness' projects, producing audio-visual resources and hosting exhibitions, mosque open days and interfaith events.

Other groups that are similarly involved in *da'wa* activities likewise see *da'wa* as an Islamic duty. FOSIS, for example, runs an annual Islam Awareness Week in collaboration with the Islamic Education and Research Academy (iERA). In its guide for the event organisers, FOSIS states that the 'first and foremost reason' for conducting such an event is 'that it is obligatory upon to Muslims to call others to Islam. It is narrated that the Prophet Muhammad (pbuh) said "convey Islam to the people even if it were by a single ayah".' By organising an Islam Awareness Week,' it states, 'you will have something to show Allah on the Day of Judgement. This is without doubt the most important reason to participate in dawah.'[70] iERA itself is a very active organisation dedicated to *da'wa* work. It conducts training courses and develops resources for *da'wa* under its Mission Dawah initiative, and has a programme aimed at supporting new Muslims with the fundamentals of their new faith. Another organisation, the Islam Channel is conceived by its founder, Mohamed Ali Harrath, as a powerful modern vehicle for *da'wa*. The channel was established as a part of Harrath's Dawah Project, the website of which states: '"Dawah" (inviting others to Islam) is an obligation upon all Muslims. Thus, it is our duty to educate people about Islam, subsequently to have a better understanding of the Muslim way of life.'[71]

The conception of *da'wa* as a duty is shared by key figures in the revivalist network, including Muhammad Abdul Bari, Suhaib Hasan, Omer El-Hamdoon and Anas Altikriti. Adbul Bari writes that 'the most important duty of Muslims is to create awareness, bearing witness to God's message among people'.[72] Consistent with this, Hasan asserts that,

> *Da'wa*, which means the propagation of Islam, the word of Allah, is a duty upon every Muslim. According to his means and abilities, he should do *da'wa*. Because as long as I think that Islam is good for everyone, and as long as I think that it is a way of your salvation on the day of judgment, then I should not hold it, I should not confine it to myself, I should propagate it.[73]

El-Hamdoon also sees *da'wa* as a duty for Muslims, but emphasises that it is something that ought to be conducted from the heart. 'The message has not been clear,' he says,

> because when people talk about *da'wa*, inviting others to Islam, they always talk it about it as a duty. At MAB, however, we want to take it to a different level, where its not just your duty, but it is something that you really do genuinely, sincerely.[74]

He cites the Muslim scholar al-Ghazali (1058–1111), who criticised some Muslims' worship of God as 'the worship of traders or businessmen', conducted because they calculate paradise will be rewarded to them in return. 'The higher level of worship,' says El-Hamdoon, 'is conducted by people who worship God because He deserves to be worshipped. Even if there was no Paradise, if there was no Hellfire, they would still worship God because He is worthy of worship.'

This notion of the duty of *da'wa* is one in which it is conducted not merely from a rational acknowledgement of its importance or a calculation of its rewards, but from a natural inclination, an unconsciously embodied and 'heartfelt' understanding of its importance. It resonates with the view of *da'wa* expressed by Khurram Murad, who wrote, 'Da'wah, prior to everything, is a state of mind, a world view, an attitude to life, indeed a kind of life.'[75] In this sense, *da'wa* is more than just the conscious act of presenting and promoting Islam to non-Muslims, for example through organised activities. It is also a way of conducting oneself in every action. It is unsurprising, then, that this is how Khurram Murad's son, Farooq Murad, views *da'wa*. While conceding that the MCB's official remit does not include *da'wa*, he asserts:

> But *da'wa* is a very broad concept and can be done in many ways. If I live my values of Islam of decency, respect, kindness and generosity, I may be doing the best kind of *da'wa* possible. I think you are doing *da'wa*

> without consciously, actively doing *da'wa*. If you live Islam, you cannot but be doing *da'wa*.[76]

Altikriti echoes these sentiments, emphasising the comprehensive nature of *da'wa* as permeating all of the various domains of human action. Social work, public relations, teaching and all other kinds of work, he states, may be classified into their respective categories only from a practical point of view, but all of them fall into the one category of *da'wa*:

> All that we do, every single activity that we engage with, every single rhetoric that we issue, every statement that we publish, every person that we meet, every party that we hold an alliance with – everything – everything around us rotates around the central and focal meaning of *da'wa*.[77]

From this point of view, *da'wa* involves a state of mind *and* a state of being, in which Islam permeates every conscious thought and unconscious action. According to this perspective, activities strategically dedicated to promote Islam, those consciously explicative of the virtues of Islam as a way of life, are considered to be but one form of *da'wa* alongside actions that unconsciously promote Islam by exemplary behaviour. Manazir Ahsan supports this interpretation, asserting, 'Witnessing by word, *Shahadah bil qaul*, and reinforcing it by action, *Shahadah bil amal*, are two sides of the same coin – both are complementary and necessary to the other.'[78]

Da'wa is not a matter of rational advocacy seeking an intellectual conversion, but a holistic presentation of the faith, both consciously, through reflection and explication, and unconsciously, through embodied action. Yet, even strategic activities that seek to make explicit the appeal of Islam as a way of life, are required – as *da'wa* – to be conducted in a certain way that unconsciously embody the values of Islam. This is because *da'wa* is not considered merely as a means of changing people's thinking, but a way of changing their unconsciously held attitudes and dispositions, as well as their behaviour.

From a revivalist perspective, *da'wa* is fundamentally remedial in serving to combat 'incorrect' ways of thinking concerning Islam as a way of life. One of the functions of *da'wa*, maintains Farooq Murad, 'is to remove misconceptions' about Islam.[79] Zahid Parvez concurs. He states that *da'wa* 'helps in removing misconceptions, builds respect and tolerance for Islam and Muslims'.[80] The website for Harrath's Dawah Project expresses a similar point of view, extolling the power of the media to 'dispel the misconception some have about Islam'. Under the auspices of the Dawah Project, Harrath plans to open an International Dawah Centre to fulfill what he describes as Muslims' 'obligatory duty of Dawah [to] counter the ever increasing misconceptions about Islam and to promote understanding amongst each other'.[81]

However, *da'wa* is not just deemed as a corrective to wrong *notions* about Islam. It is also considered, more fundamentally, as a remedy to what Parvez refers to as 'false consciousness' and 'the influences of false gods and wrong ways' that affect a person's outlook on life.[82] Thus, it is considered to address not just specific, incorrect propositions, but wrong ways of seeing things. It is deemed to transform, in Pierre Bourdieu's words, the unconsciously held dispositions and orientations of the habitus.[83] Parvez contends that

> the purpose of sharing the message of Islam and offering a critique of wrong notions is to awaken people to the realities of life, to challenge their preconceived ideas and beliefs, to agitate their thoughts and attitudes and to support them in seeing the world and social issues from an Islamic perspective. Thus, the aim of *dawa* is to counteract the harmful social conditioning which a people may be under-going, to invite them into the fold of God's Way and to help them discover their true purpose in life and the multiple dimensions of their existence.[84]

Given Parvez's former leadership role in UKIM for so many years, it is unsurprising that UKIM adopts an identical position on *da'wa*. In fact, much of the description of UKIM's work on its website, including its aims, approach and programmes, appears to be derived from Parvez's book, *Building a New Society: An Islamic Approach to Social Change*, published by the Islamic Foundation in 2000. Consistent with this book – which is without doubt the most comprehensive manifesto for Islamic revivalism in Britain – UKIM describes *da'wa* as one of the key components of its methodology for attaining an Islamic society in Britain. It is conceived not just as an important means of changing the way people see and understand their social and political realities, but also as a crucial way of changing such realities by transforming social and political institutions. Its website asserts, 'Without being actively engaged in calling people to the Islamic message and way of life, Islamic ideas and values will not be heard or appreciated by society, and positive changes based on Islam cannot be accomplished.'

A shared sense of the importance of *da'wa* – directed to both non-Muslims and Muslims – may be considered as a distinguishing feature of the revivalist network in Britain. The concept of *da'wa* as a duty for all Muslims is expressed consistently throughout the network, despite the varying ways individuals or groups may see themselves meeting this duty in practice. This is related to a shared sense of the purpose of *da'wa* – to present and propagate 'authentic' Islam through peaceful and non-coercive means – and a shared sense of Islam as a way of life that leaves no aspect of human existence untouched. Far from being merely concerned with ideas or ideology, *da'wa*, as revivalists see it, is a process of transforming people's ways of perceiving, thinking about and evaluating social reality. It has perceptual, cognitive and moral dimensions. It affects not just what or how one sees, but how one judges what one sees. It affects not just what or how one thinks, but how one is disposed to certain ideas. It also concerns imparting the 'correct' morality to individuals and the society as a whole.

'Enjoining the Good and Forbidding the Wrong'

In addition to viewing themselves as dutifully educating Muslims on Islam as a way of life and inviting non-Muslims to 'return' to the fold of Islam, individuals and groups within the revivalist network share a common view of their work in terms of the Qur'anically prescribed duty known as *al-amr bi-l-ma 'ruf wa-l-nahi 'an al-munkar,* Enjoining the Good and Forbidding the Wrong (EGFW).[85] This duty is often explicitly referred to as guiding their actions, yet it also seems to help form a set of dispositions and orientations that are shared within the network. These include a proactive stance towards social change. It also helps constitute a constellation of inter-connected concepts – including *da'wa, umma, shari'a* and *jihad* – through which the world is seen and made sense of, and through which their actions are guided.

Acknowledgement of the duty of EGFW was expressed in the joint statement made by numerous figures in the revivalist network in Britain at the aforementioned 'Muslims in Europe Conference' held in Istanbul in July 2006. Attendees – including Khurshid Ahmad, Manazir Ahsan, Iqbal Sacranie, Mohammed Abdul Aziz, Iqbal Asaria, Said Ferjani, Wakkas Khan, Mohamed Mukadam, Anas al-Shaikh-Ali, and Ahmed al-Rawi – declared: 'Islam calls upon all Muslims to promote the common good and welfare (*maslaha*) of society as a whole and prevent what is wrong (*munkar*).'[86] This duty is also acknowledged by individuals and particular groups in the network, including the MCB, the MAB, the Islamic Foundation, IFE and UKIM.

In the preamble of its constitution, the MCB states that its members aspire 'to be a community "enjoining what is right, forbidding what is wrong, and believing in Allah" (The Qur'an, 3:110)'.[87] This verse is also one of three cited at the start of the document, reading, 'You are the best community raised up for mankind – you enjoin what is right, forbid what is wrong, and believe in Allah.'[88] All member organisations have to subscribe to this aspiration, in addition to the MCB aims, in order to be eligible for membership. Considering that there are 6,236 verses in the Qur'an, its selection and prominent placement in the MCB constitution is significant. It highlights not only a sense of vanguardism on the MCB's part but also a strong sense of moral activism at the core of its *raison d'être*. This moral activism is inseparable from a sense of mission, however conceived as best implemented, to universalise Islam for the benefit of society at large.

Farooq Murad, the former MCB secretary general, while acknowledging that the MCB's official remit does not include *da'wa*, recognises EGFW as a form of *da'wa*.[89] This recognition suggests that the MCB's aspiration to be a proactive moral authority – one that assumes its position to judge 'right' and 'wrong' – is inseparable from a mission to present Islam to the broader society with a view to spreading the faith. Writing as president of the Islamic Society of Britain (ISB), Murad lauds this mission as 'the establishment of *deen* [Islamic way of life]' and laments its neglect amongst British Muslims. He also invokes EGFW, citing a *hadith* in which the prophet Muhammad exhorts social and political activism towards the fulfilment of this mission. Murad asks: 'Did not the Messenger of Allah (saw) say, "*If anyone of you sees an evil let him change it by his hands* ..." (Muslim)?'[90] Zahid Parvez, the current director of the Markfield Institute of Higher Education, also invokes the term 'changing by hand', which, he concedes 'is implied by scholars as possessing political power – the arm of the law, the ability to effect change; the power to enjoin good (*maruf*) and forbid wrong (*munkar*)'.[91]

Murad and Parvez's reference to the use of 'hands' to effect social change, in fact, has a rich history in Islamic literature. It is commonly understood as a kind of *jihad*, the effort or struggle towards the consummation of Allah's will on Earth. According to Michael Cook, a scholar of Islamic history, EGFW is 'an integral part of the mainstream scholastic tradition of Islamic societies' and was frequently linked by the Muslim scholars with *jihad*. Some considered it a part of *jihad*, others considered *jihad* a part of it.[92] '*Jihad* of the hand' was just one kind of *jihad* linked to the doctrine, albeit the dominant one. Although this typically meant military force – both defensive and offensive – in modern times it seems to highlight the various ways it may be implemented physically. Another form of *jihad* – that 'of the tongue' – highlights the importance of language and symbolic struggles for the legitimisation and naturalisation of Islam throughout society. This type of *jihad* is extolled by Yusuf al-Qaradawi, who states,

> *Jihad* for the sake of God includes supporting His cause by writing, and speaking as much as by fighting. *Jihad* may be educational, journalistic, social, economic, or political *jihad* as much as military *jihad*. We must remember that in all kinds of *jihad*, the essential condition is that the action helps make God's word supreme on earth.[93]

Thus, it is no coincidence that EGFW is referred to by Parvez as a form of *jihad* and a key component of the methodology required to usher in an Islamic revival in Britain. He writes,

> In Islamic terminology, *jihad* refers to well thought-out, strategic and organised actions, guided by Islamic values and principles, taken by an Islamic movement to enjoin good (*maruf*), forbid wrong practices (*munkar*) and remove obstacles in the way of advancing positive social change.[94]

EGFW is widely considered as a fundamental Islamic duty within the revivalist network by groups other than the MCB and by prominent individuals, including Muhammad Abdul Bari, Omer El-Hamdoon, Abdur Rashid Siddiqui, and Ghulam Sarwar. Of EGFW, El-Hamdoon, president of the MAB, asserts: 'The doctrine itself is a Qur'anic doctrine. It is something that God tells us, we cannot reject it in any way.'[95] Siddiqui, the vice chair of the Islamic Foundation and former secretary general of UKIM, states,

> Commanding good and forbidding evil is one of the most important injunctions imposed upon an individual Muslim as well as upon the *ummah* as a whole. Its importance can be gauged by the fact that it is mentioned at least nine times in the Qur'an.[96]

As with the concept of *da'wa*, with which it is intimately connected, Siddiqui asserts, 'The duty of commanding good and forbidding evil is such an important part of Islamic teachings that it permeates all the affairs of a Muslim's life.'[97] Furthermore, EGFW is seen as essentially concerned with addressing not merely one's own moral righteousness but *social* morality. 'Muslims are duty bound,' claims Siddiqui, 'to get actively involved in working for the social betterment of the society in which they live.' Abdul Bari similarly understands EGFW as an obligation for social activism at the heart of Islam. He writes:

> [S]ocial activism … comes from Islam's teachings that, as vice-regents of Allah on earth, human beings are accountable to Him on the Day of Judgement. Islam motivates its adherents to flourish spiritually and be active socially – to create a better world, with balance and harmony. *'Enjoining what is right and forbidding what is wrong' (Al-Qur'an 3:110) has been the cornerstone of a Muslim social life.*[98]

From UKIM's perspective, EGFW is one of the 'most significant components' of its methodology for achieving its stated aim of reviving Islam within British society.[99] The Qur'anic verse 3:110 cited by Adbul Bari, and more fully in the MCB's constitution, was selected and placed prominently on a banner at UKIM's 50th anniversary event in September 2012.[100] EGFW also features prominently in the work of UKIM Youth. The first of its four official aims is 'To seek the pleasure of Allah by enjoining the good and forbidding the evil'.[101]

Other organisations in the revivalist network see their work in relation to EGFW. The Association of Muslim Lawyers, for example, refers to the doctrine in its description of the role Islam has allegedly played in the regulation of social morality through legal reform. 'Based on divine revelation,' it claims,

> Islam has always acted as a filter – which retains what is good in a society while removing what is harmful … . Part of this process of change and transformation is the review of existing laws and the introduction of new ones, particularly as regards those regulating religious discrimination.[102]

Ghulam Sarwar, the longtime director of the Muslim Educational Trust, states that the second of eleven objectives of Islamic education is to 'Ensure the promotion of *Mar'af* (good) and the prevention of *Munkar* (evil) in a society'.[103] He conceives of EGFW as a religious duty that is required to achieve the goals of Islamic education, which include the spread of Islam throughout society. 'This duty,' states Sarwar, 'is universal and must be acted upon for the benefit of human kind [*sic*]'.[104]

Sarwar's understanding of humanity as the ultimate beneficiary of Islam expresses a commonly held point of view within revivalist circles. UKIM, for example, describes Islam as 'a mission and a social and political movement for establishing peace, justice and harmony in society and the entire world'. In addition to *da'wa*, it views EGFW as a duty required for the fulfilment of this mission:

> They must also *enjoin good and forbid all forms of wrongs and injustices prevalent in society.* Even a cursory reading of the Glorious Quran will indicate clearly that the Muslim community is charged with this noble and challenging purpose and mission.[105]

UKIM then cites the Qur'an, verse 3:104, 'And let there be [arising] from you a nation inviting to [all that is] good, enjoining what is right and forbidding what is wrong, and those will be the successful.' This verse is cited by Abdul Bari in a report produced for the Cordoba Foundation to encourage Muslims in Britain to be part of the group taking up this obligation.[106] According to El-Hamdoon, this verse provides the basis for the *collective* nature of the duty to 'enjoin good and prevent wrong': As long as there are some from within the Muslim *umma* who are undertaking this duty, it is not an obligation for each individual.[107] This interpretation is shared by Siddiqui, who writes that although EGFW 'is the responsibility of the entire *ummah*, Allah, in His Mercy, has given this allowance whereby there must be at least a group of people who are exclusively devoted to this task'.[108] This, he notes, has a basis in Islamic jurisprudence.

However, some groups and individuals within the revivalist network appear to present EGFW as a duty applicable to each and every Muslim individual. IFE's website, for example, states:

> In an Islamic society the individual cannot be indifferent. He is enjoined to play an active part in the establishment of sound social morals by way of *inviting to the good and combating evil in any form with all lawful means at his disposal.* In so doing, not only does he shun evil and do good but also helps others to do the same. The individual who feels indifferent to his society is a selfish sinner; his morals are in trouble, his conscience is in disorder, and his faith is undernourished.[109]

Haitham al-Haddad, a former judge at the Islamic Sharia Council, similarly asserts:

> It is clearly evident to any Muslim who possesses a basic understanding of Islam that the greatest and most important aim of Islamic law is the

> deterrence of evil … and the attainment of good … [I]t is an obligation upon every Muslim to achieve this aim, whether in part or in its totality.[110]

Thus, there is some difference of emphasis upon where the duty for EGFW lies, but common within the network is an understanding of the general applicability of the duty as well as its importance.

Most references to EGFW do not specify *what* is 'good' or 'wrong'. Zahid Parvez, however, asserts that 'Enjoining good includes the promotion of Islamic values in society'.[111] These include, he says, 'truth, honesty, chastity, family values, respect and care for the elderly, care and proper upbringing for the young, a moral and balanced education, just social policies, the equitable distribution of wealth, care for orphans and support for the poor'.[112] Parvez's list of Islamic values appear equally shareable by non-Muslims, though he adds that 'efforts for change should be motivated by a strong faith in Allah, to win his good pleasure'.[113]

Suhaib Hasan, chair of the Islamic Sharia Council, further emphasises the role of the framework of religious belief within which such values are given their meaning. Citing the Qur'an, verse 9:71, Hasan explains that 'good' (*al-Ma 'ruf*) denotes 'Islamic Monotheism and all that Islam orders one to do' and that 'wrong' (*al-Munkar*) denotes 'polytheism and disbelief of all kinds, and all that Islam has forbidden'.[114] Hasan thus emphasises not so much *what* is valued but rather the *value system itself*, the structure of belief that gives specific values, such as care for the poor, their practical sense and ultimate worth. His view resonates with that of Siddiqui, who states that 'the criteria for *ma 'ruf* and *munkar* is provided by the *Shari'ah*'.[115] This is consistent with a *shari'a* manual lauded as reliable by El-Hamdoon, which defines 'good and bad' strictly in terms of 'Sacred Law'.[116]

Within the revivalist network is a shared perception of the applicability of EGFW beyond the individual to society at large: it is generally a collective duty whose ultimate beneficiary is humanity. It is clear that, at least for some, this extends to the state too. As Zahid Parvez asserts, 'acting on such good in one's private life is not enough according to Islam. Public life and the state must conform to equitable and moral principles.'[117] He adds, 'the followers of Islam are charged with a mission to realise the vision of Islam in social life and the state'.[118] But not only is the state desired to conform to Islamic morality, it is also – if it becomes an *Islamic* state – expected to enforce it. Siddiqui writes:

> Due to the importance accorded to *al-amr bi al-ma 'ruf wa al-nahy 'an al-munkar* it is also one of the duties that an Islamic State is required to enforce … . Hence, the Islamic State is duty-bound to see that its citizens are adhering to the code of life and behaviour required by Islam.[119]

Likewise, Sarwar writes that the implementation of EGFW is one of the functions of the Islamic state.[120]

Similar thinking resounds in the work of Muhammad Taqi Usmani, a regular visitor to Britain who has played a major role in Islamic finance in Britain and globally. Usmani was a member of HSBC Amanah's Shariah Board in Britain, has sat on MIHE's international advisory council,[121] and led the 'first Shariah Finance Course in the UK' hosted by the Islamic Foundation in 2006.[122] Although only a 'part-time' member of the revivalist network in Britain, Usmani shares with Siddiqui and Sarwar the view that the Islamic state has a duty to implement EGFW. For the attainment of an Islamic social order – which he envisages to occur first in Pakistan prior to globally – he stresses the necessity of 'a permanent government department for enforcing "what is commanded" and "restraining from what is forbidden". (*Amr e bil maaroof and nahi anil munkir*)'. This department, he says, should be staffed by 'God-fearing, practicing Muslims devoted entirely to creating the spirit of Islam among the masses'.[123]

The question then arises, dealt with in the following chapter, regarding how the Islamic state features in the imaginations and aspirations within the revivalist network in Britain. Before addressing the critical issue of the Islamic state, however, it is worth noting that EGFW is not exclusive to revivalists. For example, Hizb ut-Tahrir – which differs from revivalists in rejecting participation in democratic politics – also sees it as a duty. Outlining its 'methodology for change', it states:

> Enjoining *Ma'rouf* and denying *Munkar* is a duty upon Muslims in every situation, whether there is a *Khilafah* state [caliphate] or not, and whether the rules of Islam are implemented in the government or not. Both enjoining *Ma'rouf* and forbidding *Munkar* existed at the time of the Prophet and at the time of the *Khulafah* [caliph] after him, and the other *Khulafah* who followed, and it will continue to exist until the end of time.[124]

For Hizb ut-Tahrir, however, while EGFW may help to revive Islamic morality within society, this is insufficient to usher in an Islamic way of life. What is required, from Hizb ut-Tahrir's perspective, is a political revolution. 'Resuming the Islamic way of life,' it asserts, 'would not be achieved *except* by establishing the Khilafah.'[125] As will be shown, some revivalists share with Hizb ut-Tahrir a view that Islam needs to be institutionalised in the state, though they generally differ from Hizb ut-Tahrir in their view of the state: whereas Hizb ut-Tahrir sees the Islamic state as a necessary tool to universalise an Islamic way of life, revivalists tend to see it as a natural and inevitable result of the widespread adoption of an Islamic way of life, and therefore not as something that needs to be aimed for in itself. These different conceptions of the Islamic state problematise, if not undermine, the categorisation of the Ikhwan and Jama'at as 'participationists' and Hizb ut-Tahrir as 'rejectionists' under the broad banner of 'Islamism', united in the goal of an Islamic state but merely separated by strategy. For, if their conception of the Islamic state is so different – a goal for Hizb ut-Tahrir, but a bi-product of an Islamic society for the revivalists – then it is questionable whether they are merely separated by their methods.

Notes

1 Pew Forum (2010), p. 20.
2 Denny (1975), p. 36.
3 Ibid., p. 55.
4 Abdul Bari (2013), p. 8, fn. 1.
5 Adbul Bari (2005), p. 84.
6 Hewitt (2004), p. 59.
7 Parvez (2007), pp. 266, 54.
8 'The Topkapi Declaration', Amman Message website, 2 July 2006. http://ammanmessage.com/index.php?option=com_content&task=view&id=39&Itemid=34.
9 'Muslims in Britain Come Together and Confirm their Commitment to Unity, and Working for a Just and Fair Society for all', MCB website, 15 June 2011. www.mcb.org.uk/muslims-in-britain-come-together-and-confirm-their-commitment-to-unity-and-working-for-a-just-and-fair-society-for-all/.
10 'Staging the Ummah: An Evening with Wajahat Ali', event listing, Cordoba Foundation website, 24 September 2012. www.thecordobafoundation.com/events.php?id=1&art=81.
11 Maréchal (2008), p. 322.
12 Interview with Daud Abdullah, 10 February 2012.
13 Sarwar (2006), p. 198.
14 Ibid., p. 199.
15 Zahid Parvez, 'The Crux of the Matter', *Trends*, vol. 2, no. 3, 1988, p. 14.
16 'About Us', IIIT-UK website. www.iiituk.com/about.htm.
17 'Introducing IUMS', IUMS website. http://iumsonline.org/en/iums123/introductionen/.
18 Ibid., emphasis added.
19 Interview with Irshad Bacqui, 22 February 2012.
20 Interview with Anas al-Shaikh Ali, 17 January 2013.
21 Interview with Ibrahim Mogra,29 August 2012.
22 'RESPONSE TO THE CONTEMPORARY CHALLENGES-BR ANAS AL TIKRITI', YouTube, 25 December 2012. www.youtube.com/watch?v=_KkWltn07VE.
23 Ibid.
24 Interview with Ibrahim Mogra, 29 August 2012.
25 This metaphor appears in the two most popular collections of *hadiths*, in Sahih Bukhari (number 5665) and Sahih Muslim (number 2586). See Abu Amina Elias, 'Hadith on Brotherhood: The believers are like one body in their love, mercy, and compassion for each other', Daily Hadith website, 3 March 2012. http://dailyhadith.abuaminaelias.com/2012/03/03/hadith-on-brotherhood-the-believers-are-like-one-body-in-their-love-mercy-and-compassion-for-each-other/.
26 Abdul Bari (2005), p. 85.
27 Ahsan (1977), p. 22.
28 'MCB and the Holocaust Memorial Day', MCB website, 23 January 2005. http://web.archive.org/web/20050211155329/http://www.mcb.org.uk/archivenews.php.
29 'Programme transcript' (for 'A Question of Leadership' documentary), BBC website, 16 September 2005. http://news.bbc.co.uk/2/hi/programmes/panorama/4171950.stm.
30 Abdul Bari (2005), p. 84.

31 Ibid., p. 81.
32 Sacranie (2006), p.29.
33 Ahsan (1977), p. 22.
34 Abdul Bari (2005), pp.78–79.
35 'Dawah Report 2012', UKIM website, 7 August 2012. https://web.archive.org/web/20130810090143/http://www.ukim.org/ukimdata/256/UKIM-DAWAH-REPORT-2012.pdf.
36 'UKIM Outreach Services', Alfurqan Mosque website, 2 August 2014. https://web.archive.org/web/20150222201614/http://www.alfurqanmosque.com/index.php/departments/outreach.
37 Interview with Farooq Murad, 7 October 2013.
38 Ahsan (1977), p. 42.
39 Abdul Bari (2005), pp. 124, 127.
40 Muhammad Abdul Bari, 'Secretary General's Address To the Annual General Meeting of the General Assembly', p. 6, MCB website, 16 June 2007. http://web.archive.org/web/20111105152829/http://www.mcb.org.uk/uploads/SGAGM2008.pdf.
41 Ibid.
42 'Working for the common good' is the motto of MCB. See 'MCB Constitution', p.6, available at www.mcb.org.uk/wp-content/uploads/2014/04/MCBCON2002.pdf.
43 Abdul Bari (2005), p. 85.
44 Zahid Parvez, 'Why Fasting?', UKIM Facebook page, 29 July 2012. www.facebook.com/UKIMBfd/posts/392971687419445.
45 Murad (1986), p. 16.
46 This distinction was first legally codified by Abu Hanifa (d. 767), founder of one of the four schools of Islamic jurisprudence, as recorded by Muhammad ibn al-Hasan al-Shaybani in his *Kitab al-Siyar al-Kabir*. See Nyazee (2002), p. 172, and Khadduri (1955), pp. 52–53.
47 Ramadan (1999).
48 Interview with Abdullah Faliq, 5 September 2012.
49 Interview with Farooq Murad, 7 October 2013.
50 Suleiman (2009), p. 36.
51 Ibid., p. 35.
52 Interview with Ibrahim Mogra, 29 August 2012.
53 'MCB Constitution', p. 6.
54 Interview with Mohammed Abdul Aziz, 3 September 2012.
55 Interview with Farooq Murad, 7 October 2013.
56 Iqbal Sacranie, 'Secretary General's Report', p. 11, MCB website, 14 May 2005. http://web.archive.org/web/20111105153148/http://www.mcb.org.uk/downloads/Secretary_General_2005.pdf.
57 Ahsan (2002).
58 Interview with Irshad Bacqui, 22 February 2012.
59 Ibid.
60 'Muslim Scholars: Making a positive contribution to society by Dr Zahid Parvez', MIHE website, 7 November 2017. www.mihe.ac.uk/node/305.
61 Interview with Omer El-Hamdoon, 14 February 2012.
62 'About Us', IFE website, webpage captured 25 September 2015. https://web.archive.org/web/20150925121500/http://www.islamicforumeurope.com/live/ife.php?doc=intro.
63 'Education Projects', UKIM website, webpage captured 6 October 2015. https://web.archive.org/web/20151006143017/http://www.ukim.org/education/. *Madari* refers to evening and weekend schools.

64 'The Methodology of UKIM', UKIM website, webpage captured 10 May 2015. http://web.archive.org/web/20150510235215/http://www.ukim.org:80/ukim/methodology/.
65 MEND (2014), p. 4.
66 'Electing to Deliver – British Muslims Launch Election Strategy and Programme', MCB website, 18 April 2005. www.mcb.org.uk/electing-to-deliver-british-muslims-launch-election-strategy-and-programme/.
67 'Not in our Name: British Muslims Condemn the Barbarity of ISIS', MCB website, 20 August 2014. www.mcb.org.uk/not-in-our-name-british-muslims-condemn-the-barbarity-of-isis/.
68 'About Us', IFE website.
69 'Introduction To Women's section', IFE website, webpage captured 26 September 2015. https://web.archive.org/web/20150926121150/http://www.islamicforumeurope.com/live/ife.php?doc=womens.
70 FOSIS, 'Islam Awareness Week – a brief guide', p. 1, undated, available at: www.youblisher.com/p/91965-Please-Add-a-Title/.
71 'About Us', Dawah Project website, webpage captured 6 August 2015. https://web.archive.org/web/20150806163100/http://www.thedawahproject.com/about-us/.
72 Abdul Bari (2005), p. 127.
73 Interview with Suhaib Hasan, 9 February 2012.
74 Interview with Omer El-Hamdoon, 14 February 2012.
75 Murad (1986), p. 10.
76 Interview with Farooq Murad, 7 October 2013.
77 'RESPONSE TO THE CONTEMPORARY CHALLENGES-BR ANAS AL TIKRITI'.
78 Ahsan (1989), p. 14.
79 Interview with Farooq Murad, 7 October 2013.
80 Parvez (2007), p. 154.
81 'About Us', Dawah Project website.
82 Parvez (2007), p. 154.
83 On the habitus, see Bourdieu (1989) and (1990).
84 Ibid.
85 There are various translations into English from the Arabic phrase. These include 'enjoining the good and forbidding the evil,' and 'commanding right and forbidding wrong'.
86 'The Topkapi Declaration'.
87 'MCB Constitution', p. 6.
88 Ibid., p. 4.
89 Interview with Farooq Murad, 7 October 2013.
90 Farooq Murad, 'Our Vision of the Future', *Trends*, vol. 6, no. 1., undated, p. 10.
91 Cook (2003), p. 165.
92 Ibid. See also Cook (2000), pp. 38–39.
93 Yusuf al-Qaradawi, *Fiqh Al Zakah (Volume II): A Comparative Study of Zakah, Regulations and Philosophy in the Light of Qur'an and Sunnah* (Jeddah, Saudi Arabia: Scientific Publishing Centre, King Abdulaziz University [1999]), Monzer Kahf (trans.), pp. 76, 70, emphasis added; available online at www.scribd.com/doc/18089833/Fiqh-al-Zakah-Vol-2 (accessed July 2010).
94 Parvez (2007), p. 158.
95 Interview with Omer El-Hamdoon, 14 February 2012.
96 Siddiqui (2013), p. 177.
97 Ibid., p. 181.
98 Muhammad Abdul Bari, 'Islam-Inspired Social Activism: A Vision for the Common Good', Amana Parenting website, 26 July 2011. www.amanaparenting.com/?p=128.

99 'The Methodology of UKIM', UKIM website.
100 Photo of banner at UKIM's annual convention celebrating the 50th anniversary of the organisation, 16 September 2012, https://theislamicfarrightinbritain.files.wordpress.com/2012/09/ukim-annual-convention-2012.jpg; 'UKIM Newsletter', October 2012, p. 7, available at http://web.archive.org/web/20140309065824/http://www.ukim.org/ukimdata/newsletters/UKIM-NewsLetter_2012-10.pdf.
101 UKIM Youth website homepage, www.ukimyouth.com.
102 'About Us', AML website, webpage captured 4 June 2014. http://web.archive.org/web/20140604195835/http://aml.org.uk/aboutaml/.
103 Sarwar (2001), p. 44.
104 Ibid., p. 32.
105 'UK Islamic Mission – Our Struggle', UKIM website, webpage captured 6 October 2015. https://web.archive.org/web/20151006143020/http://ukim.org/ukim-struggle.
106 Abdul Bari (2013), p. 22.
107 Interview with Omer El-Hamdoon, 14 February 2012.
108 Siddiqui (2013), p. 176.
109 'A Constructive, Unified Society', IFE website, 10 December 2003. https://web.archive.org/web/20040224204311/http://www.islamicforumeurope.com/live/ife.php?doc=articleitem&itemId=95.
110 Haitham Al-Haddad, 'Advice To British Muslims Regarding The Coming Elections', Islam21c website, 16 October 2006. www.islam21c.com/politics/216-advice-to-british-muslims-regarding-the-coming-elections/.
111 Parvez (2007), p. 251.
112 Ibid., p. 251.
113 Ibid., p. 257.
114 Suhaib Hasan, 'The Current Problems of the Muslim Ummah and their Solution in Light of the Purified Seerah', 8 April 2014. http://sheikhsuhaibhasan.blogspot.co.uk/2014/04/the-current-problems-of-muslim-ummah.html.
115 Siddiqui (2013), p. 178.
116 al-Misri (1994), a1.4, a1.5, pp. 2–3.
117 Parvez (2007), p. 251.
118 Ibid., p. 256.
119 Siddiqui (2013), p. 181.
120 Sarwar (2006), p. 170.
121 Sookhdeo (2008), p. 107.
122 Islamic Foundation, 'First Ethical stage First UK Shariah Finance Course at the Islamic Foundation', *Islamic Foundation Newsletter*, July 2006, p. 3.
123 Usmani (2001), p. 30.
124 Hizb ut-Tahrir (1999).
125 Ibid., p. 15, emphasis added.

References

Abdul Bari, Muhammad (2005). *Race, Religion, & Muslim Identity in Britain*. Swansea: Renaissance Press.

Abdul Bari, Muhammad (2013). 'Meet the challenge, make the change: A call to action for Muslim civil society in Britain'. *Cordoba Papers*, vol. 2, no. 1. Cordoba Foundation, London

Ahsan, Muhammad Manazir (1977). *Islam: Faith and Practice*. Leicester: The Islamic Foundation.

Ahsan, Muhammad Manazir (1989). 'Dawa and its significance for the future'. In Merryl Wyn Davies and Adnan Khalil Pasha (eds), *Beyond Frontiers: Islam and Contemporary Needs*: 13–21. London: Mansell Publishing.

Ahsan, Muhammad Manazir (2002). 'Foreword'. In Abdur Rashid Siddiqui, *Key to Al 'Imran: Resurgence of the Ummah*. Markfield: The Islamic Foundation.

Bourdieu, Pierre (1989). 'Social space and symbolic power'. In *Sociological Theory*, vol. 7, no. 1: 14–25.

Bourdieu, Pierre (1990). *The Logic of Practice*. Trans. Richard Nice. Cambridge: Polity Press.

Cook, Michael (2000). *Commanding Right and Forbidding Wrong in Islamic Thought*. Cambridge: Cambridge University Press.

Cook, Michael (2003). *Forbidding the Wrong in Islam: An Introduction*. Cambridge: Cambridge University Press.

Denny, Frederick Mathewson (1975). 'The meaning of "ummah" in the Qur'ān'. In *History of Religions*, vol. 15, no. 1: 34–70.

Hewitt, Ibrahim (2004). *What Does Islam Say?* 4th edition. London: Muslim Educational Trust.

Hizb ut-Tahrir (1999). *The Methodology of Hizb ut-Tahrir for Change*. London: Al-Khilafah. Available online at: www.hizb-ut-tahrir.info/info/files/Books-eng/13_The_Methodology_of_HT_for_Change.pdf.

Khadduri, Majid (1955). *War and Peace in the Law of Islam*. Baltimore, MD: Johns Hopkins University Press.

Maréchal, Brigitte (2008). *The Muslim Brothers in Europe: Roots and Discourse*. Leiden: Brill.

MEND (2014). *Activity Report 2014*. http://mend.org.uk/wp-content/uploads/2014/12/MEND_Activity_Report_2014_Low_Res.pdf.

al-Misri, Ahmad ibn Naqib (1994). *'Umdat al-Salik – Reliance of the Traveller, A Classic Manual of Islamic Sacred Law*. Ed. and trans. Nuh Ha Mim Keller. Beltsville: Amana Publications.

Murad, Khurram (1986). *Dawah Among Non-Muslims in the West*. Leicester: The Islamic Foundation.

Nyazee, Imran Ahsan Khan (2002). *Theories of Islamic Law: The Methodology of Ijtihad*. 2nd edition. Kuala Lumpur: The Other Press.

Parvez, Zahid (2007). *Building a New Society: An Islamic Approach to Social Change*. Markfield: Revival Publications.

Pew Forum on Religion and Public Life (2010). *Muslim Networks and Movements in Western Europe*. Washington, DC: Pew Research Center.

Ramadan, Tariq (1999). *To Be a European Muslim*. Leicester: Islamic Foundation.

Sacranie, Iqbal (2006). 'Engagement and exchange of ideas are vital'. In Philip Parvin and Declan McHugh (eds), Democracy Series no. 1, '*Democracy and Islam*': 28–31. Hansard Society, London.

Sarwar, Ghulam (2001). *Islamic Education: Its Meaning, Problems and Prospects*. London: The Muslim Educational Trust.

Sarwar, Ghulam (2006). *Islam: Beliefs and Teachings*. 8th edition. London: Muslim Educational Trust.

Siddiqui, Abdur Rashid (2013). *Living in Allah's Presence: Aspects of Islamic Spirituality*. Markfield: Kube Publishing.

Sookhdeo, Patrick (2008). *Faith, Power and Territory: A Handbook of British Islam*. McLean, VA: Isaac Publishing.

Suleiman, Yasir (2009). *Contextualising Islam in Britain: Exploratory Perspectives.* Cambridge: University of Cambridge in association with the universities of Exeter and Westminster.

Usmani, Muhammad Taqi (2001). *Our Socio-Economic Order.* Trans. Shakir Rizwani. Lahore, Pakistan: Idara-e-Islamiat.

4 Social and political orientations

Shari'a, jihad and the Islamic state

The revivalist network, as chapter 3 has shown, is bonded by a shared sense of community and territory, as well as a perceived set of collective responsibilities, which include speaking for Muslims and Islam, calling both Muslims and non-Muslims to the 'right path' of Islam, and taking a proactive moral stance towards social change expressed in the doctrine of *Enjoining the Good and Forbidding the Wrong*. These aspects of the cultural solidarity shared by members of the global Muslim Brotherhood network are related to a cluster of social and political orientations hinged upon the central concept of an Islamic revival.

This chapter shows how the concept of an Islamic revival features strongly in their way of thinking. It shows how revivalists in Britain broadly share an understanding of their work in terms of fulfilling God's divine will, from matters of personal conduct to those at the level of society at large. Revivalists share a perception of themselves as oriented towards a comprehensive transformation of society that, while not explicitly aiming for an Islamic state, will ultimately culminate in one as a reward for piety. A shared value placed upon non-compulsion is accompanied by a shared understanding of gradualism as the ideal approach, along with a shared perception of the future as belonging to Islam in line with religious prophecy.

The Islamic revival and the Islamic Movement

In September 2011, the Islamic Foundation organised a two-day meeting entitled, 'Islamic Revival in the UK: Past, Present and Future'. The purpose of the event, described in a Foundation newsletter, was to discuss the history and prospects of 'Islamic revival in the UK, as well as the wider scene of Islamic activism' with a view to gauging lessons for the Foundation.[1] Present at the meeting were numerous revivalist figures, including Khurshid Ahmad, Manazir Ahsan, Muhammad Abdul Bari and Mohammed Abdul Aziz. The keynote speech, 'Islamic Revival in the UK: Past, Present and Future', was delivered by Ahmad, who sees in the Islamic revival a 'reawakening of the Islamic faith and destiny' for nothing less than an alternative world order.[2] Asked to explain meaning of the phrase 'Islamic revival', Islamic Foundation executive director Irshad Bacqui fumbles uncomfortably with words before stating that it relates to the application of 'Islamic values' in contemporary Britain.[3]

The Islamic revival may indeed be interpreted by key figures in the network as an application of Islamic values throughout society, but contrary to Bacqui's denial that it has any 'political agenda', other individuals and groups in the network make very clear that it does relate to politics, as this chapter will show. For them, it inevitably relates to politics since Islam is considered as the alternative basis for a complete way of life, including personal conduct but also matters of governance, encompassing politics, education, law and economics.

For example, according to journalist Andrew Gilligan, in the transcript of an IFE training course, Muhammad Rabbani – a trustee of IFE's youth wing, the Young Muslim Organisation UK – informs IFE's new members,

> Our goal is not simply to invite people and give *da'wah*. Our goal is to create the True Believer, to then mobilise those believers into an organised force for change who will carry out *da'wah, hisbah* and *jihad*. This will lead to social change and *iqamatud-deen.*[4]

In Islamic scholarly works, *hisbah* denotes the injunction to enjoin the good and forbid the wrong. In this context, *jihad* denotes the legal obligation upon Muslims to strive – through violent or non-violent means – towards the universal fulfilment of Allah's divine will. And *Iqamatud-deen*, according to Jama'at-i-Islami itself, translates as the 'Islamization of life'.[5] Gilligan also obtained internal IFE documents that explicitly state its strategic objective as 'the establishment of a global society, the *Khilafah* [caliphate] … comprised of individuals who live by the principles of … the *Shari'ah*'.[6] They state that it is dedicated to changing the 'very infrastructure of [Western] society, its institutions, its culture, its political order and its creed … from ignorance to Islam'. Abdullah Faliq, IFE's press secretary, denies that such aspirations represent IFE's 'corporate view' – unsurprisingly, since it would be politically unwise for any organisation to hold such an official line – though he concedes that there may be some within IFE who hold this perspective.[7]

Irrespective of how mainstream the desire for an Islamic revival is within IFE, there are other groups and leading individuals within the network who express the desire for it, for what they see as a comprehensive transformation of society based upon Islamic values. The London-based Islamic Human Rights Commission (IHRC), for instance, declares as one of its key aims the promotion of 'a new social and international order'.[8] The alternative nature of this order relates to an alternative understanding of human rights based upon Islam. IHRC states its foremost aim is to champion human rights – and duties – conceived as 'divinely granted' and 'revealed for human beings' by Allah. This suggests an affinity with the Cairo Declaration on Human Rights in Islam (or the Islamic Declaration of Human Rights), rather than the UN

Universal Declaration of Human Rights. The Cairo Declaration states that *all* rights and freedoms are 'are subject to the Islamic Sharia'.[9]

Ghulam Sarwar, the director of the Muslim Educational Trust (MET), whose lifetime work has consisted in the promotion of Islamic education in Britain, states, 'Islamic education and a global Islamic revival are inextricably connected.'[10] He writes, 'The introduction of an Islamic education system should be an integral part of the efforts worldwide to establish Islam as an all-encompassing way of life.'[11] Islamic education, for MET, is a tool in the service of a higher objective: the 'Islamisation of society,' beginning with Muslim communities in Britain and culminating on a global scale.[12]

Abdur Rashid Siddiqui, the secretary and treasurer of the Islamic Foundation, states that 'the Islamic moral system … does not demand reform only in an individual's personal life. Rather, it seeks to transform the entire collective social life'.[13] The Islamic revival, he writes, will not be able to commence without the most valued sacrifice, the submission of individuals' egos 'to the dictates of the Shariah'.[14] Such a social transformation was conceived by Siddiqui's contemporary, the late Khurram Murad, as the calling of 'the Islamic movement', which he described as 'an organised struggle to change the existing society into an Islamic society based on the Qur'an and the Sunna, and make Islam, which is a code for the entire life, supreme and dominant'.[15]

The notion of the Islamic Movement is shared by other revivalists. Ahmad, for example, states, 'Islam is a movement for social change'.[16] This movement, he believes, is responsible for establishing 'a new world order' based on Islam:[17]

> Islam also launches a social movement, an international movement requiring all those who accept these [Islamic] ideals and values to establish the new world order. Islam is eager to establish this new model in any part of the world … . Once this model is established somewhere in the world, the experiment can be shared with everyone else, just as sunshine is shared by all.[18]

Zahid Parvez, the director of the Islamic Foundation's Markfield Institute of Higher Education, echoes this in describing Islam as 'a global movement'.[19] He writes extensively on the notion of the Islamic Movement as a necessary, practical means to usher in such an order, dedicating an entire book chapter to its ideal characteristics.[20] Demonstrating that this perspective is shared across ethnic lines, in a speech in July 2005 to a Muslim audience in Britain, Anas Altikriti, the director of the Cordoba Foundation, asserts: 'Islam, and the *da'wa* of Islam, is by definition a reform movement, *harakat al-islah*'.[21] He laments that the Islamic Movement, however, has come short of 'leading the way towards shaping events' in line with Islamic principles and in response to the contemporary situation.

Altikriti perceives the need for a comprehensive social transformation based upon Islamic values similarly to the other figures above. Altikriti, who established the Cordoba Foundation to address what he sees as a false dichotomy between Islam and the West, believes that because of a crisis of multiple dimensions – including politics, economics, science and morality – a comprehensive social transformation is required and that Muslims must play an active role in it. The message of Islam, he states, is about 'transforming people's realities'.[22] To a young Muslim audience, he implores:

> It is vital that we fulfil our role as individuals that we work together with our brothers, with our sisters, within our community, within our societal structure, for the benefit not only of ourselves – we Muslims we are not selfish, we don't do this just for ourselves. This is in order to create that transformation *on a worldwide level*.[23]

This transformation, states Altikriti, is not just about politics, education, finance or spirituality, but *every* aspect of human existence. 'Every single part of life,' he insists, 'needs to be touched, needs to be affected, needs to be changed, needs to be reformed.'[24] When interviewed, Altikriti plays down the Islamic character of the key values he deems needed in modern society, preferring to describe them as 'universal'.[25] This is, he says, because he sees them as not exclusive to Islam, but as shared by non-Muslims. In a talk given in 2005, however, he describes non-Muslims' sharing of such values favourably as a pathway to them becoming Muslims.[26] In another talk given in September 2011 to the Federation of Islamic Student Societies (FOSIS) in the wake of the Arab uprisings, he is clear in seeing Islam as the driving force behind the comprehensive social transformation he calls for:

> We need to touch on every single sphere and with that we can bring our message. When we say that Islam is a way of life, a comprehensive way of life, we would have acted it. We practice it, we don't need to preach about it anymore. When we talk about the excellence, the perfection, the accuracy, the precision of Islam, we would have acted it, we don't need to talk about it anymore, we don't need to theorise anymore.[27]

The belief that Islam is a comprehensive way of life and also a liberatory force for a civilizational crisis affecting mankind is shared by others including Manazir Ahsan, the chairman of the Islamic Foundation, who writes that Islam 'provides a complete and comprehensive code' for human conduct 'in all social, economic, political, moral and spiritual aspects of life'.[28] He elaborates:

> Islam, being the universal religion meant for mankind of all races, colours and times, is as relevant today as it was fourteen hundred years ago. It has been a great liberating force in the past and has the potential for leading man out of the contemporary crisis of human civilization … In the context of contemporary spiritual and cultural crises, Islam provides

> an alternative basis for the development of the human personality and the organization of human society.[29]

Likewise, for Islamic Foundation founder Khurshid Ahmad, the world is experiencing a civilisational crisis. He states that 'the dominant secular-humanistic civilisation of the West, despite its material affluence and military prowess, is in the throes of a serious crisis'. The solution, he proffers, is the 'Islamic alternative', a 'new paradigm for life', beginning with reform of the individual, passing through reform of society and culminating in reform of the world order.[30] Parvez similarly bemoans today's 'complex social, economic and political problems and global crisis'.[31] An important component of this crisis is the perceived breakdown of morality and religiosity in the West. Ahmad argues that the predicament of Muslims in Western societies is not just about 'socio-political and economic ills'.[32] '[T]he Islamic resurgence,' he insists, is not reducible to 'the angry reaction of under-privileged Muslims against Western affluence'.[33] It fundamentally concerns faith and morality. Such a view is expressed by IFE, which states that it 'is in Europe because it is this continent, despite all the furore about its achievements, which has a moral and spiritual vacuum'.[34]

Despite the perception of moral and spiritual bankruptcy within Britain and the West, and despite the understanding of the Islamic revival as addressing much more than political frustration, politics is nevertheless seen as a part of the problem and, thus, the solution. Ahmad gives voice to this sentiment, asserting, 'It is part of our religious mission to harness political and economic power for the fulfilment of moral objectives … . Islam wants to bring political power under the control of its moral ideals.'[35] In an article penned while president of Young Muslims UK, Farooq Murad writes that political power for Islam follows the people's complete embrace of Islam as a way of life.[36] Echoing this, Zahid Parvez declares:

> [I]n order to administer justice and establish a peaceful society, *political power is essential in the eyes of Islam*. In fact, Islam obligates its followers to engage with power and enjoins social and political participation. It sees power as a moral and civilising force if it is utilised in accordance with God's law [*shari'a*]. A just social order cannot be established through sermons and preaching only.[37]

Political power, states Parvez, is something to be 'brought under God, and utilised for realising His Will in society and state; for reforming and transforming society and the state for the common good'.[38] Politics is seen as an important part of Islam because Islam is seen not just as a matter of belief but as a way of life that includes the governance of society. In the words of Muhammad Faruq Khan, 'Since a total change is sought, the political order cannot be disregarded'.[39] The inseparability of politics and religion is expressed in a promotional video for UKIM by the organisation's then president Muhammad Sarfraz Madni, who explains:

> We strongly believe that politics is part of religion. We want to introduce the religion that was introduced by our beloved prophet Mohammed. We don't pick and choose. We are not limited to some issues. We take Islam completely. And we want to live Islam completely and convey that message of Islam completely. The whole Islam.[40]

Understanding the role of politics, including the Islamic state, in the revivalist habitus is important to get a sense not just of their aspirations but also their way of thinking within which their aspirations are formed. This matter is the subject of the following and final section of the chapter.

Shari'a and the Islamic state

The typical view in the academic, think tank and news media literature on what characterises Islamists is expressed by Alexander Meleagrou-Hitchens, who writes, 'all want to create an Islamic state, but they are at odds with each other about how best to achieve this, and where they should start'.[41] Bassam Tibi shares this view. He claims that there are two kinds of Islamism – 'institutional Islamism and jihadism' – which both 'share the very same ideological goal of establishing an Islamic shari'a state'.[42] Only tactics, he claims, separates them.

However, it is more accurate to say that all Islamists want an Islamic society organised according to Islamic principles and values and that they are at odds with each other about whether the state is primarily a *tool* to achieve this or the natural *outcome* of it. They are also at odds with each other about whether *shari'a* – Islamic ethics and law – is to be adopted and enforced by the state prior to, or after, the attainment of a Muslim majority that demands as much. These differences are more subtle and instructive than the simplistic mainstream conception of Islamists divided over strategic approaches.

A distinguishing characteristic of Islamic revivalists is their understanding of Islam as a way of life that cannot be imposed through state structures but which, once adopted by a majority population, requires state institutionalisation for its protection and maintenance. The individuals and groups in the revivalist network mapped out in chapter 2 broadly share this understanding. They also broadly share an understanding of *shari'a*, and of its importance, as an ethical code applicable to every aspect of Muslims' lives and as a legal code to be adopted, eventually, by the Islamic state.

Shari'a*: from the personal to the political*

Islamic revivalists understand the *shari'a* as a code of conduct applicable at the progressively ascending levels of the individual, society and the state: it encompasses both a fixed set of laws, such as the prohibition of financial interest and alcohol consumption, and a number of ethical principles that may be codified into law in various ways depending on the time and place. To Islamic revivalists, the *shari'a* takes precedence over the Islamic state: The state merely facilitates and consummates its application.

This is consistent with the orthodox Islamic position as explained by the late Majid Khadduri, who writes, '[Islamic] Law … precedes the State: it provides the basis of the State'.[43] In describing the classical position, Khadduri explains that 'the fundamental loyalty of the Muslim is given not to the imam [caliph] but to the *shari'a*'.[44] This view extends back at least as far as the classical period. Ibn Khaldun (1332–1406), the 'greatest of Islamic political thinkers,' described 'the true meaning of the caliphate [Islamic state]' as bringing 'the whole people to conform themselves to [the] ordinances [of Revealed Laws, i.e. the *shari'a*] in all matters of this world and the next'.[45] For contemporary revivalists, allegiance to the *shari'a* takes precedence over the establishment of an Islamic state, but such a state is generally seen as desirable and as a natural outcome of achieving a Muslim majority population.

Shari'a is commonly understood as beginning with personal conduct, applying to Muslims' each and every action. In an interview with the book author, Ibrahim Mogra, then assistant secretary general of the Muslim Council of Britain (MCB), affirms, 'Everything that a Muslim does is governed by *shari'a*. My sitting with you this morning also is governed by *shari'a*.'[46] Likewise, Farooq Murad professes, 'I live this term on a daily basis.'[47] Abdullah Faliq of the Cordoba Foundation and the Islamic Forum of Europe echoes this, stating, 'It does govern my every activity and my every thought.'[48] The president of the Muslim Association of Britain (MAB), Omer El-Hamdoon, highlights the personal dimension of *shari'a* in observing that 'The first things to appear in the books on *shari'a* concern purification. That's a personal thing.'[49] Consistent with this understanding, the application of *shari'a* to Muslims' personal lives is the priority for the Islamic Sharia Council. Highlighting this priority, but intimating the possibility of broader application in the future, its chair, Maulana Abu Sayeed describes the personal aspect of *shari'a*, including marriage and divorce, as the 'bare minimum requirement' for Muslims.[50]

The Islamic Sharia Council's secretary, Suhaib Hasan, likewise highlights Muslim personal law as the priority area within *shari'a* for application in Britain. But, like others in the revivalist network, he sees *shari'a* as far more comprehensive than can be currently implemented. '*Shari'a* covers all the aspects of a Muslim's life', he explains. But not only does it cover all matters of personal conduct, such as worship, eating and dress, it also covers all aspects of criminal and international law: 'Everything is covered by *shari'a*', he says.[51] This is because, in Abu Sayeed's words, *shari'a* is 'God's revealed *system of life*'.[52] Mogra agrees, noting, 'Muslims see Islam as a way of life. That would mean that everything is lumped into that way of life, including politics.'[53] In Murad's words, *shari'a* is the 'code of your conduct, your affairs: personal, social, political, your whole social conduct as a collective entity'.[54] Ahmad Thomson, the co-founder of the Association of Muslim Lawyers, similarly sees *shari'a* as applicable beyond personal conduct. He bemoans efforts to reform Islam into a secular religion that leaves the 'political and economic spheres of human activity … unaffected and impervious to the way of Islam'.[55]

El-Hamdoon recommends as an authentic guide to *shari'a* a book entitled *Umdat al-Salik* (*The Reliance of the Traveller*).[56] This tome, officially endorsed by the International Institute of Islamic Thought and the most prestigious institution of learning in the Sunni Muslim world, Al-Azhar University, clearly articulates rulings applicable within the realm of state politics.[57] These include corporeal (*hudud*) punishments, such as the cutting of hands and feet for theft, as well as dictates for the conduct of warfare and state administration. Numerous prominent figures in the network, including El-Hamdoon, Hasan, Parvez, Mogra, Faliq and Altikriti acknowledge and do not seem to reject such punishments, preferring to underplay their significance by noting that they constitute just a fraction of *shari'a* rulings.[58] 'We believe in God, and we believe in *shari'a* and we do not give up *shari'a*,' states El-Hamdoon. 'We don't believe *shari'a* is discriminatory, that *shari'a* is prejudiced.'[59] Mogra and Parvez both emphasise that prior to such punishments being applied, Islam has to be firmly embraced within society and *shari'a* established as lived morality.[60] This aspect of *shari'a* is not applicable in Britain, explains Faliq:

> When it comes to ruling, it doesn't apply to us here. We don't have an Islamic system of government, so *hudud* punishments shouldn't even arise as a question. You follow the law of the country, as long as it doesn't make you compromise your Islamic faith.[61]

The Islamic state: a reward not an objective

In academic, think tank and news media literature, Islamists are consistently characterised as bonded by their desire for an Islamic state. Peter Mandaville, for example, defines Islamism in fairly typical terms as 'forms of political theory and practice that have as their goal the establishment of an Islamic political order in the sense of a state whose governmental principles, institutions, and legal system derive directly from the shari'ah'.[62] But the individuals and organisations in Britain who are typically classified as 'non-violent Islamists' – in this book referred to as Islamic revivalists – express a consistent understanding of the Islamic state as a matter of *secondary* importance in relation to the attainment of society in which Islamic values and principles prevail. The Islamic state, as several prominent figures explain, is not an objective but, rather, a promise in reward for piety and righteousness. Farooq Murad expresses this as follows:

> We forget that not once does the Qur'an make *Khilafah* [the Islamic state] the aim and the goal of Muslim struggle. Rather it promises the glory of political power, help and victory [only] when we invite and prepare people to live for complete Islam.[63]

Suhaib Hasan provides additional clarity to this view of a promise. Firmly believing that Islam will one day become established as the dominant religion in the world, he writes:

> Succession on the Earth is Allah's promise [to the Muslim *umma*] … *but it is not the highest aim or objective* … The implementation of [a] divinely ordained Caliphate [Islamic state] is only a part of Islam's aggregated system *not the objective itself* … . Our view is that the objective should be kept as the objective and the promise as the promise.[64]

In an interview, he elaborates:

> The *main* objective of a Muslim is to please Allah and to worship Allah … Now comes the *secondary* issue. When you are a group of people living at a certain place, you have to organise your matters. On what basis you are going to organise yourselves? [The Islamic state] comes as a natural outcome of a Muslim gathering at any place, as it came to Medina where the Prophet moved and then he was accepted as a ruler and he started implementing the *shari'a* of Allah. So, this comes as a gradual process, *but it is not the objective.* We have to differentiate between the objectives and the requirements of any community wherever they are living.[65]

Mogra concurs with Hasan that the Islamic state is not an objective. 'I don't believe it is a requirement for Muslims to have an Islamic state,' he says. While not rejecting the notion of an Islamic state, he emphasises, 'For me, it is more important that God's law is *lived* by individuals in whichever political set up they are living in.'[66]

El-Hamdoon shares this understanding of the primacy of the embrace of Islam throughout society over the creation of an Islamic state: 'MAB does not look to establish a state here in Britain. As Muslims here in Britain we want to worship God and we want to introduce people to God'.[67] He emphasises, 'We want to make clear that we are not here in Britain to establish an Islamic state *because the realisation* [of Islam as a way of life] *has to come from within.*' Thus, according to El-Hamdoon, the MAB is not focused on establishing an Islamic state but, rather, on what may eventually lead to it, namely, the widespread adoption of Islamic beliefs and practice of Islamic values within society. Nevertheless, although claiming the MAB doesn't officially have any political objectives, he admits, 'As a Muslim, irrelevant of where I am living, *one of my objectives is to establish an Islamic state.* Islam is comprehensive and since the problems are comprehensive, the solution has to be comprehensive.'[68]

Elaborating his position, he explains that establishing an Islamic state is not unique to Islam, since all people want some form of government to maintain order. All people, he says, want a government system that is based on their values.

> But when you ask me as a Muslim, 'What kind of state do you want?', I'm going to say to you, 'An Islamic state', a state which is ruled by God's rules because God created us and knows what's good for us.

Putting this back into the context of *da'wa*, he cautions, 'If you just focus on the Islamic state and you don't focus on changing the individual, the state will not survive because the state is made out of individuals.'

In the rhetoric of some revivalists, the aspiration of a society organised according to Islamic principles is inseparable from that of an Islamic state. Yusuf al-Qaradawi, for example, links the goal of an Islamic society with that of the Islamic state proclaiming, 'The most important form of *jihad* today is serious, purposive organized work to re-build the Islamic society and state and to implement the Islamic way of life in the political, cultural, and economic areas.'[69] Zahid Parvez similarly connects the two in repeating the call for the fulfilment of 'the vision of Islam in social life and the state'.[70] He asserts, 'all human beings have a God-given right to justice and an Islamic state is commanded by the Quran to ensure that this is rooted in all social and economic policies and fully implemented'.[71]

However, consistent with the perspective taken by Hasan, El-Hamdoon and others, Parvez prioritises the attainment of a society based upon Islamic principles over that of an Islamic state. Such a state, he cautions, cannot arise except as an embodiment of religious, moral values:

> An effective Islamic change requires the cultivation of faith, God-consciousness, morals, correct attitudes and patience, and *its systems of society evolve from these seeds, and not the other way round.* As a general principle, a legal, political or an economic system must be compatible with the social life which it is seeking to regulate and direct, otherwise it will inevitably be rejected by it.[72]

Others in the revivalist network who idealise Islam as a way of life do not express a desire for an Islamic state or even doubt its relevance. For example, when questioned regarding al-Qaradawi's bold claim that Islam will 'conquer' Europe through non-violent means, Mogra responds:

> Islam is not about conquering people. Islam is about people finding peace in a lifestyle, which is all about submission to God's will. For me, it is more God conquering the hearts of his people than Islam as a religion

> conquering geographical pieces of land. It is not about the land. I don't even believe we need an Islamic government, so to speak. It is about people *living Islam*. [73]

Altikriti believes that calls of an Islamic state should 'not scare us … or bring about a negative reaction',[74] but, like Mogra, he underplays its importance in an interview with the book author. 'I don't think the Islamic state even figures on the radar or priorities for Muslims,' he opines. 'But if it's established, it's established through the dominance of *values*.'[75] Citing Rashid al-Ghannushi, Altikriti asserts, '*Shari'a* is justice.' He adds, 'And if I have a state where justice prevails, that to me is an Islamic state.' Faliq echoes this sentiment, stating, 'As long as Islamic values are in place – that the governor has to uphold justice, freedom *et cetera* – any system of government is fine.'[76]

Several individuals who have been very active within the network more firmly dismiss the necessity of an Islamic state altogether. Mohammed Abdul Aziz, for example, concedes that he 'probably held on to the idea of an Islamic state' until as recently as 2007.[77] The notion of the Islamic state as propounded by Mawdudi and Qutb, he says, was coloured by their experiences of colonialism. An Islamic state, he adds, is not a Qur'anic requirement. Yet, Abdul Aziz still regards himself as a 'Jama'ati' because of the social circles he moves within and because of the social welfare orientation of the Jama'at-associated organisations he works with. Abdul Aziz dismisses the goal of an Islamic state for Britain, but believes that the ideal purpose of such a state – to propagate Islamic values and deliver social welfare – remains important and can be fulfilled within society governed by a secular state.

Dilwar Hussain, a former president of the Islamic Society of Britain (ISB), also advocates a secular state as the best model for negotiating 'the reality that there are [people of] other faiths and those with none'.[78] Describing himself as a 'post-Islamist', he emphatically rejects the goal of an Islamic state altogether. Under his leadership, the ISB left the group of revivalist groups clustered in the Coordination Committee of Islamic Organisations, as described in chapter 2, because of a transformation of values within the ISB away from the revivalist aspirations held by the committee.[79] After many years of involvement, Hussain has departed from organisations within the revivalist network, including the ISB and the Islamic Foundation, and his perspective upon Islam's place in contemporary Britain is not typical within the network. His personal journey is significant, however, along with that of Mohammed Abdul Aziz, in showing that there is a degree of fluidity within the network in how the Islamic state is understood, particularly in relation to aspirations for Islam as a way of life in Britain.

Non-compulsion and the matter of majority rule

Given that *shari'a* is understood by individuals within the revivalist network as comprehensive and therefore inclusive of matters of governance, the question arises regarding the possibility that *shari'a* might remain restricted to personal matters and not be applied by the state: How can such a scenario fulfil God's will? How can revivalists be content with this scenario? To this, they present a consistent response that Islam cannot be imposed.

Ahmad Thomson of the Association of the Muslim Lawyers states that 'a system of law other than the Shari'ah which incorporates some aspects of the Shari'ah into it but not others' is 'unpalatable'.[80] Yet, he affirms, 'The Shari'ah can only be established where it is the will of a community's or society's members to be governed in accordance with the Shari'ah'. Abdul Aziz articulates a similar sentiment, as follows:

> *Shari'a* is God's will from a Muslim perspective but God has also given every individual the right not to obey him. Islam is submission, but you choose to obey God, but God has given everyone the right to obey or not to obey him. For those who choose not to obey him, you cannot force them – 'there is no compulsion in religion'.[81]

Farooq Murad echoes this, asserting,

> There is no compulsion in religion. This is a basic fact of the Qur'an. Islam is a voluntary idea of life. If God wanted to make all of us Muslims he could have done it. He decided not to. He wants to test us, check or see who wants to please him, who wants to come to his ways. This is absolutely a fundamental principle. So we begin from that.[82]

Abu Sayeed concurs. Even though he perceives 'man-made law' as inferior to 'God's law', he emphasises that 'Islam does not want to impose an Islamic system on people who are not in favour of Islam'.[83] He contends, 'In Muslim-minority countries, Muslims will not and should not try to implement Islam in centrality [*sic*], apart from [in] private life where worship and family aspects are concerned, because Islam believes in personal choice.' He adds, 'A military coup for Islam would not do for an Islamic state.' Faliq, likewise, asserts:

> Any system of government has to be liked by the people, at least the majority. It has to come via elections. If a radical Muslim group imposes *shari'a* via a coup in Egypt or elsewhere, like Hizb ut-Tahrir, al-Muhajiroun or al-Qaeda, I'll go against them. That's not Islam for me. Those who put the system of government first, they don't understand that that has to come by the will of the people, they have to willingly embrace it.[84]

Although the issue of non-compulsion is clear-cut within the network, the issue of the conditions under which the state would become governed by and adopt *shari'a* principles is somewhat vague. A shared belief in non-compulsion doesn't answer the question as to how a society may become comprehensively Islamic, including its system of government. Faliq says that 'at least the majority' of people have to endorse a system of government. Similarly, Hasan contends that an Islamic system of government may emerge with a simple majority in favour. Abu Sayeed agrees, stating, 'it is the majority's wishes that are to be fulfilled'. Regarding the Islamic state, he claims, 'Once people have chosen Islam as their life system, then automatically it should come.' El-Hamdoon, however, doesn't think it is so straightforward. Although he doesn't believe everyone has to have embraced Islam for the emergence of an Islamic state, he doesn't think the emergence of such a state can simply follow majority support from the electorate or parliamentarians.[85]

Gradualism and prophecy

In addition to the assertion of non-compulsion, another response to the question of *shari'a* not being comprehensively applied in Britain, some individuals and groups emphasise that Muslims are under no obligation to apply *shari'a* beyond matters of personal conduct, since this lies beyond their capabilities. Related to this, some believe that a gradual approach will ensure that Islam will eventually be embraced as an alternative way of life. Hasan, for example, states that the Qur'an implores Muslims to implement *shari'a* only according to their ability.[86] Abu Sayeed agrees, affirming that while Muslims are the minority in a society, they cannot promulgate *shari'a* in its entirety.[87] This chimes with the statement of the European Council for Fatwa and Research (ECFR), of which both Hasan and Abu Sayeed are members:

> According to Shari'ah, Muslims are not obliged to establish the civil, financial and political status of Shari'ah in non-Muslim countries, *as these lie beyond their capabilities.* Allah, Most High, does not require people to do things that are beyond their capacity.[88]

Even though Muslims may not be in a position to establish *shari'a* beyond the level of personal conduct, there is a shared view that they must approach a more comprehensive application of *shari'a* incrementally. Al-Qaradawi exhorts such an approach as follows:

> If we want to establish a real Muslim society, we should not imagine that such an end can be achieved by a mere decision issued to that effect by a king or a president or a council of leaders or a parliament. Gradualism is the means through which such an end can be fulfilled. Gradualism here refers to preparing people ideologically, psychologically, morally, and socially to accept and adopt the application of the Shari'ah in all aspects of life … .[89]

IFE appears to endorse the same view. Its website includes an article that states, 'The Ummah is in a real need to … [r]e-introduce to the youth the *Fiqh At-Tadarrug* (Fiqh of Gradualism) in which people are trained bit by bit on how to lead a true balanced Islamic life.'[90] Parvez articulates a gradual approach, citing the incremental changes in law at the time of Muhammad:

> [A]ll the noble Prophets of Allah worked according to the set priorities of Islam and introduced change gradually so that it could become firm in people's hearts and minds … . Once people begin to respond to Islamic values and ideas, the door to change is opened.[91]

Abu Sayeed shares Parvez's long-term perspective of the Islamic mission, also referring to Muhammad's example:

> God did not make any kind of obligation on the Muslims to apply *shari'a – full* shari'a – in the early period. It took twenty-three years. The first wave of the Prophet Muhammad's life at Mecca was just the stage of *the purification of ideas.* [92]

Muslims in Britain, Abu Sayeed says, don't feel restricted in Britain because they know that it took a long time for Muhammad to establish Islam. His reference to the precise number of years it took for Muhammad to consolidate Islam is also cited by Manazir Ahsan, who similarly warns, 'Everything cannot be achieved at once. Was not the Quran revealed piecemeal over a period of twenty-three years so that people and society could adopt Islam step-by-step and become firmly rooted in it through a gradual process?'[93] Indeed, Ahsan, Abu Sayeed and others in the revivalist network take a long-term view regarding Islam's place in Britain. This appears connected to a firm conviction in Islam's future triumph, based upon Islamic prophecy. Al-Qaradawi expresses this vision most assertively as follows:

> Constantinople was conquered in 1453 by a 23-year old Ottoman named Muhammad ibn Murad, whom we call Muhammad the Conqueror. Now what remains is to conquer Rome. That is what we wish for, and that is what we believe in. After having been expelled twice, Islam will be victorious and reconquer Europe … I am certain that this time, victory will be won not by the sword but by preaching and [Islamic] ideology … The conquest of Rome and the spread of Islam East and West will be the fruit of the seed we plant and entail the return of the Caliphate, which treads the straight path [of Islam] and is based on the path of the prophets … [The Caliphate] is worthy of leading the nation to victory.[94]

Abu Sayeed agrees with al-Qaradawi's optimistic view of Islam's future 'conquest', referring to the allegedly high rates of Muslim conversion in Britain.[95] Altikriti, in an interview with John Ware, also expresses firm conviction in al-Qaradawi's vision. 'I believe in it because that is the prophecy of the Prophet,' he admits. 'It's not an invention of Sheikh Qaradawi.'[96] Suhaib Hasan likewise voices a firm conviction in the future triumph of Islam not just in

Europe but worldwide. Regarding the return of the caliphate, Hasan contends, 'It will come because it is prophecised by the Prophet.'[97]

Jihad, a collective duty

The global Muslim Brotherhood's conviction that Islam will triumph Britain, the rest the Europe, and eventually the world is not unconditional. Islam's rise as the dominant religion and organising factor for social and political life in Britain and beyond depends, for those who believe in Islam's revival, upon the collective effort of Muslims to live piously, engage in *da'wa*, and enjoin the good and forbid the wrong. This effort is otherwise known as *jihad*.

The two founding fathers of the revivalist movement, Hasan al-Banna and Abu al-A'la Mawdudi, as noted in chapter 1, both glorified *jihad* as a collective duty for Muslims to usher in an Islamic revival. Both saw the shirking of this duty as a sin.[98] Al-Banna's understanding of *jihad* as supported in the Qur'an, the *sunna*, and the four schools of classical Sunni Islamic law, was shared by Mawdudi. Both acknowledged the prevailing conception of *jihad* within Islamic jurisprudence and throughout Islamic history as a military endeavour to expand the reach of Islam. Both described *jihad* as a defensive doctrine designed to protect Islam from attack or obstruction. But both also advocated *jihad* to further Islam through non-violent means, including physical or mental exertion, and the expenditure of one's wealth. Their understanding of *jihad* is consistent with its formulation in classical Islamic scholarship into three types: *jihad* of the sword (*jihad bi-al-saif), jihad* of the tongue (*jihad al-kalima*), and *jihad* of the heart (*jihad al-qalb*).[99]

In classical Islamic law, *jihad* of the sword is the preponderant military type and is classified into defensive and offensive legal categories. Offensive *jihad* is a collective obligation (*fard kifaya*) upon the Muslim *umma* as a whole to propagate Islam until it reigns supreme. This assumes there is an Islamic state, since only the caliph, the leader of the Islamic state, can declare offensive *jihad*.[100] But when Islam is attacked – or when Muslim land is occupied – *jihad* becomes an individual obligation (*fard 'ayn*) binding upon each and every Muslim. No caliph is required to wage such a defensive *jihad*. The other types of *jihad* are non-violent, but each kind of *jihad* is devoted, directly or indirectly, to further the spread of Islamic values and law.

Cultural jihad *for the Islamic revival*

Al-Qaradawi is the most prominent advocate of a non-violent, cultural *jihad* in the West today. He calls for a new kind of *jihad* relevant to the Muslim predicament, one that adopts a range of non-violent methods in the service of a revived caliphate, including what might be considered as a modern variant of the *jihad* of the tongue. He also makes it very clear that non-violent forms of *jihad* cannot be restricted to individual struggles with desire or sin, as *jihad* of the heart is described. This is because no form of *jihad* can be detached from the overall effort to universalise the *shari'a* on earth:

> The most important form of *jihad* today is serious, purposive organized work to re-build the Islamic society and state and to implement the Islamic way of life in the political, cultural, and economic areas … I believe that cultural, educational, and informational *jihad* in the way of God should be given priority today, *as long as such* jihad *is a purely Islamic effort that aims at re-establishing the Islamic state.*[101]

Ghulam Sarwar, the director of the Muslim Educational Trust, describes *jihad* in consistent terms. In a book distributed to Muslim schools in Britain, Sarwar describes *jihad* as 'the use of all our energies and resources to establish the Islamic system of life, in order to gain Allah's favour'.[102] Ibrahim Hewitt, the chairman of Interpal, the Palestinian Relief and Development Fund, and former MCB assistant secretary general concurs. He writes,

> Of all the precepts of Islam, it is perhaps *Jihad* that is most often misquoted, misused and misunderstood. The word itself means 'to strive or struggle in the way of Allah', not the more popular but incorrect usage, 'holy war' … Of course, a 'struggle in the way of Allah' may mean warfare, *but any personal or communal struggle to establish an Islamic lifestyle is Jihad.*[103]

Hewitt adds that another manifestation of the 'real meaning' of *jihad* is a 'counter-culture to that presented as the norm by the Western media (and frequently aped by the Muslim media)'.[104] He laments what he sees as an attack on 'the cultural heritage of Islam and Muslims and its superiority over much of what today passes as culture in non-Muslim society'. The necessary effort to promote and protect Islam as a way of life, he describes as 'the cultural *Jihad*'. For Hewitt and others in the revivalist network, *jihad* is primarily a non-violent effort or struggle to advance Islam within society through challenging ways of thinking and acting. In the words of Zahid Parvez, director of the Markfield Institute of Higher Education, *jihad* aims at '[i]ntellectually challenging ideologies, beliefs and ways of life that conflict with God's Way'. It also aims at '[i]nfluencing positive social, economic and political change in society according to Islamic ideals'.[105]

As seen in chapter 3, *jihad* is intimately connected to the doctrine of Enjoining the Good and Forbidding the Wrong (EGFW). Hewitt, for example, links *jihad* with EGFW in describing the former as '[s]triving to establish Good and remove Evil from society, to gain Allah's pleasure'.[106] Sarwar likewise sees a connection between *jihad* and EGFW. He describes EGFW as the 'comprehensive *jihad*' to establish Islam as a way of life. Consistent with classical Islamic scholarship, Sarwar describes this 'as a continuous process', beginning with what amounts to *jihad* of the heart.[107] He writes:

> In its first phase a Muslim learns to control his own passions and intentions. We need to strive hard to achieve this. This is *Jihad* within ourselves and is the basis for the comprehensive *Jihad* which is concerned with establishing *Ma'ruf* (right) and removing *Munkar* (evil) from our lives and from society in which we live. It demands the use of all our material and mental processes. Eventually, when the need arises, we even have to give our life for Allah's sake … . We cannot think of Islam without *Jihad*. [108]

Demonstrating a shared understanding across ethnic lines of the importance of the *jihad* of the heart as the starting place for a revival of Islamic values, this view is expressed in similar terms by Altikriti. Echoing the view with Farooq Murad that '*jihad*' has become a 'dirty word' in the Western media,[109] Altikriti opines, 'The word "*jihad*" is very central to Islam, extremely central to Islam. It's a very noble, very humane notion. Ultimately, starting with you fighting your own desires to do wrong. That's the very central piece of *jihad*'.[110] Asked where *jihad* ends, Altikriti remarks,

> Islam is not a pacifist religion. But Islam is never about instigating or initiating offence, never. But when you are attacked, you are called to defend yourself. You are called, and if someone attacks you by force, you are called – you are allowed – if you wish to sacrifice yourself peacefully, then that's your prerogative. But you absolutely, absolutely, have the duty to defend others, to defend your land, to defend your home, simply because to give up your own life, that's your choice, but to give up someone else's life, that's not yours.[111]

Altikriti states that *jihad* is about helping the poor, giving to charity and doing good deeds – as expressed in the doctrine of EGFW – but an important part of it, he admits, is self-defence. Altikriti's view that *jihad* should not involve initiating offence but is a duty for Muslims when attacked is fairly typical of the global Muslim Brotherhood. Altikriti, as with numerous other revivalist figures, sees the Israeli-Palestinian conflict in these terms.

Defensive **jihad**, *Palestine and Hamas*

To revivalists, as to other kinds of Islamists, Israel is viewed as an illegal, occupying force and Palestinian 'resistance' groups, such as Hamas, are seen to be fulfilling their duty to engage in defensive *jihad* to fight oppression and reclaim Muslim land. To Western audiences, this is presented in the language of justice and human rights, but underlying the pro-Palestinian cause shared by revivalist individuals and groups is a religiously informed understanding of the conflict. Such an understanding is held by Daud Abdullah, director of the Middle East Monitor and a former assistant secretary general of MCB. Abdullah says he has dedicated the rest of his life to the Palestinian cause.

Although he says that the conflict is not one between Muslims and Jews, when asked why he is so passionate about this particular political issue, he admits that his understanding of it is framed by his faith:

> As a Muslim, first of all, I understand it in a certain way. I understand that the importance of Palestine – Palestine is unique – Palestine was the land to which Abraham sought refuge, after he left his homeland in Iraq. And it is written about in the Qur'an. The city of Jerusalem and the mosque of, Al-Aqsa Mosque, is mentioned in the Qur'an. The Prophet Muhammad, peace be upon him, he made a miraculous journey, from Mecca to Jerusalem, and he was taken into the heavens. We believe this as Muslims, you see, and it all happened in Palestine. So, the issue of Palestine is inter-twined in Muslim belief. And for me, I understand it in this way: It belongs to the Muslims.[112]

When asked if he is referring to Jerusalem or the whole land, he says, 'the whole land, the whole land. The Palestinians are custodians. They lived there for centuries, thousands of years.' The notion that Israel has usurped Muslim, not just Palestinian, land is informed by, or at least consistent with, the classical Islamic doctrine of irredentism and the concomitant legal obligation placed upon each Muslim to wage defensive *jihad*. This viewpoint was expressed by al-Qaradawi, with specific reference to Israel, as follows:

> We are fighting them in the name of Islam, because Islam commands us to fight whoever plunders our land, and occupies our country. All the schools of Islamic jurisprudence – the Sunni, the Shi'ite, the Ibadhiya – and all the ancient and modern schools of jurisprudence – agree that any invader who occupies even an inch of land of the Muslims must face resistance … *They must not allow anyone to take a single piece of land away from Islam.* That is what we are fighting the Jews for … . Our religion commands us … We are fighting in the name of religion, in the name of Islam, which makes this *jihad* an individual duty, in which the entire nation takes part … . We do not disassociate Islam from the war. On the contrary, disassociating Islam from the war is the reason for our defeat. *We are fighting in the name of Islam.*[113]

This doctrine of irredentism – once Muslim land, always Muslim land – was explicitly expressed by Hasan al-Banna.[114] It is based upon perceived historic precedent. Its formalisation into a tenet of Islamic jurisprudence was based on the decisions and decrees of the second and fourth 'rightly guided' caliphs, Umar ibn al-Khattab (r. 634–644) and 'Ali ibn Abi Talib (r. 656–661).[115] It applies to all lands once conquered by *jihad*, but applies most forcefully to Israel, perhaps because of its location in the heart of what was once the *dar al-Islam* and the enduring conception of Jews in the Qur'an, *hadiths, sira* (Muhammad's biographies), and Qur'anic commentary as the most contemptuous and hostile people towards the believers.[116]

The understanding that the land that Israel 'occupies' is primarily Muslim (rather than Palestinian) is expressed in the founding charter of Hamas, the Palestinian wing of the Muslim Brotherhood organisation. Article 11 of the charter states that such land legally constitutes 'an Islamic *waqf* [endowment] for all generations of Muslims until the Day of Resurrection'.[117] Demonstrating the specifically religious conception of the conflict over the land that Israel allegedly occupies, the charter describes it locked into a 'struggle against the Jews' (not Israelis), against whom it invokes the apocalyptic *hadith* (Sahih Muslim, Book 40, Number 6985), which notes that if a Jew seeks refuge under stones or trees, these objects will be able to speak, informing a Muslim, 'There is a Jew behind me, come and kill him!'[118]

The individuals comprising the global Muslim Brotherhood in Britain do not support Salafi-Jihadist groups, such as al-Qaeda and the Islamic State, and they condemn Islamist terrorism in the West. But their view of the Israeli-Palestinian conflict and their religiously informed solidarity with Hamas and other Palestinian 'resistance' groups is something that bonds them. This aspect of their solidarity is obviously controversial. Hamas has been designated as a terrorist group by the United States, the European Union, Israel and other powers. In Britain, its military wing, the Izz al-Din al-Qassem Brigades, is proscribed as such. The revivalists' support for Hamas has occasionally attracted a critical light on them, as expressed in the British government's 2015 review of the Muslim Brotherhood, which stated:

> Muslim Brotherhood-related organisations and individuals in the UK have openly supported the activities of Hamas. People associated with the Muslim Brotherhood in the UK have applauded suicide bombing by Hamas, in some cases against civilians. Hamas terrorist activities have not been publicly disowned or condemned.[119]

The most public criticism of a revivalist group's support for Hamas came in February 2009, when Abdullah, then the deputy secretary general of MCB, signed the Istanbul Declaration. This document supporting Hamas urged the Muslim *umma* to wage *jihad* against Israel 'until the liberation of all of Palestine'. It also defined as a 'declaration of war' any country's support for Israel or deployment of forces in the 'Muslim waters' facing Gaza preventing the smuggling of arms and supplies.[120] For this reason, the British government, which was considering deploying naval forces to the Gaza coastline, suspended ties with MCB, although this decision was reversed in January 2010.[121]

In addition to Abdullah, other revivalist figures in Britain are closely connected to Hamas or at least express solidarity with it. In November 2017, Mohammed Sawalha, a founder of the MAB and former director of both the British Muslim Initiative and Muslim Welfare House, was reported to be a member of the political bureau of the group.[122] Previously, in 2006, the BBC's

Panorama programme had described him as a former senior figure in Hamas, 'said to have masterminded much of Hamas's political and military strategy' from London.[123] Azzam Tamimi, another MAB founding member, who has often been described as a Hamas spokesman in the West, famously said in a BBC interview that he would willingly martyr himself for the Palestinian cause.[124] Altikriti has written in Britain's mainstream media in support of the Hamas, distinguishing the group from al-Qaeda and urging the British government to speak directly to it.[125]

But it is not just Arab revivalists in Britain that support Hamas. Hewitt, in addition to being a former senior MCB official, is the chairman of Interpal, the Palestinian Relief and Development Fund, which has long been alleged to serve the group.[126] In 2003, the US government classified Interpal as a Specially Designated Global Terrorist organization due to allegations of funding Hamas in the Gaza Strip.[127] And in 2006, the BBC's *Panorama* claimed that Interpal was providing funds to charities in the Palestinian territories run by senior Hamas officials.[128] Hewitt has played a key role in the 'Miles of Smiles' aid convoys to the Gaza Strip which support Hamas, met with senior Hamas leaders, and paid his respects to the late Hamas founder, Sheikh Ahmed Yassin, while visiting his grave in Gaza City.[129]

Iqbal Sacranie, the founding secretary general of MCB, is another non-Arab figure in the revivalist network who has expressed support for Yassin and Hamas. He attended a memorial service for Yassin at the Central Mosque in London just after his death, and has referred to Hamas as 'freedom fighters'.[130] In an interview with the BBC in 2005, Sacranie compared Yassin to Gandhi, despite Yassin having provided theological justifications for terror attacks against civilians and being 'directly implicated in authorizing, directing, funding, and providing foot soldiers for Hamas terrorist operations'.[131] More recently, Azad Ali, MEND's head of community development, expressed admiration for Ismail Haniyeh, a senior Hamas leader.[132] No doubt other revivalists similarly support Hamas, but prefer to keep their support out of public view lest they attract criticism for supporting a terrorist group or for holding antisemitic views.

Jihad, for the global Muslim Brotherhood in Britain, is the legitimate duty of resistance against the occupation of Muslim land, most clearly expressed in their support for the Palestinian cause. Most fundamentally, however, it is a sacred collective obligation to propagate Islam as a complete way of life through *da'wa*. Along with a commitment to EGFW, the belief in non-compulsion and the eventual reward of Islam's triumph in Britain and the world, *jihad* is an important element of revivalist solidarity and conceptual component of the revivalist worldview.

Solidarity, habitus and ideology

The late Italian social movement theorist, Alberto Melucci, wrote, 'Solidarity is the capability of an actor to share a collective identity, that is, the capability of recognizing and being recognized as a part of the same system of social relationships.'[133] This chapter and the previous one have shown how individuals and groups in the revivalist network possess solidarity in this sense. These two chapters have shown how the cultural solidarity between revivalists is constituted by shared ways of classifying themselves as part of a religious community and the territory in which they live; shared ways of understanding their work and its purpose; and shared ways of perceiving the moral and political dimensions of their faith. They are connected by their understanding of the role and responsibilities they see themselves possessing as Islam's vanguard within British society. Their sense of distinction as a group is expressed in their perception of non-Muslims as part of the broader community of humanity to which they have a duty to deliver Islam. Their group solidarity is also expressed in their perception of other Muslims as either mistaken in isolating themselves from Britain's non-Muslim mainstream or integrating themselves seamlessly within it. It is also expressed in their perceived distinction from yet other Muslims who place the goal of an Islamic state prior to the attainment of a society infused with Islamic beliefs and values.

The cultural solidarity of the revivalist network is inseparable from certain concepts enabled by a vocabulary of terms rooted in Islamic tradition and expressed in particular theological doctrines. This cuts across sectarian and ethnic lines. Most observers of the individuals and organisations comprising this network refer to this expression of religious notions, particularly where they have political implications, as *ideological*. Most observers describe the social activism of these people and groups, labelled 'Islamists', as motivated by an ideology that fuses religion and politics. They describe the goals of these individuals and organisations as determined to perpetuate such an ideology. Action is assumed to be both motivated by and dedicated to the reproduction of a certain consciously accepted framework of ideas, including diagnoses of social and political problems, as well as their solutions.

Yet, what bonds the network is not ideology in the sense in which this term is typically used in academic and think tank literature. The network is not held together or driven by an explicitly articulated set of beliefs, values and ideas dedicated to predetermined political ends. It is held together or driven, rather, by precisely what makes the explicit articulation of beliefs, values and ideas possible – namely, a collective habitus. The concepts that they share, and their understanding of who they are, what they are working towards, and what rewards are in store for them, are dependent upon a shared perceptual schemata that is never fully transparent to conscious reflection and a related, unquestioned manner of evaluating social and political realities. Their shared way of classifying themselves and others – indeed, their way of proactively propagating such classifications, which constitutes a key mark of their cultural solidarity – is not the result of a conscious ideological commitment or of rational calculation. It is, rather, an expression of a shared habitus, a culturally inherited 'socialised subjectivity'.[134]

What connects the revivalist network – a similar way of perceiving and evaluating the social world – also forms the *stakes* of their struggle. What is at stake for revivalists is not just a social transformation, even less a political revolution, but a transformation in how the world is perceived and evaluated. This is contended, as the next two chapters will show, not just in the external, 'objective' institutions comprising the social and political order, but also in the internal, 'subjective' categories of perception and cognition.

Notes

1 'Islamic Revival in the UK – Past, Present and Future', *Islamic Foundation Newsletter*, October 2011, p. 9.
2 Ahmad (1995).
3 Interview with Irshad Baqui, 22 February 2012.
4 Andrew Gilligan, 'Inextricably linked to controversial mosque: the secret world of IFE', *The Telegraph*, 28 February 2010. www.telegraph.co.uk/news/newstopics/politics/labour/7333487/Inextricably-linked-to-controversial-mosque-the-secret-world-of-IFE.html.
5 See 'Philosophy', Jamaat-e-Islami Pakistan website, webpage captured 6 October 2013. https://web.archive.org/web/20131006065213/http://jamaat.org/beta/site/page/8.
6 Gilligan, 'Inextricably linked to controversial mosque: the secret world of IFE'.
7 Interview with Abdullah Faliq, 5 September 2012.
8 'Aims & Objectives', IHRC website. www.ihrc.org.uk/about-ihrc/aims-a-objectives.
9 'Cairo Declaration on Human Rights in Islam', OIC website, 5 August 1990. Webpage captured 4 February 2016. https://web.archive.org/web/20160204165950/http://www.oic-oci.org/english/article/human.htm.
10 Sarwar (2001), p. 52.
11 Ibid., p. 30.
12 Ibid.
13 Siddiqui (2004), p. 56.
14 Abdul Rashid Siddiqui, 'Time for Sacrifice', Moon Research Centre website, 2008. www.mrc.org.uk/sacrifice.html.
15 Murad (1981), p. 3.
16 Ahmad (1995), p. 46.
17 Ibid., p. 47.
18 Ibid., p. 50.
19 Parvez (2007), p. 197.
20 Ibid., chapter 9.
21 'RESPONSE TO THE CONTEMPORARY CHALLENGES-BR ANAS AL TIKRITI', YouTube, 25 December 2012. www.youtube.com/watch?v=_KkWltn07VE.
22 'Young and the Brave: Roles and Responsibilities By Brother Anas Altikriti', YouTube, 25 June 2011. www.youtube.com/watch?v=HOnCEiFuL4M.
23 Ibid.
24 'Anas Altikriti – A New Dawn', YouTube, 8 September 2011. www.youtube.com/watch?v=YYBCy60x3qw.
25 Interview with Anas Altikriti, 27 Febraury 2012.
26 'RESPONSE TO THE CONTEMPORARY CHALLENGES-BR ANAS AL TIKRITI'.
27 'Anas Altikriti – A New Dawn'.

28 Ashan (1977), p. 21.
29 Ahsan (1977), p. 42.
30 Ahmad (1995), pp. 46–47.
31 Parvez (2007), p. 85.
32 Ahmad (1995), p. 52.
33 Ibid.
34 Gilligan, 'Inextricably linked to controversial mosque: the secret world of IFE'.
35 Ahmad (1995), pp. 47, 49.
36 Murad, 'Our Vision of the Future'.
37 Parvez (2007), p. 39.
38 Ibid.
39 Khan (2004), p. 29.
40 'The UK Islamic Mission', The Islamic Far Right in Britain blog, undated. https://tifrib.wordpress.com/uk-islamic-mission/.
41 Alexander Meleagrou-Hitchens, 'The Islamic Forum of Europe and Political Participation', *Standpoint Magazine*, 1 April 2010. http://standpointmag.co.uk/node/2901.
42 Tibi (2009), p. 152.
43 Khadduri (1955), p. 16.
44 Khadduri and Liebesny (2009), p. 14, italics added.
45 Ibn Khaldun, cited in ibid., p. 13.
46 Interview with Ibrahim Mogra, 29 August 2012.
47 Interview with Farooq Murad, 7 October 2013.
48 Interview with Abdullah Faliq, 5 September 2012.
49 Interview with Omer El-Hamdoon, 14 February 2012.
50 Interview with Maulana Abu Sayeed, 16 February 2012.
51 Interview with Suhaib Hasan, 9 February 2012.
52 Interview with Maulana Abu Sayeed, 16 February 12012.
53 Interview with Ibrahim Mogra, 29 August 22012.
54 Interview with Farooq Murad, 7 October 2013.
55 Ahmad Thomson, 'Shari'a – A Way of Life', presentation given at Regents Park Mosque and Islamic Cultural Centre, 20 July 2008. Available at: www.wynnechambers.co.uk/pdf/Sharia_English_law.pdf.
56 Interview with Omer El-Hamdoon, 14 February 2012.
57 al-Misri (1994).
58 Interviews with Omer El-Hamdoon (14 February 2012), Suhaib Hasan (9 February 2012), Ibrahim Mogra (29 August 2012), Abdullah Faliq (5 September 2012) and Anas Altikriti 27 (February 2012); Parvez (2007), p. 104.
59 Interview with Omer El-Hamdoon, 14 February 2012.
60 Interview with Ibrahim Mogra, 29 August 2012; Parvez (2007), p. 105.
61 Interview with Abdullah Faliq, 5 September 2012.
62 Mandaville (2007), p. 57.
63 Murad, 'Our Vision of the Future'.
64 Suhaib Hasan, 'The Current Problems of the Muslim Ummah and their Solution in Light of the Purified Seerah'.
65 Interview with Suhaib Hasan, 9 February 2012.
66 Interview with Ibrahim Mogra, 29 August 2012.
67 Interview with Omer El-Hamdoon, 14 February 2012.
68 Ibid.
69 al-Qaradawi (1999), p. 70.
70 Parvez (2007), p. 256.
71 Ibid., p. 38.
72 Parvez (2007), p. 173, emphasis added.
73 Interview with Ibrahim Mogra, 29 August 2012.

74 James Bloodworth, 'Why is the left so blinkered to Islamic extremism?', *The Independent*, 28 June 2013. www.independent.co.uk/voices/comment/why-is-the-left-so-blinkered-to-islamic-extremism-8679265.html.
75 Interview with Anas Altikriti, 27 February 2012.
76 Interview with Abdullah Faliq, 5 September 2012.
77 Interview with Mohammed Abdul Aziz, 3 September 2012.
78 Interview with Dilwar Hussain, 29 August 2012.
79 Interview with Dilwar Hussain, 15 January 2015.
80 Thomson (2000), p. 4.
81 Interview with Mohammed Abdul Aziz, 3 September 2012.
82 Interview with Farooq Murad, 7 October 2013.
83 Interview with Maulana Abu Sayeed, 16 February 2012.
84 Interview with Abdullah Faliq, 5 September 2012.
85 Interview with Omer El-Hamdoon, 14 February 2012.
86 Interview with Suhaib Hasan, 11 June 2013.
87 Interview with Maulana Abu Sayeed, 16 February 2012.
88 Altikriti and Al-Ubaydi (2002), p. 164.
89 Yusuf al-Qaradawi, 'Gradualism in Applying the Shari`ah', On Islam website, 24 November 2011. https://web.archive.org/web/20150915164356/http://www.onislam.net/english/ask-the-scholar/shariah-based-systems/judiciary-and-police-systems/169643-gradualism-in-applying-the-shariah.html?Police_Systems=.
90 Ahmed Saad, 'Al-Wasatiyyah: The Lost Middle Path', IFE website, 30 December 2006. https://web.archive.org/web/20100903035703/http://www.islamicforumeurope.com/live/ife.php?doc=articleitem&itemId=324.
91 Parvez (2007), pp. 163–164.
92 Interview with Maulana Abu Sayeed, 16 February 2012.
93 Ahsan (1989), p. 15.
94 Yusuf al-Qaradawi, cited in Jonathan Dahoah-Halevi, 'The Muslim Brotherhood: A Moderate Islamic Alternative to al-Qaeda or a Partner in Global Jihad?', Jerusalem Center for Public Affairs, 1 November 2007. http://jcpa.org/article/the-muslim-brotherhood-a-moderate-islamic-alternative-to-al-qaeda-or-a-partner-in-global-jihad/.
95 Interview with Maulana Abu Sayeed, 16 February 2012.
96 John Ware, 'Time to Wise Up to the Muslim Brotherhood', *Standpoint Magazine*, July/August 2013. http://standpointmag.co.uk/node/5082/full.
97 Interview with Suhaib Hasan, 11 June 2013.
98 See al-Banna (1978), p. 133, and Mawdudi (1980), p. 100.
99 Cook (2009), p. 178.
100 See Peters (1996), pp. 3–4, 120–121; and Khadduri (1955), esp. pp. 60–61.
101 al-Qaradawi (1999), pp. 76, 70, emphasis added.
102 Sarwar (2006), p. 76.
103 Hewitt (2004), p. 29, emphasis added.
104 Ibid., p. 30.
105 Parvez (2007), p. 158.
106 Hewitt (2004), p. 58.
107 See Cook (2005), esp. chapter 2, and Marranci (2006), pp. 22–23.
108 Sarwar (2006), pp. 76–77.
109 Interview with Farooq Murad, 7 October 2013.
110 Interview with Anas Altikriti, 27 February 2012.
111 Ibid.
112 Interview with Daud Abdullah, 10 February 2012.
113 Yusuf al-Qaradawi, Qatar TV, 25 February 2006, English translation at *Middle East Media Research Institute*, 'Sheik Yousef Al-Qaradhawi: Our War with the

Jews is in the Name of Islam', TV Monitor Project, Clip Number 1052, www.memritv.org/clip/en/1052.htm.

114 al-Banna (1978), p. 147.

115 Bat Ye'or (2002), p. 216.

116 For a comprehensive collection of anti-Jewish motifs in Islam's foundational texts – the Qur'an, the *hadiths* (authoritative collections of accounts of Muhammad's words and deeds), and the *sira* (the early Muslim biographies of Muhammad) – as well as in the writings of influential Muslim jurists, theologians and scholars, see Bostom (2008).

117 Article 11, Hamas Covenant 1988: The Covenant of the Islamic Resistance Movement', The Avalon Project: Documents in Law, History and Diplomacy, Yale Law School. http://avalon.law.yale.edu/20th_century/hamas.asp.

118 Article 7, 'Hamas Covenant 1988'.

119 House of Commons (2015), para. 37, p. 7.

120 For the text of the Istanbul Declaration, see 'A statement by the religious scholars and proselytisers (du'a) of the Islamic Nation (ummah) to all rulers and peoples concerning events in Gaza', published online at: http://hurryupharry.org/wp-content/uploads/2009/03/istpdf.pdf.

121 See Alan Travis, 'Hazel Blears' standoff with Muslim Council overshadows new anti-terror launch', *The Guardian,* 25 March 2000, www.guardian.co.uk/politics/2009/mar/25/muslim-council-britain-hazel-blears; and Nicholas Watt, 'Government restores links with biggest Muslim group', *The Guardian*, 15 January 2010, www.guardian.co.uk/politics/2010/jan/15/government-relations-muslim-council-britain-mcb.

122 David Brown, 'Finsbury mosque leader Mohammed Sawalha part of Hamas politburo', *The Times*, 7 November 2017. www.thetimes.co.uk/article/finsbury-mosque-leader-mohammed-sawalha-part-of-hamas-politburo-0cdn3gs80.

123 'Faith, hate and charity', *Panorama*, BBC, originally broadcast 30 July 2006, http://news.bbc.co.uk/2/hi/programmes/panorama/5234586.stm.

124 *The Telegraph*, 19 January 2010. www.telegraph.co.uk/news/uknews/terrorism-in-the-uk/7019734/Hamas-supporter-who-condones-suicide-bombing-to-speak-at-Birmingham-University.html.

125 Anas Altikriti, 'Hamas is not al-Qaida', *The Guardian*, 21 September 2009. www.theguardian.com/commentisfree/2009/sep/21/hamas-al-qaida.

126 Steve Merley, 'The Union of Good: INTERPAL and the U.K. Member Organizations', The NEFA Foundation, 23 March 2009. https://globalmbwatch.com/wp-content/uploads/2013/04/27722268-The-Union-of-Good-Interpal-and-the-UK-Member-Organizations-NEFA-Foundation.pdf.

127 'U.S. Designates Five Charities Funding Hamas and Six Senior Hamas Leaders as Terrorist Entities', U.S. Department of Treasury website, 22 August 2003. www.treasury.gov/press-center/press-releases/Pages/js672.aspx.

128 'Faith, hate and charity', *Panorama*, BBC.

129 See 'Seniors in Interpal, a British fund that supports Hamas, play a major role in sending aid convoys to Gaza', The Meir Amit Intelligence and Terrorism Information Center, 3 August 2011, www.terrorism-info.org.il/Data/pdf/PDF_11_172_2.pdf; and Samuel Westrop, 'UK: Hamas-linked Interpal Enjoys Mainstream Support', Gatestone Institute, 15 December 2014, www.gatestoneinstitute.org/4953/interpal-mainstream-support.

130 'Sacranie, Yassin and Gandhi', MCB Watch blog, 17 October 2005. http://mcbwatch.blogspot.in/2005/10/sacranie-yassin-and-gandhi.html.

131 Matthew Levitt„ 'Shaykh Yassin and Hamas Terror', Washington Institute website, 23 March 2004. www.washingtoninstitute.org/policy-analysis/view/shaykh-yassin-and-hamas-terror.

132 Azad Ali, 'Amir al-Mu'mineen', IFE blog, September 25, 2008. http://web.archive.org/web/20120430044855/http://blog.islamicforumeurope.com/2008/09/25/amir-al-mu%E2%80%99minun/.
133 Melucci (1985), pp. 794–795.
134 Bourdieu and Wacquant (1992), p. 126.

References

Ahmad, Khurshid (1995). 'Man and the future of civilization: an Islamic perspective'. *Encounters*, vol. 1, no. 1: 39–55.

Ahsan, Muhammad Manazir (1977). *Islam: Faith and Practice.* Leicester: The Islamic Foundation.

Ahsan, Muhammad Manazir (1989). 'Dawa and its significance for the future'. In Merryl Wyn Davies and Adnan Khalil Pasha (eds), *Beyond Frontiers: Islam and Contemporary Needs*: 13–21. London: Mansell Publishing.

Altikriti, Anas Osama and Shakir Nasif Al-Ubaydi (trans.) (2002). *Fatwas of the European Council for Fatwa and Research.* Cairo: Islamic INC.

al-Banna, Hasan (1978). *On Jihad*, in Charles Wendell (trans. and annot.), *Five Tracts of Hasan al-Banna (1906–1949): A Selection from the Majmu'at Rasa'il al-Imam al-Shahid*: 133–161. Berkeley: University of California Press.

Bat Ye'or (2002). *Islam and Dhimmitude: Where Civilizations Collide.* Cranbury, NJ: Farleigh Dickinson University Press.

Bostom, Andrew G. (ed.) (2008). *The Legacy of Islamic Antisemitism: From Sacred Texts to Solemn History.* New York: Prometheus Books.

Bourdieu, Pierre, and Loïc J. D. Wacquant (1992). *An Invitation to Reflexive Sociology.* Cambridge: Polity Press.

Cook, David (2005). *Understanding Jihad.* Berkeley and Los Angeles: California University Press.

Cook, David (2009) 'Islamism and jihadism: the transformation of classical notions of jihad into an ideology of terrorism'. In *Totalitarian Movements and Political Religions*, vol. 10, no. 2: 177–187.

Hewitt, Ibrahim (2004). *What Does Islam Say?* 4th edition. London: Muslim Educational Trust.

House of Commons (2015). *Muslim Brotherhood Review: Main Findings.* HC 679. www.gov.uk/government/uploads/system/uploads/attachment_data/file/486948/53163_Muslim_Brotherhood_Review_-_PRINT.pdf.

Ibn Khaldun (1989). *The Muqaddimah: An Introduction to History.* Ed. N. J. Dawood, trans. Franz Rosenthal. Princeton, NJ: Princeton University Press.

Khadduri, Majid (1955). *War and Peace in the Law of Islam.* Baltimore: Johns Hopkins University Press.

Khadduri, Majid and Herbert J. Liebesny (eds) (2009). *Law in the Middle East, Volume One, Origin and Development of Islamic Law.* Clark, NJ: The Lawbook Exchange.

Khan, Muhammad Faruq (2004). 'Self-development and its role in life'. In Abdur Rashid Siddiqui, *Tazkiyah: The Islamic Path of Self Development*: 64–98. Leicester: Islamic Foundation.

Marranci, Gabriele (2006). *Jihad Beyond Islam.* Oxford: Berg.

Mandaville, Peter (2007). *Global Political Islam.* New York: Routledge.

Mawdudi, Abul Ala (1980). *Towards Understanding Islam.* Trans. Khurram Murad. Leicester: Islamic Foundation.

Melucci, Alberto (1985). 'The symbolic challenge of contemporary movements'. In *Social Research*, vol. 52, no. 4: 789–816.

al-Misri, Ahmad ibn Naqib (1994). *'Umdat al-Salik – Reliance of the Traveller: A Classic Manual of Islamic Sacred Law.* Ed. and trans. Nuh Ha Mim Keller. Beltsville, MD: Amana Publications.

Murad, Khurram (1981). *The Islamic Movement in the West: Reflections on Some Issues.* Leicester: The Islamic Foundation.

Parvez, Zahid (2007). *Building a New Society: An Islamic Approach to Social Change.* Markfield: Revival Publications.

Peters, Rudolph Peters (ed.) (1996). *Jihad in Classical and Modern Islam.* Princeton, NJ: Markus Weiner Publishers.

al-Qaradawi, Yusuf (1999). *Fiqh Al Zakah (Volume II): A Comparative Study of Zakah, Regulations and Philosophy in the Light of Qur'an and Sunnah.* Trans. Monzer Kahf. Jeddah, Saudi Arabia: Scientific Publishing Centre, King Abdulaziz University.

Sarwar, Ghulam (2001). *Islamic Education: Its Meaning, Problems and Prospects.* London: The Muslim Educational Trust.

Sarwar, Ghulam (2006). *Islam: Beliefs and Teachings.* 8th edition. London: Muslim Educational Trust.

Tibi, Bassam (2009). 'Islamism and democracy: on the compatibility of institutional Islamism and the political culture of democracy'. In *Totalitarian Movements and Political Religions*, vol. 10, no. 2: 135–164.

5 Politics and governance

A conflict of vision and values with the state

Chapter 2 established the existence of a network in Britain of individuals and organisations associated with Jama'at-i-Islami and the Muslim Brotherhood. Chapters 3 and 4 established a sense of cultural solidarity shared between many of the network's key protagonists, particularly in the form of shared ways of seeing themselves, their sociopolitical milieu and their mission as a vanguard community to disseminate what they deem to be 'true' Islam within and beyond Britain's Muslim population. The current chapter and the following one seek to show that, in addition to being organisationally networked and culturally bonded, the key figures and groups comprising the network are engaged in a political and cultural struggle – that is, a conflict concerning perspectives, values and a way of life, as well as the authority to determine them. They show how the revivalist network is involved in a conflict concerning the power to determine an alternative social reality, and an alternative way of seeing social reality, both for Muslims and the broader population.

Certain aspects of this conflict, highlighted by recent events in Britain, have placed Islamic revivalists at the forefront of political debate. In particular, the media spotlight shone upon the numerous British Muslims that have joined the Islamic State (IS) has led some analysts to claim that revivalist groups play a key role in the 'radicalisation' of British Muslims. Samuel Westrop, for example, writes that '"non-violent" Islamist networks', composed of groups linked to Jama'at-i-Islami and the Muslim Brotherhood, impose an 'extremist culture' and ideology upon British Muslims.[1] Because of these groups' influence in inculcating radical beliefs amongst Muslim Britons, he asserts, some have travelled abroad to fight for IS, while others who remain at home have developed a distrust of Britain, disdain for British liberal democratic values, and a victim mentality that serves to divide communities. Westrop asserts that these groups have, for a number of years, sought to impose a 'culture of extremist Islamic thought' on British Muslims by exerting their influence within local government, schools, universities, charities, prisons and even interfaith groups. 'By permitting Islamist groups to represent British Muslims, and then equipping them with funds and political recognition,' he writes, 'Britain has actually advanced intolerance – and for far too long.'

The radicalising effect of non-violent but 'extremist' groups upon British Muslims and the role of these groups in Muslim Britons joining jihadist groups abroad or in Islamist terrorism at home, as claimed by Westrop, the think tank Quilliam and others, is a contentious but key issue for the British government to handle. Membership in the ostensibly non-violent rejectionist groups appears to have a connection with involvement in Islamist violence: almost half the Islamist terror plots in Britain were found to have some connection to the Hizb ut-Tahrir offshoot, al-Muhajiroun. But no comparable connection between involvement with participationist groups and terrorism has been shown.

Such concerns have prompted the government to create, for the first time, a strategy to counter both violent *and* non-violent 'extremism', as well as a new Extremism Analysis Unit located in the Home Office.[2] On July 1, 2015, a statutory duty – the 'Prevent duty' – came into force requiring all public bodies, including schools, prisons and local councils 'to take steps to identify and tackle radicalisation'.[3] The causes of terrorism and the alleged causal relationship between non-violent and violent extremism are issues that lie beyond the scope of this book. But the debates concerning 'extremism' are inseparable from a more fundamental question that is central to this book, namely, that of a conflict of values.

Such a conflict may be seen to concern not just certain values, however, but the schemes of perception in which values make sense: it is not just a matter of *what* is right or wrong, but *how* what is right and wrong obtains its moral value. This involves different perceptions regarding the sources of authority for determining morality. The phrase 'a culture of thought' appears to capture this key stake in the conflict, but it should be emphasised that what is contested is not just a particular set of thoughts or ideas, but the culture in which they form and resonate with meaning and value. In other words, this conflict of values is less a conflict of ideas or thoughts than one concerning a *way* of thinking. Yet, more than this, it concerns a way of seeing or, better still, a way of living in which such a way of thinking is nurtured and rewarded.

There are three areas in which revivalists have been most active in contesting 'a culture of thought', in engendering a conflict of visions and values. These include *politics*, in the sense of national and local systems of representation and governance, and *education*, in the sense of the institutional provision of teaching and learning, particularly as they relate to Muslim children. There are some clear links between these two fields, particularly where advocacy is concerned, for example in the representation of Muslims' educational needs to government. But for the purposes of clarity, politics and education are treated in this book as two separate fields. The third focus area is *arbitration*, in particular the network of *shari'a* courts. This is presented in the next chapter with education, since both relate to a conflict of values occurring primarily within Muslim communities.[4]

Although politics as it relates to policymaking is treated as a distinct field of contention in this chapter, it should be noted that contention in *all* three fields is political, in the sense that authority is contested across them. This concerns the power to represent Muslims and Islam within official discourse, policy and law, as well as within Muslim communities, in Muslim schools and *shari'a* courts. In Pierre Bourdieu's terms, it concerns the possession of *symbolic capital.* This contested authority also concerns the power to shape the social order in which Muslims live and Islam is practised, through institutionalising a certain understanding of Islam and Islamic values amongst Muslims and the wider population. Thus, the political dimension of this struggle relates to contention concerning the authority to structure the social world, as well as the perception and evaluation of it. This cuts across the fields of politics 'proper', where government is concerned, and education, in relation to institutions of teaching and learning.

The field of politics referred to in this chapter relates to national and local systems of government. There are several ways in which Islamic revivalists' activism within this field demonstrates their engagement in a conflict with political and cultural dimensions. The first involves the efforts of specific organisations to serve as interlocutors for Muslims' needs and interests. There is a distributed but concerted effort to speak on behalf of Muslims at the interface with central and local government authorities. The second way involves the involvement or infiltration of certain individuals and organisations within local government authorities, exemplified by the Islamic Forum of Europe in the London Borough of Tower Hamlets. The efforts of these interlocutionary groups are contentious not only for many Muslims outside the revivalist network for determining Muslim identity, a common understanding of Islam and the needs of Muslims. They are also contentious for Britain more generally in influencing or seeking to influence government policy in support of a vision of society that, in the final analysis, clashes with that of a culturally secular liberal democracy.

Representation and advocacy: the MCB and other interlocutors

Some of the organisations and individuals comprising the revivalist network currently play, or have played, an active role in advocating for Muslims' needs and interests at the interface with government authorities. There are two senses in which this work may be understood as constituting a conflict of values contesting cultural norms and political authority, and therefore as more than mere advocacy. The first is in vying to represent the entirety and diversity of Muslims in Britain by promoting and instituting a particular understanding of Islam that is contentious amongst some Muslims in contemporary Britain. The second is in challenging mainstream liberal democratic values in the public arena of policymaking. Thus, some revivalist groups and individuals, while appearing to advocate Muslims' needs and interests, promote a particular vision of Islam within British society to the detriment of alternative visions held by other Muslims. They also promote a particular understanding of 'common' social values that clashes with their understanding in mainstream society and their articulation by the state.

Put succinctly, the conflict of values in which revivalists are engaged has two sides, one facing *Muslims*, whom they claim to represent, and one facing *society as a whole*, represented by government authorities. But it also has two aspects that cut across these two faces, one that involves *perception, belief and thought*, and one that involves *institutions* (see Figure 5.1 below). These might be thought of, respectively, as the 'software' and 'hardware' of Britain's political culture. This conflict might be termed a 'clash of narratives', but it is more than a conflict over the meaning of words. The effort to control language – particularly as it relates to Islam, 'British values', and 'extremism' – is the *symbolic* aspect of a conflict over how certain values are understood and the source of authority from which they obtain their worth. But this is connected to the conflict's *practical* aspect, which concerns how such values are most appropriately embedded within the social fabric and upheld by the state.

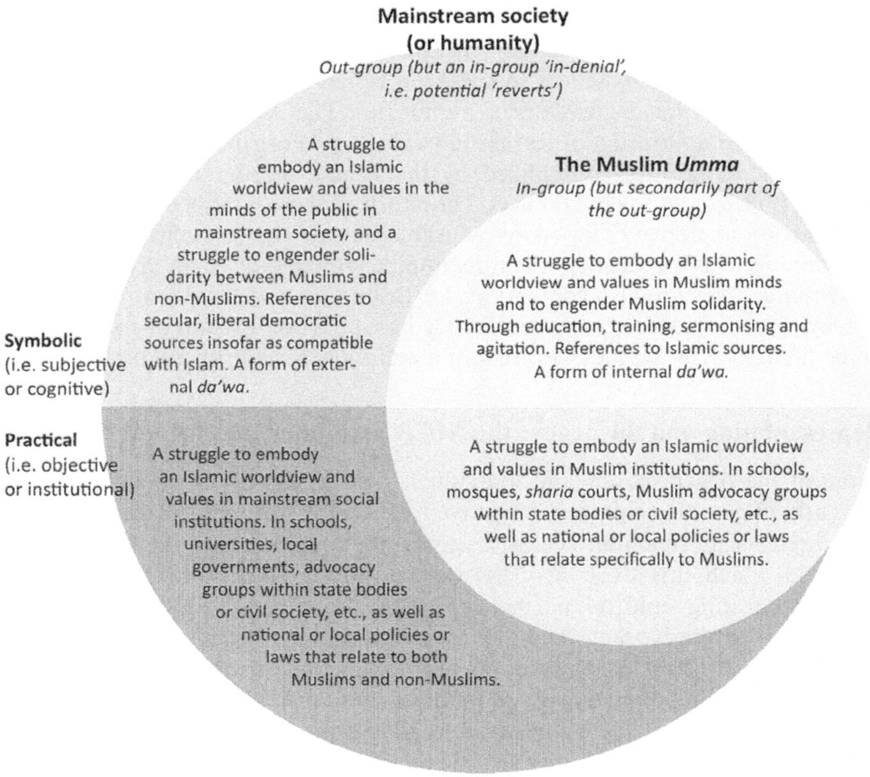

Figure 5.1 Symbolic and practical dimensions of authority contested by the revivalist movement within the Musim *umma* and across mainstream society

The Muslim Council of Britain

A clash of values and government disengagement

The Muslim Council of Britain (MCB) was the primary interlocutor between British Muslims and the British government from its creation in 1997 until 2009. For over a decade the MCB acted as the government's key consultative partner, providing 'the Muslim perspective' on national policy matters. Its fall from government favour, which began while Labour was in office, was from the government's point of view the result of a conflict of core values.

The incident that provoked the then communities secretary, Hazel Blears, to formally suspend the government's relationship with the MCB was the signing of the Istanbul Declaration by MCB deputy secretary general, Daud Abdullah. The Istanbul Declaration exhorted the Muslim *umma* to wage *jihad* against Israel 'until the liberation of all of Palestine' – in other words, to strive for Israel's annihilation. As understood by Blears, the document also 'advocat[ed] attacks on Jewish communities all around the world'.[5] Furthermore, it defined any country's support for Israel or its deployment of forces in the 'Muslim waters' facing Gaza preventing the smuggling of arms and supplies as a 'declaration of war'.[6] Since the British government was considering deploying naval forces to the Gaza coastline, it viewed this as condoning attacks on British troops. Abdullah's refusal to withdraw his signature on the declaration and the MCB's refusal to force Abdullah's resignation marked the end of the MCB's special relationship with the government.

However, there were numerous signs of a clash of values between the MCB and the British government prior to Abdullah's signing of the Istanbul Declaration. In 2001, for example, the MCB's then secretary general, Yousuf Bhailok, instigated the MCB boycotting of Holocaust Memorial Day. The MCB claimed that the occasion ought to be replaced by one that commemorates genocides other than the Nazi genocide of Jews, most notably what it dubiously referred to as 'the Palestinian genocide'.[7] The MCB lifted the boycott in 2008, but resumed it the following year in protest against Israel's Operation Cast Lead in Gaza. In 2010, it changed its position again, sending a junior representative, Shuja Shafi (who became MCB secretary general in 2014). The MCB's protest against the memorial event appears now to have been shelved. However, the initial boycott and the perceived attempt to extract political capital from it for the Palestinian cause raised concerns for some in government and the media that the MCB leadership was expressing an unacceptable antisemitic stance.[8]

Another indication of a clash of values between the MCB and the government came in August 2006, after the police arrested a group of British Muslims who planned to detonate liquid explosives on seven trans-Atlantic flights from Heathrow airport to American and Canadian cities.[9] Despite the group leader's video-recorded explanation of the plot's rationale to 'fulfill a covenant and promise with Allah the almighty, and to make his *din* [religion and way of life] reign supreme',[10] the MCB pointed solely to British and American foreign policy as the primary motivation behind it. As Martyn Frampton and Shiraz Maher observe:

> The MCB was felt to be legitimizing terrorism, drawing moral equivalences, while failing to directly confront the radicalization of some young British men. This raised fresh and troubling concerns about its suitability as a partnership organization. Subsequently, therefore, the government sought to rebalance its relationship with groups like the MCB by empowering alternative organizations at the grassroots. The new mantra in Whitehall was that it would only work with groups and individuals that accepted a set of '*non-negotiable values*'.[11]

In fact, a month prior to this, Ruth Kelly, then communities secretary, had already announced that the government would work with a broader range of Muslim groups, including the newly formed Sufi Muslim Council, which she praised for condemning 'terrorism in all its forms'.[12]

Beginning under Labour and continued by the coalition and Conservative administrations, the British government has brought the question of values to the forefront of political debate. Moreover, it has explicitly articulated the sharing of non-negotiable 'British' values as a pre-requisite for official engagement with (and the funding of) community organisations. Since 2011, with the publication of the Conservative-led coalition's revised counter-radicalisation strategy, Prevent, an explicitly values-led approach to community engagement and counter-radicalization has been adopted.[13] This is evident in the government's definition of 'extremism' as the 'vocal or active opposition to fundamental British values, including democracy, the rule of law, individual liberty and mutual respect and tolerance of different faiths and beliefs'.[14] Its definition also includes calling 'for the death of members of our armed forces, whether in this country or overseas'. MCB sidelining by Cameron's successive administrations indicated that the government saw the group as failing to uphold these core British values. Theresa May's government has not shunned the MCB altogether – the group was invited to present its views at a Home Affairs Committee inquiry into radicalisation and counter-narratives in 2016 – but it no longer enjoys the main interlocutionary role it once had. The government now consults various Muslim groups with quite diverse views.

Contesting the notion of 'British values'

The MCB's involvement in a conflict of values with the state is not just a matter of government perspective. Most evident in the policy areas of counter-terrorism and community engagement, it is belied by its attitude to the Home Office's introduction of fundamental values as a key criterion for moderation and partnership. Rather than expressing agreement and support for the government on this matter, the MCB, under Farooq Murad's leadership, dismissed the government's definition of 'extremism', and thus of 'British values', as 'arbitrary' and devised by 'neoconservative think-tanks'[15] and 'divisive pundits'.[16] This view is often echoed by other groups in the revivalist network, including Muslim Education and Development (MEND), a group that campaigns for Muslims' active political participation. The MCB's attitude to the government's criticism of Muslim groups or individuals espousing non-violent but extremist beliefs is often similarly dismissive and conspiratorial. This was evident in 2014 in its response to the Trojan Horse affair in Birmingham, which will be examined in detail in the next chapter. The MCB's response was to lambast critics of the Muslim individuals and groups involved as conducting a 'witch hunt'.[17] Perhaps this is unsurprising, since one of its former senior staff, Tahir Alam, was implicated in the scandal. As journalist John Ware observes, the MCB has 'a reflex tendency to dismiss criticism of such ['extremist'] beliefs as "Islamophobic" and motivated by a right-wing "neo-con" agenda'.[18]

This denial of Muslim 'non-violent extremism', as defined by the government in terms of a rejection of British values, may be interpreted as concealing certain realities, such as the preaching of enmity for non-Muslims in MCB-affiliated mosques and the unequal treatment of women at MCB-affiliated *shari'a* councils. But it may also be interpreted as a denial of the *way* in which such realities are classified and understood. Denials of non-violent but 'extremist' acts committed by Muslims are effectively *a rejection of the government's monopoly on the discourse of values.* They express a symbolic conflict in which the stakes include the way in which Muslims and Islam are perceived, as well as how 'Britishness' may be understood. Reflecting on the MCB's fall from government favour, former MCB leader Daud Abdullah opines, 'It was a one-way, one-track process: These are the rules, our values, you take it or leave it.'[19] The MCB and the government are not merely engaged in a conflict of values, but also a conflict of vision relating to the fundamental way in which the social world is seen and in which such values obtain their worth.

MCB leaders have sometimes publicly endorsed 'British values', but done so by absorbing them into their own narrative as *Islamic* values. In January 2015, for example, MCB secretary general Shuja Shafi gave a talk at a conference organised by the 100 Group entitled 'British Values are Islamic Values'.[20] Citing David Cameron's description of British values as including belief in freedom, the tolerance of others, personal and social responsibility, and respect for the rule of law, Shafi stated that such values are 'indeed Islamic values and we should champion them'. British values are thus re-classified as Islamic values. That the latter takes precedence in terms of providing the perceptual and moral framework in which the former make sense is suggested in Shafi's statement that – while the MCB has 'no objection to British values' – what inspires Muslims 'to seek the common good' are '*the values of our faith*'.[21] Others in the revivalist network, such as Muhammad Abdul Bari, similarly conceive of British values as Islamic in the language of 'universal values'.[22] Anas Altikriti, who also champions universal values, goes as far to say that the term 'British values' has 'no meaning whatsoever'.[23]

Contesting the notion of 'extremism'

The concept of British values was introduced into political parlance in the context of security concerns and in this context is inseparable from a certain concept of extremism. In the same way that the notion of British values is a point of contention for the government and the MCB, so is that of extremism. The MCB associates extremism with violence and it therefore renounces and disassociates itself from it. But, it asserts, 'Anyone who eschews violence and wants to engage by democratic means should be encouraged to do so, no matter how difficult their opinions may be for some.'[24] The MCB is 'against the singling out of particular mosques, imams, charities, or student societies', regardless of their possibly radicalising effects. Non-violent extremism is rejected out of principle, rather than as an empirical matter. This is because, in Murad's words, much of the prevalent vocabulary, concepts and theories in relation to terrorism and radicalisation 'remain deeply muddled and misguided'.[25]

Perhaps this is unsurprising, for the MCB's concept of extremism stems from a different intellectual lineage than the government's. It has an Islamic epistemological heritage. Using the terminology of the Muslim Brotherhood's spiritual guide, Yusuf al-Qaradawi, the MCB views itself as taking a 'middle path' between 'extremism' and what it calls 'rejection'. This was apparent in March 2009, when the umbrella group convened a meeting of over 200 Muslim activists and community leaders to discuss proposed changes to the government's counter-terrorism strategy.[26] In addition to contesting the government's definition of extremism – which it declared was 'dictated by xenophobic commentators' – it stated that, 'Islam is the religion of the middle way that rejects any form of extremism'. In May 2015, the MCB organised a seminar to explore 'the implications of increasing counter terror legislation and rising extremism, and how peaceful Muslims caught in the middle can navigate the terrain drawing on the middle path traditions of Islam'.[27] Former MCB secretary general Muhammad Abdul Bari gave the keynote talk on the subject of 'Islam's Middle Path: Between Rejection & Extremism', again drawing upon al-Qaradawi's frame of reference. In November of the same year, MCB held a conference entitled, 'Terrorism and Extremism: How Should British Muslims Respond?'. One of its resolutions included the recognition that it had to do more to convey the message that 'the normative understanding of Islam' rejects violence and upholds 'the middle path'.[28]

Abdul Bari articulates the MCB's notion of extremism succinctly as 'rigidity, fanaticism, and radicalism'.[29] Muslims may be extremists by 'misunderstanding' their faith either by committing violent acts or isolating themselves from the mainstream society. Neither may be condoned from this point of view because of the belief that Islam ought to be spread beyond the Muslim population without coercion. Abdul Bari describes 'rejection', on the other hand, as a 'libertarian attitude, laxity, or so-called liberalism'. In fact, both of these positions are viewed as extremes. Between what amounts to violence or self-segregation and secularism – all of which are deemed extremist – he asserts, 'we have to take the middle path, the path that Allah *subhanahu wa ta'ala* has given us'. This understanding of extremism, shared by the Islamic Forum of Europe,[30] is inextricable from a certain Islamic perspective: what the MCB deems as extreme is measured not in relation to what the government describes as British values, but in relation to the proper practice of Islam, which serves as the middle ground. 'Extremism' thus obtains its meaning from an entirely different normative basis.

Contesting the symbolic authority to speak for Islam

For revivalist Muslims, contention over the concept of extremism is inextricable from contention over the understanding of Islam. While the government has often expressed the view that Islam is a 'religion of peace' and that Islam-inspired terrorism or extremism is a 'misunderstanding' of the faith – a view shared by the MCB – the umbrella body sees itself in a struggle with the state to control the representation of Islam.[31] The MCB says that it agrees with the government that those who call for the murder of innocent civilians present 'a distorted interpretation of Islam', but it firmly rejects the government's authority to classify Islam. Expressing concern 'as to who will be the judge of what a "distorted interpretation of Islam" really is', it professes that 'the idea of the state or police arbitrating theological "distortion" is especially worrying'.[32] Any effort by the government to classify what Islam is or isn't, states the MCB, amounts to the promotion of 'state-sponsored sectarianism'. In response to Peter Clarke's report on the Trojan Horse affair, the MCB contested the observation that 'a hardline and politicised strand of Sunni Islam'[33] was being pushed in some Birmingham schools, asserting, 'It is not for the state to define the theological boundaries of the Islamic faith and to create an "approved version of Islam".'[34]

The MCB's conflict of vision and values with government authority is inseparable from a symbolic conflict with other Muslims over the representation of their faith. This relates not just to the right to advocate changes in policy on behalf of British Muslims, but to the possession of the symbolic authority to influence the public perception and understanding of Islam. Murad states that 'the MCB cannot represent anyone but its many affiliates'.[35] But the MCB clearly seeks to represent more than the 500 or so organisations under its umbrella by presenting itself as the most authentic voice for British Muslims and by striving to establish an understanding of Islam – one consistent with a long-term vision of a society in which it is willingly embraced by all – that is contentious from a variety of other Muslim perspectives.

The MCB's engagement in a symbolic conflict with other Muslims is apparent in its consistent rejection of the association of violent acts with

Islam by Muslims who see such acts as *jihad* for the sake of pleasing Allah. It is also apparent in Murad's rejection of the practice of *takfir*, the declaration of Muslims as non-Muslim made most commonly by violent jihadists and non-violent rejectionist groups such as Hizb ut-Tahrir.[36] Decrying the 'arrogance' of those who 'claim that they can pronounce on the relationship that any of the rest of us have with Allah', Murad is blind to the irony of his own declarations that such Muslims have themselves misunderstood Islam and hijacked it for merely political ends.

Furthermore, under Sacranie's leadership, the MCB was adamant in classifying Ahmadi Muslims as non-Muslims, a position it has not publicly disavowed.[37] In April 2016, responding to pressure to clarify its position, the MCB stated that since 'the Ahmadi community' does not subscribe to the 'cornerstone' tenet of Islam that Muhammad is its final messenger, it could not represent the Ahmadis as Muslims.[38] Stopping short of explicitly declaring Ahmadis to be non-Muslim, it added that Muslims should not be obliged to classify Ahmadis as 'Muslim'.

The MCB has also clashed with secular, reformist Muslim groups, such as Quilliam and the Sufi Muslim Council, for whom Islam ought to be a matter of personal worship, rather than a religious moral code arbitrated by the state in the public space, for example in schools.[39] Such clashes have occasionally spilled out into the media.

In 2008, for example, the MCB initially supported a marriage contract produced by the Muslim Institute for use by Muslims wishing to have an Islamic marriage (*nikah*). As Ed Husain, co-founder of Quilliam, explains, 'The new Muslim marriage contract sought to update and develop *fiqh*, or Muslim personal jurisprudence, by shifting the power balance in a marriage to empower women to trigger divorce, feel safe from rape or abuse, prevent husbands from taking second wives, and set up accommodation separated from a husband's parents.'[40] Traditionally, Muslim women require a *wali*, or male guardian, to oversee and consent to the marriage, plus male witnesses. The new contract waived the requirement for a *wali* and stipulated that witnesses can be women and even non-Muslims. The MCB quickly withdrew its support for the contract, clarifying that it had misplaced its trust in those leading the initiative, whose attempts to 're-invent' *shari'a* towards a 'modern' or 'reformist' view it described as 'misguided' and 'incorrect'.[41] Ibrahim Mogra, the MCB's former assistant secretary general, defended the decision, asserting that *shari'a* is the domain of Muslim theologians and jurists, and that they are 'clear' that Muslim brides-to-be are required in Islamic law to be represented by their male guardians.[42]

Contesting the symbolic authority to represent Muslims

The MCB's claim to represent a diversity of Islamic perspectives is dubious, as is its assumption that it provides the most authentic voice for Britain's Muslims. Ignoring the other Muslim groups that the government has engaged with in recent years, Mogra portrays the MCB as the necessary voice for British Muslims that is provided neither by Muslim politicians, who represent their constituents rather than Muslims' needs, nor the mosques. In sidelining the MCB, says Mogra, the government is denying Muslim communities of political representation.[43] His view is echoed by others, including Saleem Kidwai, the secretary general of the Muslim Council of Wales. '[Y]ou must talk to the Muslim Council of Britain,' states Kidawi, 'because it is the largest organization. You can talk to think-tanks but they are not the grassroots groups – the MCB has got the mandate from 500 organizations who represent Muslims from all walks of life.'[44]

However, the MCB's representativeness is questionable in terms of how many mosques fall within its network and how many British Muslims view it as representing their interests. Mehmood Naqshbandi calculates that mosques managed by MCB affiliates total just 12 per cent of all mosques in Britain.[45] The MCB represents half or more of all Jama'at- and Ikhwan-related mosques in the country, but less than half of the mosques belonging to any other 'faction'. Deobandi mosques comprise the largest number of MCB-affiliated mosques, but these comprise a small proportion of the total in Britain. Perhaps more significant in indicating the representativeness of the MCB as a national interlocutionary body, according to a 2007 survey, only 6 per cent British Muslims consider the MCB as representing their views.[46] A more recent poll, conducted by ICM in 2016, found that the MCB 'was identified by just 9% of those who preferred to engage via Muslim organisations', which was 20 per cent of all Muslims polled. This proportion, it was noted, 'amounts to just 2% of the Muslim sample population'.[47]

Humayun Ansari, in his comprehensive history of Muslims in Britain, *The Infidel Within*, states that the MCB has 'made no claim to be the "sole" representative of "true" Islam or the "whole" of the British Muslim community'.[48] This is not quite accurate. While it may not have publicly declared as such, the MCB quite clearly views itself as speaking for Muslims as an entire group, rather than for just its affiliates. In the description of its aims and vision it consistently refers to 'the' Muslim community as the singular constituency it seeks to advocate for, unify and empower.[49] The same assumption that it represents all British Muslims is apparent in the language it employs in official lobbying. 'The Muslim community', it has advocated in parliament, 'would like to see the early introduction of a law that makes it a criminal offence to vilify any religious belief'.[50] In its 2016–17 annual report, the MCB also describes as 'vital' its work 'representing the voice of the Muslim Community'.[51]

Furthermore, in deriding some Muslim groups as unrepresentative of British Muslims and presenting itself as the most authoritative alternative – without which Muslims would lack a political voice – the MCB quite clearly seeks to speak for all British Muslims, rather than a select few. And in denouncing some Muslim groups as misrepresenting Islam and in judging what is a correct or incorrect interpretation of *shari'a*, the MCB clearly claims the authority to speak for Islam. The authority it vies for is both political, in seeking legal and policy changes, and symbolic, in seeking recognition for its point of view from both government officials and Muslim communities. As noted above, this authority has been challenged by the government, as it casts the MCB within a narrative of national values and non-violent extremism. It has also been challenged by observers who note its slim base of support within the overall Muslim population.

Other revivalist interlocutors

The MCB is not the only revivalist group that has an interlocutionary role with the government regarding Muslims' interests in Britain. While not receiving media attention comparable with MCB, there are other, smaller organisations that specialise in certain sectors, including education, law and policing, which have a history of engagement with the authorities. Some of these are highlighted below. Each of these organisations brings to the interface with government a mode of advocacy that, while legal and non-violent, is framed by a vision of society and a set of values that ultimately clash with Britain's liberal democratic culture.

The Muslim Educational Trust

The Muslim Educational Trust (MET), an affiliate of the MCB, began lobbying and advising central and local governments from the early 1970s for specific arrangements in schools for Muslim children and for revisions of the national school curriculum according to Islamic principles. In Britain, each Local Education Authority (LEA) is required by law to have a Standing Advisory Council on Religious Education (SACRE). MET representatives have served on SACREs all over Britain. In 1993, it obtained government approval for an Islamic studies syllabus in secondary schools, for which it has provided teachers and teaching materials. Urfan Khaliq notes that MET participates and assists in Islamic studies lessons 'in the majority' of schools in the Midlands.[52] MET states that it has persuaded LEAs to recognise and accept the 'special needs' of Muslim pupils in state schools, including halal food, 'appropriate' dress for Muslim girls, dress for sports for Muslim boys and girls, exemption from mixed-sex swimming lessons, exemption from some aspects of sex education, facility for prayers, and the inclusion of its approved Islamic books in school libraries.[53] Ansari concurs with this, attributing changes in schools, including the provision of Islamic religious education, to MET.[54]

Yet, in some respects, MET's work is highly contentious in presenting a set of values and a vision of society that clearly conflict with that of the liberal democratic mainstream. In an introductory text on Islam – which, according to Ed Husain, is used widely in British Muslim schools – MET founder and director Ghulam Sarwar presents Islam as a 'complete system of life' in which politics of a highly contentious nature and religion are inextricable.[55] This book, *Islam: Beliefs and Teachings*, commends the Muslim Brotherhood and Jama'at-i-Islami for working towards the 'establishment of Allah's law in Allah's land', confessing a hope that 'a real Islamic state will emerge from these efforts' for the benefit of the world.[56] As Husain recalls,

> In my school, a Jamat-e-Islami activist named Abdul Rabb represented the MET and awarded us trophies and medals for our performance in MET exams. Ostensibly it all seemed harmless, but the personnel all belonged to Jamat-e-Islami front organizations in Britain. Their key message was that Islam was not merely a religion but also an ideology that sought political power and was beginning to make headway.[57]

For Sarwar, 'The introduction of an Islamic education system should be an integral part of the efforts worldwide to establish Islam as an all-encompassing way of life.'[58] In his book used in British schools, he describes such an ideal way of life as including the legal sanction of polygamy and arranged marriages and the prohibition of the 'free mixing of grown-up boys and girls'. Children in British schools learning about Islam from this resource are taught that men and women have different duties defined by Allah, and that to aspire for 'total equality between a man and a woman' goes 'against nature'.[59]

This teaching strikes a chord with Mawdudi's view of the different roles of men and women assigned to them by nature, which he detailed in his book *Purdah and the Status of Women in Islam*.[60] It is shared by other revivalists in Britain, such as Zahid Parvez, the director of the Islamic Foundation's Markfield Institute of Higher Education. He states,

> Men and women due to their biological differences are assigned different primary but complementary roles by Islam, and any confusion in these roles will inevitably lead to internal tensions and a decline in the family … . As a norm, men are the bread-winners and women attend to the children and domestic work.[61]

An 'over emphasis on rights' and a 'confusion in gender roles', says Parvez, is weakening the family unit, the most important building block for the rebuilding of society in accordance with Allah's divine will.[62]

The Association of Muslim Schools UK

In recent years, advocacy for Muslim education has become the domain of the Association of Muslim Schools UK (AMS-UK), also an MCB affiliate. Unlike MET, AMS-UK is a national membership organisation. As such, it has been able to build on MET's advocacy work by developing relationships with and representing the 150-odd independent Muslim schools throughout Britain. Its influence is suggested by its formal recognition by the Department for Education (DfE) as the national representative body for Muslim faith schools in the country. In 2005, it was given financial support by DfE's precursor, the Department of Education and Skills, to the sum of £100,000, to assist 60 or so of its affiliated schools integrate into the state maintained sector.[63] AMS-UK has played an active lobbying role for increased funding for its affiliate schools. Furthermore, along with the Christian Schools Trust (CST), it was successful lobbying the government for a separate inspections body for faith schools. In 2008, AMS-UK and CST jointly established the Bridge Schools Inspectorate, which until recently conducted inspections of their affiliate schools on behalf of the government. Some of AMS-UK's leaders have enjoyed roles advising the government on other educational issues. In 2010, for example, AMS-UK's former chairman, Mohamed Mukadam, and its current chair, Ashfaque Choudhury, helped co-author a report for the Department for Communities and Local Government, entitled, *The training and development of Muslim Faith Leaders: Current practice and future possibilities.*[64]

AMS-UK's website claims that 'British values', 'such as democracy, the rule of law, mutual respect, tolerance, freedom of speech and freedom of association', are examples of 'universal values'.[65] This is the same phrase used by the MCB and revivalist individuals such as Anas Altikriti. But AMS-UK suggests that such values derive from the 'traditional authentic Islamic values as taught in the Qur'an and through the example of the Prophet Muhammad'. And, although the organisation does not openly challenge the state, there are indications that its leadership sees itself as promoting a vision of society and a set of values that differ significantly with the liberal democratic values that the state strives to uphold. Josephine Squires observes that AMS-UK claims the government 'wishes to maintain a Judeo-Christian monopoly in controlling the minds of youth in the state education system'.[66] AMS-UK seems to view itself as fighting an ideological battle against the state and the liberal democratic culture of Britain for not just the minds of young Muslims but also their souls. Mukadam, states that Muslim children need to be 'saved' from a secular educational environment.[67] The 'first and foremost' duty of Muslim parents, he asserts, is the transference of Islamic faith and values to their children, without which they would enter 'the fire of hell'. For Mukadam, the prioritisation of Islam as a religion over the human rights of individuals who happen to be Muslim is further expressed in his belief that Muslim apostates in an Islamic state must be killed, since this is the penalty ordained by Allah and prescribed by the *shari'a*.[68]

Mukadam was AMS-UK chairman at the time that an AMS-UK member school's website stated in terms inimical to 'British' values and social integration – 'If we oppose the lifestyle of the West, then it does not seem sensible that the teachers and the system which represents that lifestyle should educate our children.''[69] In 1999, the school under Mukadam's own leadership was criticised by Ofsted (the government's Office for Standards in Education,

Children's Services and Skills) for 'its failure to prepare pupils to take their place in the wider society'.[70] In another AMS-UK school, undercover filming 'discovered that Muslim children are being taught religious apartheid and social segregation'.[71] Although AMS-UK cannot be held responsible for what goes on in any particular school, it has been accused of whitewashing such 'extremism' in its role within the Bridge Schools Inspectorate (BSI).[72] These concerns appeared well founded when in June 2015 the government announced its plans to close BSI later that year for failing to identify 'warning signs of extremism and radicalisation in school settings'.[73] In 2014, *The Sunday Times* reported that AMS-UK was being investigated by the Department for Education 'amid claims that some of their inspectors support fundamentalist Islamic beliefs'.[74]

AMS-UK's inspectors include its vice-chair, Tahir Alam.[75] A former assistant secretary general of the MCB, Alam is linked to the Trojan Horse scandal, which will be covered in chapter 6. Another inspector – a co-founder and executive committee member of AMS-UK – is Ibrahim Hewitt. A former assistant director at MET and a former MCB official, Hewitt is the head of Al-Aqsa school in Leicester. He advocates that, in an ideal Islamic state, adulterers should be stoned to death and that homosexuals and fornicators should be lashed.[76] Muslim schools, for Hewitt, are not just for educational purposes, but for safeguarding the future of the Muslim *umma*: Islam as a way of life takes priority over its Muslim adherents; the 'community' or nation takes priority over individuals.[77] Hewitt is also a trustee of IBERR, the International Board of Educational Research and Resources, which was established to implement the aims of the First World Conference on Islamic Education held in Makkah in 1977.[78] The conference statement affirmed the 'complete submission to Allah on the level of the individual, the community and humanity at large' as the 'ultimate aim of Muslim Education'.[79]

The founder of AMS-UK, Mohammed Akram Khan-Cheema, is also linked to IBERR. He is the chairman of IBERR's executive committee. At the AMS-UK 2013 conference, consistent with a revivalist perspective in which Islam is viewed as an alternative way of life, he gave a workshop entitled 'Islamification of the whole school curriculum'.[80] Also speaking at this conference was Farah Ahmed, a founding trustee of the Islamic Shakhsiyah Foundation and former member of Hizb ut-Tahrir. She has attacked the National Curriculum for 'pushing the idea of religious tolerance' and its 'systematic indoctrination' of Muslim children, while criticising 'attempts to integrate Muslim children' into British society as an effort 'to produce new generations that reject Islam'.[81]

Despite its rhetoric of upholding British values, AMS-UK and at least some of its schools have a very different understanding from mainstream views in Britain of what constitutes sex discrimination. In October 2017, a court of appeal ruled that one of AMS-UK's schools, Al-Hijrah, a mixed-sex state school, had caused unlawful discrimination by formally segregating boys and girls from the age of nine.[82] The school's segregation policy prevented any mixing of girls and boys, in classrooms, corridors, play areas, at school clubs or on school trips. The appeal was made by the government's schools inspection body, Ofsted, which argued successfully that the school had breached the 2010 Equalities Act. The judgment, welcomed by the Equality and Human Rights Commission, overturned an earlier high court ruling which found that Ofsted inspectors were wrong to penalise the school for sex-segregating children.

The inspectors reported a serious failure of leadership at the school and the discovery of 'extremist' literature in the school library. According to the inspection report, these books 'included derogatory comments about and the incitement of violence towards women'.[83] According to the court judgment, one of the books stated 'that a wife is not allowed to refuse sex to her husband'. This echoes the view of Sheikh Maulana Abu Sayeed, president of the Islamic Sharia Council, that rape within marriage is impossible.[84] It is also supported by orthodox interpretations of *shari'a*, as articulated in a book recommended as a reliable guide to *shari'a* by MCB deputy secretary general, Omer El-Hamdoon.[85] Another book in the school's library stated, in line with MET's view, 'that women are commanded to obey their husbands and fulfil their domestic duties'. A further two books stated that a husband may in certain circumstances beat his wife, 'provided that this is not done 'harshly''. This is consistent with the view articulated by Yusuf al-Qaradawi, the spiritual guide of the global Muslim Brotherhood and chair of the European Council for Fatwa and Research, the main body providing guidance for Muslims to live *shari'a*-compliant lives in Europe's Muslim-minority context.[86]

Speaking after the appeal court's decision, Amanda Spielman, Her Majesty's Chief Inspector of Schools, said, 'This is discrimination and is wrong. It places these boys and girls at a disadvantage for life beyond the classroom and the workplace, and fails to prepare them for life in modern Britain.'[87] A month after the ruling, in November 2017, AMS-UK attempted to join a legal action to seek leave to appeal to the supreme court for a review of the ruling, but this was rejected by an appeal court judgment.[88] After the final court ruling, AMS-UK's chairman, Ashfaque Choudhury, warned that it may create a conflict between the association's role to ensure its member schools obey the law and its role to ensure they act in accordance with Islamic teachings and practices.

The final court judgment on sex-segregation marks an important point in a conflict of values between revivalist groups and Britain's liberal democracy. Following the ruling, no mixed-sex state school is legally allowed to apply such policies. A month after the appeal court's decision, however, AMS-UK admitted that more of its affiliated schools were still operating strict sex-segregation policies. The appeal court judges said that because the education secretary and Ofsted had failed to identify the problem earlier, the affected schools could have time to 'put their houses in order'.[89] But Ofsted has made it clear that 'it will apply a consistent approach to all similarly organised schools'. This ruling presents a legal challenge to sex-segregation in Islamic schools, but also to the religious values – as espoused by Sarwar, Parvez and other revivalists involved in education – that underpin such practices. However, according to Colin Diamond, the education chief of Birmingham city council that runs the school, it may lead to an increase in home schooling, sex-segregation and exposure to 'extremist ideologies'.[90]

The Association of Muslim Lawyers

The Association of Muslim Lawyers (AML) was established in 1993 to 'promote the legal rights of Muslims and the availability of advice in accordance with the Shari'ah of Islam'.[91] According to its own literature, it has worked with the Commission for Racial Equality, City Hall, the Home Office, the House of Commons and the House of Lords, as well as other Muslim organisations including the MCB, of which it is an affiliate. Although neither as active as AMS-UK, nor as connected to government agencies as MSF has been, AML has played a key role in advocating changes in law in the interests of Britain's Muslims. Most notably, it campaigned for an extension of England's (now abolished) blasphemy law to cover Islam and a redefinition of the crime of incitement to hatred to protect Muslims. AML states that the government has a duty 'to secure the basic rights of freedom of religion, freedom to practice one's religion and freedom to educate one's children in accordance with one's religion'.[92] For AML, this duty entails the full incorporation of Muslim personal law into English law, so that the 'decisions of properly constituted Shari'a courts will have to be recognised by the English civil courts as being legally binding and enforceable'.[93]

Much of AML's campaign work has been led by its co-founder and former deputy chair, Ahmad Thomson, who is a committee member of the London-based Islamic Sharia Council. In 2002, on behalf of AML, he made written and oral representations to the House of Lords Select Committee on Religious Offences. These proposals clearly conflict with liberal democratic values, including the freedom of speech and equality before the law. Anti-blasphemy legislation, he urged, ought to be updated to criminalise behaviour that is 'likely to shock and outrage the feelings of the general body of believers'.[94] He added, 'it is not just the people who follow the religion, but it is *the religion itself* which has to be protected'.[95] This prioritisation of group rights over individual rights clearly conflicts with a fundamental tenet of liberal democratic law and culture.

These lobbying efforts, which have their roots in the 1989 Rushdie Affair, were part of a campaign involving the MCB, ICHR, MSF and others, to criminalise the criticism of Islam, the Qur'an and Muhammad, with a prison sentence of up to seven years. Although new offences 'involving stirring up hatred against persons on racial or religious grounds' were created in the Racial and Religious Hatred Act 2006, in the interests of free expression, clauses criminalising the insulting and abuse of religion were removed from the final draft of the act.[96] Under the act, religious hatred has to be shown to be intentionally stirred up.

In his representations to the select committee, Thomson lobbied to have some aspects of *shari'a* incorporated into English law. These included the statutory right of Muslims to have prayer breaks at work and for Islamic marriages to be legally recognised, as well as that of Muslim men to marry up to four wives.[97] He also argued that the 'freedom of religion' trumps gender and sexuality equality:

> [W]here there is such a conflict of rights – for example, between the right to freely practice one's religion on the one hand, and on the other hand, the right not to be treated less favourably because of one's gender or sexual orientation – there is a statutory requirement to pay particular regard to the former rather than the latter.[98]

In other words, according to Thomson, institutionalised discrimination against women and homosexuals should be legally sanctioned if it is part of religious practice. Furthermore, religious schools, he asserted, have the right to discriminate in not employing those who do not share their faith. The assumption is that religion ought to be taught not critically but doctrinally, that the teaching of religion itself ought to be religious rather than disinterested and educational.

Thomson cites the European Convention on Human Rights and the Human Rights Act 1998 (HRA) as the basis of the British government's duty to protect the 'freedom of religion' and incorporate the personal aspects of Islamic law into state law. He refers to Article 9 of the HRA to justify separate legal jurisdictions for different religious groups, including Muslims. Yet, paradoxically, Thomson views 'secular human rights law' as an imposition 'in the name of equality'.[99] He considers 'man-made' law – which includes all Western legal systems and statutes – as inferior to Islamic law. He believes that the *shari'a* – which, he confesses, allows '*humane* slavery'[100] – is the final 'legal modality' of civilisation and one that his lobbying efforts are presumably directed to.[101] Thomson views the legal changes that he has lobbied for in Britain on behalf of AML as practical 'for the time being' until 'the democratic wish of the majority of its people' is for British law to be fully compliant with the *shari'a*.[102]

The Muslim Safety Forum

The Muslim Safety Forum (MSF) was, until recently, 'the key advisory body for the Police Service', providing advice 'on matters of safety and security from *the* Muslim perspective'.[103] It was established, in its own words, to challenge the 'unfair focus on the Muslim community when it came to policing activities and enforcement of anti-terror policing legislation'.[104] As an indication of its influence, it met on a regular basis with senior representatives of the Association of Chief Police Officers, the Metropolitan Police Service (MPS), the Home Office, the Crown Prosecution Service and other official bodies. The agreement between the Metropolitan Police Service and MSF stated that the police will 'use the MSF as a consultation body to help formulate policy or practice'.[105] Composed of numerous other revivalist organisations, including the MCB, the Federation of Student Islamic Societies (FOSIS), the Islamic Forum of Europe (IFE) and the East London Mosque, MSF was accused of being 'anti-establishment' and unrepresentative of Britain's diverse Muslim communities. Subsequently, in 2012, it was replaced by the London Muslim Communities Forum (LMCF).

On The Islam Channel's 'Politics and Media Show' in July of that year, MSF chair, Azad Ali, claimed not to know why MSF had been side-lined by the newly formed LMCF.[106] Yet, his political views had for some years been troubling to government officials and other observers, who had noted his 'strong track record of extremism'.[107] He had praised the al-Qaeda-linked cleric Anwar al-Awlaki; denied that the Mumbai *jihad* terror attacks were terrorism; and quoted, apparently approvingly, a statement advocating the killing of British troops in Iraq made by Huthaifa Azzam, son of the architect of the global *jihad*, Abdullah Azzam, upon whom he has also lavished praise.[108] For these comments, he was suspended from his job as a civil servant in January 2009, but returned to work in June of that year after being cleared in an internal investigation. Ali, a senior member of IFE, addressed a Muslim readership on the organisation's website, stating, 'we are all working our socks off, in different ways, for the resurgence of the Khilafa [caliphate]'.[109] Writing on the political blog, *Harry's place*, David Toube states that Ali's 'politics are as great a threat to our democratic, liberal and pluralist system as any white fascist or far left extremist'.[110]

Although MSF has been marginalised by the government, Ali remains its chairman and is very active in numerous other groups. According to the website for Muslim Engagement and Development (MEND), in which he plays a leading role, he also sits on the National Accountability Board for Schedule 7 Stops with the police and Home Office. He is a member of the Independent Police Complaints Commission's Community Advisory Group and the Home Office's Trust and Confidence Community Panel.[111] As detailed in chapter 2, he has also been a member of the MCB's Central Working Committee and was the chair of its Membership Committee.

The National Association of Muslim Police

The National Association of Muslim Police (NAMP) was launched by the MCB in 2007 to support Muslim officers and staff within the police service. Like other organisations in the revivalist network, it has a *da'wa* role. It seeks to 'promote understanding and awareness of Islam' within the police by advising on cultural and religious issues. Yet, similarly to MSF, NAMP's aspirations include 'bridging the gap between the police and the Muslim community', as well as tackling 'Islamophobia'.[112] Prior to MSF's marginalisation, the two organisations collaborated on some issues. According to

Azad Ali, the two organisations worked together to improve the recruitment and retention of Muslim police officers. NAMP has also collaborated with LMCF, which appears to some extent to have taken MSF's concern with Islamophobia forward.

Composed of local police associations and serving police officers, NAMP, unlike the other organisations highlighted in this section of the chapter, is situated within the institutional structure of the state. Perhaps because of this, it has a less contentious relationship with the government. However, its choice of organisational partners and attitudes towards government policy, particularly regarding counter-terrorism, suggest it is at least sympathetic to a view that contests both the authority of the state to determine the national values upon which British society is based and the mainstream understanding of Islam in Britain.

One of NAMP's key organisational partners is MEND. In November 2014, the two organisations held a joint conference, 'Challenging Islamophobia: Building Communities', at which NAMP's president, Asif Sadiq, was a keynote speaker.[113] LMCF promoted the event. Sadiq was also a speaker at MEND's rebranding launch earlier in the year.[114] In its previous incarnation as iEngage, notes Andrew Gilligan, MEND 'consistently defended fundamentalist organisations such as the East London Mosque and the Islamic Forum of Europe'.[115] It also undermined and discredited spokespeople for secular interpretations of Islam, 'defended the right of radical Muslim preachers to come to Britain … and opposed the ban on extremist group Hizb-ut-Tahrir from university campuses'.[116] MEND's founder and managing director, Sufyan Ismail, is a promoter of Haitham al-Haddad, a preacher and former judge at the Islamic Sharia Council.[117] Al-Haddad states that women are inferior to men and that wives ought to obey their husbands; that homosexuality is a 'crime against humanity'; that adulterers found guilty ought to be stoned to death; and that once an Islamic state is in place, it is obliged to wage 'proactive' *jihad* to establish Islam as a global force.[118]

NAMP has also a close relationship with the London-based Islamic Human Rights Commission (IHRC), recommending British Muslims to report crimes to it.[119] However, for its alleged links to the Iranian regime it has been described as a 'promoter of Khomeini jihadism in the UK'.[120] IHRC openly supports Hezbollah and holds an annual Al-Quds Day, where protesters call for the annihilation of Israel. Some of its advisers, including Hamid Algar, are advocates of *jihad* for Islam's eventual global hegemony.[121] IHRC is also a loyal supporter of Yusuf al-Qaradawi, who advocates suicide bombings in Israel and calls for the Muslim conquest of Europe through non-violent *jihad*. At the time of the cleric's visit to Britain in 2004, the metropolitan police commissioner passed a dossier on al-Qaradawi's sermons to the Crown Prosecution Service with a view to prosecution. Raza Kazim, an IHRC spokesman and trustee of its charitable trust, considered this as an 'insult' and in protest walked out of a meeting with the police, with which it used to meet regularly regarding 'the treatment of Muslims at the hands of the police and others'.[122]

Both MEND and IHRC encourage a perception in Britain that Muslims are under siege. A government-commissioned review into opportunity and social integration published in December 2016 stated that 'the influence of extremist organisations who promote a grievance narrative' was likely one of the reasons for a concerning divergence of views of some Muslims from the general population on, for example, 'sympathy for extremist or radical actions'.[123] Although no organisation is named in the review, MEND and IHRC do promote such a narrative, stoking negative Muslim sentiment towards the British government if not integration within Britain. NAMP's close relationship with these two groups suggests it too is involved in, or at least condones, the aggravation of negative attitudes towards Britain amongst British Muslims. Along with MEND and IHRC, NAMP seeks to change not just government policy, but also a public (and Muslim) mind-set. Indicating its involvement in a symbolic struggle to speak for Islam, NAMP blames the government's foreign policy and 'Islamophobia' for terrorism in Britain committed by Muslims in the name of their faith.[124] Echoing the narrative of MEND and IHRC, it denies the documented religious inspiration for these attacks and plots. In accord with these groups, it also condemns the government's preference to engage with Muslim organisations other than the MCB, such as Quilliam.

Local government: the Islamic Forum of Europe

True to their characterisation as 'participationists', some of the groups in the revivalist network – including MEND, the MCB, the Islamic Forum of Europe (IFE) and the Muslim Association of Britain (MAB) – have campaigned for Muslims' active participation in electoral politics. The Electoral Commission made MEND an 'official partner' for registering Muslim voters for the 2015 general election, despite its endorsement of Muslim clerics, such as Abu Eesa Niamatullah and Haitham al-Haddad, who, while condoning democratic elections, preach against secularism and liberal democratic values.[125] At least ten Labour and Conservative MPs joined the launch of the MEND's 'Muslim manifesto' in the House of Commons in March 2015.[126] That wasn't the first time the organisation had been embraced by the government. Its precursor, Engage, led by the MCB's Inyat Bunglawala, was invited to be the secretariat of a new All-Party Parliamentary Group on Islamophobia, whose inaugural meeting was held in the House of Commons in November 2010.

Some groups have been more directly involved in politics by supporting the election of local government councillors, mayors and members of parliament. IFE, for example, was instrumental in the success of George Galloway's Respect Party in the 2005 general election,[127] where Galloway – a supporter of Hamas and Hezbollah – won the seat for the London Borough of Bethnal Green and Bow.[128] At a dinner shortly after his victory at the East London Mosque, the home of IFE, he was recorded as saying, 'I am indebted more than I can say – more than it would be wise *for them* for me to say – to the Islamic Forum of Europe. I believe they played the decisive role.'[129] Some of the MAB's leading activists were also involved in the Respect Party. Anas Altikriti, for instance, gave up his MAB presidency to stand for Respect in Yorkshire and Humberside in the 2004 European Parliamentary elections. IFE was also involved in a group called 'Muslims 4 Ken', which unsuccessfully campaigned for Ken Livingstone's re-election as the mayor of London in 2008. The group was run by Azad Ali, IFE's community affairs co-ordinator, and Altikriti, an 'IFE ally'.[130]

But the most significant involvement of revivalist Islam in British politics was with IFE's infiltration of the Labour Party within the London Borough of Tower Hamlets and its involvement in Lutfur Rahman's successful campaign to become the mayor of the borough.[131] While it is difficult to measure the precise extent of the impact of IFE and Rahman's involvement in Tower Hamlets' local government, it has certainly empowered and encouraged groups whose values conflict with Britain's liberal democratic culture.

Rahman was elected as a Labour party councillor in 2008 and soon after won the leadership of the borough council. In October 2010, he became the borough's mayor after running as an independent candidate. Labour had dropped him as its party candidate over 'serious allegations' over both 'the eligibility of participating voters' and his 'conduct'.[132] Rahman governed the borough for five years until he was removed from office in April 2015 when a High Court hearing found him guilty of electoral fraud. Throughout this time, evidence emerged of his links with IFE, whose literature describes its commitment to change the 'very infrastructure of [Western] society, its institutions, its culture, its political order and its creed … from ignorance to Islam'.[133]

In his court judgement, Richard Mawrey QC asserted that the court had 'not heard a shred of credible evidence linking Mr Rahman with any extreme or fundamentalist Islamist movement'.[134] But if the court understood 'extreme' or 'fundamentalist' as connected with violence, then it is no surprise that it did not consider IFE in such terms. IFE is a revivalist, *dawa*-oriented organisation that operates within the law. The notion of and concern about *non*-violent extremism, which the government has begun to incorporate into government policy, is not necessarily shared throughout the political and legal establishments. Because of its legality, it was probably not a concern for the High Court.

However, despite Mawrey's dismissal of the claim that Rahman was linked to an 'extremist' movement, there are indications that Rahman was linked to IFE. Rahman was said by seven serving and former councillors to have gained his post as council leader with the help of IFE. The petition that led to the establishment of a directly elected mayor for Tower Hamlets was organised by the IFE activist Abjol Miah, who subsequently took a leading role in Rahman's 2010 campaign for mayorship. The manager of Rahman's campaign to become mayor, Bodrul Islam, admits Rahman enjoyed a 'strategic relationship' with IFE.[135] Most of his campaigners, he states, were 'either Respect or IFE activists'. Prior to Rahman's success in becoming mayor, another IFE activist, Abu Talha, confessed to an undercover reporter for Channel 4's *Dispatches* programme that IFE was planning to get 'one of our brothers' into that position.[136] He named Azad Ali, community affairs coordinator for IFE and a member of the MCB's central working committee, as one possible candidate.

Independently of the relationship between IFE and Rahman, there were indications that the organisation had infiltrated the council. In the *Dispatches* programme broadcast in March 2010, Abjol Miah, then a Tower Hamlets councillor as well as an IFE leader, was caught boasting on secret camera, 'We've consolidated ourselves now. We've got a lot of influence and power in the council, councillors, politicians'.[137] His IFE colleague, Abu Talha, claimed, 'Our brothers have gone into positions of influence, council positions.' These may include up to 30 councillors, the number of Muslim councillors in Tower Hamlets according to IFE's head of media and public relations, Abdullah Faliq.[138] IFE activists Miah and Talha, recorded by undercover reporters, described Tower Hamlets council – with its 15,000 staff and £1.1 billion budget – as their most impressive political achievement.[139] Such entryism was confirmed by Jim Fitzpatrick, then the Environment Minister and MP for Tower Hamlets. Interviewed by Andrew Gilligan for *Dispatches*, Fitzpatrick claimed that IFE had become, in effect, a secret party within Labour and other political parties:

> They are acting almost as an entryist organisation,' he said, 'placing people within the political parties, recruiting members to those political parties, trying to get individuals selected and elected so they can exercise political influence and power, whether it's at local government level or national level.[140]

Rahman wasn't the only IFE-linked individual to secure an elite political position in the borough council. In 2008, Lutfur Ali was appointed its assistant chief executive, the second highest civil servant position in the council with responsibility for grant funding. Ali's appointment was controversial, since he was hired by Rahman despite apparently lacking the proper credentials for the job. In this role, Ali oversaw a marked re-direction of funds from a variety of Muslim community organisations, including secularists such as Udichi Shilpi Ghoshthi, to those with ties to IFE.[141] These included Blyda and Elite Youth, which were closely linked to IFE in sharing numerous trustees and staff. Under Ali's leadership, the council decided to hand over its entire youth service for the west of the borough to a consortium in which Blyda and Elite Youth were to play a key role. Gilligan's reporting on these matters helped prompt Ali's resignation in March 2010.

Rahman too channelled millions of pounds into sympathetic groups, including 'IFE front organizations'. Gilligan reports that 'there was a clear diversion of funding away from secular bodies serving the whole community to faith-based or religious groups serving only sections of the community'.[142] While Muslims make up only 34.5 per cent of the borough's population, Muslim organisations received £858,500 (70%) of the £1,235,000 grants for community and economic engagement, and £334,500 (64%) of the £526,000 grants for children, schools and families. A similar pattern was evident in the allocation of grants for a community faith buildings support scheme, study support schemes, mother-tongue classes, youth and career advice services, and lifelong learning. Throughout his mayorship, Rahman never appointed one non-Muslim to a cabinet post, despite Muslims being a minority in the borough. According to Gilligan, Rahman was 'hostile or indifferent' to the non-Muslim heritage of the borough, one example being the attempted sell-off of the local history library, which was prevented by a backlash of protest.[143]

The beneficiaries of Rahman's Muslim favouritism – what Theresa May, then home secretary, referred to as 'divisive community politics' – included a number of 'IFE fronts' including the Osmani Trust.[144] Created from the merging of Blyda and Elite Youth, the Osmani Trust runs weekend schools, organises workshops in primary schools and works to 'help young people into education'.[145] Through this work, however, it likely that government money has helped pay for the dissemination of a worldview and moral values in young Muslims that clashes with Britain's liberal democratic culture. One of the managers at the trust, Muhammad Rabbani, trained recruits for IFE, informing them:

> Our goal is not simply to invite people and give *da'wah* [the call to Islam]. Our goal is to create the True Believer, to then mobilise those believers into an organised force for change who will carry out *da'wah, hisbah* [enforcement of Islamic morality] and *jihad* [struggle for Islam].[146]

He added that this will lead to 'social change and *iqamatud-deen*', which is translated by Jama'at-i-Islami as the 'Islamization of life'.[147] Rabbani now leads CAGE, an organisation that campaigns for Muslim prisoners, including convicted terrorists, and espouses the divisive view that Islam is under attack in Britain. In May 2017, he was charged under the Terrorism Act after refusing to provide police at Heathrow airport with the passwords to his mobile phone and laptop.[148]

Another IFE-related beneficiary of Rahman's largesse was the London Muslim Centre, which is closely linked to the East London Mosque (ELM) and serves as IFE's base. The centre and mosque has a documented history of promoting speakers who espouse a vision of the world and ethical values antithetical to liberal democracy and universal human rights.[149] These include Anwar al-Awlaki, al-Qaeda's late chief ideologue, alleged to have mentored the Fort Hood jihadist, Nidal Hasan, and the Detroit Bomber, Umar Farouk Abdulmutallab.[150] Al-Awlaki espoused the view that the goal of Islamic *jihad* is not just victory in Palestine, Iraq or Afghanistan, but the collapse of the 'system of *kufr* [unbelief] with global reach'.[151] Other speakers include Bilal Philips, an unindicted co-conspirator in the 1993 World Trade Center bombing, who advocates death for homosexuals and 'defends child marriages, wife beating, polygamy and killing apostates';[152] Abdullah Hasan, an IFE activist who praises Osama bin Laden and describes Jews as 'devil-worshippers';[153] Murtaza Khan, a primary school teacher and a keen advocate of the *shari'a*, including the punishment of stoning to death for adulterers;[154] and Abdul Rahman al-Sudais, a Saudi cleric who believes Muslims are locked in 'a war of faith, identity and existence' with Jews, who he describes as the 'worst of mankind'.[155]

The supremacy of Muslim over non-Muslim culture, misogyny, homophobia and antisemitism have been recurrent themes in many of the sermons of these and other speakers at ELM, which is intimately connected to IFE through overlapping trustees and staff. In March 2015 the then home secretary Theresa May noted these as serious concerns across Tower Hamlets, the only borough referred to by name in her speech that made explicit the government's new thinking on extremism.[156] Dean Godson of the think tank Policy Exchange describes IFE as 'a key ideological influence in Tower Hamlets'.[157] Without further research, however, it is difficult to ascertain the impact of IFE's political influence in the council upon local Muslim attitudes. But it is less problematic to observe both IFE's entryism into council politics and a conflict of vision and values that its activists and associates have often expressed.

This conflict is apparent in some of the borough's schools, including the London East Academy, which is managed by ELM. The school was warned by the then education secretary Nicky Morgan in November 2014, along with five other Muslim private schools in Tower Hamlets, to make urgent changes or face closure.[158] She claimed the schools were 'failing to prepare children for life in modern Britain'. This came in the wake of Ofsted chief Sir Michael Wilshaw's report, following unannounced inspections, that pupils were 'vulnerable to extremist influences and radicalisation'.[159] This was borne out in March 2015, when it was reported that Zubair Nur, a graduate of the London East Academy, had joined the Islamic State.[160]

Notes

1 Samuel Westrop, 'How to Radicalize an Entire London Borough', The Gatestone Institute, 5 May 2015. www.gatestoneinstitute.org/5677/tower-hamlets.

2 HM Government (2015).

3 'PM statement on Tunisia and European Council', British Government website, 29 June 2015. www.gov.uk/government/speeches/pm-statement-on-tunisia-and-european-council.

4 It should be noted that these are not the only fields of contention where a clash of values is apparent. Universities, prisons and mosques present three other kinds of institution in which such a clash has been reported and recognised by the government. Because of limited space, however, this book has had to omit consideration of these arenas of cultural conflict.

5 Hazel Blears, 'Our shunning of the MCB is not grandstanding', *The Guardian*, 25 March. www.theguardian.com/commentisfree/2009/mar/25/islam-terrorism.
6 For the text of the 'Istanbul Declaration', see 'A statement by the religious scholars and proselytisers (du'a) of the Islamic Nation (ummah) to all rulers and peoples concerning events in Gaza', published online at: http://hurryupharry.org/wp-content/uploads/2009/03/istpdf.pdf.
7 See MCB, 'Holocaust Memorial Ceremony MCB Regrets Exclusion of Palestinian Tragedy', MCB website, 25 January 2002, www.mcb.org.uk/holocaust-memorial-ceremony-mcb-regrets-exclusion-of-palestinian-tragedy/; and MCB, 'Holocaust Day: MCB regrets exclusion of Palestinian genocide', MCB website, 27 January 2003, www.mcb.org.uk/holocaust-day-mcb-regrets-exclusion-of-palestinian-genocide/.
8 Vikram Dodd, 'Muslim Council ends Holocaust memorial day boycott', *The Guardian*, 3 December 2007. www.theguardian.com/uk/2007/dec/03/secondworldwar.religion.
9 Duncan Gardham, 'Airline terror trial: The bomb plot to kill 10,000 people', *The Telegraph*, 7 September 2009. www.telegraph.co.uk/news/uknews/terrorism-in-the-uk/6153243/Airline-terror-trial-The-bomb-plot-to-kill-10000-people.html.
10 BBC News, '"Suicide videos": What they said', 4 April 2008. http://news.bbc.co.uk/2/hi/uk_news/7330367.stm.
11 Maher and Frampton (2013), p. 38.
12 Dominic Casciani, 'Minister backs new Muslim group', BBC News, 19 July 2006. http://news.bbc.co.uk/2/hi/uk_news/5193402.stm.
13 Toby Helm, 'Back British values or lose grants, Kelly tells Muslim groups', *The Telegraph*, 12 October 2006. www.telegraph.co.uk/news/uknews/1531226/Back-British-values-or-lose-grants-Kelly-tells-Muslim-groups.html.
14 Home Office (2011), p. 107.
15 MCB, 'Stigmatising Muslim civil society won't avert terrorism – Prevent strategy still flawed', MCB website, 7 June 2011. www.mcb.org.uk/stigmatising-muslim-civil-society-wont-avert-terrorism-prevent-strategy-still-flawed/.
16 MCB, 'Secretary General Calls for Fresh Thinking on Extremism at MCB AGM 2013', MCB website, 29 July 2013. www.mcb.org.uk/secretary-general-calls-for-fresh-thinking-on-extremism-at-mcb-agm-2013/.
17 MCB, 'Education and Muslims: End this Witch-Hunt of British Muslims', MCB website, 17 April 2014. www.mcb.org.uk/education-and-muslims-end-this-witch-hunt-of-british-muslims/.
18 John Ware, 'Inside The World Of "Non-Violent" Islamism', *Standpoint Magazine*, March 2015. http://standpointmag.co.uk/node/5936/full.
19 Interview with Daud Abdullah, 10 February 2012.
20 MCB, 'Speech by Dr Shuja Shafi on British and Islamic Values', MCB website,29 January 2015. www.mcb.org.uk/shuja-shafi-speech-british-values-290115/.
21 MCB, 'Muslim Council of Britain Elects New Leadership and Discusses British Values', MCB website, 15 June 2014. www.mcb.org.uk/muslim-council-of-britain-elects-new-leadership-and-discusses-british-values/.
22 Muhammad Abdul Bari, 'Who Does Not Agree With British Values That Are Universal?', *The Huffington Post*, 18 June 2014. www.huffingtonpost.co.uk/muhammad-abdul-bari/british-values_b_5506138.html. See also AMS-UK, 'Iqra Slough Governor discusses Islamic and British Values', AMS-UK website, 10 April 2014. http://ams-uk.org/iqra-slough-governor-discusses-islamic-and-british-values/.
23 'Young and the Brave: Roles and Responsibilities By Brother Anas Altikriti', YouTube, 25 June 2011. www.youtube.com/watch?v=HOnCEiFuL4M.
24 MCB, 'Secretary General Calls for Fresh Thinking on Extremism at MCB AGM 2013'.
25 Ibid.

26 MCB, 'Muslims Unite for Civil Liberties: Consultation Meeting', MCB website, 23 March 2009. www.mcb.org.uk/muslims-unite-for-civil-liberties-consultation-meeting/.
27 MCB, 'Seminar – Navigating Extremes: Muslims in the Middle', MCB website, 11 May 2015, www.mcb.org.uk/navigating-extremes-muslims-in-the-middle/.
28 MCB, 'British Muslims Explore Community-led Responses to Terrorism and Extremism', MCB website, 12 November 2015. www.mcb.org.uk/counterterrorconf2015/.
29 'Dr Muhammad Abdul Bari – Between Ignorance and Extremism', lecture transcript, 10 February 2006. Available at: www.scribd.com/document/47470171/Dr-Muhammad-Abdul-Bari-Between-Ignorance-and-Extremism.
30 Ahmed Saad, 'Al-Wasatiyyah: The Lost Middle Path', IFE website, 30 December 2006. https://web.archive.org/web/20100116093531/http://www.islamicforumeurope.com/live/ife.php?doc=articleitem&itemId=324.
31 See, for example, 'PM speech at the UN General Assembly 2014', British Government website, 25 September 2014. www.gov.uk/government/speeches/pm-speech-at-the-un-general-assembly-2014.
32 MCB, 'Fear and Loathing is not the Best Response to Terrorism: Muslim Council of Britain Responds to Extremism Task Force Proposals', MCB website, 5 December 2013. www.finsburyparkmosque.org/news/mcb-press-release-fear-and-loathing-is-not-the-best-response-toterrorism-muslim-council-of-britain-responds-to-extremismtask-force-proposals/.
33 'Oral statement by Nicky Morgan on the "Trojan Horse" letter', British Government website, 22 July 2014, www.gov.uk/government/speeches/oral-statement-by-nicky-morgan-on-the-trojan-horse-letter, and Clarke (2014), p. 48.
34 MCB, 'The Muslim Council of Britain Responds to Peter Clarke's "Trojan Horse" Letter Report', MCB website, 23 July 2014. www.mcb.org.uk/the-muslim-council-of-britain-responds-to-peter-clarkes-trojan-horse-letter-report/.
35 MCB, 'Secretary General Calls for Fresh Thinking on Extremism at MCB AGM 2013'.
36 Ibid. For an interesting take on 'non-violent' takfirism, see James Brandon, 'By denouncing ISIS as "not Muslims", moderate Muslims risk making things worse', 9 September 2014. Left Foot Forward blog. http://leftfootforward.org/2014/09/by-denouncing-isis-as-not-muslims-moderate-muslims-risk-making-things-worse/.
37 MCB, 'Qadiyani Centre not Mosque', MCB website, 2 October 2003. Original link (www.mcb.org.uk/qadiyani-centre-not-mosque/) removed, but available at: www.rabwah.net/wp-content/uploads/2015/09/muslim_council_britain_antiahmadiyya_website.png.
38 MCB, 'Position Statement: The Muslim Council of Britain and Ahmadis', MCB website, 6 April 2016. www.mcb.org.uk/position-statement-the-muslim-council-of-britain-and-ahmadis/.
39 For example, see Oliver King, 'Criticism for new Muslim organisation', *The Guardian*, 19 July 2006. www.theguardian.com/politics/2006/jul/19/immigrationpolicy.religion; and George Readings, 'British Islamism's Black Knight Strikes Again', 16 June 2009, Harry's place blog, http://hurryupharry.org/2009/06/16/british-islamisms-black-knight-strikes-again/.
40 Ed Husain, 'Frustrated love and forced marriage', *The Guardian*, 20 August 2008. www.theguardian.com/commentisfree/2008/aug/20/islam.religion.
41 MCB, 'STATEMENT: Muslim Marriage Certificate', MCB website, 15 August 2008. http://web.archive.org/web/20080824221846/http://www.mcb.org.uk/article_detail.php?article=announcement-734.
42 Allen Esterson, 'The MCB and the Muslim Marriage Contract', 24 August 2008. Butterflies & Wheels blogwww.butterfliesandwheels.org/2008/the-mcb-and-the-muslim-marriage-contract/.

43 Interview with Ibrahim Mogra, August 29, 2012.
44 'Anti-Terror Measures Foster Extremism: MCB', On Islam website, 2 September 2014. http://web.archive.org/web/20150920033214/http://www.onislam.net/english/news/europe/476971-anti-terror-measures-foster-extremism-mcb.html.
45 Naqshbandi (2014).
46 Mirza, Senthilkumaran and Ja'far (2007).
47 Frampton, Goodhart and Mahmood (2016).
48 Ansari (2004), p. 365.
49 MCB, 'About MCB', MCB website, 16 April 2014. www.mcb.org.uk/about-mcb/.
50 MCB (2003), 2.2.
51 MCB (2017), p. 14.
52 Khaliq (2004), p. 257.
53 MET, 'Achievements', MET website. Webpage captured 3 May 2008. http://web.archive.org/web/20080503042942/http://www.muslim-ed-trust.org.uk/achievements.php.
54 Ansari (2004), p. 386.
55 Husain (2007), pp. 20–21. Sarwar (2006), p. 169.
56 Sawar (2006), p. 171.
57 Husain (2007), p. 22.
58 Sarwar (2001), p. 30.
59 Sarwar (2006), p. 160.
60 Mawdudi (1979), cited in Mayer (2007), p. 144.
61 Parvez (2007), p. 240
62 Ibid., pp. 239, 280.
63 Conway (2009), p. 5.
64 Department for Communities and Local Government (2010).
65 AMS-UK, 'FAQ', AMS-UK website. http://ams-uk.org/faq/.
66 Squires (2003), p. 88.
67 Jamal and Panjwani (2011), p. 81.
68 Faisal, 'The penalty for apostasy', Spittoon blog. 30 March 2010. http://web.archive.org/web/20100407163056/http://www.spittoon.org/archives/5719.
69 Andrew Gilligan, 'Ofsted praises Islamic schools which oppose Western lifestyle', *The Telegraph*, 6 November 2010. www.telegraph.co.uk/education/educationnews/8114452/Ofsted-praises-Islamic-schools-which-oppose-Western-lifestyle.html.
70 Conway (2009), p. 22.
71 Tazeen Ahmad, 'Shame of Britain's Muslim schools: Secret filming shows pupils being beaten and "taught Hindus drink cow p***"', *The Daily Mail*, 13 February 2011. http://www.dailymail.co.uk/news/article-1356361/Shame-Britains-Muslim-schools-Secret-filming-shows-pupils-beaten.html#ixzz3bV4ri2fB.
72 Gilligan, 'Ofsted praises Islamic schools which oppose Western lifestyle'.
73 Andrew Gilligan, 'Schools watchdog with links to extremists shut down', *The Telegraph*, 14 June 2015. www.telegraph.co.uk/education/educationnews/11673313/Schools-watchdog-with-links-to-extremists-shut-down.html.
74 Richard Kerbaj and Sian Griffiths, 'Two Muslim school inspectorates face axe', *The Sunday Times*, 11 May 2014. www.thesundaytimes.co.uk/sto/news/uk_news/Education/article1409438.ece.
75 'Controversial schools inspectorate reportedly forced to close following successful BHA campaigning', Humanists UK website, 16 June 2015. https://humanism.org.uk/2015/06/16/controversial-schools-inspectorate-reportedly-forced-to-close-following-successful-bha-campaigning/.
76 Tom Worden and Abul Taher, 'Private school chief linked to Islam Trojan Horse plot says: Stone all adulterers to death', *The Daily Mail*, 19 April 2014. www.dailymail.co.uk/news/article-2608662/Private-school-chief-linked-Islam-Trojan-Horse-plot-says-Stone-adulterers-death.html.

77 Hewitt (1996), p. 78.
78 This information was available on IBERR's main website until at least November 2010 (at 'About IBERR', http://iberr.co.za/index.php?option=com_content&task=view&id=14&Itemid=2), but has subsequently been removed. However, it is still available on its Russian website at http://iberr.chat.ru/iberr1.htm.
79 Statement from The First World Conference on Muslim Education, 1977, Mecca, quoted in Sarwar (2001), p. 29.
80 John Ware, 'The Plot to Islamise Birmingham's Schools', *Standpoint Magazine*, September 2014. http://standpointmag.co.uk/node/5696/full.
81 'When tolerance is taken too far', *The Telegraph*, 12 December 2009. www.telegraph.co.uk/comment/telegraph-view/6798250/When-tolerance-is-taken-too-far.html; Andrew Gilligan, 'Muslim extremists, and a worrying lesson for us all', *The Telegraph*, 16 March 2014. www.telegraph.co.uk/education/educationopinion/10700041/Muslim-extremists-and-a-worrying-lesson-for-us-all.html.
82 Richard Adams, 'Islamic school's gender segregation is unlawful, court of appeal rules', *The Guardian*, 13 October 2017. www.theguardian.com/education/2017/oct/13/islamic-school-gender-segregation-unlawful-court-of-appeal.
83 BBC News, 'School's legal bid to block Ofsted report continues', 8 November 2016. www.bbc.com/news/education-37899565.
84 Tim Ross, 'Rape within marriage is "impossible", claims Muslim cleric', *The Telegraph*, 15 October 2010. https://web.archive.org/web/20101018071909/http://www.telegraph.co.uk/news/newstopics/religion/8064571/Rape-within-marriage-is-impossible-claims-Muslim-cleric.html.
85 Interview with Omer El-Hamdoon, 14 February 2012. Asked for a recommendation of a manual that describes the rules of *shari'a*, El-Hamdoon named the Shafi'ite manual of *shari'a, 'Umdat al-Salik*. Authorised in 1991 by Sunni Islam's highest learning institution, al-Azhar University in Egypt, it states that if a woman is asked at home and can physically endure it, it is 'obligatory for a woman to let her husband have sex with her'. The husband has the 'full right to enjoy his wife's person … in what does not physically harm her' (al-Misri (1994), pp. 526, 527).
86 Steven Stalinsky and Y. Yehoshua, 'Muslim Clerics on the Religious Rulings Regarding Wife-Beating', MEMRI website, 22 March 2004. www.memri.org/reports/muslim-clerics-religious-rulings-regarding-wife-beating. See also Vidino (2006), pp. 38–39.
87 BBC News, 'Birmingham Islamic faith school guilty of sex discrimination', 13 October 2017. www.bbc.com/news/uk-england-birmingham-41609861.
88 Sally Weale, 'Some Islamic schools in England still segregating children', *The Guardian*, 7 November 2017. www.theguardian.com/education/2017/nov/07/some-islamic-schools-in-england-still-segregating-children.
89 BBC News, 'Birmingham Islamic faith school guilty of sex discrimination'.
90 Camilla Turner, 'End of segregation in schools could increase risk of radicalisation, Birmingham council chief warns', *The Telegraph*, 24 November 2017. www.telegraph.co.uk/education/2017/11/24/end-segregation-schools-could-increase-risk-radicalisation-birmingham/.
91 AML, 'Aims and Objectives', AML website, webpage captured on June 4, 2014 (the current website omits this information). http://web.archive.org/web/20140604195835/http://aml.org.uk/aboutaml/.
92 AML, 'In Practice', AML website, webpage captured on September 1, 2014 (the current website omits this information). http://web.archive.org/web/20140901195742/http://aml.org.uk/aboutaml/in-practice/.
93 Ibid.
94 Association of Muslim Lawyers (2002b), n. 18.1.1.
95 Ibid., n. 23, emphasis added.

96 See Cox and Marks (2006), p. 132–133; and Raab (2009), p. 59.
97 Association of Muslim Lawyers (2002a), n. 88.
98 Ibid., n. 43.
99 Thomson (2010), p. 13.
100 Ibid., p. 5, emphasis added.
101 Ibid., p. 18
102 Association of Muslim Lawyers (2002a), n. 95.
103 IFE, 'Attempted car bombings in London', Muslim Safety Forum press release, IFE website, 30 June 2007. https://web.archive.org/web/20070728085322/http://www.islamicforumeurope.com/live/ife.php?doc=articleitem&itemId=350, emphasis added.
104 Andrew Gilligan, 'Police Muslim forum headed by Islamic extremist', *The Telegraph*, 24 July 2010. www.telegraph.co.uk/journalists/andrew-gilligan/7908273/Police-Muslim-forum-headed-by-Islamic-extremist.html.
105 Andrew Gilligan, 'Sir Ian Blair's deal with Islamic radical', *The Telegraph*, 1 March 2010. www.telegraph.co.uk/news/uknews/law-and-order/7339604/Sir-Ian-Blairs-deal-with-Islamic-radical.html.
106 'Politics and Media Show', Islam Channel, broadcast on 2 July 2012, available at: www.youtube.com/watch?t=122&v=HFLi8ZTVmsM.
107 Gilligan, 'Sir Ian Blair's deal with Islamic radical'.
108 See Andrew Gilligan, 'Mayor gives £30,000 of taxpayers' money to Muslim group led by "extremist"', *The Evening Standard*, 12 March 2009, www.standard.co.uk/news/mayor-gives-30000-of-taxpayers-money-to-muslim-group-led-by-extremist-6938333.html; and habibi (pseud.), 'Azad Ali: The Jihad Lover and the Civil Service', Harry's place blog, 20 November 2008, http://hurryupharry.org/2008/11/20/azad-ali-the-jihad-lover-and-the-civil-service/.
109 Shiraz Maher, A reduction of reality at the Guardian?', *Standpoint Magazine*, 5 August 2010. http://standpointmag.co.uk/node/3267. Ali's original post is archived at: http://web.archive.org/web/20081005054141/http://blog.islamicforumeurope.com/?p=89.
110 David T., 'Defend Azad Ali', Harry's place blog, 18 January 2009. http://hurryupharry.org/2009/01/18/defend-azad-ali/.
111 MEND, 'MEND Team', MEND website. https://mend.org.uk/about-mend/meet-the-team/
112 NAMP website homepage (no longer active). Webpage captured 17 October 2013. https://web.archive.org/web/20131017000847/https://www.nampuk.org.
113 MEND (2014), p. 12.
114 Ibid., p. 16.
115 Andrew Gilligan, 'Islamists establish a bridgehead in Parliament', Andrew Gilligan's blog (originally on *The Telegraph* website), 25 November 2010. https://andrewgilliganblog.wordpress.com/2010/11/25/islamists-establish-a-bridgehead-in-parliament/.
116 Martin Bright, 'Anti-Islamophobia parliamentary group drop "Islamist" secretariat', *The Jewish Chronicle*, 8 December 2010. www.thejc.com/politics/42307/anti-islamophobia-parliamentary-group-drops-muslim-secretariat.
117 Harry Black, 'MEND – The Rebranding of iENGAGE', Harry's place blog, 11 July 2014, http://hurryupharry.org/2014/07/11/mend-the-rebranding-of-iengage/. See also Andrew Gilligan, 'Muslim group with links to extremists boasts of influencing election', *The Telegraph*, 4 April 2015, www.telegraph.co.uk/news/general-election-2015/11515630/Muslim-group-with-links-to-extremists-boasts-of-influencing-election.html.
118 Al-Haddad's statements have been sourced from video recordings of al-Haddad's lectures available at: http://tifrib.com/haitham-al-haddad/.

119 Douglas Murray, 'The Government should ignore the National Association of Muslim Police', *The Telegraph*, 21 January 2010. https://web.archive.org/web/20160331113857/http://blogs.telegraph.co.uk/news/douglasmurray/100023218/the-government-should-ignore-the-national-association-of-muslim-police/
120 Melanie Phillips, 'Hezbollah cells await Iran's orders', *The Spectator*, 2 August 2006. www.spectator.co.uk/features/24356/hezbollah-cells-await-irans-orders/.
121 Joseph D'Hippolito, 'A Front For Jihad', *Frontpage Magazine*, 22 September 2004. http://archive.frontpagemag.com/readArticle.aspx?ARTID=11339.
122 'Islamic Human Rights Commission 2007: A Decade of Fighting Injustice', Innovative Minds website. www.inminds.com/ihrc10years.php.
123 Casey (2016), p. 71.
124 NAMP (2010).
125 Andrew Gilligan, 'The baroness, Islamic extremists and a question of free speech', *The Telegraph*, 22 March 2015. www.telegraph.co.uk/news/uknews/11488175/The-baroness-Islamic-extremists-and-a-question-of-free-speech.html.
126 Ibid.
127 Andrew Gilligan, 'The infiltration of Labour', *The Telegraph*, 28 February 2010. www.telegraph.co.uk/news/newstopics/politics/labour/7333470/The-infiltration-of-Labour.html.
128 On Galloway's support for Hamas and Hezbollah, see 'George Galloway', Mark Humphrys' blog. http://markhumphrys.com/galloway.html.
129 Andrew Gilligan, '"Britain's Islamic republic": full transcript of Channel 4 *Dispatches* programme on Lutfur Rahman, the IFE and Tower Hamlets', Andrew Gilligan's blog, (originally on *The Telegraph* website), 22 October 2010. https://andrewgilliganblog.wordpress.com/2010/10/22/britains-islamic-republic-full-transcript-of-channel-4-dispatches-programme-on-lutfur-rahman-the-ife-and-tower-hamlets-the-full-transcript/comment-page-1/.
130 Andrew Gilligan, 'Islamists got voters out for Livingstone', *The Telegraph*, 6 March 2010. www.telegraph.co.uk/news/politics/7386900/Islamists-got-voters-out-for-Livingstone.html.
131 At the forefront of journalism covering these matters has been Andrew Gilligan (formerly at *The Telegraph* and now at *The Sunday Times*). His work is referred to in this chapter more than that of other journalists, since it provides the cutting edge of reporting on Islamism in Tower Hamlets and across Britain more widely. His reporting on the Trojan Horse affair in Birmingham, covered in the next chapter, is referred to for the same reason. No other journalist has covered these issues so extensively.
132 BBC News, 'Lutfur Rahman wins Tower Hamlets mayoral election', 22 October 2010. www.bbc.com/news/uk-england-london-11604108.
133 Andrew Gilligan, 'Inextricably linked to controversial mosque: the secret world of IFE', *The Telegraph*, 28 February 2010. www.telegraph.co.uk/news/newstopics/politics/labour/7333487/Inextricably-linked-to-controversial-mosque-the-secret-world-of-IFE.html.
134 Erlam & Ors v Rahman & Anor [2015] EWHC 1215, para. 186. Judgement available at: https://trialbyjeory.files.wordpress.com/2015/04/judgment.pdf.
135 Andrew Gilligan, 'Lutfur Rahman: the "chief coordinator" of his election campaign says he has "strategic relationship" with extremist IFE', Andrew Gilligan's blog (originally on *The Telegraph* website), 23 November 2010. https://andrewgilliganblog.wordpress.com/2010/11/23/lutfur-rahman-one-of-his-former-supporters-says-he-has-strategic-relationship-with-extremist-ife/
136 Gilligan, 'Islamists got voters out for Livingstone'.
137 Andrew Gilligan, 'Radicals with hands on the levers of power: the takeover of Tower Hamlets', *The Telegraph*, 28 February 2010. www.telegraph.co.uk/news/

newstopics/politics/labour/7333537/Radicals-with-hands-on-the-levers-of-power-the-takeover-of-Tower-Hamlets.html.

138 Interview with Abdullah Faliq, 5 September 2012.

139 Gilligan, 'Radicals with hands on the levers of power: the takeover of Tower Hamlets'.

140 Andrew Gilligan, 'Islamic radicals "infiltrate" the Labour party', *The Telegraph*, 27 February 2010. www.telegraph.co.uk/news/newstopics/politics/labour/7333420/Islamic-radicals-infiltrate-the-Labour-Party.html.

141 See Gilligan, 'Radicals with hands on the levers of power: the takeover of Tower Hamlets'; and Gilligan, '"Britain's Islamic republic": full transcript of Channel 4 Dispatches programme on Lutfur Rahman, the IFE and Tower Hamlets'.

142 Andrew Gilligan, 'Lutfur Rahman's Muslim favouritism: the evidence', Andrew Gilligan's blog (originally on *The Telegraph* website), 3 April 2014. https://andrewgilliganblog.wordpress.com/2014/04/03/lutfur-rahmans-muslim-favouritism-the-evidence/.

143 Andrew Gilligan, 'Lutfur Rahman: 30 things you need to know about the extremist-linked mayor of Tower Hamlets', Andrew Gilligan's blog (originally on *The Telegraph* website), 21 May 2014. https://andrewgilliganblog.wordpress.com/2014/05/21/lutfur-rahman-what-you-should-know/.

144 *The Spectator*, 'Theresa May's speech on terrorism and extremism – full text and audio', 30 September 2014. http://blogs.spectator.co.uk/coffeehouse/2014/09/theresa-mays-speech-on-terrorism-and-extremism-full-text-and-audio/.

145 Westrop, 'How to Radicalize an Entire London Borough'.

146 Gilligan, 'Inextricably linked to controversial mosque: the secret world of IFE'.

147 See 'Philosophy', Jamaat-e-Islami Pakistan website, webpage captured 6 October 2013. https://web.archive.org/web/20131006065213/http://jamaat.org/beta/site/page/8.

148 Ewen MacAskill, 'Cage director charged under Terrorism Act after failing to hand over passwords', *The Guardian*, 17 May 2017. www.theguardian.com/uk-news/2017/may/17/cage-campaign-group-director-muhammed-rabbani-charged-under-terrorism-act.

149 Hasan Afzal, 'Extremism in Abdul Bari's Mosque', *The Huffington Post*, 20 September 2011. www.huffingtonpost.co.uk/hasan-afzal/extremism-in-abdul-baris-_b_971232.html.

150 Bill Roggio, 'US-born cleric Awlaki "proud" to have taught al Qaeda operatives', *The Long War Journal*, 27 April 2010. www.longwarjournal.org/archives/2010/04/usborn_cleric_awlaki.php.

151 Shaykh Anwar al-Awlaki, *44 Ways to Support Jihad*, p. 1. Available online at: http://ebooks.worldofislam.info/ebooks/Jihad/Anwar_Al_Awlaki_-_44_Ways_To_Support_Jihad.pdf.

152 See Nadia Moharib, QMI Agency, 'Controversial Muslim preacher to speak in Calgary', *Canoe News*, 9 June 2012. http://cnews.canoe.com/CNEWS/Canada/2012/06/09/19858731.html; and Stewart Bell, 'Islamic former guitarist now preaches against music', *The National Post*, 15 February 2011. http://web.archive.org/web/20110301184748/http://www.nationalpost.com/news/Islamic+former+guitarist+preaches+against+music/4290981/story.html.

153 Stand for Peace, 'Bin Laden supporter, anti-gay preacher speaks at East London Mosque', Stand for Peace website, 14 October 2014. http://standforpeace.org.uk/bin-laden-supporter-anti-gay-preacher-speaks-at-east-london-mosque/.

154 See Khan's lecture, 'Free Love', recorded in June 2007 and released on a DVD, *A Menace II Society*, available on YouTube at: www.youtube.com/watch?v=sF1zErRdn4U.

155 'Shaykh Abdur Rahmaan As-Sudays', Al Haramain Sermons website, 19 April 2002. Webpage captured on 12 April 2008. http://web.archive.org/web/

20080412023817/http://www.alharamainsermons.org/eng/modules.php?name=News&file=article&sid=71

156 'A Stronger Britain, Built On Our Values', British Government website, 23 March 2015. www.gov.uk/government/speeches/a-stronger-britain-built-on-our-values.

157 Dean Godson, 'David Cameron and Theresa May are to be congratulated for their strategy on tackling Islamist extremism', Conservatives website, 7 June 2011. www.conservativehome.com/platform/2011/06/dean-godson-david-cameron-and-theresa-may-are-to-be-congratulated-for-their-strategy-on-tackling-isl.html.

158 Ibid.

159 Michael Wilshaw, 'Advice note from Her Majesty's Chief Inspector, Sir Michael Wilshaw, to the Secretary of State for Education, Rt Hon. Nicky Morgan MP, on school inspections in the London Borough of Tower Hamlets', UK Government website, 21 November 2014. www.gov.uk/government/uploads/system/uploads/attachment_data/file/386594/Tower_20Hamlets_20advice_20note.pdf.

160 David Churchill and Anna Davis, 'Zubair Nur: Teen feared to have joined Isis attended private Muslim school where students were "vulnerable to radicalisation"', *The London Evening Standard*, 27 March 2015. https://web.archive.org/web/20150711172643/http://www.standard.co.uk/news/london/zubair-nur-teen-feared-to-have-joined-isis-attended-private-muslim-school where-students-were-vulnerable-to-radicalisation-10138534.html.

References

Ansari, Humayun (2004). *The Infidel Within: Muslims in Britain Since 1800*. London: Hurst & Co.

Association of Muslim Lawyers (2002a). 'Memorandum from The Association of Muslim Lawyers'. Minutes of Evidence. Select Committee on Religious Offences in England and Wales, House of Lords. https://publications.parliament.uk/pa/ld200203/ldselect/ldrelof/95/2101710.htm.

Association of Muslim Lawyers (2002b). 'Memorandum by the Association of Muslim Lawyers'. Minutes of Evidence. Select Committee on Religious Offences in England and Wales, House of Lords. https://publications.parliament.uk/pa/ld200203/ldselect/ldrelof/95/2101711.htm.

Casey, Louise (2016). *The Casey Review: A Review into Opportunity and Integration*. Department for Communities and Local Government. www.gov.uk/government/uploads/system/uploads/attachment_data/file/575973/The_Casey_Review_Report.pdf.

Clarke, Peter (2014). *Report into Allegations Concerning Birmingham Schools Arising from the 'Trojan Horse' Letter*. House of Commons. www.gov.uk/government/uploads/system/uploads/attachment_data/file/340526/HC_576_accessible_-.pdf.

Conway, David (2009). *Disunited Kingdom: How the Government's Community Cohesion Agenda Undermines British Identity and Nationhood*. London: Civitas. www.civitas.org.uk/pdf/DisunitedKingdom.pdf.

Cox, Caroline, and John Marks (2006). *The West, Islam and Islamism: Is Ideological Islam Compatible with Liberal Democracy?* 2nd edition. London: Civitas.

Department for Communities and Local Government (2010). *The Training and Development of Muslim Faith Leaders: Current Practice and Future Possibilities*. www.gov.uk/government/uploads/system/uploads/attachment_data/file/6155/1734121.pdf.

Frampton, Martyn, David Goodhart and Khalid Mahmood (2016). *Unsettled Belonging: A Survey of Britain's Muslim Communities*. London: Policy Exchange. https://policyexchange.org.uk/wp-content/uploads/2016/12/PEXJ5037_Muslim_Communities_FINAL.pdf.

Hewitt, Ibrahim (1996). 'The case for Muslim schools'. In Ghulam Sarwar (ed.), *Issues in Islamic Education*: 72–78. London: Muslim Educational Trust.

HM Government (2015). *Counter-Extremism Strategy*, Cm 9148. www.gov.uk/government/uploads/system/uploads/attachment_data/file/470088/51859_Cm9148_Accessible.pdf.

Home Office (2011). *Prevent Strategy*, Cm 8092. www.gov.uk/government/uploads/system/uploads/attachment_data/file/97976/prevent-strategy-review.pdf.

Husain, Ed (2007). *The Islamist*. London: Penguin.

Jamal, Arif A. and Farid Panjwani (2011). 'Having faith in our schools: struggling with definitions of religion'. In Myriam Hunter-Henin, *Law, Religious Freedoms and Education in Europe*: 69–87. Ashgate: Farnham.

Khaliq, Urfan (2004). 'Islam and the European Union: Report on the United Kingdom'. In Richard Potz and Wolfgang Wieshaider (eds), *Islam and the European Union*: 221–262. Leuven: Peters.

Maher, Shiraz, and Martyn Frampton (2009). *Choosing our Friends Wisely: Criteria for engagement with Muslim Groups*. London: Policy Exchange. https://policyexchange.org.uk/wp-content/uploads/2016/09/choosing-our-friends-wisely-mar-09.pdf.

Mawdudi, Abul Ala (1979). *Purdah and the Status of Women in Islam*. Lahore: Islamic Publications.

Mayer, Ann Elizabeth (2007). *Islam and Human Rights: Tradition and Politics*. Boulder, CO: Westview.

MCB (2003). 'Memorandum from the Muslim Council of Britain (404)'. Minutes of Evidence. Select Committee on Religious Offences in England and Wales, House of Lords. https://publications.parliament.uk/pa/ld200203/ldselect/ldrelof/95/2101707.htm.

MCB (2017). 'Annual report: July 2016–June 2017'. www.mcb.org.uk/wp-content/uploads/2017/07/Annual-Report-2017.pdf.

MEND (2014). 'Activity report 2014.' http://mend.org.uk/wp-content/uploads/2014/12/MEND_Activity_Report_2014_Low_Res.pdf.

Mirza, Munira, Abi Senthilkumaran and Zein Ja'far (2007). *Living Together Apart: British Muslims and the Paradox of Multiculturalism*. London: Policy Exchange. www.policyexchange.org.uk/wp-content/uploads/2016/09/living-apart-together-jan-07.pdf.

NAMP (2010). 'Memorandum from NAMP (National Association of Muslim Police) (PVE 71)'. In 'Preventing violent extremism, sixth report of session 2009–10': Ev. 223–227. Communities and Local Government Committee, House of Commons. https://publications.parliament.uk/pa/cm200910/cmselect/cmcomloc/65/65.pdf.

Naqshbandi, Mehmood (2014). 'UK mosque statistics / masjid statistics'. Published online at: www.muslimsinbritain.org/resources/masjid_report.pdf.

Pantucci, Raffaello (2015). *'We Love Death As You Love Life': Britain's Suburban Terrorists*. London: Hurst & Co.

Parvez, Zahid (2007). *Building a New Society: An Islamic Approach to Social Change*. Markfield: Revival Publications.

Raab, Dominic (2009). *The Assault on Liberty: What Went Wrong with Rights*. London: Fourth Estate.

Sarwar, Ghulam (2001). *Islamic Education: Its Meaning, Problems and Prospects*. London: Muslim Educational Trust.

Sarwar, Ghulam (2006). *Islam: Beliefs and Teachings*. 8th edition. London: Muslim Educational Trust.

Squires, Josephine E. (2003). 'The significance of religion in British politics'. In William Safran (ed.), *The Secular and the Sacred: Nation, Religion and Politics*: 78–95. Frank Cass: London.

Thomson, Ahmad (2010). 'Human rights in Islam'. Paper presented at London Muslim Centre, 20 August. Published online at: www.wynnechambers.co.uk/pdf/Human_Rights_in_Islam_20AUG10.pdf.

Vidino, Lorenzo (2006). 'Aims and methods of Europe's Muslim Brotherhood'. In *Current Trends in Islamist Ideology*, vol. 4: 22–44. The Hudson Institute Center on Islam, Democracy, and the Future of the Muslim World. www.hudson.org/research/9776-aims-and-methods-of-europe-s-muslim-brotherhood.

6 Education and arbitration

A clash of values within Muslim communities

Within Muslim communities, education and arbitration are two key fields of contention where a conflict with Britain's liberal democratic values, championed by the state, can be observed. In the classrooms of Muslim schools and in the court rooms of *shari'a* councils, a worldview and associated set of values are being taught or implemented that conflict with liberal democracy and human rights legislation.

The British government recognises these two domains, in addition to universities and prisons, as problematic in the fight against 'extremism'. In a speech in March 2015, Theresa May, then home secretary, identified the 'Trojan Horse plot' in Birmingham schools as an example of how 'extremists use entryist tactics to infiltrate legitimate organisations to promote their own agendas'.[1] She also singled out *shari'a* councils' use of *shari'a* law to discriminate against women as an example of the rejection of 'British values'. To address these two issues, she announced that the newly formed Extremism Analysis Unit in the Home Office would develop a counter-entryist strategy for 'government, the public sector and civil society as a whole' and commission an independent investigation into 'the application of Shari'a law in England and Wales'.[2] The government's counter-extremism strategy, published in October 2015, reiterated this dual commitment.[3] The inquiry into *shari'a* law was formally launched in May 2016. Its report, which recommended the regulation of *shari'a* councils, was published in February 2018.[4] Regarding its counter-entryist strategy, the Home Office, states that 'Reviews of several sectors have been concluded and Ministers are being advised of the findings and options for implementation'.[5]

This chapter details this conflict of values in these two key fields of contention where Muslims' lives are being directly affected. It shows how a key stake in this conflict is the authority to legitimise competing visions of an ideal society and the values associated with it, both in the minds and institutions of British Muslims.

Muslim schools: influencing Muslim minds

According to Michael Whine, of all the campaigning issues of concern for Islamist groups in Britain, the education of Muslim children is the most important.[6] For such groups, schooling is seen as the most effective way of inculcating religious belief and safeguarding Muslim identity against the pernicious influences of Britain's decadent, secular society. There have been numerous reports in recent years demonstrating this. They show that in some British Muslim schools a worldview and set of values antagonistic to liberal democracy is being propagated. For example, John Ware reported in November 2010 that some 40 British Muslim schools are teaching the Wahhabi-Islamist curriculum of Saudi Arabia to around 5,000 children.[7] He showed how young Muslim children are being taught to regard Britain as an enemy of Islam and to hate non-Muslims – especially Jews, about whom these children are taught conspiracy as fact, and homosexuals, for whom the death penalty is taught in accordance with the *shari'a*. For Andrew Gilligan and other observers, the spread of illiberal and anti-integrationist ideology in Muslim schools is 'the single most worrying aspect of Islamist and radical activity in Britain'.[8]

This chapter does not consider the influence of Wahhabi Islam in Britain's schools, but limits its focus to individuals and groups within the revivalist network and their role in a clash of values in the field of education. It first regards the Trojan Horse affair in Birmingham, what Sam Westrop refers to as 'a concerted attempt by Islamist groups to infiltrate and Islamize British schools'.[9] It then details how this may be viewed as part of a long-term strategy within a wider network of Islamic activists to 'Islamise knowledge' for a global Islamic revival.

The Trojan Horse affair

In November 2013, a document was sent anonymously to Birmingham City Council describing a strategy it alleged was being implemented for the takeover of a number of schools and their governance according to 'strict Islamic principles'. The strategy involved identifying target schools in predominately Muslim areas, selecting groups of 'Salafi' parents to join governing bodies, identifying key staff to 'disrupt' schools from within, and removing non-Muslim teachers from positions of influence. The information contained in the document, which had no addressee and no signature, demonstrated a detailed knowledge of events in certain schools. The document came to be known as the Trojan Horse letter. After receiving the letter from the Home Office, the Department for Education instigated an investigation into the schools of concern to understand the implications for the school system in Birmingham and more widely. Former deputy assistant police commissioner, Peter Clarke, was appointed to the task, while Birmingham City Council began its own investigation headed by Ian Kershaw. By June 2014, five of the schools were placed in special measures.

Clarke's report concluded there had been 'co-ordinated, deliberate and sustained action' by a number of individuals to introduce an 'intolerant and aggressive Islamic ethos' into a number of Birmingham schools.[10] This had been achieved, he wrote, by such individuals gaining influence on the governing bodies, installing sympathetic head teachers and senior staff, appointing like-minded people to key positions and removing heads who were not compliant with their religiously inspired agenda. There is clear evidence, he asserted, that 'there are a number of people, associated with each other and in positions of influence in schools and governing bodies, who espouse, endorse or fail to challenge extremist views'.[11]

Clarke identified a 'disconcerting pattern reaching across a number of schools', which included 'the reinforcement of Muslim identity to the exclusion and disparagement of others', 'the introduction of conservative Islamic practices into school life', and changes in the curriculum by governing bodies taken over by 'like-minded' people.[12] The agenda that Clarke found being pursued, however, went beyond mere religious conservatism, and was clearly in conflict with the liberal democratic vision and associated values of human rights:

> In the context of schooling, it manifests itself as the imposition of an aggressively separatist and intolerant agenda, incompatible with full participation in a plural, secular democracy. Rejecting not only the secular and other religions but also other strands of Islamic belief, it goes *beyond* the kind of social conservatism practised in some faith schools which may be consistent with universal human rights and respectful of other communities. It appears to be a deliberate attempt to convert secular state schools into exclusive faith schools in all but name.[13]

In March 2015, the House of Commons Education Committee produced its own report into the Trojan Horse affair. The report asserted, 'All our witnesses also accepted that they had found no evidence of extremism in schools.'[14] This is incorrect, however. Although Clarke – a key witness – reported no evidence of 'terrorism, radicalisation or violent extremism', he reported clear evidence of 'a number of people, associated with each other and in positions of influence in schools and governing bodies, who espouse, endorse or fail to challenge extremist views'.[15] Supposedly supporting its claim, the committee report cited the then education secretary Nicky Morgan's admission to the House of Commons in July 2014 that there had been 'no evidence of direct radicalisation or violent extremism'. Yet, while conceding that there was no evidence of children becoming radicalised or of violence being promoted, she added that 'there is a clear account in the [Clarke] report of people in positions of influence in these schools, who have a restricted and narrow interpretation of their faith, not promoting British values and failing to challenge the extremist views of others'.[16]

The report also cites Michael Wilshaw, then Ofsted chief, who stated: 'We did not see extremism in schools. What we did see was the promotion of a culture that would, if that culture continued, have made the children in those schools vulnerable to extremism because of ... the disconnection from wider society and cultural isolation.'[17] Thus, claims the committee report, whilst the promotion of a culture that may lead to extremism was evident in some schools, extremism itself was not. This is a remarkable distinction for it places extremism at the far end of a convoluted sequence in which cultural disconnection, and prior to that the promotion of such disconnection, precedes it: The assumption is that practices that express a disconnection from British mainstream culture do *not* constitute extremism, and neither does the advocacy of such practices. 'Extremism' in the education committee report, it seems, refers only to the *violent* kind.

However, this is not consistent with the government's view that extremism is not confined to violent acts but includes the 'vocal or active opposition' to the values that underpin British society, as first articulated in the revised Prevent counter-radicalisation strategy in 2011.[18] Such values, it says, include 'the mutual respect and tolerance of different faiths and beliefs'.[19] And yet Wilshaw himself has criticised Birmingham City Council for its 'failure to support schools in their efforts to keep pupils safe from the risk of extremism', noting that in some schools 'children are not being encouraged to develop tolerant attitudes to other faiths and other cultures'.[20] As Morgan remarked, 'Teachers have said they fear children are learning to be intolerant of difference and diversity'.[21] Wilshaw also noted that boys and girls are being treated unequally and that in one school, an extremist preacher was invited to address schoolchildren.

Other behaviours equally interpretable as extremist according to the government's own thinking have been observed at Trojan Horse schools – none of which are designated as faith schools – as documented by Peter Clarke. These include the teaching, in sex and relationships education (SRE) lessons, that rape is permissible in marriage; the alteration of the curriculum along Islamic lines prohibiting music, drama and the figurative arts; the banning of Christmas, Easter and Diwali celebrations; and misogynistic attitudes towards women expressed in the lack of training opportunities and promotion, as well as disparaging comments by teachers and governors. Attitudes expressed by senior staff, stemming from 'a shared ideological basis to their faith', espoused anti-Western and homophobic views; divided the world between 'us' (Muslims) and 'them' (non-Muslims or Muslims who disagree); and perceived 'a worldwide conspiracy' against Islam.[22] Whether these behaviours and attitudes constitute 'extremism' may be debated between supporters of the government's position and others who dissent from it. In any case, they certainly indicate a conflict of vision and values with the British liberal democratic mainstream. And they are certainly not consistent with a human rights perspective.

Such a conflict also involves the authority to legitimise competing visions of an ideal society and the values associated with it. The governance and management of schools is the ideal battleground for such authority. The education committee's report, however, seems to obfuscate this. It states, 'we have seen no evidence to support claims of an organised plot to take over

English schools'.[23] Upon the publication of this report in March 2015, and leaning heavily upon its conclusions, the BBC incorrectly stated that a 'series of official investigations' found claims that 'extremists had tried to take over several schools in Birmingham to advance radical interpretations of Islam' to be 'groundless'.[24] These assertions have been taken by certain groups in the revivalist network in Britain as grounds to declare that there has been no collectively organised effort to Islamise schools in Birmingham. For example, Islam21c, a project created by the Muslim Research and Development Foundation, stated, 'there was no evidence of any "radical" or "extremist" plot'.[25] MEND similarly stated that 'the "plot" has been declared a sham idea'.[26]

But both the committee's report and the BBC have ignored what Morgan recognised in Clarke's report as 'compelling evidence of a determined effort by people with a shared ideology to gain control of the governing bodies of a small number of schools in Birmingham' and introduce within them 'the segregationist attitudes and practices of a hardline and politicised strand of Sunni Islam'.[27] This effort, Clarke reported, has been 'co-ordinated, deliberate and sustained' by a network of individuals.[28] 'The tactics used,' he wrote, 'are too similar, the individuals concerned too closely linked' and their behaviour 'too orchestrated for there not to be a degree of co-ordination and organisation behind what has happened'.[29] Wilshaw also acknowledged the reports of numerous head teachers 'that there has been an organised campaign to target certain schools in Birmingham in order to impose a narrow faith-based ideology and alter the school's character and ethos'.[30] *The Telegraph* conducted its own inquiry into the controversy and concluded, similarly to Clarke, that 'there is indeed an organised group of Muslim teachers, education consultants, school governors and activists dedicated to furthering what one of them describes as an "Islamising agenda" in Birmingham's schools'.[31]

In November 2017, MEND organised an event in Birmingham for educators, parents and others to discuss what it describes as the 'Trojan hoax'.[32] But this event, rather than demonstrating that Trojan Horse has nothing to do with extremism or Islamism, demonstrates quite the converse. Trojan Horse, as this event shows, has become a key rallying point for Islamist extremists or supporters of extremists in defence of illiberal Islamic practices and in protection of their authority to control the narrative of values.

The MEND event was supported by the Muath Trust in allowing the event to be held at the Bordesley Centre, which it owns. The director of the trust, Irshad Baqui, is the former executive director of one of the most important revivalist organisations in Britain, the Islamic Foundation. In 2014, the Muath Trust was criticised for hosting Yasir Qadhi, an American Salafi scholar, who argues that under an Islamic state, homosexuals should be killed, *hudud* punishments enforced and *jihad* declared against non-Muslims if, after being invited to Islam, they refuse to convert or pay the *jizya*, a protection tax.[33] The Trust, which has received hundreds of thousands of pounds in government grants, has also supported the group CAGE, which held an event at its Bordesley Centre in April 2015.[34] Reportedly, the premise doors were locked to raise cash donations for CAGE – described by some as a 'pro-terrorist group' – since its bank account had been frozen in 2014, when one of its senior staff, Moazzam Begg, was arrested on suspicion of terrorism offences linked to Syria.[35]

The leaflets advertising MEND's November 2017 event complained, in provocative and unsubstantiated terms, of 'the stigmatisation of a community' – a phrase homogenising Muslims in Britain – and promised to present 'the facts'. But the event was cancelled after MEND was 'accused of attempting mislead the local community'.[36] Birmingham City Council responded in robust terms to MEND's effort to reframe events concerning the Trojan Horse controversy. 'What happened in the schools caught up in Trojan Horse in 2014,' it stated, 'is clearly established and we must not shy away from challenging those who seek to deny there was a serious problem at that time.'[37] The authority referred to Clarke's report and the report it commissioned, produced by Ian Kershaw.

According to Kershaw's report, although there was insufficient evidence of a 'conspiracy to promote an anti-British agenda, violent extremism or radicalisation in schools', there was evidence of 'a determined effort to change schools, often by unacceptable practices, in order to influence educational and religious provision for the students served'.[38] According to Kershaw, there was no 'systematic plot to take over schools', but there were sufficiently 'clear patterns of behaviour' amongst the individuals involved to infer that they were connected. Furthermore, he found evidence of the 'improper manipulation of school governance' and pressure applied to head teachers 'to modify curriculum provision which denies students their right to a broad and balanced curriculum, including the right to understand of other world religions and the right to sex and relationship education'.[39]

The Trojan Horse letter outlines a five-step plan to take over schools and ensure they are run according to Islamic principles.[40] Kershaw noted that in many of the schools under investigation some, if not all, of the five steps outlined had been or were evident. Kershaw's acknowledgement of such evidence, and his description of a 'determined effort to change schools' according to an 'improvement agenda' for the schools involved, seems to contradict his denial of a 'systematic plot to take over schools'. Whether the collective effort of certain 'activist governors' and other perpetrators to 'improve' schools through the institutionalisation of illiberal Islamic principles may be described as an attempt to effectively take them over ought to be a straightforward matter. Likewise, whether or not Trojan Horse could be described as a 'plot' ought to be uncontroversial: efforts to introduce a divisive Islamic ethos into schools were determined, organised and ideologically motivated. However, although Kershaw's findings were consistent with Clarke's less cautiously worded conclusions, his choice of language has been seized on by revivalist groups as evidence that there was no religiously-informed effort to introduce illiberal ideas and practices into schools.

According to Clarke, 'At the centre of what has happened are a number of individuals who have been, or are, associated with either Park View School or the Park View Educational Trust' (PVET), the latter of which he described as 'the incubator for much of what has happened and the attitudes and behaviours that have driven it'.[41] The most important of these individuals is Tahir Alam who, until his resignation in July 2014, was the director and chair of the trust. In this role, Alam was responsible for the management of three schools at the centre of the Trojan Horse affair, including Park View, which 'appeared to act as a blueprint for [other schools], exhibiting all the behaviours which cause concern'.[42]

Alam – who the Trojan Horse letter describes as having 'fine-tuned the "Trojan Horse" [operation] so that it is totally invisible to the naked eye and allows us to operate under the radar' – is a former senior MCB official.[43] He was the organisation's assistant secretary general between 2006 and 2008 and the chair of its education committee during the same period. He co-authored the MCB's 2007 paper, *Meeting the Needs of Muslim Pupils in State Schools*, which critics have described as a blueprint for the Islamisation of British schools. Alam was also an executive committee member of the Association of Muslim Schools-UK (AMS-UK), as well as one of its inspectors. Furthermore, as *The Sunday Times* revealed, Alam was 'the leader of HISAM, an organisation which believed in imposing Islamic law and promoting gender segregation'.[44] In September 2015, Morgan, banned Alam from having any involvement with schools. The barring decision was made on the grounds that he had been involved in activities aimed at 'undermining fundamental British values of democracy, the rule of law, individual liberty, and mutual respect and tolerance of those with different faiths and beliefs'.[45]

Alam, who was one of the scheduled speakers at the cancelled MEND event in November 2017, maintains that the Trojan Horse letter is a hoax and denies the existence of a plot. The MCB has stepped to Alam's side in taking the same view. However, as Clarke wrote in his report, whether the letter is a hoax 'misses the point. The important issue is not who wrote it or whether it is a genuine extract from a letter between co-conspirators, but whether the events and behaviours have actually happened'.[46] Clarke noted that 'the behaviour described in the "Trojan Horse" letter has been seen at a number of schools over a long period of time and particularly more recently', and that allegations about a plot to Islamise schools pre-existed the letter.[47]

The MCB stated in melodramatic and obfuscatory terms that failures in governance and procedures do not equate to a 'khalifate-takeover'.[48] The implicit distinction drawn here between mere bad governance and the more problematic promotion of an extremist religious agenda in schools is supported by the education committee report, which states that the Trojan Horse affair 'is less about extremism than about governance'.[49] But this is a naïve and contrived distinction that obscures the religious motivations behind the numerous cases of governance malpractice and the religious basis of the behaviour and attitudes documented that clearly clash with Britain's liberal democratic, human rights-based culture.

This clash of values is inextricable from clashing perceptions regarding the social order and humanity's place within the universe, as well as the nature of truth, knowledge and morality. Such clashing perceptions inevitably relate to how the Trojan Horse affair itself is understood. The MCB's response to it – that it is a fabrication that amounts to an Islamophobic attack – indeed exhibits signs of cognitive dissonance, but also demonstrates that it is involved in a conflict over the authority to establish a way of seeing social and political reality. This is most apparent in its denial of the government's authority to pronounce on matters relating to Islam. In an effort to control the language and conceptualisation of the matters at hand, the MCB stated:

> We are however concerned about the phrase 'particular strand of Sunni Islam': given how diverse our Muslim communities are, it is unwise for any of us to pass judgement on the acceptability of certain strands of Islam over others. It is not for the state to define the theological boundaries of the Islamic faith and to create an 'approved version of Islam'. Such an aim is contrary to the spirit of our free society and beyond the scope of debate on education of children in school. We are troubled that Mr Clarke delves into intricacies of Muslim theological debate raising serious allegations against a number of national Muslim organisations including the MCB.[50]

It should be noted that Clarke's report was not in any way representative of the state's view and made no judgement of what constitutes authentic or inauthentic Islam, merely noting that *an* understanding of Islam implicitly or explicitly informed much of the thinking behind the actions and attitudes he observed. The MCB, assuming for itself the symbolic authority to determine the religious nature of what Clarke had seen, passed off such behaviour as mere religious conservatism rather than an 'ideology and agenda to "Islamise" secular schools'.[51] This may be a deliberate attempt to conceal the truth but, regardless, it reflects a conflict of vision with the state, in trying to impose an understanding that certain actions and attitudes belong within the acceptable limits of the social and political order, and are not thus 'extremist' or subversive. This clash of perceptual schemas – in which, for example, the nature and purpose of education, or the roles of men and women, mean something very different – escapes the government's definition of extremism. But such a clash is what *underlies* the 'vocal or active' undermining of values that extremism is defined by.

In December 2016, Dame Louise Casey published her government-commissioned report into opportunity and integration. She noted that the local authority's failure in accepting claims by groups of individuals to represent the views of a wider community and in not challenging their views was not unique to Birmingham.[52] In January 2017, Casey reported to the House of

Commons communities committee. Asked whether 'Trojan Horse' was happening elsewhere in Britain, she said, 'Yes, it is happening elsewhere.'[53] She added, 'In terms of some of the things that were seen in what's called the Trojan Horse, we did not find it very difficult to find things like the segregation of girls – what I would describe as *anti-equal opportunities* or *anti-liberal values.*' Her response confirmed what Clarke said after he published his findings in 2014. He stated, 'What I put in my report was the tip of the iceberg … . There were problems elsewhere which I couldn't evidence sufficiently in the time available.'[54] This seemed to be borne out more recently: in February 2017, concerns were raised about a possible Trojan Horse situation in Oldham, where a head teacher reportedly said she had started working at home after being 'subjected to a campaign of "death threats" and verbal abuse by people determined to introduce an Islamic agenda'.[55] The National Association of Head Teachers said it was 'supporting a number of members in the Oldham area with a variety of apparent Trojan Horse issues'.

Challenging the view held by the MCB and other revivalist groups that the problem is merely one of socially conservative religiosity, Casey informed the communities committee:

> Now, Trojan Horse is a set of issues – they go from girls being split off from boys, through to teachers essentially teaching *extremism* … . That's not how we bring children up in this country. It's often veiled as religious conservatism. I have a problem with the expression of 'religious conservatism' because I think often it can be *anti-equalities.* We've got to be careful that people can choose, obviously, to live the lives they live, but they can't condemn others for living differently.[56]

The accusation levelled by the MCB, MEND and others of 'Islamophobia' at anyone treating Trojan Horse seriously as an organised effort to undermine liberal democratic values in British schools seems to be working. Asked if head teachers and decision-makers in schools were afraid of standing up to community leaders pushing a religious agenda, due to a fear of being labelled 'racist', she said that many people, not just head teachers, are afraid to speak up on matters of extremism in schools due to such fears. She said that right-wing extremism is also a real problem, but one that people feel freer to talk about. The fear of being able to talk about Islamist extremism, she emphasised, was a 'disservice to thousands of people that are caught up in actually being on the receiving end of not having the start in life that they should have living in the United Kingdom'.[57]

The government's response to the Trojan Horse affair, despite the education committee's report, demonstrates an explicitly held understanding that it is involved in a *conflict of values.* The most wide-reaching of all new measures taken by the Department of Education is the active promotion of 'British values' in maintained schools, academies and nurseries. While education secretary, Nicky Morgan stated that 'actions which undermine fundamental

British values should be viewed as misconduct' resulting in teachers being 'barred from the profession'.[58] Her banning of Tahir Alam from having any involvement with schools, including being a school governor, was the first case of disciplinary action in relation to Trojan Horse and showed the government's new resolve to combat extremism in schools. In October 2017, Morgan's successor, Justine Greening, admitted, 'Trojan Horse was a shocking wake-up call for all of us, about how these people who peddle these extremist views are actually looking to do so in schools'.[59] She said, 'we have a stronger focus on helping children understand their British values', but added that the Department of Education is looking to reform the disciplinary procedures for teachers accused of misconduct, since they may not be adequate for dealing with such complex cases.

The British government is engaged in a conflict of values with individuals and groups who share what it refers to as an 'extremist ideology'. But, as the Trojan Horse affair has shown, this conflict of values concerns more than differences in political perspectives or objectives. It involves what Casey refers to as a 'regressive Islamic religiosity'.[60] This problem is not reducible to ideology or ideas, although it does involve them in the organised and self-conscious efforts to articulate and institutionalise a particular (and, for some Muslims, contentious) understanding of Islam. Implicit to the values the government struggles to articulate and defend – and underlying the values of the 'Islamists' with which it clashes – is a taken-for-granted way of seeing the world, a cognitive framework comprised of a set of unquestioned assumptions and self-evident 'truths', including those that relate to human nature, individual and group identity, social and political organisation, and scientific knowledge.

The Islamisation of knowledge

The Trojan Horse affair may be viewed as part of a global Islamic revivalist phenomenon that contests the Western, liberal democratic understanding of the role of education. Clarke argued that the Trojan Horse agenda 'appears to stem from an international movement to increase the role of Islam in education', supported by AMS-UK and the International Board of Educational Research and Resources (IBERR), both of which have been mentioned in chapter 5, as well as the MCB. 'The movement,' he stated, 'provides practical advice and religious legitimisation to those who, in the words of the IBERR, seek to "*Islamise the provision of educational services*"'.[61] Clarke did not elaborate on this point but it is worth doing so, since it is an important one. This is because the actions and attitudes he observed in Birmingham indeed have historical origins dating back at least four decades and national, as well as global, dimensions.

As noted, the MCB produced a paper in 2007 entitled, *Meeting the Needs of Muslim Pupils in State Schools*.[62] Co-authored by Alam, this document advocates what may be described as the voluntary Islamisation of education in British schools. It proposes that Muslim pupils ought to be separated from their non-Muslim peers in numerous areas of the curriculum. It also advocates that schools adjust numerous classes according to Islamic principles – including music, dance, drama, art, sports, and sex education – or grant Muslim parents the right to withdraw their children from them. Religious education, the report urges, ought to include greater attention to Islam for both Muslims and non-Muslims. Remarkably, the report states that the adoption of a policy where religion is treated as a private matter 'makes it more difficult for schools to appreciate and respond positively to meeting some of the distinctive spiritual, moral, social and cultural needs of Muslim children'.[63] It appears that the provision of special arrangements in schools are proposed not merely to meet the allegedly distinct needs of Muslim children – which the MCB treats homogeneously – but to inculcate such needs.

MCB's paper recommends for schools a book, *Islam: Beliefs and Teachings*, by the director of the Muslim Educational Trust (MET), Ghulam Sarwar. This book describes Islam as a code of conduct for 'personal and private affairs, including social, political, economic, moral and spiritual activities'.[64] As noted earlier, it praises Jama'at-i-Islami and the Muslim Brotherhood for working to establish a global Islamic state, condones polygamy, and states that men and women have different roles in society due to their different natures. Sarwar believes Islamic education ought to be 'an integral part of the efforts worldwide to establish Islam as an all-encompassing way of life'.[65]

In 2004, MET published a paper, 'A Programme for Muslim Education in a Non-Muslim Society', by Sahib Mustaqim Bleher.[66] This states that critical thinking can occur 'only on the basis of knowledge from the original sources', namely the Qur'an and Muhammad's *sunna*.[67] Bleher describes Islamic education as a tool to secure the permanence of the Muslim community in a non-Muslim environment. What is needed, he states, 'is much more of an *Islamic socialisation process,* rather than simply Islamic teaching'.[68] This theme was echoed at a European conference convened by the AMS-UK in 2002 by Musharraf Hussain, who asserted, 'The *raison d'être* of Muslim schools is vigorously stated by its founders as follows: to prevent the assimilation of the new generation.'[69] The problem identified by Hussain was the secular National Curriculum that is compulsory for all schools including Muslim ones. His proposed course of action is to embed the National Curriculum within an 'Islamic milieu' by instilling an Islamic ethos in schools, and then by gradually working to Islamise its contents.[70] This approach is strikingly similar to what Clarke observed in Birmingham schools.

This concept of Islamic education, which elevates the Muslim social collective above the Muslim individual, conflicts with the core liberal democratic principle of individual liberty by devaluing the independence of mind and inhibiting the spirit of rational inquiry. It is based upon orthodox Islamic precepts. J. Mark Halstead, who has written at length about Islamic education, observes that, 'Independence of thought and personal autonomy do not enter into the Muslim thinking about education, which is more concerned with the progressive initiation of pupils into the received truths of the faith'.[71] Islamic education, he affirms, is a vehicle for helping children become fulfilled adults, but such fulfilment hinges upon a particularly Islamic notion of human nature in which humanity is geared towards the 'realization on earth of divinely ordained moral imperatives'.[72]

The Islamisation of education can be understood as a cultural and political strategy, employed within the arc of the global Islamic revivalist movement, to dissolve the separation of the secular and religious spheres of human society, by subordinating rational inquiry and the pursuit of scientific knowledge in schools to the dogma of what is perceived as divine revelation. Halstead describes it as 'a key process in countering the influence of western secularism and purging Muslim institutions of insidious western influences'.[73] This is borne out by the attitudes expressed by key individuals in the revivalist network in Britain, including Ibrahim Hewitt, Ghulam Sarwar and Mohamed Mukadam. This strategy as it applies in Britain and the West more generally is decades old and can be traced back to the First World Conference on Muslim Education held in Mecca in 1977.

The conference statement affirmed as the 'ultimate aim of Muslim Education' the 'complete submission to Allah on the level of the individual, the community and humanity at large'.[74] This aim appears verbatim in the mission statement of one of the first Muslim schools to receive state funding in Britain, the Islamia Primary School, founded in 1983 by Yusuf Islam. IBERR, also established by Islam, describes its origins in the late 1990s as 'the natural outcome of the deliberations of a core group of Muslim educationalists committed to implementing the aims and objectives' of the 1977 Mecca conference.[75] Attended by over 300 scholars and statesmen, this conference convened to address a perceived crisis facing the *umma* relating to the encroachment of Western, secular values in education upon Muslims in Muslim-majority and Muslim-minority countries. One of the speakers, S. N. al-Attas, asserted that the 'confusion and error' in knowledge resulting from the detachment of education from Qur'anic principles and Muhammad's *sunna*, was the ultimate cause of the difficulties experienced by contemporary Muslim communities.[76] This had to be addressed, he declared, by a global programme dedicated to '*the Islamization of knowledge*'.

The Islamisation of knowledge was a key theme taken up in the writings of Ismail Raji al-Faruqi, who 'saw no hope for the revival of the *umma* unless the dualism in Muslim education that separates Islamic and secular aspects be abolished once and for all'.[77] In 1981, al-Faruqi founded the International Institute of Islamic Thought (IIIT) in the US in order to advance the Islamisation of knowledge project. Ian Johnson informs us that IIIT was initiated at a meeting in Lugano, Switzerland, also held in 1977, which brought together a much smaller number of Muslim leaders from around the world, including al-Faruqi, to lay the foundations for a Islamic revivalist network in Europe and the U.S.[78] IIIT has an office in London. Although it is not involved in children's education in Britain, it sees its work as contributing to the revival of Islamic knowledge and the Muslim *umma.* By supporting research projects, organising academic conferences and publishing scholarly works, it seeks to contribute to the reform of Islamic thought and 'help Muslims regain their intellectual and cultural identity'.[79]

The Islamisation of knowledge project, despite its official conception at the Mecca conference and further formalisation in the work of IIIT, appears to have developed informally, without centralised coordination, in several directions. In Britain, while the key concern of IIIT-UK is the academic reflection upon the key concepts and methods for a revival of Islamic thought, the practical work of promoting Islamic knowledge is the focus of numerous other organisations, linked within the revivalist network, including MET, AMS-UK, IBERR and the Nida Trust. The outcome of their work within schools appears to have engendered a conflict with the very liberal democratic culture that has enabled them to operate.

This conflict has manifested in Tower Hamlets in London. As mentioned earlier in the chapter, Michael Wilshaw, while head of Ofsted, noted that hundreds of children in six of the borough's private Islamic schools are at risk of 'extremist influences and radicalisation'.[80] In November 2014, Wilshaw wrote an advice note to the then education secretary, Nicky Morgan, stating, 'All schools focused intensively on developing Islamic knowledge and understanding at the expense of other important areas of the curriculum.' He noted that all the schools had failed 'to provide an appropriately broad and balanced curriculum'. Consistent with MCB's paper on the needs of Muslim pupils, music, art and drama were rarely taught. In all six schools, he warned, 'pupils' physical and educational welfare is at serious risk'. Despite this, Muhammad Abdul Bari – the founding chairman of IFE and the former chair of the borough's East London Mosque – remarkably describes Islamic knowledge as the 'antidote to extremism'.[81] Such knowledge, if taught properly, he insists, 'increases belief in human goodness, patience and wisdom, and a belief in God's mercy'.

Shari'a councils

Shari'a courts have been operating unofficially in Britain since the 1980s, but the first recorded demand for the introduction of Islamic law into the domestic legal structure for British Muslims came from the Union of Muslim Organisations and the UK and Eire in 1975 in a petition to parliament.[82] Officially, they have been operating since August 2007 as Muslim Arbitration Tribunals (MATs) under the 1996 Arbitration Act.[83] What sparked the media's interest in these courts in 2008, and brought to light some of the pertinent issues raised by them, was their public endorsement by Rowan Williams, then archbishop of Canterbury. Williams said that it was a fact that aspects of the *shari'a* were already being implemented in Britain and that the formal incorporation of the *shari'a* 'seems unavoidable'.[84]

Shari'a courts in Britain are of two types. First, are the MAT courts whose rulings are legally enforceable under the Arbitration Act on certain conditions. Their judgements must not contravene British law and all parties must agree voluntarily to have their disputes arbitrated by them. Since criminal issues cannot be dealt with by any tribunal under the Act, these courts deal mostly with family matters, such as Islamic marriages, as well as mosque and commercial disputes. Operating under the Act since August 2007, initial reports stated that there were five such courts, in London, Birmingham, Bradford, Nuneaton and Manchester.

The London court is run by the Islamic Sharia Council, headed by Suhaib Hasan and Maulana Abu Sayeed, who are both networked with the spiritual guide of the Muslim Brotherhood, Yusuf al-Qaradawi, through their involvement in al-Qaradawi's European Council for Fatwa and Research (ECFR). The council was involved in seeking charitable status for a national federation of *shari'a* councils, called the UK Board of Sharia Councils. This body is designed to serve as 'a representative and supervisory body of individual Sharia Councils' that will look to it 'for advice and expertise in matters of Sharia law'.[85] Abu Sayeed describes a key function of the federation as providing 'a common formula and set of principles' which local *shari'a* councils must adhere to in dispensing verdicts.[86] He considers this as an achievement since, although there isn't much variation across councils, 'some aren't as strict as we are'. Via this federation, *shari'a* councils across the country are now networked to ECFR, which provides guidance on the application of *shari'a* more widely across Europe.[87]

Constituting the second type of *shari'a* court are the more numerous unofficial courts littered around the country that, according to British law, can at most provide mediation, not arbitration, where an agreement, rather than a legal judgement, can be made.[88] Denis MacEoin, in his report for the think tank Civitas, *Sharia Law or 'One Law for All'?*, claimed that there are at least 85 *shari'a* courts, including both types, in Britain.[89]

Both kinds of courts are supported by MCB. According to Ibrahim Mogra, MCB does not have a formal role to issue religious edicts, but it does 'signpost people to *shari'a* councils and *shari'a* bodies and the like'.[90] However, there are four main issues with these courts that demonstrate a conflict with human rights norms and liberal principles, including, most prominently, equality of all under the law. Underlying all of these is a conception of *shari'a* as a complete legal and ethical system, applicable to all aspects of human existence, which is superior to 'man-made' law and destined to replace it in the long term.[91]

First, *shari'a* courts are providing discriminatory verdicts on disputes that would not be supported in the civil courts. Such disputes include those relating to inheritance. Under the *shari'a*, women are discriminated against since they are entitled to just half of what their male siblings are able to inherit. Suhaib Hasan says his court does not get involved in the division of property after separation.[92] However, in September 2008 it was reported that the

Nuneaton court had ruled in exactly this way, dividing the estate of a Midlands man between three daughters and two sons.[93] In theory, the rulings of *shari'a* courts must be enforceable in English civil courts, but the civil courts are unlikely to support a ruling in an inheritance dispute on the discriminatory basis of the *shari'a*. The likely reason that *shari'a* courts can make these rulings in practice is because they are rarely sent to civil courts for enforcement.

Discrimination is also occurring in the issuing of Islamic divorces. Divorce possibly constitutes the vast majority of the cases handled by the network of MAT courts.[94] Yet, whereas for a Muslim man a divorce is automatic, for a Muslim woman complicated legal procedures are required with no guarantee of divorce. The Islamic Sharia Council in London makes clear that Islamic divorce is the right of a man, but available to a woman only with her husband's permission.[95] The council, and others including Birmingham Central Mosque's *shari'a* council, also discriminates against women by charging women more than men for obtaining a divorce.[96] This, as Charlotte Proudman notes, is 'a form of gender discrimination contrary to the Equality Act 2010'.[97]

Second, *shari'a* courts are issuing rulings on areas that lie outside their legal remit, resulting in the failure of these cases to reach the civil courts where they ought to be settled. These include criminal matters, such as domestic violence and assault.[98] In 2007, for example, a stabbing case involving Somalian youths was apparently decided upon by an unofficial *shari'a* court in Woolwich, southeast London.[99] Cases of domestic violence have also apparently been settled without justice being served to women in England's criminal courts.[100] Machteld Zee, a Dutch legal scholar who gained unprecedented access to *shari'a* courts in London and Birmingham, was told by one *shari'a* court judge that they see 600 to 800 cases a year involving 'divorce-seeking women who are on the receiving end of violence or maltreatment'.[101] *Shari'a* courts' handling of criminal matters was confirmed by Elham Manea, a Muslim academic, who published an extensive study of women and the practice of *shari'a* in Britain in 2016. Disturbingly, she found that the MAT in Nuneaton had dealt with cases of not only domestic violence but also child abuse.[102]

The third problematic aspect of *shari'a* courts in Britain is the coercion of Muslim women to use such courts. The director of the UK-based think tank Civitas, David Green, claims that 'there is a good deal of intimidation of women in Muslim communities', which prevent us from safely assuming that women use *shari'a* courts on a genuinely voluntary basis.[103] This view is shared by a number of human rights and women's rights advocates, who have collected numerous case studies of women pressured to use *shari'a* courts. One of these groups, the One Law for All Campaign, reports that 'women are often pressured by their families into going to these courts and adhering to unfair decisions and may lack knowledge of English and their rights under British law'.[104] The refusal to settle a dispute in a *shari'a* court, it warns, can lead to threats, intimidation and ostracisation. Equally, if not more, disturbing, there have also been reports of Muslim clerics' willingness 'to conduct sharia marriages involving child brides as young as 12'.[105] In 2012, *The Times* reported that, 'Almost one in seven of the estimated 8,000 forced marriages of Britons each year are believed to involve girls of 15 or under.'[106]

The fourth troubling aspect of these courts is the risk of creating parallel legal systems and communities, divided along Muslim and non-Muslim lines. For Zee, this risk is already a reality. She states, 'There are, in fact, two separate legal orders functioning [in Britain], of which one currently operates in the "shadow of the law".'[107] The retort that *shari'a* courts' rulings, in theory, have to be consistent with British law does not begin to address the problem that, in practice, rulings are issued that directly contravene basic human rights, and in many cases such rulings are not referred to civil courts for formal legal sanction. It is simply not in the interests of any *shari'a* court to seek approval within the English legal system to uphold a ruling when it is unlikely to be approved under English law. This is especially so when 'man-made' law is conceived as inferior to *shari'a*, as made explicit by Sheikh Maulana Abu Sayeed, president of the Islamic Sharia Council, and Ahmad Thomson, co-founder of the Association of Muslim Lawyers, who states that the demise of 'man-made' law is inevitable.[108]

The dichotomy in the English legal system that is opened up by the presence of a network of *shari'a* courts and tribunals is strikingly illustrated by the starkly different conceptions of crime in English secular law and orthodox interpretations of the *shari'a*. What is clearly a criminal matter under English law is, in certain important instances, not considered so from a *shari'a* perspective. Rape is a key case in point. Demonstrating a point of view that clearly conflicts with a liberal, human rights perspective, Abu Sayeed states that rape is impossible in marriage: 'In Islamic sharia,' he affirms, 'rape is adultery by force. So long as the woman is his wife, it cannot be termed as rape.'[109] This view is shared by Suhaib Hasan, the secretary of the Islamic Sharia Council, who explains that 'marital rape is a western type of emotion'.[110] Marital rape, he says, does not exist in Islam. Haitham al-Haddad, a former judge at the Islamic Sharia Council, echoes this conviction, referring to such an act as '*so-called* rape against your wife', bemoaning the prison sentence against a husband who rapes his wife as an infringement upon his liberty.[111] Far from an anomaly, this 'extremist' view has been found propagated in schools involved in the Trojan Horse affair.[112] It is part of a mindset or culture of thought that is not exclusive to the *shari'a* court network.

But this is not just the shared personal view of certain Muslim judges in *shari'a* councils. It is derived from orthodox *shari'a* precepts, and thus dissent from it has to contend with the weight of traditional authority.[113] It has also appeared in edicts issued from online *fatwa* services, so it is readily accessible.[114] Although the number of rape cases seen by *shari'a* courts may be small, this view of the legal status of rape is likely to ensure that justice for some Muslim women will never be obtained in English courts. The issue here is that these cases will be dealt with as non-criminal matters in *shari'a* courts. One of the fundamental conditions upon which *shari'a* courts have obtained their approval in England – that they will not handle criminal matters – rests upon a shared understanding of what constitutes a crime, yet this is lacking in a key area where women's human rights are concerned. This divergence in understanding of what constitutes a crime effectively creates parallel legal systems, which in turn exacerbate the problem of segregated communities.

In addition to different conceptions of crime, *shari'a* court judges' belief that they are best to resolve certain criminal matters without the need to refer them to the civil courts also contributes to a de facto divergence of legal systems. Domestic violence, as noted above, is sometimes handled without referral to the police or the country's law courts, even though it may be recognised as a criminal matter. Zee, in her observation of *shari'a* courts in operation, noted the statement of a *shari'a* court judge who said, 'Under Islam, we should reconcile marriages *even if there is violence*'.[115] The prioritisation of marriage – even at the expense of women's rights – has a religious basis in the importance placed upon the preservation of the family as the primary 'building block' for an Islamic society. This view is expressed in the literature produced by Ghulam Sarwar for the Muslim Educational Trust and by Zahid Parvez, the director of the Islamic Foundation's Markfield Institute of Higher Education. In a book designed for and distributed to Muslim schoolchildren in Britain, Sarwar opines that marriage is the basis of the Islamic family, which is the basis of Islamic society.[116] 'Divorce,' he says, 'is allowed but is regarded as the *least* desirable of *all* lawful acts.'[117] This is because marriage should lead to the fulfilment of Allah's pleasure. Like Sawar, Zahid bemoans the 'over emphasis on rights' and women's 'greater independence' as an impediment to the attainment of an Islamic society.[118]

The jurisprudence that is used in Britain's *shari'a* courts, according to Manea, is 'classical Islamic law with all its contradictions and discriminations'.[119] Its incompatibility with universal human rights standards unsurprisingly exacerbates concerns regarding a legal system operating in Muslim communities outside the control of the state. Notwithstanding the inhumane penal code of such law – which can include the death penalty for apostasy, homosexuality and adultery, amputation for theft, and flogging for a range of other offences – its civil code is comprised of numerous tenets that contravene basic human rights. The One Law for All Campaign, pioneered by Maryam Namazie in response to the discriminatory nature of *shari'a* courts in Britain, provides sufficient examples:

> Under Sharia law's civil code, a woman's testimony is worth half that of a man's; a woman's marriage contract is between her male guardian and her husband and a Muslim woman is not permitted to marry a non-Muslim. A man can have four wives and divorce his wife by simple repudiation, whereas a woman must give justifications for requesting a divorce, some of which are extremely difficult to prove. Child custody

> reverts to the father at a preset age, even if the father is abusive; women who remarry lose custody of their children even if the child has not reached the preset age; and sons are entitled to inherit twice the share of daughters.[120]

Thus, some basic human rights taken for granted in Britain, including most importantly the equality of all under the rule of law, are outlawed by the classical *shari'a*. The incompatibility between the *shari'a* and human rights has, in fact, been confirmed by the European Court of Human Rights (ECHR) and the upper house of the United Kingdom's national legislature, the House of Lords. In 2003, ECHR stated:

> *Sharia*, which faithfully reflects the dogmas and divine rules laid down by religion, is stable and invariable … . It is difficult to declare one's respect for democracy and human rights while at the same time supporting a regime based on sharia, which *clearly diverges* from Convention values, particularly with regard to its criminal law and criminal procedure, its rules on the legal status of women and the way it intervenes in all spheres of private and public life in accordance with religious precepts.[121]

In October 2008, in determining the asylum claim of a Lebanese woman who, in accordance with *shari'a* principles, risked handing over custody of her 12-year-old son to an abusive husband if returned to Lebanon, the House of Lords described the Islamic legal code as 'wholly incompatible' with human rights legislation and granted her asylum.[122]

Recognising the problems with *shari'a* courts in Britain, Baroness Cox, an unaffiliated life-peer in the House of Lords, authored a report in March 2015 that condemns what she calls 'the emergence of a rapidly developing alternative quasi-legal system, which not only promotes systematic gender discrimination, but also undermines the fundamental principle of one law for all'.[123] Several years earlier, in 2011, she introduced a private members' bill to the House of Lords – the Arbitration and Mediation Services (Equality) Bill – to address these matters. The bill, which seeks to tackle a range of legal issues including gender discrimination and domestic abuse by amending five different acts of parliament, has been introduced in the Lords for seven consecutive years. But, due to a lack of governmental support it has so far failed to pass through the parliamentary process and become law.[124] In July 2017, Cox took a different approach to the problems faced by women in *shari'a* courts. She introduced a more narrowly focused private member's bill into the Lords – the Marriage Act 1949 (Amendment) Bill, 'designed to help women in polygamous households or those who have had a religious marriage, only to find upon divorce they have little to no rights in terms of finance or property'.[125] The bill, which is yet to pass through the House of Lords, seeks to do so by ensuring that all religious marriages are recognised in England and Wales's civil law.[126]

The government has consistently argued against the need for Cox's Arbitration and Mediation Services (Equality) Bill, saying that there are adequate provisions to protect women in existing legislation. But recognising the issues raised by Cox and other advocates of human and women's rights, it has recently launched two inquiries into the application of *shari'a* law in Britain.

The first was commissioned in May 2016 by the Home Office, as promised in the government's counter-extremism strategy.[127] Upon its announcement, it was criticised by some human rights groups, such as One Law for All, on the basis that it was to be led and advised by theologians and imams, rather than 'human rights and women's rights experts including those from across the world who have confronted religious personal laws and jurisdictional challenges in the furtherance of human rights'.[128] The inquiry published its report in February 2018. It made three recommendations.[129]

The first recommendation is the introduction of legislative changes 'to ensure that civil marriages are conducted before or at the same time as the Islamic marriage ceremony'.[130] No reference is made to Cox's Marriage Act 1949 (Amendment) Bill, but the panel's recommendation similarly seeks to penalise the failure to civilly register Islamic marriages. This recommendation, which was made by Louise Casey in her review into opportunity and integration in 2016, aims to ensure that Muslim women who obtain an Islamic divorce are legally entitled to the protections given divorced women under civil law, including financial redress.[131] It is based on the assumption or hope that *shari'a* courts will process Islamic divorces automatically upon the presentation of a decree absolute, which would prevent Muslim women from suffering unfairly difficult and protracted procedures. But – as the report acknowledges as an aspect of bad practice in *shari'a* councils – 'even with a decree absolute a religious divorce is not always a straightforward process and the council will consider all the evidence again'.[132]

The report notes that its first recommendation to register Islamic marriages and link them to civil marriages represents 'a significant cultural and legal change' and that its success is therefore dependent on changing Muslim attitudes and values. It concedes that 'cultural change is required within Muslim communities', particularly with regard to women's rights. This admission is significant, since it recognises, albeit implicitly, that the *shari'a* court network is exacerbating a problem of religious culture that clashes with the country's liberal values.[133] To address the matter of 'cultural change', the panel's second recommendation proposes measures to raise Muslims' education about and awareness of women's civil rights and the importance for women to register their Islamic marriages. However, the report fails to provide an indication of how a 'very clear message' can be communicated effectively in Muslim communities about the negative consequences of the 'non-registration of Islamic marriages'. It also fails to discuss the most appropriate means to monitor and evaluate the effectiveness of such messaging. As such, the report stops short of where the hard thinking needs to begin regarding the interface between the discriminatory practices of a minority religious culture and the political institutions of an 'extremist' ideological movement that aspires to perpetuate and ultimately expand such a culture.

The panel's third recommendation calls for the state to create a body to regulate *shari'a* councils. Such a body, it proposes, would be responsible for implementing a code of practice to ensure *shari'a* councils only deal with Islamic marriages and divorces, refer other family matters to the civil justice system, and adopt standardised policies and procedures for greater fairness and transparency. The body, it proposes, would include *shari'a* council representatives and be self-regulating. Interestingly, the inquiry panel members failed to unanimously agree on this recommendation. One unnamed panel member objected, writing in the report that the government's involvement in a regulatory body would give undue legitimacy to the 'quasi-legal status' of the councils. He or she added, 'The creation of state endorsed regulation sends the message that certain groups have separate and distinct needs and further that sharia councils are an appropriate forum for resolution of family disputes. In short, it would perpetuate the myth of separateness of certain groups.'[134]

The allegedly 'mythical' status of group separateness is not something to take for granted, as the 2016 Casey Review made clear. There are genuine concerns for both residential and school concentrations of Muslims in Britain, particularly those from Pakistani and Bangladeshi ethnic backgrounds, which clearly amount to social segregation.[135] The government' endorsement of a body to regulate *shari'a* courts would not just give credence to the mere perception of Muslim separateness; it would legitimise the institutions that perpetuate the reality of this very separateness, particularly so if the body is self-regulating and influenced by *shari'a* council members.

In its response to the inquiry panel's report, the Home Office echoed the dissenting view of the unnamed panellist, rejecting the report's third recommendation. It noted, 'We will not be taking forward the review's recommendation to regulate Sharia councils. Sharia law has no jurisdiction in the UK and we would not facilitate or endorse regulation, which could present councils as an alternative to UK laws'.[136] It added that the Home Office will 'consider carefully the review's findings and its remaining recommendations'.[137]

The second inquiry into *shari'a* in Britain was launched by the House of Commons Select Committee in June 2016.[138] Written and oral evidence has been submitted to the committee from a variety of individuals and groups, including those recommending the reform of *shari'a* courts and those arguing for their abolition.[139] The inquiry has closed but no report has yet been published.

Political and cultural conflict

This chapter and the preceding one have demonstrated that the global Muslim Brotherhood in Britain is engaged in a conflict of values with the country's liberal democratic culture, particularly as represented by the state. This conflict has both practical and symbolic dimensions. The stakes of this conflict include the institutionalisation of competing worldviews – Islamic and liberal democratic – and related values within the structure of civil society, as well as in government policy and state law. This practical dimension of the conflict is evident, as this and the previous chapter have shown, in the fields of political advocacy and local governance, as well as education and arbitration, particularly where Muslim communities are concerned. It concerns the institutional and legal structures that regulate peoples' lives. Inseparable from the practical dimension of this conflict, there is also a symbolic or cognitive dimension. The stakes thus also include the institutionalisation of competing worldviews and related values within the minds of people, whether they are policymakers, British Muslims or the general public. This dimension of the conflict is evident in competing efforts to classify – and to command the authority to classify – the 'correct' understanding of core social values ('British' or 'universal' values), and Islam.

The practical and symbolic dimensions of this conflict overlap. The attempt to influence the minds of children and foster an Islamic identity in Muslim schools, for example, is inseparable from attempts to influence government policy in the area of educational provision for Muslims, as well as the structure of schools' governing boards. The arbitration of disputes in *shari'a* courts does not just have practical consequences for people's lives, it also establishes the symbolic authority of the courts to establish a particular understanding of Islam in Muslim communities that is contrary to how many secular, liberal Muslims understand and practise their faith. This overlapping may also be seen in revivalist groups' efforts to undermine the government's counter-extremism strategy both symbolically, where concepts such as 'extremism' are contested, and practically, where changes in government policy is sought through protest, advocacy or testimony.

A clash of values and the authority to determine them

A clash of values has been discernible in a practical sense since the Rushdie Affair in 1989, when the MCB's precursor organisation initiated a campaign to criminalise what it perceived as the 'vilification' of Islam and its prophets, what its liberal opponents see as their right to criticise, satirise or even insult religion. Other groups, such as the Islamic Human Rights Commission (IHRC) and MEND, have supported MCB's effort.[140] This campaign has been unsuccessful, but it conflicts in principle with a key tenet of liberal democracy, that of the freedom of speech, as well as its bedrock assumption of individual rather than group rights.

The MCB fell from government favour after its boycotting of Holocaust Memorial Day and Daud Abdullah's signing of the Istanbul Declaration in 2009. While these acts were understood by the government as a betrayal of 'non-negotiable' values, the clash they underline may also be understood in terms of conflicting perceptions of social and political reality. Rather than arguing for the legitimate value of the declaration, the MCB contested the government's understanding of it. Vigorously denying communities secretary Hazel Blears' view of it as endorsing attacks on Jews, the MCB called such a view 'outrageous'.[141] The MCB added that it is 'completely opposed to all forms of prejudice'. The MCB does not perceive as prejudicial its support for *shari'a* councils and its rejection of the model marriage contract produced by the Muslim Institute, both of which imply an acceptance of the religiously sanctioned discrimination against women.

This indicates not a straightforward clash of values in the sense that it is contested whether a certain act or kind of act may be classified as good or bad. It indicates clashing perceptual and evaluative frameworks where it is contested whether or not a given act has taken place at all, or whether a kind of act may be considered as such in the first place. A more striking example of this contention is how rape within marriage is understood by the leaders of *shari'a* councils: there is simply no such thing. In a clash of worldviews and their related moral frameworks, there is no shared understanding of the key terms to allow for an agreement to disagree. Terms are shared, like 'extremism' and 'universal values', but their meanings are different because they are situated in different perceptual schemes informed by different cultures of knowledge.

As chapter 5 has shown, the practical aspects of this clash of values is evident in the fields of political and legal advocacy in relation to central government, where the MCB and other revivalist interlocutors have sought to influence domestic and foreign policy in line with an Islamic revivalist worldview. Some groups in the network have taken a more activist approach to challenge the government over foreign policy, either through street demonstrations or protest campaigns. The Muslim Association of Britain, for example, played a key role in the anti-war demonstrations of 2002 and 2003, but in recent years its activism has been eclipsed by other, newer groups such as MEND and CAGE. However, more often than not, government policy has been contended quietly through advocacy work by sector-specific groups working in various fields, most importantly, education. While appealing to Britain's equality legislation to justify their causes – for example, for the right of Muslims to have more state-maintained schools – the worldview and values that fundamentally guide such efforts are clearly antagonistic to the liberal democratic basis of Britain's society and mode of government.

Beyond such advocacy work, the practical aspects of this clash of values is evident in local government, as observed in the London Borough of Tower Hamlets where individuals connected to the revivalist Islamic Forum of Europe (IFE) played an important role in directly obtaining or influencing political power. The IFE-linked mayor, Lutfur Rahman, has been deposed, but other, less prominent revivalists possibly remain in office in the borough. Their influence is difficult to gauge without a thorough investigation. But it is also difficult to disassociate the cultural dispositions and long-term political aspirations of IFE – which are clearly antagonistic to liberal democratic values and its secular model of government – and the fact that hundreds of children in six of the borough's Islamic schools are recognised by the government of being at risk of 'extremist influences and radicalisation'.[142]

The symbolic dimension of the conflict has become more apparent in recent years as the British government has become increasingly clear regarding the importance of targeting what it refers to as the 'ideology' of 'Islamist extremists'. From the revision of the Prevent counter-radicalisation strategy in June 2011, which first defined 'extremism' as the 'vocal or active opposition to fundamental British values',[143] through the publication of Britain's first counter-extremism strategy in October 2015,[144] to current plans to develop a 'fundamental British values curriculum' for teachers to build resilience to extremism in schools,[145] the government has increasingly sought to confront what it deems as an ideological challenge to the values that underpin the British way of life.

Since 2011, the government has explicitly viewed the key battleground for combatting terrorism as ideological. The first of the three objectives of the revised Prevent strategy is to 'respond to the ideological challenge of terrorism and the threat we face from those who promote it'.[146] But, while countering 'extremist' ideology remains at the heart of the government's counter-terrorism programme, it has also begun to view the ideological problem it faces beyond its function as a precursor to violence, as a matter affecting social cohesion and institutional entryism.

The government's concern with the extent to which extremist ideology has spread throughout various public institutions was made clear in December 2013 in a report by the Task Force on Tackling Radicalisation and Extremism. This report identified schools, universities and prisons as vulnerable to 'the ideology of Islamist extremism'.[147] Drawing on the recommendations of the report, the then home secretary Theresa May delivered a speech in March 2015 in which she noted 'increasing evidence' of a rejection of British values amongst some British people.[148] Highlighting some of the problems with non-violent extremism beyond its link to terrorism, she warned of the dangers of segregated communities and discrimination on the basis of sex, sexuality and race. She cited 'the Trojan Horse plot' as an example of the infiltration of extremism within British public institutions and singled out Tower Hamlets as a borough with 'extremist' issues.

In July 2015, Cameron delivered an address setting out the four pillars of the government's new counter-extremism strategy. Highlighting the first pillar – countering 'extremist ideology' – he stated, 'What we are fighting, in Islamist extremism, is *an ideology*.'[149] The new strategy is the first of its kind that aims to tackle both violent and non-violent 'extremism'. Importantly, it lays out an approach to combat 'non-violent extremism' not just as a pathway to terrorism, but also as a contributing factor to a range of other issues, which were touched on in May's March 2015 speech. These include 'isolated communities' (which can lead to 'alternative values, structures and authorities');

'alternative systems of law' (including *shari'a*) that discriminate against women; the non-participation in or rejection of democracy; and 'harmful and illegal practices' (such as female genital mutilation, honour-based violence and forced marriage).

Also in 2015, indicating its firm commitment to combating the ideological basis of terrorism and these kinds of 'non-violent extremism', the government established the Extremism Analysis Unit (EAU) in the Home Office. Significantly, the EAU is the first body of its kind in the world that pools resources for the study and combatting of violent and non-violent manifestations of 'extremism'. Just after it was created, May said the new unit will 'inform the development of a counter-entryism strategy' to protect key British institutions, and will likely play a role in an independent investigation into *shari'a* courts in England and Wales.[150]

The reaction of Islamic revivalist groups to these developments has been hostile, casting the government as intent on dividing British society between Muslims and non-Muslims. The MCB, for example, has suggested that, for the government, 'Muslims and Islam are inherently apart from British society'.[151] Contesting the terms 'radicalisation' and 'extremism' – as the MCB has done – IHRC produced a statement in March 2015 against the 'ongoing demonisation of Muslims in Britain' and 'their values', which was signed by numerous revivalist groups and individuals.[152] It described the government's inclusion of 'non-violent extremism' within its revised counter-terrorism strategy as the 'criminalisation of Islam'. IHRC proclaimed that the government's criticism of *shari'a* councils – which it says are 'an essential institution in the Muslim community' – was an assault on Islam: 'In our view the focus on Shariah councils is part of a wide, insidious and relentless attack on the whole Muslim way of life under the pretext of security and anti-terrorism.'[153] Ignoring the criticisms levelled at *shari'a* councils, the MCB defended them, saying:

> When it comes to 'Shari'ah courts' or arbitration panels it is important to realise that for those who choose to use them, they provide a valuable service for dispute resolution, as do religiously-mandated forums in other faiths. We reject notions that Muslims want 'parallel legal systems' or even a 'Shari'ah state'. They must certainly operate within the law of this land, and Muslim communities must work together to ensure their services offered are of a high standard in modern Britain.[154]

Other groups, such as MEND, have defended *shari'a* councils in similar terms.[155] MEND has, in fact, become one of the most ardent critics of government policy within the revivalist network, eclipsing the MAB, which now defers to MEND's work in articulating its own dissent.[156] Another very vocal critic of the government is CAGE. Echoing the MCB's point of view described earlier, it has stated:

> The British government, advised primarily by those who are inclined toward neoconservatism, are re-defining what constitutes genuine Islam. This idea that a British government can interfere with, define and regulate the Islamic faith and ideology is insulting to Muslims.[157]

Asim Qureshi, CAGE's research director, declares of Prevent, 'It's always been a social engineering programme to legitimise the government sponsored version of Islam only.'[158] He describes the government's counter-extremism approach as 'criminalising thought'. Standing shoulder-to-shoulder with CAGE is the Federation of Islamic Student Societies (FOSIS). At a CAGE event in March 2015, its vice president of student affairs, Ibrahim Ali, described the work of FOSIS and CAGE as part of a 'broad coalition' on university campuses dedicated to disseminating the message that, 'Prevent in itself is a racist agenda; it's an Islamophobic agenda'.[159] The government has recognised universities as important sites in this clash of values, but is yet to effectively evaluate and confront it. Similar sentiments have been expressed by Ibrahim Hewitt, a prominent figure within the revivalist network, who states that the government's targeting of non-violent extremism amounts to a war on Islam:

> Claims that the government is pursuing an 'anti-extremism' agenda are wearing thin; it is anti-Islam, period. It's fine for Muslims to have their faith as long as they keep it to themselves and out of the public domain. In other words, the neo-conservatives want Islam to be shorn of its 'complete way of life' guidelines. This is dangerous territory.[160]

Islamophobia is perceived as an attack on Islam as a 'way of life' carried out through not just government policy but also through a variety of social institutions. Iqbal Sacranie encapsulates this view, asserting, 'Islamophobic prejudice is prevalent in the mainstream on display in political life, in the media and in the attitudes of the police and the courts.'[161] In particular, journalists and research organisations that highlight the detrimental effects of Muslim groups and individuals upon civil liberties and social harmony in Britain are commonly attacked as being 'Islamophobic'. Targets include critics of Islamism, such as John Ware and Andrew Gilligan and the think tanks Policy Exchange and the Centre for Social Cohesion.[162] They also include human rights advocates such as Pragna Patel of Southall Black Sisters, who has campaigned for the abolition of religious tribunals in Britain. She writes, 'Those of us who try to challenge religious laws – on the basis of long-established secular feminist principles, international human rights and gender equality laws – are increasingly labelled "anti-faith", "unrepresentative" or "Islamophobic".'[163]

According to a former Islamic activist, the term 'Islamophobia' was invented by the International Institute for Islamic Thought to stifle the criticism of Islam, particularly its political, revivalist interpretations.[164] Abdur-

Rahman Muhammad, a former member of IIIT, has stated, 'This loathsome term is nothing more than a thought-terminating cliché conceived in the bowels of Muslim think tanks for the purpose of beating down critics.'[165] This claim, echoed by the French scholar Gilles Kepel, is difficult to ascertain.[166] However, whether intentional or not, the widespread use of the term effectively blurs the distinction between the legitimate criticism of certain orthodox Islamic doctrines and practices – including those, recognised by Muslim reformists, that undermine liberal values and human rights – and the bigoted discrimination against Muslims. Revivalist organisations have never articulated or even acknowledged this distinction. The government has so far not invited or challenged them make this distinction, perhaps because it has consistently claimed that Islam is a 'religion of peace' and does not wish to be seen as critical of Islam for fear of inciting further social division along lines it cannot control.

Indeed, commanding the authority to speak on matters of social division – to determine the principles of such division – is a key arena of conflict in which Islamic revivalists and the government, as the most powerful representative of Britain's liberal democracy, clash: Islamic revivalist groups claim the government is sowing the seeds of social division with its counter-extremism policies, branding non-violent, law-abiding Muslims as 'extremists' (or 'the other').

This trend was observable in the MCB's response to the government's announcement that it was developing a counter-extremism strategy. It voiced its over-riding concern as the possibility that all Muslims will be labelled 'extremist' and the perpetuation of 'a deep misunderstanding of Islam'.[167] When the strategy was published, in October 2015, MCB secretary general, Shuja Shafi, stated that it was based on a 'flawed analysis'.[168] He said it risked alienating Muslim communities and restricting the freedom of thought and expression. 'For over 10 years,' he added, 'we have had to contend with a misguided "conveyor-belt theory" analysis that conflates terrorism with subjective notions of extremism and Islamic practices.' On the government's plans to close mosques hosting 'extremist' speakers, Shafi questioned the government's authority to classify any mosque as 'extremist'.

The government, on the other hand, claims that the MCB and other revivalist groups inculcate a victim mentality amongst British Muslims, exacerbating the problem of radicalisation. As it has begun to articulate a problem with non-violent extremism – not just as a potential stepping-stone to terrorism, but as a threat to civil liberties and social cohesion – revivalist groups have become increasingly vocal in their opposition. The struggle to distinguish an 'in-group' – whether it be model British citizens or Muslims – from an 'out-group' is inextricable from a clash regarding the authority to establish social values. This couldn't have been more clearly articulated than when Theresa May, as home secretary, stated:

> Extremists often talk about a 'them' and 'us' – often described as a war between the West and Islam – and we do not challenge that successfully or often enough. Promoting the values *we* believe in will allow *us* to define the 'them' and 'us' on *our* terms … .[169]

Both the government and the revivalist groups use the language and concepts of the other to accrue symbolic authority. On one hand, the government, while characterising extremism as a rejection of British values, uses the notion of a 'genuine' Islam to identify its enemy: Islam is a 'religion of peace' that extremists have hijacked for their violent ends. But the MCB and other revivalist groups, while making exactly the same claim, deny the government the authority to pronounce on this.[170] On the other hand, revivalist groups, while characterising Islamophobia as a rejection of Islam and Muslims' freedom to practice it, use the liberal notions of bigotry and racism to identify an enemy, an oppressor. This most importantly includes the government and its policies, which are characterised as breaching human rights and the liberal democratic principles of equality and justice.

Yet, this use of each other's terminology is somewhat asymmetrical due to an imbalance in symbolic power in favour of the state. While revivalist groups explicitly deny the government the symbolic authority to represent Islam – even when it disassociates Islam from violence – the government does not explicitly deny the MCB and other revivalist groups the authority to determine what constitutes bigotry. Instead, it simply asserts its own authority to do so most clearly in the language of British values and extremism, as well as in legal reform, most notably in the area of counter-terrorism.

The MCB's explicit attack on the state's authority to classify Islam is in part a reflection of its weakness: if the government has the symbolic authority to classify Islam as non-*violent* – even though the MCB agrees with and expresses this view – then it is a short step to it possessing the authority to classify Islam as non-*extremist*. The government so far has not taken this step to classify Islam as such, although revivalist groups assume the contrary. Doing so would exacerbate the symbolic aspect of this clash. It would cast what the MCB and its allied groups consider as 'socially conservative' Muslim practices to be *un*Islamic and perhaps even illegal. It would render groups that support such practices, including the MCB and numerous others, beyond the pale of engagement, if not the law. Moreover, it would also undermine the MCB's authority to command respect and recognition within the Muslim population for its particular vision of society, its understanding of Islam and of the task of Muslims to usher in an Islamic revival.

To conclude this chapter and the previous one, it suffices to note that, in addition to being connected by the bonds of organisational networking and cultural solidarity, the key figures and groups comprising the global Muslim Brotherhood in Britain are engaged in a conflict with the state as the key representative of liberal democratic values and an associated way of viewing the world. This conflict of vision and values is both cultural and political. It concerns communal identity and a way of life, which includes how children are educated and how government policy is conducted, as well as the authority to articulate it and protect it by law. This conflict of values concerns the institutionalisation of competing worldviews within the structure of society and, ultimately, the state.

Islamic revivalism presents to the British state not mere advocacy for change within its liberal democratic framework, but a programme for a peaceful transformation of it. In this sense, it may be described as *metapolitical*. This conflict may be considered as a form of political subversion, but not in the sense conceived in the Security Service Act of 1989, as the undermining or overthrowing of 'parliamentary democracy'.[171] The political subversion of Islamic revivalism is not concerned with usurping the organs of government, as such, but with contesting the authority to represent and institutionalise the framework of moral values and mode of knowledge upon which the political order rests. It may be thought as the subversion of the cultural edifice upon which the political system is based. This concerns fundamental values, but these depend upon the way in which the world is perceived. As the late political sociologist Pierre Bourdieu observed of all collective struggles, 'political subversion presupposes cognitive subversion, a conversion of the vision of the world'.[172]

Notes

1 'Theresa May speech, 'A Stronger Britain, Built on our Values: A New Partnership to Defeat Extremism', Conservatives website, 23 March 2015. http://press.conservatives.com/post/115395299770/theresa-may-speech-a-stronger-britain-built-on.
2 Ibid.
3 HM Government (2015), p. 19.
4 'Independent review into sharia law launched', Government website, 26 May 2016, www.gov.uk/government/news/independent-review-into-sharia-law-launched; Home Office (2018).
5 Home Office, official inquiry response, correspondence by email, 27 December 2017.
6 Whine (2005), p. 54.
7 'British Schools, Islamic Rules', *Panorama*, BBC. Originally broadcast on 22 November 2010. www.bbc.co.uk/programmes/b00w8kwz. See also BBC News, 'Saudi school lessons in UK concern government', 22 November 2010. www.bbc.co.uk/news/uk-11799713.
8 Andrew Gilligan, 'Extremist Muslim schools: Islamism's most worrying manifestation of all', Andrew Gilligan's blog (originally on *The Telegraph* website), 22 November 2010. https://andrewgilliganblog.wordpress.com/2010/11/22/extremist-muslim-schools-islamisms-most-worrying-manifestation-of-all/.
9 Samuel Westrop, 'Britain Funding Separateness, Not Integration', Gatestone Institute, 5 March 2015. www.gatestoneinstitute.org/5323/trojan-horse.
10 Clarke (2014), p. 14.
11 Ibid., p. 95.
12 Ibid., p. 10.

13 Ibid., p. 48, emphasis added.
14 Education Committee (2015), p. 6.
15 Clarke (2014), p. 12.
16 Education Committee (2015), p. 6.
17 Ibid.
18 Home Office (2011), p. 107.
19 Ibid.
20 Gary Marks, 'Trojan Horse: Sir Michael Wilshaw's statement in full', *The Birmingham Mail*, 9 June 2014. www.birminghammail.co.uk/news/midlands-news/trojan-horse-sir-michael-wilshaws-7240705.
21 'Oral statement by Nicky Morgan on the "Trojan Horse" letter', British Government website, 22 July 2014. www.gov.uk/government/speeches/oral-statement-by-nicky-morgan-on-the-trojan-horse-letter.
22 Clarke (2014), pp. 11, 49.
23 Education Committee (2015), p. 7.
24 Patrick Howse, 'Overlapping "Trojan Horse" inquiries criticised by MPs', BBC News, 17 March 2015. www.bbc.co.uk/news/education-31905704.
25 Yusuf Patel, 'Gove's Trojan Horse Hoax finally exposed by Education Select Committee', Islam21c, 18 March 2015. www.islam21c.com/politics/goves-trojan-horse-hoax-finally-exposed-by-education-select-committee/.
26 MEND, 'Home Secretary announces new counter-extremism strategy', MEND website, 24 March 2015. https://mend.org.uk/news/home-secretary-announces-new-counter-extremism-strategy/.
27 'Oral statement by Nicky Morgan on the "Trojan Horse" letter', and Clarke (2014), p. 48.
28 Clarke (2014), p. 14.
29 Ibid., p. 96.
30 Marks, 'Trojan Horse: Sir Michael Wilshaw's statement in full'.
31 Gilligan, 'Muslim extremists, and a worrying lesson for us all'.
32 MEND, 'Trojan Hoax', event promotional video, 3 October 2017, MEND website. https://mend.org.uk/videos/trojan-hoax/.
33 Stand for Peace, 'Taxpayer-funded Muath Trust hosts hate preacher in aid of terror-linked charity', Stand for Peace website, 13 June 2014. http://standforpeace.org.uk/muath-trust-hosts-hate-preacher-in-aid-of-terror-linked-charity/. For videos and transcripts of Qadhi's views on homosexuality, non-Muslims, *jihad, hudud* punishments, etc., see also 'Yasir Qadhi', The Islamic Far Right in Britain blog, undated. https://tifrib.com/yasir-qadhi/.
34 Luke Heighton, and Shashi Singh, 'Event hosted by Muslim charity fundraised for Cage', *The Telegraph*, 6 January 2016. www.telegraph.co.uk/news/investigations/12085794/Event-hosted-by-Muslim-charity-fundraised-for-Cage.html.
35 Douglas Murray and Robin Simcox, 'The evidence shows that Cage is a pro-terrorist group', *The Telegraph*, 21 July 2014. www.telegraph.co.uk/news/uknews/law-and-order/10981050/The-evidence-shows-that-Cage-is-a-pro-terrorist-group.html.
36 Jonathan Walker, 'Anger over debate asking whether "Trojan Horse" plot to take over Birmingham schools really happened', *The Birmingham Mail*, 2 November 2017. www.birminghammail.co.uk/news/midlands-news/anger-over-debate-asking-whether-13849408.
37 Jonathan Walker, 'Birmingham Council insists Trojan Horse did happen and promises to challenge those who deny it', *The Birmingham Mail*, 3 November 2017. www.birminghammail.co.uk/news/midlands-news/birmingham-council-insists-trojan-horse-13852775.
38 Kershaw (2014), p. 4.
39 Ibid., pp. 4, 8.

40 These include identifying target schools; selecting a small group of activist parents – 'those most committed to Islam' – to pressure head teachers regarding the 'corrupting' influences of sex education, teaching about homosexuals, Christian prayers and mixed swimming and sports; installing a governor to 'drip feed' ideals for an Islamic school; identifying staff to disrupt schools from within so that the head teacher resigns or is removed; and instigating a letter and public relations campaign to governors, local MPs, education authorities, Ofsted, Governor Support, local media and the Department for Education, to pressure the head teacher, weakening their resolve until they give up. See Kershaw (2014), p. 6, and Clarke (2014), pp. 111–112.
41 Clarke (2014), p. 14.
42 Ibid., p. 119.
43 Ibid., p. 21.
44 Richard Kerbaj and Sian Griffiths, 'Trojan Horse kingpin led fundamentalists', *The Sunday Times*, 1 June 2014. www.thesundaytimes.co.uk/sto/news/uk_news/Education/article1417360.ece.
45 'Direction: Tahir Alam barred from managing independent schools', Government website, 9 September 2015. www.gov.uk/government/publications/direction-tahir-alam-barred-from-managing-independent-schools.
46 Clarke (2014), p. 8.
47 Ibid., pp. 6, 75.
48 MCB, 'Speech by Dr Shuja Shafi on British and Islamic Values', MCB website, 29 January 2015. www.mcb.org.uk/shuja-shafi-speech-british-values-290115/.
49 Education Committee (2015), p. 29.
50 MCB, 'The Muslim Council of Britain Responds to Peter Clarke's "Trojan Horse" Letter Report', MCB website, 23 July 2014. www.mcb.org.uk/the-muslim-council-of-britain-responds-topeter-clarkes-trojan-horse-letter-report/.
51 Ibid. See also MCB (2015), p. 15.
52 Casey (2016), n. 7.47, p. 116.
53 'The Communities and Local Government Committee questions Dame Louise Casey about her report on social integration', 9 January 2017. www.parliament.uk/business/committees/committees-a-z/commons-select/communities-and-local-government-committee/news-parliament-2015/integration-review-evidence-16-17/.
54 Andrew Gilligan, 'Trojan Horse "just the tip of the iceberg"', *The Telegraph*, 12 October 2014. www.telegraph.co.uk/education/educationnews/11157116/Trojan-Horse-just-the-tip-of-the-iceberg.html.
55 Henry Bodkin, 'Second Islamist "Trojan Horse" scandal feared after Oldham headteacher reports death threats', *The Telegraph*, 19 February 2017. www.telegraph.co.uk/news/2017/02/19/second-islamist-trojan-horse-scandal-feared-oldham-headteacher/.
56 'The Communities and Local Government Committee questions Dame Louise Casey about her report on social integration', 9 January 2017.
57 Ibid.
58 'Oral statement by Nicky Morgan on the "Trojan Horse" letter'.
59 Jonathan Walker, 'New teacher disciplinary procedures to deal with "Trojan Horse" attempts to infiltrate schools', *The Birmingham Post*, 2 October 2017. www.birminghampost.co.uk/news/regional-affairs/new-teacher-disciplinary-procedures-deal-13704242.
60 Casey (2016), n. 8.25, p. 128.
61 Clarke (2014), p. 48, emphasis in original.
62 MCB (2007).
63 Ibid., p. 18, emphasis added.
64 Sarwar (2006). p. 13.

65 Sarwar (2001), p. 30.
66 Bleher (1996), pp. 61, 64.
67 Ibid., p.64.
68 Ibid., emphasis added.
69 Musharraf Hussain, quoted from Association of Muslim Social Scientists UK, Muslim Education in Europe Conference, 27–29 September 2002, p. 36, cited in MacEoin (2009a), p. 50.
70 Ibid.
71 Halstead (2004), p. 519.
72 Ibid., p. 523.
73 Ibid., pp. 521–522.
74 Statement from The First World Conference on Muslim Education, 1977, Mecca, quoted in Sarwar (2001), p. 29.
75 This information was available on IBERR's main website until at least November 2010 (at 'About IBERR', http://iberr.co.za/index.php?option=com_content&task=view&id=14&Itemid=2), but has subsequently been removed. However, it is still available on its Russian website at http://iberr.chat.ru/iberr1.htm.
76 Halstead (2004), p. 521.
77 Bat Ye'or (2005), p. 254.
78 Johnson (2008), p. 77; Johnson (2010), pp. 195–196.
79 'About Us', IIIT-UK website. www.iiituk.com/about.htm.
80 Michael Wilshaw, 'Advice note from Her Majesty's Chief Inspector, Sir Michael Wilshaw, to the Secretary of State for Education, Rt Hon. Nicky Morgan MP, on school inspections in the London Borough of Tower Hamlets', UK Government website, 21 November 2014. www.gov.uk/government/uploads/system/uploads/attachment_data/file/386594/Tower_20Hamlets_20advice_20note.pdf.
81 Muhammad Abdul Bari, 'Religious Middle Way Is the Antidote to Extremism', *The Huffington Post*, 3 June 2015. www.huffingtonpost.co.uk/muhammad-abdul-bari/religious-extremism_b_7483840.html.
82 Nielsen (1992), p. 109.
83 See, for example, Richard Edwards, 'Sharia courts operating in Britain', *The Telegraph*, 14 September 2008. www.telegraph.co.uk/news/uknews/2957428/Sharia-law-courts-operating-in-Britain.html; and Abdul Taher, 'Revealed: UK's first official sharia courts', *The Times*, 14 September 2008. https://web.archive.org/web/20080917152241/http://www.timesonline.co.uk/tol/news/uk/crime/article4749183.ece.
84 Riazat But, 'Uproar as archbishop says sharia law inevitable in UK', *The Guardian*, 8 February 2008. www.guardian.co.uk/politics/2008/feb/08/uk.religion.
85 'UK Board of Shariah Councils', London Central Mosque and Islamic Cultural Centre website, undated. www.iccuk.org/page.php?section=media&page=ukboard_sharia_councils. This was confirmed in interviews with Maulana Abu Sayeed, 16 February 2012, and Suhaib Hassan, 9 February 2012.
86 Interview with Maulana Abu Sayeed, 16 February 2012.
87 Interviews with Maulana Abu Sayeed, 15 February 2012, and Suhaib Hassan, 9 February 2012.
88 Addison (2009), pp. xiii–xv.
89 MacEoin (2009b), p. 69.
90 Interview with Ibrahim Mogra, 29 August 2012.
91 Interviews with Maulana Abu Sayeed, 16 February 2012, and Suhaib Hassan, 9 February 2012; Thomson (2000 and 2001).
92 Interview with Suhaib Hassan, 9 February 2012.
93 Edwards, 'Sharia courts operating in Britain', and Taher, 'Revealed: UK's first official sharia courts'.
94 Perhaps indicative of how divorce features in the majority of disputes referred to *shari'a* courts in Britain, the Leyton Islamic Sharia Council, which has operated

an unofficial *shari'a* court since 1982, claims that 95% of the 7,000 cases it has dealt with since its inception relate to divorce. See Ahmed and Gibb, 'From Leyton to Dewsbury, Sharia courts are already settling disputes'.

95 'WHAT IS KHUL'A?', Islamic Sharia Council website, undated. Webpage captured on 1 April 2009. http://web.archive.org/web/20090401224229/http://www.islamic-sharia.org/divorce-khula/what-is-khula-2.html.

96 Proudman (2012), pp. 29, 39, 47, 73.

97 Charlotte Proudman, 'A Practical and Legal Analysis of Islamic Marriage, Divorce and Dowry', Family Law Week, 31 January 2012. www.familylawweek.co.uk/site.aspx?i=ed95364.

98 Domestic violence was actually listed on MAT's website one type of case that it deals with. See Muslim Arbitration Tribunal website: http://web.archive.org/web/20111004220746/http://www.matribunal.com/cases.html.

99 Murad Ahmed and Frances Gibb, 'From Leyton to Dewsbury, Sharia courts are already settling disputes', *The Times*, 8 February 2008. www.thetimes.co.uk/tto/faith/article2098953.ece.

100 Edwards, 'Sharia courts operating in Britain', and Taher, 'Revealed: UK's first official sharia courts'.

101 Senay Boztas, 'Sharia in the UK: The courts in the shadow of British law offering rough justice for Muslim women', *The Independent*, 4 December 2015. www.independent.co.uk/news/uk/home-news/sharia-in-the-uk-the-courts-in-the-shadow-of-british-law-offering-rough-justice-for-muslim-women-a6761221.html.

102 Manea (2016), pp. 224–226.

103 Green (2009), p. 4.

104 Namazie, Atasheen and Waters (2010), p. 16.

105 Mazher Mahmood and Marie Woolf, 'Revealed: scandal of child brides', *The Times*, 9 September 2012. https://web.archive.org/web/20160509161906/http://www.thesundaytimes.co.uk/sto/news/uk_news/Society/article1122316.ece.

106 Ibid.

107 Senay Boztas, 'Sharia courts in Britain lock women into "marital captivity", study says', *The Independent*, 4 December 2015. www.independent.co.uk/news/uk/home-news/sharia-courts-in-britain-lock-women-into-marital-captivity-study-says-a6761141.html.

108 Interview with Maulana Abu Sayeed, 16 February 2012; Thomson (2001), p. 6.

109 Tim Ross, 'Rape within marriage is "impossible"', claims Muslim cleric', *The Telegraph*, October 15, 2010. https://web.archive.org/web/20101018071909/http://www.telegraph.co.uk/news/newstopics/religion/8064571/Rape-within-marriage-is-impossible-claims-Muslim-cleric.html.

110 Proudman (2012), p. 74.

111 Al-Haddad cited from audio and video recordings available at 'Haitham al-Haddad', The Islamic Far Right in Britain blog, undated. http://tifrib.com/haitham-al-haddad/.

112 BBC News, 'School's legal bid to block Ofsted report continues', 8 November 2016. www.bbc.com/news/education-37899565.

113 According to orthodox interpretations of the *shari'a*, a married woman is obliged to accommodate her husband's sexual advances and needs. See, for example, the Shafi'ite manual of *shari'a, 'Umdat al-Salik*. This was authorised in 1991 by Sunni Islam's highest learning institution, al-Azhar University in Egypt and recommended as a guide to the *shari'a* by the president of the Muslim Association of Britain to the author of this book. It states that it is 'obligatory for a woman to let her husband have sex with her' if 'he asks her', if they are 'at home', and if 'she can physically endure it'. The husband has the 'full right to

enjoy his wife's person … in what does not physically harm her' (al-Misri (1994), pp. 526, 527).

114 See, for example, the *fatwa* of Shaykh Ibn 'Uthaymeen (1925–2001), the prominent Saudi scholar of Islamic law, who wrote around 50 books on the subject. This is still posted on the Web and referred to as authoritative. Unless a woman is ill, he states, 'It is obligatory upon the woman to respond to her husband if he calls her to his bed.' See Shaykh Ibn 'Uthaymeen, 'Husband calls his wife to bed, but she is ill and unable to respond to his call', 24 June 2001. www.fatwa-online.com/husband-calls-his-wife-to-bed-but-she-is-ill-unable-to-respond-to-his-call/.

115 Senay Boztas, 'Sharia in the UK: The courts in the shadow of British law offering rough justice for Muslim women', emphasis added.

116 Sarwar (2006). p. 157.

117 Ibid., p. 159.

118 Parvez (2007), p. 239.

119 Manea (2016), p. 129.

120 Namazie, Atasheen and Waters (2010), p. 7.

121 European Court of Human Rights, Refah Partisi and Others v. Turkey BAILII (ECHR 87). 13 February 2003, emphasis added. www.bailii.org/eu/cases/ECHR/2003/87.html.

122 Afua Hirsch, 'Sharia law incompatible with human rights legislation, Lords say', *The Guardian,* 23 October 2008. www.guardian.co.uk/world/2008/oct/23/religion-islam.

123 Cox (2015).

124 Amin Al-Astewani, 'Why has Baroness Cox's Bill failed to become law?', Law and Religion blog, 4 April 2016. www.lawandreligionuk.com/2016/04/04/why-has-baroness-coxs-bill-failed-to-become-law/.

125 'Timeline', Equal and Free website, undated. http://equalandfree.org/timeline/.

126 See 'Marriage Act 1949 (Amendment) Bill [HL] 2017–19', Parliament website, undated. https://services.parliament.uk/bills/2017-19/marriageact1949amendment.html.

127 'Independent review into sharia law launched', Government website.

128 'Open letter to the Home Secretary: The law and not religion is basis of justice for citizens', One Law for All website, 4 July 2016. http://onelawforall.org.uk/open-letter-to-the-home-secretary/.

129 Home Office (2018).

130 Ibid., p. 5.

131 Casey (2016), n. 8.50, p. 135.

132 Home Office (2018), p. 16.

133 Ibid., p. 6.

134 Ibid., p. 21.

135 Casey (2016), n. 1.31–1.32, p. 11.

136 'Home Office in the media: 02 February 2018', Home Office blog, 2 February 2018. https://homeofficemedia.blog.gov.uk/2018/02/02/home-office-in-the-media-02-february-2018/.

137 Ibid.

138 'Sharia councils inquiry launched', Parliament website, 24 June 2016. www.parliament.uk/business/committees/committees-a-z/commons-select/home-affairs-committee/news-parliament-2015/160623-new-inquiry-sharia-councils/.

139 'Sharia councils inquiry – publications', Parliament website, undated. www.parliament.uk/business/committees/committees-a-z/commons-select/home-affairs-committee/inquiries/parliament-2015/inquiry6/publications/.

140 Gilligan, 'Muslim group with links to extremists boasts of influencing election'.

141 MCB, 'MCB Rejects Hazel Blears' Baseless Accusations About Attacking Jewish Communities', MCB website, 26 March 2009. www.mcb.org.uk/mcb-rejects-hazel-blears-baseless-accusations-about-attacking-jewish-communities/.
142 Wilshaw, 'Advice note'.
143 Home Office (2011), p. 107.
144 HM Government (2015).
145 Freddie Whittaker, 'Government developing "fundamental British values curriculum"', 27 October 2017. https://schoolsweek.co.uk/government-developing-fundamental-british-values-curriculum/.
146 Home Office (2011), p. 7.
147 Cabinet Office (2013), p. 1.
148 'Theresa May speech A Stronger Britain, Built on our Values: A New Partnership to Defeat Extremism'.
149 'Extremism: PM speech', British Government website, 20 July 2015. www.gov.uk/government/speeches/extremism-pm-speech, emphasis added.
150 'Theresa May speech A Stronger Britain, Built on our Values: A New Partnership to Defeat Extremism'.
151 Patrick Wintour, 'Muslim Council of Britain objects to Pickles letter to Islamic leaders', *The Guardian*, 19 January 2015. www.theguardian.com/politics/2015/jan/19/uk-muslim-council-objections-eric-pickles-letter.
152 IHRC, 'Muslim community rejects the State's criminalisation of Islam and condemns moves to silence legitimate critique and dissent', IHRC website, 11 March 2015. http://ihrc.org.uk/news/comment/11381-muslim-community-rejects-the-states-criminalisation-of-islam-and-condemns-moves-to-silence-legitimate-critique-and-dissent-.
153 IHRC, 'A letter to Nick Clegg regarding the government's proposed new plans to "combat Islamic extremism"', IHRC website, 11 March 2015. www.ihrc.org.uk/activities/campaigns/11382-a-letter-to-nick-clegg-regarding-the-governments-proposed-new-plans-to-combat-islamic-extremism.
154 MCB (2015), p. 11.
155 MEND, 'Home Secretary announces new counter-extremism strategy'.
156 For example, see Mariam Amir Hassan, 'Diverse and Strong Voices Emerging – 15,000 Stood Up to Racism and Fascism in the UK', MAB website, 30 March 2015. www.mabonline.net/diverse-and-strong-voices-emerging-15000-stood-up-to-racism-and-fascism-in-the-uk/. This refers to MEND's document that sought to stop the Counter-Terrorism and Security Bill, MEND (2014).
157 Mohammed and Siddiqui (2013), p. 9.
158 Karen Jayes, 'The PREVENT Policy: a politically motivated programme', CAGE website, 5 August 2014. http://cageuk.org/article/prevent-policy-politically-motivated-programme.
159 Stuart (2015), p. 22.
160 Ibrahim Hewitt, 'Crusade against British Muslims in education', *Aljazeera*, 12 May 2014. www.aljazeera.com/indepth/opinion/2014/05/crusade-against-british-muslims-201451018411814899.html.
161 Murtaza Ali Shah, 'Muslims call for change in UK blasphemy laws', *The International News* (Pakistan), 14 November 2012. www.thenews.com.pk/Todays-News-2-142770-Muslims-call-for-change-in-UK-blasphemy-laws.
162 See Miller, Griffin and Miller (2011).
163 Pragna Patel, 'Sharia courts have no place in UK family law. Listen to women who know', *The Guardian*, 14 December 2016. www.theguardian.com/commentisfree/2016/dec/14/sharia-courts-family-law-women.
164 Claire Berlinski, 'How the Term "Islamophobia" Got Shoved Down Your Throat', *Ricochet*, 24 November 2010. http://ricochet.com/main-feed/

Moderate-Muslim-Watch-How-the-Term-Islamophobia-Got-Shoved-Down-Your-Throat.

165 Ibid.

166 Kepel (2017), p. 17.

167 MCB, 'Prime Minister's Speech on Extremism: Muslim Council of Britain Makes Initial Response', MCB website, 20 July 2015. www.mcb.org.uk/prime-ministers-speech-on-extremism-muslim-council-of-britain-makes-initial-response/.

168 MCB, '"One Nation Counter-Extremism Strategy" Risks Further Undermining Fight Against Terrorism', MCB website, 19 October 2015. www.mcb.org.uk/one-nation-counter-extremism-strategy-risks-fight-against-terrorism-191015/.

169 'Home Secretary speech at summit on countering extremism', British Government website, 20 February 2015. www.gov.uk/government/speeches/white-house-summit-on-countering-violent-extremism, emphasis added.

170 For example, MCB, 'MCB Condemns Day of Violence', MCB website, 26 June 2015. www.mcb.org.uk/mcb-condemns-day-of-violence/.

171 Gill (1994), p. 120.

172 Bourdieu (1991), pp. 127–128.

References

Addison, Neil (2009). 'Foreword: Sharia tribunals in Britain – mediators or arbitrators?'. In Denis MacEoin, *Sharia Law or One Law for All?* (ed. David G. Green): viii–xv. London: Civitas. www.civitas.org.uk/pdf/ShariaLawOrOneLawForAll.pdf.

Bat Ye'or (2005). *Eurabia: The Euro-Arab Axis.* Cranbury, NJ: Fairleigh Dickson University Press.

Bleher, Sahib Mustaqim (1996). 'A programme for Muslim education in a non-Muslim society'. In Ghulam Sarwar (ed.), *Issues in Islamic Education*: 61–65. London: Muslim Educational Trust.

Bourdieu, Pierre (1991). *Language and Symbolic Power.* Ed. John B. Thompson, trans. Gino Raymond and Matthew Adamson. Cambridge: Polity Press.

Cabinet Office (2013). 'Tackling extremism in the UK', Report from the Prime Minister's Task Force on Tackling Radicalisation and Extremism. www.gov.uk/government/uploads/system/uploads/attachment_data/file/263181/ETF_FINAL.pdf.

Casey, Louise (2016). *The Casey Review: A Review into Opportunity and Integration.* Department for Communities and Local Government. www.gov.uk/government/uploads/system/uploads/attachment_data/file/575973/The_Casey_Review_Report.pdf.

Clarke, Peter (2014). 'Report into allegations concerning Birmingham schools arising from the 'Trojan Horse' letter'. HC 576. House of Commons. www.gov.uk/government/uploads/system/uploads/attachment_data/file/340526/HC_576_accessible_-.pdf.

Cox, Caroline (2015). 'A parallel world: confronting the abuse of many Muslim women in Britain today'. Bow Group, London. www.bowgroup.org/sites/bowgroup.uat.pleasetest.co.uk/files/Bow%20Group%20Report%20-%20A%20Parallel%20World%20-%20Confronting%20the%20abuse%20of%20many%20Muslim%20women%20in%20Britain%20today%2024%2003%2015.pdf.

Education Committee (2015). 'Extremism in schools: the Trojan Horse affair'. Seventh Report of Session 2014–2015. HC 473. House of Commons. www.publications.parliament.uk/pa/cm201415/cmselect/cmeduc/473/473.pdf.

Frampton, Martyn, David Goodhart and Khalid Mahmood (2016). *Unsettled Belonging: A Survey of Britain's Muslim Communities.* London: Policy Exchange.

https://policyexchange.org.uk/wp-content/uploads/2016/12/PEXJ5037_Muslim_Communities_FINAL.pdf.

Gill, Peter (1994). *Policing Politics: Security Intelligence and the Liberal Democratic State*. London: Frank Cass.

Green, David G. (2009). 'Editor's introduction'. In Denis MacEoin, *Sharia Law or One Law for All?* (Ed. David G. Green): 1–8. London: Civitas. www.civitas.org.uk/pdf/ShariaLawOrOneLawForAll.pdf.

Halstead, J. Mark (2004). 'An Islamic concept of education'. In *Comparative Education*, vol. 40, no. 4: 517–529.

HM Government (2015). *Counter-Extremism Strategy*, Cm 9148. www.gov.uk/government/uploads/system/uploads/attachment_data/file/470088/51859_Cm9148_Accessible.pdf.

Home Office (2011). *Prevent Strategy*. Cm 8092. www.gov.uk/government/uploads/system/uploads/attachment_data/file/97976/prevent-strategy-review.pdf.

Home Office (2018). *The Independent Review into the Application of Sharia Law in England and Wales*. Cm 9560. www.gov.uk/government/uploads/system/uploads/attachment_data/file/678473/6.4152_HO_CPFG_Report_into_Sharia_Law_in_the_UK_PRINT.pdf.

Johnson, Ian (2008). 'The Brotherhood's westward expansion'. In *Current Trends in Islamist Ideology*, vol. 6: 71–84. The Hudson Institute Center on Islam, Democracy, and the Future of the Muslim World. www.hudson.org/research/9853-the-brotherhood-s-westward-expansion.

Johnson, Ian (2010). *A Mosque in Munich: Nazis, the CIA and the Rise of the Muslim Brotherhood in the West*. New York: Houghton Mifflin Harcourt.

Kepel, Gilles (2017). *Terror in France: The Rise of Jihad in the West*. Princeton, NJ: Princeton University Press.

Kershaw, Ian (2014). 'Investigation report: Trojan Horse letter'. Northern Education. www.birmingham.gov.uk/downloads/file/1579/investigation_report_trojan_horse_letter_the_kershaw_report.

MacEoin, Denis (2009a). *Music, Chess and other Sins: Segregation, Integration, and Muslim Schools in Britain*. London: Civitas. www.civitas.org.uk/pdf/MusicChessAndOtherSins.pdf.

MacEoin, Denis (2009b). *Sharia Law or One Law for All?* Ed. David G. Green. London: Civitas. www.civitas.org.uk/pdf/ShariaLawOrOneLawForAll.pdf.

Manea, Elham (2016). *Women and Shari'a Law: The Impact of Legal Pluralism in the UK*. London: I. B. Taurus.

MCB (2007). *Meeting the Needs of Muslim Pupils in State Schools: Information and Guidance for Schools*. London: Muslim Council of Britain. www.religionlaw.co.uk/MCBschoolsreport07.pdf.

MCB (2015). *Fairness, Not Favours: British Muslim Perspectives at the 2015 General Election*. London: Muslim Council of Britain. www.mcb.org.uk/wp-content/uploads/2015/03/fairnessnotfavours-MCB.pdf.

MEND (2014). 'Counter Terrorism and Security Bill briefing 2014'. Published online at: https://mend.org.uk/wp-content/uploads/2017/03/CTSB2014_Briefing_Paper_v361.pdf.

Miller, Tom, Tom Griffin and David Miller (2011). *The Cold War on British Muslims: An Examination of Policy Exchange and the Centre for Social Cohesion*. London: Spinwatch. www.thecordobafoundation.com/attach/SpinwatchReport_ColdWar12.pdf.

al-Misri, Ahmad ibnNaqib (1994). *'Umdat al-Salik – Reliance of the Traveller, A Classic Manual of Islamic Sacred Law.* Ed. and trans. Nuh Ha Mim Keller. Beltsville: Amana Publications.

Mohammed, Jahangir and Adnan Siddiqui (2013). 'The Prevent strategy: a cradle to grave police-state'. Ed. Louise De Menthon. CAGE, London. https://cage.ngo/wp-content/uploads/A4_PREVENT_CAGE_REPORT_WEB.pdf.

Namazie, Maryam, Yassi Atasheen and Anna Waters (2010). *Sharia Law in Britain: A Threat to One Law for All and Equal Rights.* London: One Law for All. www.onelawforall.org.uk/wp-content/uploads/New-Report-Sharia-Law-in-Britain_fixed.pdf.

Nielsen, Jørgen (1992). *Muslims in Western Europe.* Edinburgh: Edinburgh University Press.

Parvez, Zahid (2007). *Building a New Society: An Islamic Approach to Social Change.* Markfield: Revival Publications.

Proudman, Charlotte Rachael (2012). *Equal and Free? Evidence in Support of Baroness Cox's Arbitration and Mediation Services (Equality) Bill.* London: House of Lords. www.secularism.org.uk/uploads/equal-and-free-16.pdf.

Sarwar, Ghulam (2001). *Islamic Education: Its Meaning, Problems and Prospects.* London: Muslim Educational Trust.

Sarwar, Ghulam (2006). *Islam: Beliefs and Teachings.* 8th edition. London: Muslim Educational Trust.

Stuart, Hannah (2015). 'Understanding CAGE: a public information dossier'. Centre for the Response to Radicalisation and Terrorism, Policy Paper No. 5. Henry Jackson Society, London. http://henryjacksonsociety.org/wp-content/uploads/2015/04/Understanding-CAGE.pdf.

Thomson, Ahmad (2000). 'Questions and answers on the Shari'ah'. Published online at: www.wynnechambers.co.uk/pdf/Qs&As.pdf.

Thomson, Ahmad (2001). 'Divine Law and man-made law'. *Al-Karam Muslim Magazine*, vol. 3, no. 2. Available online at: www.wynnechambers.co.uk/pdf/DivineLaw.pdf.

Whine, Michael (2005). 'The penetration of Islamist ideology in Britain'. In *Current Trends in Islamist Ideology*, vol. 1: 50–67. The Hudson Institute Center on Islam, Democracy, and the Future of the Muslim World. www.hudson.org/research/9886-the-penetration-of-islamist-ideology-in-britain.

Zee, Machteld (2016). *Choosing Sharia?: Multiculturalism, Islamic Fundamentalism and Sharia Councils.* Utrecht, Netherlands: Eleven International Publishing.

Conclusion

Islamism, 'non-violent extremism' and the 'battle of ideas' in Britain

The individuals and groups associated with the Muslim Brotherhood and Jama'at-i-Islami in Britain, as this book has shown, are organisationally networked, bonded with the ties of cultural solidarity, and engaged in a conflict of values with Britain's mainstream liberal democratic culture as well as the British political authorities. Collectively, they form a social movement.

This is not a social movement in the sense in which the term is most commonly understood in the popular imagination or in the academic study of social movements. It does not have a central leadership structure with clearly identifiable spokespeople, it is not primarily driven by a desire to address inequalities within the political system, and the conflict in which it is involved is not merely with the state. But it is a social movement nonetheless. It is decentralised, but very well networked and organised. It is concerned with what its protagonists perceive as injustices within Britain's political and legal apparatus, but this concern drives deeper to the taken-for-granted values underlying and sustaining this apparatus. It is engaged in a conflict with the state but, more importantly, it is opposed to the culture – political, legal, economic, scientific and social – that the state represents and protects. It is a social movement but, to emphasise its concern with both a way of life and the authority to present and maintain it, it is perhaps better described as a cultural and political movement.

The individuals that feature prominently in this revivalist movement do not constitute a clear vanguard, in the sense of a unified front directing its strategic direction. There is no hierarchical central command structure but, rather, a multiplicity of overlapping leadership structures. In each distinct field of contention there are clearly positioned leaders or clusters of leaders with specialist knowledge and experience. Without a central or dominant leadership structure it may be asked whether the network of revivalists is engaged in disconnected and diverse struggles, and thus whether it is a movement at all. But what makes this a singular struggle, as opposed to a plurality of struggles, is not only the overlapping organisational connections between the key protagonists, but also the singularity of stakes in the various fields in which they conflict.

For the protagonists of the revivalist movement – whether advocating for changes in government policy and legislation, influencing the education of Muslim children, arbitrating disputes in Muslim communities or acquiring political power in local government – the stakes are the same: the embodiment of a distinct Islamic worldview and associated values within the social and political structures of the British state, and within the cognitive structures of its people. This involves the religious identity not only of Muslims and Muslim social institutions but also – on a timescale of no immediate concern to them – of would-be Muslims and would-be Muslim social institutions. For the authorities of the state, including central and local government, the stakes involve the protection of the liberal democratic worldview and associated values within Britain's social and political order, as well as in the minds of its citizenry.

The conflict in which the revivalist movement in Britain is engaged is networked or distributed throughout the social order in various fields, including education, media, governance and law. The *raison d'être* of the work of all revivalists is to defend and promote Islam as a way of life in Britain. This includes an epistemology and an ethics – an approach to knowledge and a moral code – that conflicts with the liberal democratic status quo and the powers that preside over it. Because a way of life has a multiplicity of expressions – such as how people educate their children and how they settle disputes – there is a multiplicity of antagonisms or potential antagonisms with the authorities protecting the liberal democratic status quo where these individuals and groups are active. These include the subtle contention of 'British values' in campaigns to influence government policy or law, for example in the Muslim Council of Britain (MCB) and others' efforts seeking the criminalisation of 'blaspheming' Islam[1] or special provisions for Muslim schoolchildren in state schools that elevate the collective (specifically the *umma*) above the individual. They also include more confrontational campaigns agitating Muslim sentiment against the government, for example in CAGE and FOSIS's collaborative work in British universities undermining its counter-radicalisation strategy, Prevent.[2]

Contesting Muslim identity and Islamic values

According to Lorenzo Vidino, all global Muslim Brotherhood organisations in the West possess two goals. The first, he says, is 'the preservation of an Islamic identity among Western Muslims'.[3] This alludes to a crucial feature of the movement. But these groups, as this book has shown, do not simply seek to 'preserve' Muslim identity. They seek to define and practically engineer it. If there is something as an Islamic identity of Muslims in the West perceived in need of protection from the corrupting influences of decadent secular culture, then it is also something that is contested between Muslims with very different perceptions of their faith and its role in contemporary Western societies. Muslim identity is not something to be taken for granted, but something that is actively produced and contested within a web of often conflictual relationships.

The revivalists' claims about what it is to be a Muslim, or what constitutes the Islamic values that a Muslim should follow, are contentious for other Muslims. For some Muslims, their faith does not determine the curriculum that their children ought to learn, the rules regarding who should be a witness to their marriage, or the way they ought to understand and live out gender roles. For others, Islam does play a role in determining these things, but does so in a way that is compatible with liberal democratic norms. During the Trojan Horse affair, numerous Muslim parents objected to the 'Islamising agenda' being put in place in Birmingham schools. For doing so, some were reportedly referred to as 'shaitans [devils] running out to make mischief'.[4] According to an ICM poll of Muslim attitudes in Britain conducted in 2016, 'the most important question [for Muslims] when contemplating education is its quality, rather than any emphasis on ensuring children receive a specifically *Muslim* education'.[5] A clear majority of Muslims want their children to be taught art and music, contrary to both the efforts of 'activist governors' to alter the curriculum in Trojan Horse schools and the principles expressed in the MCB's guidance. In analysing this poll, Frampton, Goodhart and Mahmood write, 'such measures were being enforced against the wishes of a clear majority of Muslim parents, whose desire for their children to receive a holistic, secular education was the principal casualty of that conspiracy'.[6] The same poll also showed how, contrary to the Trojan Horse agenda and the revivalist Islamisation of knowledge programme, most Muslim parents wish their children to learn their Islam outside school.[7]

The institutionalisation of a particular and contentious understanding of Islam has not just been a stake in schools in Birmingham and in the advocacy work of revivalist groups such as the Muslim Educational Trust (MET) and the Association of Muslim Schools UK (AMS-UK). It is also a stake in *shari'a* courts, where Islam is presented, through the application of classical *shari'a* principles, in a way that is disputed by other Muslims, including those who are learned on the subject of Islamic law.

Elham Manea, a self-identified Muslim scholar who spent four years researching *shari'a* and its impact on women in Britain, says the type of Islamic law that is dispensed in Britain's *shari'a* courts is derived from 'the medieval jurisprudence tradition, which freely violates human rights and the concept of gender equality'.[8] She finds this remarkable given that 'the trend in Arab and Islamic countries is to push for the reform of Islamic law'.[9] Demonstrating that this is possible from a Muslim perspective, she cites the Tunisian reformer al-Taher al-Haddad, whose work, including the 1930 book *Our Women in Shari'a and Life*, influenced legal reforms in post-independence Tunisia addressing the inferior status of women. Manea also cites another Muslim scholar in favour of modernising *shari'a*, Abdullahi Ahmed An-Na'im, who argues that 'the principles of shari'a – sanctioning serious and unacceptable discrimination on the grounds of gender and religion – are untenable today and violate the constitutional principles of equality before the law'.[10] An-Na'im insists not only that Islamic law needs reform but also that the state should treat individuals in terms of their citizenship only, and not in terms of their membership of a religious community.

The second goal that Vidino sees the global Muslim Brotherhood groups as possessing is to become the official or de facto interlocutors for Muslims in their respective countries.[11] This claim also intimates an important point, but it is somewhat concealed by a slight empirical inaccuracy: not all groups in the movement aspire to represent Muslims' interests to the state authorities officially or unofficially. In Britain, some groups, such as the UK Islamic Mission and the Islamic Forum of Europe, do not have any communicative channels to the government and prefer to work within Muslim communities, leaving the MCB to act as the primary interlocutor and other groups, such as the AMS-UK, to represent Muslim needs in specialist fields such as education.

Nevertheless, while only some groups have an official or unofficial intermediary role with the state, all of the individuals and groups comprising the global Muslim Brotherhood in Britain are engaged in symbolic work that might be thought to 'represent' Islam and Muslims, whether in relation to the state or within Muslim environments. Yet, in the same sense in which these actors are engaged in engineering (rather than merely protecting) Muslim identity, they are also engaged in determining (rather than merely representing) Muslims' needs. Strictly speaking, the revivalist actors – who may be public interlocutors, local community activists below the radar of media interest, or both – are involved in a symbolic struggle not to represent Islam as a way of life, but to *present* it as such.

Vidino's two goals highlight two key aspects of the revivalists' struggle, one relating to Muslim communities and the other relating to the secular authorities. Respectively, these may be seen as internal and external *da'wa*. But we must add that these two aspects are linked.

For the revivalist movement in Britain, the struggle within Muslim milieus is arguably more important than that in the social and political mainstream. Muslims are viewed by revivalists as an important vanguard for *da'wa* and bringing Islam to the British people, so activities that impart a certain Islamic worldview and set of values which can affect concentrations of Muslims are particularly significant. But this struggle is inevitably connected with the state, since the state is the guardian of policies, regulations and laws that affect Muslims as a distinct 'community' and that affect them as citizens of the state along with everyone else. Much of the work of the revivalist movement focuses on Muslims, but this necessarily involves a relationship with the state, not just as the regulator of policy that affects British Muslims as British citizens, but also as 'the ultimate source of symbolic power' that protects a dominant worldview and associated values perceived to be antagonistic or obstructive to Islam as a way of life.[12]

Islamism, ideology, and the 'battle of ideas'

Underlying the description of revivalist individuals and groups as 'Islamists' is the unquestioned assumption that they share a political ideology whose goal is an Islamic state, as well as a gradualist, bottom-up methodology. As this book has shown, however, these individuals and groups generally consider the Islamic state not as a goal but as a reward, as a natural outcome of a society infused with Islamic values. Strictly speaking, the Islamic state is not an objective in itself, but a promise – a promised reward for widespread piety. If it may be said to be strived for, then it is only inasmuch as it is a component or bi-product of a society that has fully embraced Islam as a comprehensive 'system' of life that cannot leave matters of political organisation untouched.

While 'Islamist' does not really apply to the revivalist movement without the aforementioned qualification, neither does the term 'post-Islamist', which involves a conscious and explicit rejection of the Islamic state as a model of government. Revivalists in no way eschew what they view as the inevitable long-term result of their cultural *jihad* for an alternative society, but neither do they prioritise it as an objective. Their immediate concerns are not a mere means to this end but, rather, goals in themselves. These include education for Muslim children in accordance with teachings from the Qur'an and *sunna*; national legislation that prohibits the 'vilification' of Islam and its prophet Muhammad; and the arbitration of disputes between Muslims under *shari'a*.

To the extent that the term 'Islamist' is misleading, the classification of these individuals and groups as 'participationist' is problematic. This is because it is predicated upon their distinction from 'rejectionists', such as Hizb ut-Tahrir, and, more importantly, based on the assumption that they both share the same goal of an Islamic state. Their most important point of difference is deemed to be in their choice of methods, which is secondary to what binds them. This, however, not only overplays the importance of the goal of an Islamic state but also underestimates the importance of their approaches, which are, in fact, integral to their particular Islamic worldview and identity. Far from being incidental to their religiously conceived long-term goal of a society based on Islam, the revivalists' approach to spreading their religion through education, advocacy and participation in secular politics, as well as their rejection of cultural isolation and violence, is a key constitutive element of their political ideology and religious solidarity.

Just as the notion of an Islamic state is overemphasised by both political analysts and British government leaders, so is the notion of ideology to make sense of what drives and unites politically active Muslims in Britain, including 'non-violent extremists'. Not only are the specific characteristics of these groups' ideology sometimes mischaracterised, the underlying concept of ideology that is used is inherently doctrinaire and therefore fails to accommodate the cultural dimension of 'Islamism'. These are two mistakes in the struggle to champion and strengthen a liberal democratic and human rights-oriented culture in Britain.

Mischaracterising Islamism

In a landmark speech in Birmingham on 20 July 2015, David Cameron outlined the government's new five-year counter-extremist strategy, which was subsequently published in October 2015. He stated, 'The root cause of the threat we face is the extremist ideology itself'.[13] Several months earlier, in September 2014, the then home secretary Theresa May asserted, 'We need to defeat the ideology that lies behind the [terrorism] threat', and outlined this ideology as follows:

> The extremists believe in a clash of civilisations – a fundamental incompatibility between Islamic and Western values, an inevitable divide between 'them and us'. They demand a caliphate, or a new Islamic state, governed by a harsh interpretation of Shari'ah law. They utterly reject British and Western values, including democracy, the rule of law, and equality between citizens, regardless of their gender, ethnicity, religion or sexuality. They believe that it is impossible to be a good Muslim and a good British citizen. And they dismiss anybody who disagrees with them – including other Muslims – as non-believers.[14]

This description of the ideology Britain faces from what the government calls 'Islamist extremism' is derived from the report of the prime minister's Task Force on Tackling Radicalisation and Extremism, 'Tackling extremism in the UK', published in December 2013.[15] It is repeated in the new counter-extremism strategy. It is problematic since it blurs many important points of contention that divide those considered as Islamists. In relation to the 'non-violent extremists' of the global Muslim Brotherhood it is, in fact, wrong on almost every point.

While violent jihadist groups liberally cast other Muslims as apostates, reject Western values and prioritise the attainment of an Islamic state, the revivalist Brothers, as this book has shown, believe some Western values are Islamic values, assert the compatibility of Muslim and British identity, and reject the notion of a clash of civilisations. This is because, unlike the militant jihadists, they view Islam as a way of life that can and should be propagated from within secular, liberal democratic societies. Unlike the jihadists and the 'non-violent' rejectionists, such as Hizb ut-Tahrir, they do not reject democracy as an electoral system and encourage Muslims to vote, although they idealise the *shari'a* as the model for government policy and law for their prophesised situation of a Muslim majority. They tend to believe that Muslim identity can accommodate national identity, as long as the latter does not determine the former. Rather than rejecting and isolating themselves from non-Muslim culture and identity, the revivalists are generally disposed to transforming it from within. This is not merely tactical, since it is linked to their mission of *da'wa*. And as mentioned, an Islamic state is a secondary concern in relation to an Islamic society.

Given the importance that the government places upon 'non-violent extremism' as a stepping-stone to 'violent extremism', the error in classifying revivalist groups ideologically with other 'Islamists' is a grave one. By conflating distinct forms of Islamic activism under the heading of 'Islamist extremism', the government makes itself an easy target of criticism by Muslim activists and their sympathisers who can quite readily reject its faulty accusations. This hugely undermines the government's symbolic and moral authority to make judgments of Muslim groups and pronounce upon national values. It significantly undercuts the government's credibility and ability to identify and tackle 'extremism'.

Beyond ideas: a conflict of culture

The government's understanding of the ideology of 'Islamism' as expressed by the then home secretary Theresa May and the new counter-extremism strategy – particularly of 'non-violent extremism' – is flawed. But it's very reference to ideology carries problems of its own. This is because the conflict with what it calls 'Islamist extremism', violent or non-violent, is typically viewed as a 'battle of ideas' that may be resolved through the triumph of argumentation and reason. Such a view expresses a very limited understanding of the 'battleground', and thus the resolvability, of the conflict.

In the *Counter-Extremism Strategy*, the then prime minister David Cameron refers to the 'fight against Islamist extremism' not only as 'one of the great struggles of our generation' but also as a 'battle of ideas' in which 'the case' for British values has to be made.[16] This framing of the problem as an Oxford Union debate or a legal prosecution ignores the cultural and social dimension of ideas and practices that conflict with Britain's human rights-oriented liberal democracy. It wrongly assumes that the key concepts and rules of the 'debate' are shared across a divide of understanding, yet it is precisely these that are stake.

Unsurprisingly, this view is shared by a number of 'counter-extremism' analysts and government advisers, including Ed Husain, co-founder of Quilliam, a think tank that advised the government's counter-extremism strategy. Husain writes, 'Winning the long-term battle of ideas against Islamist radicals is the only solution. Muslim and other communities are in dire need for support to defeat the ideology that produces terror.'[17] Maajid Nawaz, Quilliam's chairman, asserts that the organisation 'works to critique and refute this ideology wherever it is found'.[18] He states that 'we are indeed engaged in an ideological war' with Islamism, which must be 'intellectually terminated'.[19] A similar perspective is expressed by Rashad Ali, the director of another London-based 'counter-extremism' think tank, Centri. In criticising the government's proposals in 2015 to introduce banning orders on alleged 'extremist' groups, Ali stated:

> The Government is obsessed with legislation but this is not something you can defeat by legislation. It is a battle of ideas and we have to defeat these ideas by argument … What we need, far more than any new law, is a counter-argument and a policy which can inspire [Muslim] society to defeat extremist ideas.[20]

Ali put this view into practice by co-authoring a theological 'rebuttal' of jihadist ideology, drawing upon Islamic sources to question the jihadist interpretation of the Qur'an and other scriptures.[21]

Ideas and ideals undeniably form part of the phenomenon of 'Islamist extremism', whether violent jihadism, non-violent rejectionism, or non-violent revivalism. But what this approach fails to grasp is that what is considered as an ideological battle is not equivalent to the rational competition between rival ideas settled through the logic of reason. With Islamic revivalism in Britain, the government is engaged not in a contest of argument and counter-argument, but in a conflict of worldviews and values waged upon different levels of consciousness and acted out in practice in social settings. The notion of a 'battle of ideas' in which 'extremists' might be 'de-radicalised' (or potential 'extremists' swayed) through the rebuttal of certain ideas ignores the complex, unconscious and social factors that enable the production, meaningfulness and appeal of such ideas.

Such factors include a taken-for-granted worldview and an associated set of values. The primary battleground that makes ideological warfare possible is at the level of what the late French sociologist Pierre Bourdieu calls the *habitus*, the unconsciously embodied dispositions and 'mental structures' through which people apprehend the social world as natural and self-evident. These, he observed, are generated socially in experience, inculcated through a mixture of subtle processes and overt methods.

The most important predispositions that enable the embrace of a certain ideological outlook include a range of unquestioned distinctions through which an in-group and others outside the group are relatively viewed and judged. The basis of the Islamic revivalist outlook is a vision of humanity clearly divided between Muslims and non-Muslims. Although Muslims are viewed within the broader family of humankind, they are distinguished internally, since only Muslims have embraced the truth of revelation and possess the divine duty to spread Islam, albeit through non-coercive means. Non-Muslims may or may not be explicitly cast as inferior due to their ignorance or rejection of their 'true' Muslim nature, but Islam is deemed as a superior way of life that will one day prevail and, as carriers of the message of Islam, for revivalists there is an implicit but distinct sense of superiority in Muslim identity.

An important factor that enables such an outlook to take shape in consciousness as an ideology – in addition to a shared set of tacitly held dispositions and perceptual categories expressed in everyday social settings – are specific social and political constraints or events perceivable as grievances.

Cameron is wrong to dismiss what he calls 'the grievance justification' and focus only on 'ideology'.[22] Revivalists are quite genuine in pointing to certain grievances, such as British foreign policy in Iraq, as motivating Muslim dissent and even terrorism. Eliza Manningham-Buller, former director-general of MI5, recognised this in 2010 when she told the Chilcot inquiry that Britain's involvement in Iraq and Afghanistan had 'radicalised' Muslims who saw such involvement as 'an attack upon Islam'.[23]

However, critics of the government, such as Arun Kundnani, who altogether reject the role of ideology or religious belief as an explanatory factor for understanding Muslim dissent and even terrorism are equally mistaken.[24] Positing religious ideology and political grievances as two mutually exclusive factors that might explain Muslim dissent, radicalisation or violence, as Cameron and Kundnani both do in their own ways, sets up a false choice. The political grievances of non-violent Muslim activists or Islamist terrorists are perceived through the lens of a religious ideology or worldview. It is through such a lens that grievances take on their full significance. This is exemplified by the martyrdom video of Ibrahim Savant, one of the terrorist cell caught by the British police plotting to blow up trans-Atlantic airliners in 2006. After complimenting his co-plotters' rants about British and American forces in Iraq and Afghanistan, he added,

> I, Savant, have sacrificed my life cheaply, within the sake of Allah, not to save myself from a life of trials and tribulations but to fulfill a covenant and promise with Allah the almighty, and to make his *Deen* [religion and way of life] reign supreme.[25]

Crucially, for an ideology to take shape and for religious identity to become politicised – whether this leads to non-violent or violent conflict with the prevailing cultural and political orthodoxy – grievances need to be articulated as such by an elite of professional activists and ideologues. The entertainment of an ideology and the recognition of oneself as part of an oppressed group depends upon the trust willingly invested in the symbolic authority of the figures articulating an ideological vision of the group, its oppression and its struggle. So, any effort to combat an ideology needs to undermine the value of this kind of symbolic investment, not just the value of the ideas propagated. The 'battle of ideas' is better thought as a battle for symbolic power, which commands the recognition of certain social and political realities, including one's identity and one's place in the world. The key is not so much the assent of individuals and groups to certain ideas that conflict with liberal democracy. It is, rather, their assent to an *alternative authority* that they can identify with that pronounces the value of such ideas. It is their deference to an alternative, unquestioned source for the legitimation of ideas and values, one with which they can collectively identify.

This is not the simple result of a rational calculation, but of a symbolic and psychological investment in an alternative source of cultural and political legitimation, enabled by pre-political, cultural dispositions and a context of cultural strain or dislocation. From an alternative perspective, this entails a symbolic and psychological *dis*investment from the cultural and political orthodoxy, which cannot be fully explained by reference to specific unfavourable social norms or government policies. A loss of faith in liberal democratic culture and its political system may facilitate a new-found or rejuvenated faith in Islam understood as an alternative way of life and form of governance. But this is not the simple result of a rational calculation. It is the outcome, rather, of a more inclusive psychological transformation occurring within fields of social activity involving competing symbolic authorities.

Symbolic struggles are inextricable from practical struggles in social environments. Thus, it is a serious error to locate this ideology solely in the heads of individuals and assume its *modus operandi* consists in ideas and arguments. David Cameron states, 'What we are fighting, in Islamist extremism, is an ideology. It is an extreme doctrine. And like any extreme doctrine, it is *subversive*.'[26] But the ideology that the government is concerned with – or one of the ideologies that it is concerned with, since 'Islamism' is a multiplicity – is part of a larger, social and cultural problem that cannot be separated from its practice. Underlying the conscious elaboration of any distinct form of Islamism as a doctrine, Islamist ideology, as it were, is expressed in practice throughout numerous fields of social activity. This book has only highlighted local government, education and arbitration as fields relevant to the revivalist movement in Britain, but there are undoubtedly other fields in which a conflict of values is being played out – for example, charities, prisons, mosques and universities.

Tackling Islamist ideology, as the government wishes to do, will be partial at best if it is treated simply as a doctrine. A more complete approach requires a conceptual leap from preventing 'extremism' as a precursor to 'radicalisation', which is focused on vulnerable individuals, to preventing the subversion of liberal democratic culture, which concerns vulnerable institutions, governmental and non-governmental, and communities. It is not just '*ideas* which are hostile to basic liberal values such as democracy, freedom and sexual equality' that matter.[27] Arguably of more importance is the embodiment of these hostile ideas in social institutions and cultural practices that effectively undermines those values and, in some cases, the laws that are supposed to protect them.

In recent years, 'counter-narratives' (and 'alternative narratives') have become a large part of preventing and countering violent extremism (PVE and CVE) programmes worldwide.[28] But, according to a report by the European Commission's Radicalisation Awareness Network (RAN), 'Most [PVE/CVE] programmes tackle ideology as a *secondary* issue and focus'. There are a few simple lessons that can be learned from these programmes. These include the importance of engaging with families and local community networks as bulwarks against the allure of 'extremist' groups, and identifying alternative credible sources of authority to speak on religious and political matters, including identity and grievances. The explicit tackling of ideology, for example through theological refutations, is often delayed until trust is built between the key stakeholders, i.e. until the ground is laid for the reception of alternative perspectives and ideas. Although PVE and CVE work is aimed at tackling violent, not non-violent, 'extremism' – and therefore is primarily concerned with recruitment into terrorist groups – it nevertheless highlights the role of social and cultural factors in the creation and politicisation of 'radical' identities and the assent to 'extremist' ideologies.

Political and cultural subversion

The revivalist movement in Britain is subversive, but not as traditionally understood by the British government or the few academics that have written about Islamist subversion. That is, it is neither primarily geared to overthrowing parliamentary democracy nor primarily a problem in presenting a conduit for violence.[29] It is subversive in the sense of presenting an organised but decentralised programme of cultural propagation whose success entails the undermining or transformation of liberal democratic values and institutions, particularly as they affect Muslim communities. The British government has begun to articulate the importance of safeguarding what it refers to as 'British values' and the 'British way of life', and, in doing so, implicitly recognises the threat of subversion from 'non-violent Islamist extremism'. As noted, Cameron, when prime minister, described 'Islamist extremism' as a 'subversive doctrine'.[30] But the government does not use the term 'subversion'. To do so would require a radical reconception of subversion from its Cold War-era formulation.

Today, the official view of the British government on subversion remains framed by the concerns of the era in which the term first entered the modern political vocabulary. Subversion was defined in 1975 by the Labour minister Lord Harris of Greenwich, as activities 'which threaten the safety or well being of the state and which are intended to undermine or overthrow parliamentary democracy by political, industrial or violent means'.[31] This definition remains today as it appears in the Security Service Act of 1989. Although it does not use the word 'subversion', the Act directly borrows Lord Harris's terms to define the function of the domestic security service, MI5, as follows:

> The function of the Service shall be the protection of national security and, in particular, its protection against threats from espionage, terrorism and sabotage, from the activities of agents of foreign powers and from actions *intended to overthrow or undermine parliamentary democracy by political, industrial or violent means.*[32]

Thus, included in the legal definition of the role of MI5 is the protection of national security from subversive threats. The Act relates these to the protection of 'parliamentary democracy' and, in doing so, considers the system of government (or in David Maxwell-Fyfe's terms, the state) as the key target for subversive threats to national security.[33] This focus on the political system of the state, and blindness to the cultural edifice of liberal democratic values that underlies it, is out-dated. But it is understandable. The key concern at the time of the Act's drafting was of Britain being subverted by, and into, an undemocratic, authoritarian communist regime. This concept of subversion as of mere historical interest has not changed in the official view of the security service, so the only possible kind of subversive threat it sees is equivalent to a communist one. Accordingly, in MI5's view, there is no threat of subversion in Britain today. Until recently, MI5's website had a dedicated page on subversion. It stated, 'Since the late 1980s, especially following the end of the Cold War and the collapse of Soviet communism, the threat from subversion has declined. It is now considered to be negligible. We do not currently investigate subversion.'[34] Subversion is mentioned on its current website, but as part of the organisation's history. Counter-subversion work would only resume, it states, 'if our monitoring of emerging threats suggested an increase in the subversive threat'.[35]

Counter-subversion: protecting a 'way of life'

Despite the government's official neglect of reassessing or updating the concept of subversion, in the last ten or so years it has begun to recognise, albeit implicitly, the need to protect against cultural forms of subversion, as presented by Islamic revivalism, which is one form of what it calls 'non-violent Islamist extremism'. The origins of this recognition can be traced to the publication of Britain's national security strategy in 2008, which marked a significant break from the decades-old paradigm influenced by Cold War concerns.[36] David Omand describes the most fundamental shift in the strategy as 'the definition of *security itself*'.[37] This is expressed in the document as one from a state-centric concept of security to what Omand describes as a new 'human view of national security' in which people and communities are central. The strategy explicitly emphasises the protection of the state's citizens and their 'way of life'.[38] This new broader concept of national security was again central to the 2010 version of the strategy, which states: 'Above all, we act to maintain our way of life: to protect our people and the freedoms we have built for ourselves, and the values of our society and institutions.'[39] The most recent iteration of the strategy, published in 2015, re-affirms this commitment to protect a 'way of life' and states that 'core British values' are the foundation of the country's security and prosperity. It lists them as:

> Democracy, the rule of law, open, accountable governments and institutions, human rights, freedom of speech, property rights and equality of opportunity, including the empowerment of women and girls, are the building blocks of successful societies.[40]

The strategy adds, 'We will continue to uphold these values against those who are intent on undermining them. We will prevent those who seek to spread extremist ideologies through our communities from doing so'.[41]

The importance of protecting or, more accurately, promoting British core values, such as universal human rights, equality before the law and democracy, came into sharp focus in 2011 with the revision of the government's counter-radicalisation strategy, Prevent. A previous iteration of Prevent in 2009 acknowledged the importance of challenging views 'which fall short of supporting violence and are within the law, but which reject and undermine our shared values and jeopardise community cohesion'.[42] The spread of 'non-violent extremism', including a rejection of secular society and democratic government, was acknowledged as a problem, but primarily for creating 'a climate in which people may be drawn into violent activities'.[43] The importance of combating 'extremist (and non-violent) ideas' continues to be recognised in the latest iteration of Prevent, published in 2011, again from the point of view that they are 'part of a terrorist ideology'.[44] Prevent's conception of 'non-violent extremism' as a conduit to terrorism – and not as a problem for Britain's 'way of life' – is understandable given its counter-radicalisation and counter-terrorism focus.

However, since the latest revision of Prevent, the government has begun to view the importance of countering non-violent extremism beyond its function as a pathway to violence. It has begun to view 'non-violent extremism' independently from its connection with terrorism, as producing a range of problems challenging British values and key public institutions, as well as social integration.

New teachers' standards were introduced in 2012 which stipulate that 'teachers must not undermine fundamental British values, including democracy, the rule of law, individual liberty and mutual respect, and tolerance of those with different faiths and beliefs'.[45] In November 2014, all schools were subject to a new duty to 'actively promote' these values to enhance the 'spiritual, moral, social and cultural development of pupils' and guard against 'extremism'.[46] Complementing this effort to positively strengthen 'British values' and Britain's liberal democratic culture, the 'Prevent duty', introduced in 2015, places an onus on schools and other public institutions to be prepared to combat 'extremist ideology' and prevent radicalisation. In December 2013, schools, universities and prisons were all identified by the Task Force on Tackling Radicalisation and Extremism as institutions vulnerable to 'the ideology of Islamist extremism'.[47]

In July 2015, more clearly signalling that the government was taking 'extremism' seriously as a problem beyond its connection to terrorism, Cameron stated the importance of combatting '[i]deas which are hostile to basic liberal values such as democracy, freedom and sexual equality … [and] which actively promote discrimination, sectarianism and segregation'.[48] This point of view is now being incorporated into government strategy.

In the same year, as mentioned in chapter 6, the Home Office published the country's first counter-extremism strategy and established the Extremism Analysis Unit (EAU) to study and assist combat both violent and non-violent forms of 'extremism'. In May 2016, as part of this strategy, the Home Office commissioned an independent review into *shari'a* councils with regard to their impact on women's rights.[49] The report was published in February 2018.[50] The government is yet to formulate a strategic response to the report's findings and recommendations, but has noted that it will not endorse the creation of a self-regulatory body, one of the report's three recommendations.[51] The Home Office is also leading the development of a 'counter-entryism' strategy for key British public bodies. No update on this strategy has been published, but reviews of several sectors have been concluded and government ministers are being advised of the findings and options for action.[52] As Charles Moore observes, the government remains uncomfortable with the word 'subversion', but its counter-extremism strategy, particularly its 'counter-entryism' component, amounts to counter-subversion in all but name.[53]

The *Counter-Extremism Strategy* states, 'Extremists have attempted ... to subvert our democratic processes', but the examples it provides of such subversion refer solely to the efforts of rejectionist groups to dissuade Muslims from voting and the vocal rejection of the principles underpinning democratic processes.[54] It does not acknowledge the subversion of participationist groups, which is not the undermining of democracy in public speech, for they advocate engagement in democratic politics. It is, rather, the undermining of liberal democratic culture through an attempt at influencing perception and regulating action, particularly in Muslim communities, in favour of a worldview and value system that is antagonistic to liberal democratic norms. This presents a problem that isn't captured in the security service's out-dated official view of subversion: it presents a problem not so much for parliamentary democratic government but for a way of life, a phrase first highlighted in the national security strategy.

Yet, there is no trade off between securing a way of life and the state: the cultural subversion of the revivalist movement involves not just the undermining of a way of life. It also involves undermining the state as the primary power that legitimates this way of life both practically, in the political and legal structures of society, and symbolically, in the cognitive structures of the people.

The participationist movement of the global Muslim Brotherhood, as this book has shown, is both cultural and political. It is opposed not merely to a particular culture – progressive, liberal democracy – but to the social and political institutions of this culture. Contrary to the government's view, these 'extremists' do not 'demand a caliphate, or a new Islamic state', although this is what they hope to achieve when Britain and eventually the world willingly embraces Islam as a complete 'life system'.[55] And although they do not aim to topple Britain's liberal democratic political system, they are concerned with attaining or directing political authority insomuch as it relates to the governance of everyday practices – as apparent in education and arbitration – and, most importantly, as it relates to the symbolic capacity to structure knowledge and belief in line with their contentious religiopolitical worldview. The revivalists' undermining of liberal democratic culture is inseparable from the undermining of the institutions and authorities that project and protect this culture.

Distinguishing 'non-violent extremisms'

The government's public recognition of 'non-violent extremism' as problem of subversion has its origins in discussions on counter-terrorism and was first articulated in public in Munich, in February 2011, by the then prime minister David Cameron. He stated,

> As evidence emerges about the backgrounds of those convicted of terrorist offences, it is clear that many of them were initially influenced by what some have called 'non-violent extremists', and they then took those radical beliefs to the next level by embracing violence.[56]

He continued, that if we are to defeat the threat of Islamist terrorism, we need to confront all forms of the 'extremist ideology' underlying it – i.e. its violent and non-violent forms. In doing so, he said, 'We need to think much harder about who it's in the public interest to work with. Some organisations that seek to present themselves as a gateway to the Muslim community' – implying the MCB – 'are showered with public money despite doing little to combat extremism. As others have observed, this is like turning to a right-wing fascist party to fight a violent white supremacist movement'. This speech was significant in articulating a connection between non-violent and violent 'extremism'. Such a connection was highlighted again in Cameron's Birmingham 2015 speech. He stated, 'When you look in detail at the backgrounds of those convicted of terrorist offences, it is clear that many of them were first influenced by what some would call non-violent extremists.'[57]

Described somewhat inaccurately as a 'conveyor belt' theory of radicalisation by its critics, it has brought the government under fire for wrongly characterising religious 'social conservatism' – illiberal but legal views and practices – as a precursor to involvement in terrorism. But, to be clear, Cameron did not state that the connection between involvement in some non-violent Islamist groups and terrorism was *casual*. And he wasn't altogether wrong in noting such a connection: a report published in 2017 by the Tony Blair Institute for Global Change found that more than three quarters of the 113 British jihadists that it profiled had some connection to non-violent Islamist groups.[58] It noted,

> Although there is not an inevitable conveyor belt between non-violent and violent extremism, and many move away from extremist ideologies

> altogether, our sample provides clear evidence of a connection between the two. The vast majority of our sample moved towards jihadism after their exposure to non-violent Islamist ideologies.[59]

This report drew upon a study by Raffaello Pantucci published in 2015, which revealed that almost half of the terror plots carried out or foiled by police in Britain in the last twenty years or so have been connected to al-Muhajiroun, a 'non-violent extremist' group with origins in Hizb ut-Tahrir.[60] An earlier report by Hannah Stuart noted that almost one fifth of those 'convicted for Islamism-inspired terrorism offences or killed in suicide attacks in the UK between 1999 and 2010' were connected to al-Muhajiroun.[61] And the 2011 iteration of Prevent, while not naming any participationist groups, noted the involvement of al-Muhajiroun in 15 per cent of terrorism-related convictions between 1999 and 2009.[62]

However, Cameron's failure to clearly distinguish between different kinds of non-violent Islamists – his conflation of rejectionists, such as al-Muhajiroun, with participationists, such as the MCB, who have no demonstrated link with terrorism in Britain – has led many to altogether dismiss the idea of a connection between non-violent and violent 'extremism'. Such a conflation has led some critics, including those within parliament, to focus solely on the inclusion of participationists in the notion of a pathway between non-violent to violent 'extremism', and dismiss the notion on the basis of their inclusion. Ignoring the evidence of a connection between rejectionist groups and terrorism, and mischaracterising participationist groups as mere 'religious conservatives', it is understandable that such critics are wary of supporting any measures that they see as curtailing religious freedom. While discussing the government's proposed Counter-Extremism and Safeguarding Bill, the Joint Committee on Human Rights stated in July 2016:

> The Government's proposals rest on the assumption that there is an escalator that starts with religious conservatism and ends with support for violent jihadism, and that violence is therefore best tackled by curtailing or placing restrictions on religious conservatism. However, it is by no means proven or agreed that religious conservatism, in itself, correlates with support for violent jihadism. The aim should be to tackle extremism that leads to violence, not to suppress views with which the Government disagrees.[63]

This criticism is misplaced. The government has explicitly acknowledged that there is 'no single pathway to radicalisation'.[64] But its failure to distinguish between different kinds of non-violent extremism that different kinds of Islamists may be seen to present has led its critics to dismiss outright the notion of non-violent extremism, particularly as a starting point for jihadist terrorism. Revivalist groups, such as the MCB, MEND, CAGE and the Islamic Human Rights Commission (IHRC) – which defend *shari'a* courts despite their discrimination of women,[65] deny the evidence of hate-preachers in Britain's mosques,[66] and obfuscate the facts regarding the illiberal religious agenda of 'activist governors' in Trojan Horse schools[67] – are at the forefront of this line of criticism. However, while there is no evidence that religious conservatism is a way station to jihadist terrorism, there is evidence of a connection between non-violent and violent 'extremism': it is with one kind of (ostensibly) non-violent 'extremism', that associated with rejectionist Islamism. This includes agitating anti-British or anti-Western sentiment amongst Muslims, while encouraging the belief that *jihad* against British and other Western forces fighting jihadist militants in Iraq, Syria and elsewhere is a collective obligation for Muslims in line with Islamic law.

The problem in Britain with participationist Islamism – Islamic revivalism – is not as a conduit to violence. The individuals and groups comprising the global Muslim Brotherhood in Britain are unlikely suspects in providing such a conduit, since they generally condemn terrorism, at least as it occurs in Britain and the West. They typically share support for Hamas in Israel with rejectionist groups, such as al-Muhajiroun, but no data has been produced to demonstrate that involvement in revivalist groups have led to terrorism in Britain.[68] And although they often contest government policy and normative values with the state, they believe in non-compulsion as the means to ensure Islam's triumph in the West and eventually worldwide. If we must stick with the government's phrase 'non-violent extremism', the kind that they primarily present is not the promotion of an ideology that can lead to terrorism in Britain, even though they express support for (or refuse to condemn) *jihad* terrorism in Israel. It is, rather, the promotion and protection of a non-violent but illiberal worldview and set of values that in some cases breaks the law, and that may, in the long term, exacerbate social divisions.

As a key plank in the government's 2015 counter-extremism strategy, the Counter-Extremism and Safeguarding Bill was conceived to confront those 'who seek to undermine democracy or use hate speech in public places'.[69] The bill has featured twice in the Queen's Speech, in 2015 and 2016, but has stalled while ministers struggle to provide legally acceptable definitions of both 'non-violent extremism' and 'British values'.[70]

In June 2016, the Joint Committee on Human Rights met with Home Office representative Karen Bradley to discuss the government's thinking about the bill, a draft of which has not yet been drawn. Responding to the Committee's questions regarding what kind of behaviour the bill sought to target, she described such behaviour as the preaching of an intolerant ideology 'that leads to some form of crime, hatred or division in society'.[71] She said that although the counter-extremism strategy is focused on non-violent Islamist extremism that can lead to violent extremism, it is 'much wider' than that: 'It is about the promotion of ideology that leads to criminal behaviour, which might be hate crime, violence against women or girls or terrorist activity – the crime itself.'[72] The example she used was of female genital mutilation (FGM). Acknowledging that FGM is already a criminal activity,

Bradley said the government would like measures to prevent the promotion of FGM to pre-empt its occurrence, possibly through civil orders, which have a lower threshold of evidence to secure a prosecution. The Committee responded by arguing that while FGM is a clear-cut case, 'opposition to fundamental British values' is not. 'Extremism', it noted, 'is so broad, nebulous and subjective that we do not know how to assess it.'[73] It also expressed concern about the use of civil orders 'to potentially interfere with a number of human rights including freedom of religion, expression and association'.[74]

Bradley's comments demonstrate that the government's understanding of non-violent extremism is centred on the vocal promotion of an illiberal ideology that encourages violent or undesirable non-violent behaviour. Despite its commitment to combat 'extremism' in *shari'a* courts and entryism in public institutions as demonstrated by the reviews it has commissioned, and despite the inclusion of strengthening 'social cohesion' in its counter-radicalisation strategy, the government's understanding of 'non-violent extremism' remains primarily focused on speech that promotes 'harmful' ideas and activities. Despite seeming to appreciate the importance of formulating a strategic approach to tackle 'extremist' *practices* – for example, the application of Islamic law in Muslim communities, the infiltration of an illiberal Islamic ethos in schools, forced marriage and FGM – the government remains focused on the expression of 'extremist' *ideas*. It is as if all 'extremist' actions – whether terrorism or what might be considered as cultural issues, such as FGM – are dependent on the prior conscious assent to ideas that promote and justify them. Not only that, the approach the government wishes to take to tackle the expression of such ideas is through criminalisation, which as critics have rightly noted, risks undermining the very liberal democratic values that it purports to defend, particularly the freedom of speech.

The government applies the term 'non-violent extremism' to different kinds of problematic and undesirable behaviour, including incitement to terrorism, ideologically motivated institutional entryism and illegal cultural practices such as forced marriage. Although the government does not explicitly distinguish between different kinds of non-violent extremism, it may be useful to make several such distinctions.

A first kind concerns the *vocal articulation* of support for 'extremist' behaviour. This includes the kind that the government seeks to prevent in its controversial Counter-Extremism and Safeguarding Bill. It may be divided into the promotion of 'extremist' acts that are criminal or illegal (violence, terrorism, hatred, sexual discrimination, FGM and other crimes framed by an ideological point of view, which are subject to the various existing laws), and the promotion of 'extremist' acts or values that are illiberal but not prohibited or punishable by law (such as advocacy for a change in law to allow for religious freedom to override equality legislation).[75] The first kind of non-violent extremist 'speech', which promotes – or incites – criminal behaviour may be sub-divided into that which promotes violent crimes, including terrorism, and that which promotes non-violent crimes deemed 'extremist'.

The second kind of non-violent extremism is not the act of promoting an 'extremist' ideology but the *actual practice* of it, as it were. It is not the incitement of 'extremist' acts, but the acts themselves. It is not the advocacy of 'extremist' values in the public space – which can and should be debated – but the actual institutionalisation of such values, their being put into practice in real social settings. The vocal promotion of illiberal values, intolerant attitudes, or discriminatory ideas, after all, is not the same as their enactment in specific social environments.

It may be objected that the promotion of an extremist ideology includes both its explicit vocalisation and other actions that constitute its practical application. Indeed, it is difficult to separate the preaching in sermons or teaching in classrooms, for example about 'God-given' gender roles, from the practice of ideas, such as the imposition of sex-segregated spaces in mosques or the preferential treatment of boys in Muslim schools. Likewise, the vocalisation of illiberal views of women in *shari'a* courts by Muslim judges is hard to separate from the discrimination against women in such courts. But recognising the connection, in some cases, between the vocal expression of an illiberal ideology and its practice provides for a broader understanding of the 'promotion' of extremism than that expressed by the government. And, arguably, the connection between the vocal promotion and the practice of 'non-violent extremism' may be better understood if these are first recognised as distinct.

There is a difference between the vocal promotion of 'extremist' ideas or values and putting them into practice. While incitement laws or public debates may be relevant for tackling the former, more comprehensive and imaginative solutions are required for the latter. With so much emphasis on combatting extremist speech, the government risks not only impinging on civil liberties. It also risks overlooking extremist acts or practices, as well as the relationship between such acts and the vocal promotion of them. As with the vocal articulation of an 'extremist' ideology, 'extremist' practices may be beyond the pale of the law or not. Clearly, the government needs to assess which kinds of acts it deems 'extremist' are already criminal or illegal, which are not, and, of those that are not, which might require new legislation without compromising the liberal democratic values it seeks to uphold and defend. This requires clarity on what 'extremism' consists in and what it is precisely that needs defending and promoting in safeguarding our 'way of life'. It also requires clarity on what cluster of legislation may be deemed to legally protect 'British values', and what other means, beyond laws, that may be used to strengthen these values.

The government has not expressed an understanding of these distinctions. Its definition of 'extremism' seems to distinguish between 'vocal' and 'active' forms, but this isn't extrapolated upon in its counter-extremism strategy. The distinction it seems keenest to make is that between different vocal forms of 'extremism'. In response to the Joint Committee on Human Rights' consideration of the Counter-Extremism and Safeguarding Bill, the government articulated a distinction between the justification of *violent* extremism and the justification of *non-violent* extremism. It stated,

> Extremists of all types seek to normalise attitudes and behaviours which run contrary to the values and freedoms which make our society so successful. One of those harms is the use, or justification, of violence (terrorism) to achieve political or social change. But, the harms extremists seek to justify are not limited to this use [or] justification of violence. We see evidence of extremists drawing on ideology to seek to justify:
>
> - the purposeful segregation of communities – a rejection of integration based on differences in race, religion or denomination;
> - the discrimination against women and girls and creating or supporting an environment in which illegal cultural practices are more likely to go unchallenged, including female genital mutilation (FGM), forced marriage and so called honour based violence;
> - the hatred of others on basis of race, religion, denomination, or sexual orientation – which can lead to hate crime including violence; and,
> - The rejection of the core concept and institutions of democracy and rule of law.[76]

FGM and honour-based violence, it may be argued, are better understood as '*violent* extremism', though the distinction being made here, it seems, is between the incitement to terrorism and the incitement to other forms of extremism. In any case, a more comprehensive 'counter-extremism' approach would consider not just the ideological promotion of such 'extremist' acts and attitudes, but also the acts themselves, and whether they are (or should be legislated as) criminal. It would also consider, where such acts are not criminal, what kinds of measures, other than prosecution, might be used to prevent or counter them.

The government's need to clarify 'non-violent extremism' has become more apparent in the last few years at least in part because of the criticisms it has received from revivalist individuals and groups who contest the state's authority to determine normative values. When the counter-extremism strategy was published in October 2015, the MCB's secretary general, Shuja Shafi, said it risked alienating Muslims and restricting the freedom of thought and expression. He claimed that the strategy was based on a flawed analysis 'that conflates terrorism with subjective notions of extremism and Islamic practices'.[77] The claim that non-violent extremism is mere social conservatism that risks being criminalised through Prevent, and more specifically the Prevent duty, due to the incorrect notion that it inevitably leads to terrorism is a mistaken but recurrent one, expressed often by revivalists.

In February 2016, for example, in a paper published by the Cordoba Foundation that described 'Islamic radicalisation' as a 'myth', Abdullah Faliq penned an introductory note that claimed 'religious observations and conservative Islamic practices are conflated with extremism', and 'leaders of the community as well as mainstream Islamic organisations are being targeted and tarred with the brush of extremism'.[78] And in March 2015, IHRC produced a statement that denounced the government's counter-terrorism approach, including the Prevent duty, as the 'criminalisation of Islam', which was signed by numerous revivalist groups and individuals.[79] The statement said,

> [I]t is unacceptable to label as 'extremist' numerous normative Islamic opinions on a variety of issues, founded on the Quran and Sunnah of Prophet Muhammad (peace be upon him), implying there is a link between them and violence, using such labels as an excuse to silence speakers.[80]

This is unsurprising, since the spotlight on the dissemination of illiberal Islamic ideas and practices, such as that on *shari'a* courts, presents a threat to their religious worldview, if not their long-term political aspirations, which IHRC describes as 'a new social and international order' no doubt based on *shari'a* rather than 'man-made' law.[81] The well-organised 'Preventing Prevent' campaign led by FOSIS, CAGE and MEND within and outside of British universities has attracted the support of the National Union of Students and the University and College Union on the basis of a shared belief in the strategy's impingement on civil liberties.[82] However, in the case of FOSIS, CAGE, and MEND, the liberties they are concerned about relate to their ability to propagate an understanding of normative values and Islam that runs counter to civil liberties, for example with regard to women and homosexuals.[83]

The claim that non-violent extremism is merely social conservatism that has wrongly been conceived as an inevitable precursor to terrorism, and thus risks being criminalised, simply does not hold up to scrutiny. First, some of the views expressed by revivalist organisations and individuals are not just socially conservative, but discriminatory and illiberal, clearly challenging liberal democratic values such as equality under the law and the tolerance of other faiths. The imposition, or attempted imposition, of such views – whether preached in mosques, taught in schools, or implemented in *shari'a* courts – cross the line of religious culture into the field of political advocacy, activism or agitation in favour of an alternative social order. Second, nowhere does the government insist on an inevitable or linear pathway from non-violent to violent extremism. Its counter-extremism strategy, in fact, accepts the complexity of radicalisation.[84] Moreover, the government's counter-extremism efforts as laid out in the Prevent duty do not seek to outlaw the expression of 'non-violent extremist' views. Under the duty, public institutions, such as universities and schools, have an obligation to give 'due regard' to preventing people from being drawn into terrorism. This may mean preventing 'non-violent extremist' speakers from speaking on university campuses, for example, but *only insofar* as they present the risk of drawing people into 'violent extremism'.

In July 2017, Prevent was issued its first legal challenge. The case was brought by Salman Butt, who argued that the government's approach to combat non-violent extremism, Prevent, and specifically the Prevent duty guidance, exceeds the government's powers by going beyond the need to prevent people from being drawn into terrorism. His lawyers argued, in line with groups such as the MCB, MEND, IHRC, and CAGE, that the guidance conflicts with the right to free speech by restricting, or even criminalising, normative Islamic beliefs and political dissent. It was unclear, they alleged, 'whether characterising homosexuality as a sin or opposing UK foreign policy in the Middle East would amount to non-violent extremism' and thus be criminalisable.

Butt has a special interest in disarming the government's counter-extremism strategy. In September 2015, a press release by the Prime Minister's Office on tackling extremism in universities and colleges identified him as on record 'expressing views contrary to British values'.[85] Butt is the chief editor of the website Islam21C, which expresses the revivalist view that 'Islam is a comprehensive world view incorporating a way of life, a system of belief, a 1400 year old history and an extensive and divine system of law'.[86] Islam21C was created by the Muslim Research and Development Foundation, a think tank founded by Haitham al-Haddad, a Saudi-born scholar and former judge at the Islamic Sharia Council. Al-Haddad, also named as an 'extremist' by the Prime Minister's Office, is a contributor to Islam21C, which includes him in a promotional video for the website.[87] Al-Haddad has expressed numerous 'extremist' views. He has described homosexuality as a 'crime against humanity', stated that 'equality between the two genders is a very evil thing', referred to Jews as the 'descendants of apes and pigs', and asserted that the ultimate aim of Islam is to govern the world.[88]

The judge, Justice Ouseley, rejected Butt's case, confirming the legality of the Prevent duty and refuting the notion that it criminalises Islam and free speech. The judged said that the Prevent duty does not apply to 'non-violent extremism, however intrinsically undesirable, which does not create a risk that others will be drawn into terrorism'.[89] Prevent is not aimed at preventing socially conservative views and practices, whether called 'non-violent extremism' or not, as long as they do not incur a risk to radicalise people towards violence. The judge also rejected the notion that the duty has a 'chilling effect' on free speech in universities, since the requirement to have 'due regard' to preventing people from being drawn into terrorism 'does not override' the requirement on higher education institutions to exercise 'particular regard' of the duty to ensure freedom of speech and academic freedom.

The case significantly highlights the distinction between 'non-violent extremism' that may lead to terrorism and 'non-violent extremism' that may not.

While Prevent is only concerned with the former, the latter is the concern of the government's broader counter-extremism strategy. It is useful to separate these kinds of 'non-violent extremism'. How public service providers, parents or others can judge whether a person is at risk of being radicalised is a problem that can only be exacerbated if different kinds of 'non-violent extremism' are blurred together in the government's strategic efforts to tackle extremism and terrorism. And, likewise, how we understand non-violent forms of 'extremism' that are problematic not as a conduit for violence but for violating human rights – such as those of women in *shari'a* courts – is not helped if different strands of Islamism are conflated in the analysis that underlies counter-extremism strategy.

The government is right to be concerned about a relationship between non-violent and violent extremism, even though its understanding of this relationship requires greater clarity. But in the coming years, the links between what might be called 'political extremism' and 'cultural extremism' are likely to attract considerable interest. Although the government has effectively blurred the two in its counter-extremism strategy – which considers the subversion of public institutions and the cultural practices of FGM and forced marriage – it is significant that culture is included. In providing the seedling of a public discussion on the relationship between certain religious, cultural practices and their compatibility with 'British values', this may well become a Pandora's Box. But, in any case, greater clarity may be sought on the relationship between political (i.e. ideologically driven) and cultural 'non-violent extremism'. This task may well involve a greater spotlight on revivalist organisations, particularly those with a community membership base, since the concerns of such organisations lie precisely in the domain of culture, in nurturing and developing an Islamic 'way of life' that begins from the ground up.

Future considerations

The British government's conflict with 'non-violent Islamist extremism' is likely to continue for many years to come. Several factors compound the importance of understanding this conflict: Muslim attitudes to integration and Muslim demographics.

Recent polls consistently show a significant minority of Muslims in Britain desire *shari'a* law. In a poll conducted in 2006 by GfK NOP Social Research, despite 94 per cent of British Muslims expressing the desire not to live separately from non-Muslims, an average of 30 per cent of Muslims expressed the desire to live under *shari'a* rather than British law, peaking at 34 per cent of 18–24-year-olds.[90] Just over a quarter wanted to see Britain as an Islamic state. In the same year, a poll conducted by ICM for *The Sunday Telegraph* showed that 40 per cent of British Muslims want *shari'a* introduced into parts of Britain.[91] Similar findings were found in a poll commissioned by Policy Exchange in 2007, which found that an average of 28 per cent of Muslims wanted to live under the *shari'a*, peaking at 37 per cent of 16–24-year-olds.[92]

In 2008, YouGov conducted a poll for the Centre for Social Cohesion at 12 universities, which found that 40 per cent of Muslim students supported the introduction of *shari'a* into British law for Muslims.[93] And, more recently, a survey conducted by ICM for Channel 4 published in April 2016 found that 23 per cent of British Muslims would prefer parts of Britain governed by *shari'a* rather than British law.[94]

Another ICM poll, conducted for Policy Exchange in 2016, also revealed a high level of Muslim support for *shari'a*, with 43 per cent of its Muslim respondents expressing support for *shari'a* (16% strongly) when broadly defined.[95] Contrary to the 2007 Policy Exchange poll, it found young Muslims were relatively less in favour. Its authors noted that support for the use of *shari'a* finance was relatively low, with 55 per cent saying they would prefer not use it. The greater level of support for *shari'a* at the more abstract level, they suggest, could be because 'expressing support for Sharia is a way of saying something about one's identity and religion, rather than voicing a commitment to a specific policy and legal objective'.[96] Whether or not this is correct, there are significant differences between Muslim and non-Muslim attitudes to liberal democratic norms. The ICM/Channel 4 survey, which used a control group to compare attitudes, found 'a chasm … between those Muslims surveyed and the wider population on attitudes to liberal values on issues such as gender equality, homosexuality and issues relating to freedom of expression'.[97] It also revealed 'significant differences on attitudes to violence and terrorism'.

These attitudes are a source of concern that is likely to grow as Britain's Muslim population grows. According to the Office for National Statistics, Britain's Muslim population has grown ten times faster than the general population over the last decade, from 1.6 million in 2001 (when the British Census first began to measure religion) to 2,869,000 in 2010.[98] Demographers expect this trend to continue. In January 2011, the Pew Forum on Religion and Public Life projected that by 2030 Britain will have a Muslim population of 5.5 million, roughly 8.2 per cent of the total population.[99] That is almost double its 2010 figure of 2.8 million, at 4.6 per cent. Most of this increase will occur in areas where Muslims are concentrated, in cities such as Bradford and Oldham.[100] According to a study presented to the Royal Geographical Society in 2005, the proportion of Britons of Muslim Pakistani origin living in ethnic enclaves had already trebled in the previous ten years.[101]

Given these considerations, the problems presented by 'non-violent Islamist extremism' in Britain – from encouraging social division to inspiring jihadist terrorism – are likely to become more acute. This book cannot present policy recommendations to tackle this range of problems. But it can conclude by making several observations that might be useful for the government to consider for the development of its efforts to counter 'extremism'.

The government's official understanding of 'Islamism' fails to acknowledge key differences not just between violent jihadists and non-violent Islam-inspired groups, but also between non-violent groups that reject political participation and those that support it. In all of its announcements and reports – including 'Tackling extremism in the UK' and *Counter-Extremism Strategy* – it blurs all of these groups under the heading of 'Islamist extremism'. By articulating a more sophisticated understanding of Islamism, the government can avoid making false claims about certain groups or individuals, for example, regarding the importance of an Islamic state or attitudes to non-Muslims. Revivalist organisations do not seek to overthrow parliamentary democracy but, rather, to transform it from within to make it compliant with *shari'a* values. Some of them have given platforms to, or defend, speakers who express bigoted views of non-Muslims, Jews, homosexuals, women or other Muslims they consider apostates. Yet, they are committed to *da'wa* to spread Islam beyond the Muslim *umma* as a gift to potential 'reverts'. With a more nuanced view of Islamism, the government can target its criticisms more precisely, separating out the groups that present a risk of violence and those that present other risks, and in doing so minimise the sting to its credibility that erroneous generalisations encourage. It can also better formulate strategies to deal with the different problems that the different kinds of Islamists present.

Furthermore, by being much more specific about national values and laws – for example, those relating to women's rights – the government can make it more difficult for 'extremist' groups to deploy liberal concepts, such as 'equality', in a general way while concealing the radically different meaning such concepts have in their alternative worldview. This will, however, have the effect of forcing a clash of cultures onto the public stage.

Combating this worldview is important for the government, but the conflict that the global Muslim Brotherhood is engaged in is greater than a 'battle of ideas' that may be won by theological counter-arguments. The challenge is far bigger and more complex. It is a conflict of schemes of perception and moral judgement, and so necessarily involves the cultural institutions and forms of social practice that inculcate and reinforce them. Such institutions may include mosques, Muslim schools, study groups, community organisations, charities, *fatwa* councils and *shari'a* courts. This isn't to say that these institutions necessarily radicalise individuals. It is, rather, to say that they may foster a collective mindset or way of seeing the world for Muslim children and young adults in which distinctions between Muslims and non-Muslims, between 'authentic' and 'inauthentic' Muslims, and between men and women are prominent and unconsciously naturalised.

Most importantly, these institutions may help foster a collective Muslim identity that is deemed prior to any other form of social identification. Such an identity is one that elevates the collective above the individual, as encouraged by the European Council for Fatwa and Research (ECFR), which advises European Muslims that the integrity of the collective Muslim *umma* 'comes before anyone's individual rights'.[102] The kind of Muslim identity that ECFR and many other revivalist bodies engineer is not necessarily political, but it may serve as the seed for a politically activist mentality that consciously opposes Western liberal values and institutions.

The government's acknowledgment of the cultural factors in the development of extremist Muslim attitudes opens policy avenues that are far from risk-free. Many new problems and challenges arise, including the entire matter of faith schooling, as well as religious arbitration and mediation. The tensions between the freedom of religion and other arguably more fundamental freedoms are likely to become more acute. Any government scrutiny of Islamic institutions is bound to provoke accusations of Islamophobia from individuals and groups already active in the revivalist movement. Clarity on the values and laws that the state needs to uphold, and transparency in its application of the measures required to uphold them, will help minimise discrimination as well as the perception of it.

For the government's 'battle of ideas' to be effective, it has to target the symbolic authority of the key 'extremist' ideologues and activists. It also has to get a firm grasp on the nuances in values, worldviews and political aspirations of the various individuals and groups it deems to be 'extremist'. But even a more sophisticated official understanding of the ideology or worldview of so-called Islamist extremists will provide an insufficient basis for the development of an effective strategy to counter 'extremism' if it does not incorporate into its analysis not only the different kinds of cultural enabling environment but also the sources of the ideologues' symbolic credibility. Research into this area – that identifies the key actors, their core messages and, most importantly, what factors give them their social appeal – would fill an important knowledge gap.

The government could also acknowledge that grievances play a role in agitating Muslim 'extremism', including attacks on the symbolic authority of the state and terroristic attacks on its people. Grievances contribute to the symbolic credibility of key ideologues, but are in turn amplified by such leaders. Grievances depend upon certain ways of perceiving and evaluating the world, but also foster them. So it is important for the government to take them seriously. A greater openness to discuss grievances may allow the authorities to engage with Muslim sentiment and not just 'Islamist' ideology into which such sentiment may become channelled. Greater openness may also enable the authorities to distinguish between the legitimate criticism of government policy – where differences of view on the facts or on the value of certain actions may be disputed – and attacks on the legitimacy of the state that emanate from a radically different worldview whose source is an alternative, higher authority.

Perhaps the most important thing for the government to acknowledge is that the protection of liberal democratic values and universal human rights cannot occur simply through a battle of ideas or a war of words. They are to be protected in practice in numerous fields of social activity, including, most importantly, education. How they are to be protected is one of the most important challenges that the government, as their primary champion, faces in the coming decades. In some cases, the protective measures will be legislation, criminal or civil; in others, it will be 'positive action' in the form of programmes and initiatives that promote and institutionalise the liberal democratic values that Britain holds dear. Either way, this will require mapping out the different kinds of 'extremism', particularly 'non-violent extremism', that present a threat or challenge to these values. The government's tendency to focus on incitement, whether to terrorism or non-violent extremism (such as sex discrimination), ought not slide into the criminalisation of free speech. And it ought not overlook actual non-violent extremist practices, particularly in isolated or segregated communities where cultural attitudes, towards women for example, may be reinforced through Islamist identity politics.

There are plenty of avenues of research yet to be conducted to help inform the task of protecting liberal democratic values and human rights norms. This book has shown that an organised network of revivalist individuals and organisations are active in institutionalising an alternative worldview and set of values within Muslim milieus, but it has probably only scratched the surface.

The extent to which further Trojan Horse operations are underway in places other than Birmingham has not been the subject of serious scrutiny. Fears of Islamophobia and racism are a factor in the prevention of disclosing concerns about Islamist entryism, as well as harmful religious practices. As Louise Casey reported in her 2016 review into opportunity and integration,

> Too many public institutions, national and local, state and non-state, have gone so far to accommodate diversity and freedom of expression that they have ignored or even condoned regressive, divisive and harmful cultural and religious practices, for fear of being branded racist or Islamophobic.[103]

In August 2017, the former chair of the Equality and Human Rights Commission, Trevor Philips, expressed dismay that the same such fears had played a key role in the institutional failure to publicly admit and confront the decades-long phenomenon of Muslim sexual grooming gangs in cities such as Rotherham, Rochdale and Bradford.[104] The revivalist movement plays a key role in disseminating the Islamophobia narrative and confusing the legitimate criticism of certain Islamic doctrines and practices with outright anti-Muslim bigotry. An investigation into this 'culture of fear', incorporating an open and honest discussion, while sensitive, would be useful to begin understanding some of the more subterranean social and political anxieties that have allowed 'extremism' to go unchecked.

The impact of Islamic education (in secular and Muslim schools) on children's attitudes to social integration and national identity is likewise understudied. The dissolution of the Bridge Schools Inspectorate (which enabled a small network of revivalists to inspect their own schools) is a welcome move. But more robust and regular monitoring of the provision of religious education, with particular regard to the teaching of critical thinking, would support

'British values' in schools. Far more can be learned about the extent to which *shari'a* councils, as well as online *fatwa* forums, play a role in Muslim communities and their impact on the human rights of women and children. The recent inquiry into *shari'a* law in England and Wales was a lost opportunity to understand the extent to which discrimination is taking place in *shari'a* councils, what is driving it and how it may be combatted. While anecdotal data concerning some of the problems with *shari'a* councils exist, statistical data would provide a more robust evidence base for action.

The global Muslim Brotherhood in Britain, as this book has argued, is a decentralised but organised effort to institutionalise a particular Islamic worldview and value system in Muslim milieus and mainstream society that is at odds with the country's liberal democratic culture. Rather than presenting a risk of radicalisation, this revivalist movement presents a challenge to the state as the protector of liberal democratic values. It no doubt feeds on Muslim socially conservative attitudes, which are a concern in themselves. But, in turn, it potentially strengthens such attitudes by giving them a voice within an ideological framework that exceeds conservatism in presenting Islam as a complete civilisational alternative. The global Muslim Brotherhood may be described as ideological, but it is better described as a political and cultural movement, since it is concerned with both power and a way of life: it is concerned with obtaining the symbolic and practical authority to determine a way of seeing, evaluating, and living in the world. Its struggle to determine normative cultural values brings it into conflict not only with the state but also with alternative Muslim voices.

Notes

1 See, for example, Murtaza Ali Shah, 'Muslims call for change in UK blasphemy laws', *The International News* (Pakistan), 14 November 2012. www.thenews.com.pk/Todays-News-2-142770-Muslims-call-for-change-in-UK-blasphemy-laws. See also Association of Muslim Lawyers (2002b), n. 18.1.1.

2 See, for example, Stuart (2015).

3 Vidino (2011), p. 10.

4 Andrew Gilligan, 'Muslim extremists, and a worrying lesson for us all', *The Telegraph*, 16 March 2014. www.telegraph.co.uk/education/educationopinion/10700041/Muslim-extremists-and-a-worrying-lesson-for-us-all.html.

5 Frampton, Goodhart and Mahmood (2016), p. 84.

6 Ibid., p. 51.

7 Ibid., p. 52.

8 Manea (2016), p. 120.

9 Ibid., p. 212.

10 Ibid., p. 214.

11 Vidino (2011), pp. 12–13.

12 Swartz (2013), p. 141.

13 'Extremism: PM speech', British Government website, 20 July 2015. www.gov.uk/government/speeches/extremism-pm-speech.

14 'A Stronger Britain, Built On Our Values', British Government website, 23 March 2015. www.gov.uk/government/speeches/a-stronger-britain-built-on-our-values.

15 Cabinet Office (2013), pp. 1–2.

16 'Prime Minister Foreword', HM Government (2015), p. 5.
17 Ed Husain, 'Taking passports would only raise the jihadist threat', *The Evening Standard*, 2 September 2014. www.standard.co.uk/comment/ed-husain-taking-passports-would-raise-the-jihadist-threat-9706097.html.
18 Maajid Nawaz, 'The Way Back from Islamism', The Washington Institute, 16 July 2008. www.washingtoninstitute.org/policy-analysis/view/the-way-back-from-islamism.
19 ABC News, 'A war of ideas: An atheist and a Muslim on the future of Islam and reforming religion', 29 October 2015. www.abc.net.au/news/2015-10-28/sam-harris,-maajid-nawaz-discuss-the-future-of-islam/6892166.
20 Andrew Gilligan, 'How banning radical Islamists will play right into their hands', *The Telegraph*, 31 May 2015. www.telegraph.co.uk/news/uknews/terrorism-in-the-uk/11641188/How-banning-radical-Islamists-will-play-right-into-their-hands.html.
21 Ali and Stuart (2014).
22 'Extremism: PM speech'.
23 Richard Norton-Taylor, 'Former MI5 chief delivers damning verdict on Iraq invasion', *The Guardian*, 20 July 2010. www.theguardian.com/uk/2010/jul/20/chilcot-mi5-boss-iraq-war.
24 See Kundnani (2015).
25 BBC News, '"Suicide videos": What they said', 4 April 2008, emphasis added. http://news.bbc.co.uk/2/hi/uk_news/7330367.stm.
26 'Extremism: PM speech', emphasis added.
27 Ibid.
28 See Radsch (2016).
29 See, for example, Kilcullen (2007), Rosenau (2007), and Clutterbuck and Rosenau (2009).
30 'Extremism: PM speech'.
31 Gill (1994), p. 120.
32 Security Service Act 1989, 1.(2), emphasis added.
33 In 1952, the British home secretary Sir David Maxwell-Fyfe stated that the task of MI5 was to defend the country from both internal and external threats, including subversion: 'MI5's task is the defence of the realm as a whole, from external and internal dangers arising from attempts at espionage and sabotage, or from actions of persons and organisations whether directed from within or without the country which may be judged to be *subversive* of the State.' See Gill (1994), p. 119, emphasis added.
34 'Subversion', MI5 website, web page captured 18 September 2015. https://web.archive.org/web/20150918171700/https://www.mi5.gov.uk/home/about-us/what-we-do/the-threats/other-issues-former-threats/subversion.html.
35 'What We Do, MI5 website, undated. www.mi5.gov.uk/what-we-do.
36 Cabinet Office (2008).
37 Omand (2009), p. 4, emphasis added.
38 Cabinet Office (2008), pp. 3–4.
39 Cabinet Office (2010), p. 22.
40 HM Government (2015b), p. 10
41 Ibid.
42 HM Government (2009), p. 15.
43 Ibid.
44 Home Office (2011), p. 6.
45 Department for Communities and Local Government (2011), p. 17.
46 'Guidance on promoting British values in schools published', British Government website, 27 November 2015. www.gov.uk/government/news/guidance-on-promoting-british-values-in-schools-published.

47 Cabinet Office (2013), p. 1.
48 'Extremism: PM speech'.
49 'Independent review into sharia law launched', Government website, 26 May 2016. www.gov.uk/government/news/independent-review-into-sharia-law-launched.
50 Home Office (2018).
51 'Home Office in the media: 02 February 2018', Home Office blog, 2 February 2018. https://homeofficemedia.blog.gov.uk/2018/02/02/home-office-in-the-media-02-february-2018/.
52 Home Office, official inquiry response, correspondence by email, 27 December 2017.
53 Charles Moore, 'Islamists only want one thing. We cannot appease them', *The Telegraph*, 3 July 2015. www.telegraph.co.uk/news/worldnews/islamic-state/11717180/Islamists-only-want-one-thing.-We-cannot-appease-them.html. See also HM Government (2015a), p. 19.
54 HM Government (2015a), pp. 12–13.
55 'Theresa May speech A Stronger Britain, Built on our Values: A New Partnership to Defeat Extremism', Conservatives website, 23 March 2015. http://press.conservatives.com/post/115395299770/theresa-may-speech-a-stronger-britain-built-on.
56 'PM's speech at Munich Security Conference', British Government website, 5 February 2011. www.gov.uk/government/speeches/pms-speech-at-munich-security-conference.
57 'Extremism: PM speech'.
58 Bryson (2017).
59 Ibid., p. 23.
60 Pantucci (2015).
61 Stuart (2014), p. 5.
62 Home Office (2011), p. 20.
63 Joint Committee on Human Rights (2016a), p. 3.
64 Joint Committee on Human Rights (2016b), p. 8.
65 For example, see MCB (2015), p. 11. See also IHRC, 'A letter to Nick Clegg regarding the government's proposed new plans to "combat Islamic extremism"', IHRC website, 11 March 2015. www.ihrc.org.uk/activities/campaigns/11382-a-letter-to-nick-clegg-regarding-the-governments-proposed-new-plans-to-combat-islamic-extremism.
66 In 2010, MCB, for example, said it deplored the Home Office's barring of Zakir Abdul-Karim Naik to enter Britain. Naik was barred for preaching the death penalty for Muslim apostates and praising Osama bin Laden. See Leon Symons, 'Hate preacher banned from UK', *The Jewish Chronicle*, 18 June 2010, www.thejc.com/news/uk-news/hate-preacher-banned-from-uk-1.16302, and Lucy Lips (pseud.), 'The Zakir Naik Scandal: Farr Must Go', Harry's Place blog, 20 October 2010, http://hurryupharry.org/2010/10/20/the-zakir-naik-scandal-farr-must-go/. MCB's leadership similarly refused to denounce one of its affiliates, Al-e-Hadith, for hosting hate preachers; see 'Muslim leaders in denial claim', BBC News, 21 August 2005, http://news.bbc.co.uk/2/hi/uk_news/4166402.stm. For more on this, see also, 'Trouble at Leeds Grand Mosque', MCB Watch blog, 21 August 2005, http://mcbwatch.blogspot.in/2005/08/trouble-at-leeds-grand-mosque.html.
67 The MCB, for example, describes Trojan Horse as an example of Islamophobia; see MCB (2015), p. 13. MEND also describes it as a 'hoax'; see MEND, 'Trojan Hoax', event promotional video, 3 October 2017, MEND website. https://mend.org.uk/videos/trojan-hoax/.
68 House of Commons (2015), paras. 36–37, pp. 6–7.

69 'Counter-Extremism Bill – National Security Council meeting', British Government website, 13 May 2015. www.gov.uk/government/news/counter-extremism-bill-national-security-council-meeting.
70 Mark Townsend, 'Theresa May's counter-terrorism bill close to "sinking without trace"', *The Guardian*, 29 January 2017. www.theguardian.com/politics/2017/jan/29/theresa-may-counter-terrorism-bill-sinking-without-trace-extremism-british-values.
71 Joint Committee on Human Rights (2016c), Q. 7, p. 8.
72 Ibid., Q. 10, p. 12.
73 Ibid.
74 Joint Committee on Human Rights (2016a), p. 28.
75 As advocated, for example, by Ahmad Thomson of the Association of Muslim Lawyers to the Select Committee on Religious Offences in England and Wales in the House of Lords in 2002. See Association of Muslim Lawyers (2002a), n. 43. For more on this, see chapter 5.
76 Joint Committee on Human Rights (2016b), p. 1.
77 MCB, '"One Nation Counter-Extremism Strategy" Risks Further Undermining Fight Against Terrorism', MCB website, October 19, 2015. http://www.mcb.org.uk/one-nation-counter-extremism-strategy-risks-fight-against-terrorism-191015/.
78 Faliq (2016).
79 IHRC, 'Muslim community rejects the State's criminalisation of Islam and condemns moves to silence legitimate critique and dissent', IHRC website, 11 March 2015. http://ihrc.org.uk/news/comment/11381-muslim-community-rejects-the-states-criminalisation-of-islam-and-condemns-moves-to-silence-legitimate-critique-and-dissent-.
80 Ibid.
81 'Aims & Objectives', IHRC website, undated. www.ihrc.org.uk/about-ihrc/aims-a-objectives.
82 See Stuart (2015), Sutton (2015), Sutton (2016), and Wilson (2017).
83 See, for example, Student Rights, 'FOSIS and the issue of extremist speakers', Student Rights website, 25 November 2013, www.studentrights.org.uk/article/2138/fosis_and_the_issue_of_extremist_speakers; Andrew Gilligan, 'Cage: the extremists peddling lies to British Muslims to turn them into supporters of terror', *The Telegraph*, 28 February 2015, www.telegraph.co.uk/news/uknews/terrorism-in-the-uk/11442602/Cage-the-extremists-peddling-lies-to-British-Muslims-to-turn-them-into-supporters-of-terror.html; Lottie Moore, 'In Plain Sight: MEND, CAGE, and So-Called "Non-Violent Extremism"', Quilliam website, 30 June 2017, www.quilliaminternational.com/in-plain-sight/. On CAGE, see also Stuart (2015), and on MEND, see Wilson (2017).
84 HM Government (2015a), p. 21.
85 'PM's Extremism Taskforce: tackling extremism in universities and colleges top of the agenda', British Government website, 17 September 2015. www.gov.uk/government/news/pms-extremism-taskforce-tackling-extremism-in-universities-and-colleges-top-of-the-agenda
86 'About Us', Islam21C website, undated. www.islam21c.com/about-us/.
87 'Why does it exist? 12 influential Muslims explain…', Islam21C video, YouTube, 23 June 2016. www.youtube.com/watch?v=6YnlptpBsiw. Also at: 'Support Islam21C', Islam21C website, undated. https://www.islam21c.com/donate/.
88 Al-Haddad cited from audio and video recordings available at 'Haitham al-Haddad', The Islamic Far Right in Britain blog, undated. http://tifrib.com/haitham-al-haddad/.
89 Butt v Secretary of State for the Home Department, EWHC 1930 (Admin), 26 July 2017, sect. 30. www.bindmans.com/uploads/files/documents/CO-6361-2015_-_Butt_v_Secretary_of_State_for_the_Home_Department_-_Final…pdf.

90 GfK NOP Social Research (2006).
91 *The Sunday Telegraph*, 'Poll reveals 40pc of Muslims want sharia law in UK', 19 February 2006. www.telegraph.co.uk/news/uknews/1510866/Poll-reveals-40pc-of-Muslims-want-sharia-law-in-UK.html.
92 Mirza, Senthilkumaran and Ja'far (2007).
93 Thorne and Stuart (2008).
94 Channel 4, 'C4 survey and documentary reveals What British Muslims Really Think', Channel 4 website, 11 April 2016. www.channel4.com/info/press/news/c4-survey-and-documentary-reveals-what-british-muslims-really-think. For the full survey report, see 'ICM Muslims survey for Channel 4', ICM website, 11 April 2016. www.icmunlimited.com/polls/icm-muslims-survey-for-channel-4/.
95 Frampton, Goodhart and Mahmood (2016), p. 43.
96 Ibid., p. 47.
97 Channel 4, ibid.
98 Richard Kerbaj, 'Muslim population "rising 10 times faster than rest of society"', *The Times*, 30 January 2009. www.thetimes.co.uk/tto/news/uk/article1937685.ece.
99 For the Pew Forum report, see 'The Future of the Global Muslim Population, Projections for 2010–2030, Analysis', Pew Forum website, 27 January 2011. www.pewforum.org/future-of-the-global-muslim-population-regional-europe.aspx.
100 Ed West, 'Here's one story the Right-wing media didn't make up: in 2030 Britain will be 8.2 per cent Muslim', *The Telegraph*, 28 January 2011. https://web.archive.org/web/20160326174412/http://blogs.telegraph.co.uk/news/edwest/100073893/heres-one-story-the-right-wing-media-didnt-make-up-in-2030-britain-will-be-8-2-per-cent-muslim.
101 David Adam, 'UK Asians isolated in city enclaves', *The Guardian*, 1 September 2005. www.guardian.co.uk/uk/2005/sep/01/race.world.
102 Fatwas of the European Council for Fatwa and Research (2002), p. 31.
103 Casey (2016), n. 1.67, p. 16.
104 Trevor Philips, 'On abuse it's time to call a spade a spade', *The Telegraph*, 10 August 2017. www.telegraph.co.uk/news/2017/08/10/abuse-time-call-spade-spade/. For the most comprehensive treatment of the issue of grooming gangs in Britain, which discusses how fears of being branded 'racist' or 'Islamophobic' contributed to the authorities' failure to act, see McLoughlin (2016).

References

Ali, Rashad and Hannah Stuart (2014). 'A guide to refuting jihadism: critiquing radical Islamist claims to theological authenticity'. The Henry Jackson Society, London. http://henryjacksonsociety.org/wp-content/uploads/2014/02/Refuting-Jihadism.pdf.

Association of Muslim Lawyers (2002a). 'Memorandum from The Association of Muslim Lawyers'. Minutes of Evidence. Select Committee on Religious Offences in England and Wales, House of Lords. https://publications.parliament.uk/pa/ld200203/ldselect/ldrelof/95/2101710.htm.

Association of Muslim Lawyers (2002b). 'Memorandum by the Association of Muslim Lawyers'. Minutes of Evidence. Select Committee on Religious Offences in England and Wales, House of Lords. https://publications.parliament.uk/pa/ld200203/ldselect/ldrelof/95/2101711.htm.

Bourdieu, Pierre (1989). 'Social space and symbolic power'. In *Sociological Theory*, vol. 7, no. 1: 14–25.

Bryson, Rachel (2017). 'For caliph and country: exploring how British jihadis join a global movement'. Tony Blair Institute for Global Change, London. https://institute.global/sites/default/files/inline-files/For-Caliph-Country.pdf.

Cabinet Office (2008). 'The national security strategy of the United Kingdom: security in an interdependent world'. Cm 7291. www.gov.uk/government/uploads/system/uploads/attachment_data/file/228539/7291.pdf.

Cabinet Office (2010). 'A strong Britain in an age of uncertainty: the national security strategy'. Cm 7953. www.gov.uk/government/uploads/system/uploads/attachment_data/file/61936/national-security-strategy.pdf.

Cabinet Office (2013). 'Tackling extremism in the UK'. Report from the Prime Minister's Task Force on Tackling Radicalisation and Extremism. www.gov.uk/government/uploads/system/uploads/attachment_data/file/263181/ETF_FINAL.pdf.

Casey, Louise (2016). *The Casey Review: A review into opportunity and integration.* Department for Communities and Local Government. www.gov.uk/government/uploads/system/uploads/attachment_data/file/575973/The_Casey_Review_Report.pdf.

Clutterbuck, Lindsay and William Rosenau (2009). 'Subversion as a facet of terrorism and insurgency: the case for a twenty-first century approach'. In *Strategic Insights*, vol. 8, no. 3.

Department for Communities and Local Government (2011). *Creating the Conditions for Integration.* www.gov.uk/government/uploads/system/uploads/attachment_data/file/7504/2092103.pdf.

Faliq, Abdullah (2016). 'Welcome', in Alain Gabon, 'The twin myths of the Western "jihadist threat" and "Islamic radicalisation"', p. 5. *Cordoba Papers*, vol. 4, no. 1. Cordoba Foundation, London.

Fatwas of the European Council for Fatwa and Research (2002). Trans. Anas Osama Altikriti and Shakir Nasif Al-Ubaydi. Cairo: Islamic INC.

Frampton, Martyn, David Goodhart and Khalid Mahmood (2016). *Unsettled Belonging: A Survey of Britain's Muslim Communities.* London: Policy Exchange. https://policyexchange.org.uk/wp-content/uploads/2016/12/PEXJ5037_Muslim_Communities_FINAL.pdf.

GfK NOP Social Research (2006). *Attitudes to Living in Britain: A Survey of Muslim Opinion.* Channel 4/Dispatches, London.

Gill, Peter (1994). *Policing Politics: Security Intelligence and the Liberal Democratic State.* London: Frank Cass.

HM Government (2009). *Pursue Prevent Protect Prepare: The United Kingdom's Strategy for Countering International Terrorism*, Cm 7547. www.gov.uk/government/uploads/system/uploads/attachment_data/file/228644/7547.pdf.

HM Government (2015a). *Counter-Extremism Strategy*, Cm 9148. www.gov.uk/government/uploads/system/uploads/attachment_data/file/470088/51859_Cm9148_Accessible.pdf.

HM Government (2015b). '*National Security Strategy and Strategic Defence and Security Review 2015: A Secure and Prosperous United Kingdom*', Cm 9161. www.gov.uk/government/uploads/system/uploads/attachment_data/file/478936/52309_Cm_9161_NSS_SD_Review_PRINT_only.pdf.

Home Office (2011). *Prevent Strategy*, Cm 8092. www.gov.uk/government/uploads/system/uploads/attachment_data/file/97976/prevent-strategy-review.pdf.

Home Office (2018). *The Independent Review into the Application of Sharia Law in England and Wales*, Cm 9560. www.gov.uk/government/uploads/system/uploads/atta

chment_data/file/678473/6.4152_HO_CPFG_Report_into_Sharia_Law_in_the_UK_PRINT.pdf.

House of Commons (2015). *Muslim Brotherhood Review: Main Findings.* HC 679.

Joint Committee on Human Rights (2016a). 'Counter-extremism'. Second Report of Session 2016–17. HL Paper 39, HC 105. https://publications.parliament.uk/pa/jt201617/jtselect/jtrights/105/105.pdf.

Joint Committee on Human Rights (2016b). 'Counter-extremism: government response to the Committee's Second Report of Session 2016–17'. First Special Report of Session 2016–17, HC 756. https://publications.parliament.uk/pa/jt201617/jtselect/jtrights/756/756b.pdf.

Joint Committee on Human Rights (2016c). 'Oral evidence: legislative scrutiny: Counter-extremism Bill', HC 105, 29 June. http://data.parliament.uk/writtenevidence/committeeevidence.svc/evidencedocument/human-rights-committee/countering-extremism/oral/34800.pdf.

Kilcullen, David (2007). 'Subversion and countersubversion in the campaign against terrorism in Europe'. In *Studies in Conflict and Terrorism*, vol. 30, no. 8.

Kundnani, Arun (2015). 'A decade lost: rethinking radicalisation and extremism'. Claystone, London. www.claystone.org.uk/wp-content/uploads/2015/01/Claystone-rethinking-radicalisation.pdf.

Manea, Elham (2016). *Women and Shari'a Law: The Impact of Legal Pluralism in the UK*. London: I. B. Taurus.

MCB (2015). *Fairness, Not Favours: British Muslim Perspectives at the 2015 General Election*. London: Muslim Council of Britain. www.mcb.org.uk/wp-content/uploads/2015/03/fairnessnotfavours-MCB.pdf.

McLoughlin, Peter (2016). *Easy Meat: Inside Britain's Grooming Gang Scandal*. London: New English Review Press.

Melucci, Alberto (1985). 'The symbolic challenge of contemporary movements'. In *Social Research*, vol. 52, no. 4: 789–816.

Mirza, Munira, Abi Senthilkumaran and Zein Ja'far (2007). *Living Together Apart: British Muslims and the Paradox of Multiculturalism*. London: Policy Exchange. www.policyexchange.org.uk/wp-content/uploads/2016/09/living-apart-together-jan-07.pdf.

Omand, David (2009). 'The National Security Strategy: implications for the UK intelligence community'. The Institute for Public Policy Research, London. www.ippr.org/files/images/media/files/publication/2011/05/National%20Security%20Strategy_1675.pdf.

Pantucci, Raffaello (2015). *"We Love Death As You Love Life": Britain's Suburban Terrorists*. London: Hurst & Co.

Radsch, Courtney C. (2016). *Media Development and Countering Violent Extremism: An Uneasy Relationship, a Need for Dialogue*. Washington, DC: Center for International Media Assistance. www.cima.ned.org/wp-content/uploads/2016/10/CIMA-CVE-Paper_web-150ppi.pdf.

RAN (Radicalisation Awareness Network) (2014). 'Preventing radicalisation to terrorism and violent extremism: strengthening the EU's response'. European Commission. https://ec.europa.eu/home-affairs/sites/homeaffairs/files/what-we-do/networks/radicalisation_awareness_network/ran-best-practices/docs/collection_of_approaches_lessons_learned_and_practices_en.pdf.

Rosenau, William (2007). *Subversion and Insurgency*. Santa Monica, CA: RAND National Research Defense Institute.

Security Service Act, 1989 (chapter 5). www.legislation.gov.uk/ukpga/1989/5/pdfs/ukpga_19890005_en.pdf.

Stuart, Hannah (2014). 'Disrupting extremists: more effective use of existing legislation'. Centre for the Response to Radicalisation and Terrorism, Policy Paper No. 3. Henry Jackson Society, London. http://henryjacksonsociety.org/wp-content/uploads/2014/10/Disrupting-Extremists.pdf.

Stuart, Hannah (2015). 'Understanding CAGE: a public information dossier'. Centre for the Response to Radicalisation and Terrorism, Policy Paper No. 5. Henry Jackson Society, London. http://henryjacksonsociety.org/wp-content/uploads/2015/04/Understanding-CAGE.pdf.

Sutton, Rupert (2015). 'Preventing Prevent? Challenges to counter-radicalisation policy on campus'. Henry Jackson Society, London. http://henryjacksonsociety.org/wp-content/uploads/2015/10/Preventing-Prevent_webversion3.pdf.

Sutton, Rupert (2016). 'Myths and misunderstandings: understanding opposition to the Prevent strategy'. Centre for the Response to Radicalisation and Terrorism, Policy Paper No. 7. Henry Jackson Society, London.

Swartz, David L. (2013). *Symbolic Power, Politics and Intellectuals: The Political Sociology of Pierre Bourdieu*. Chicago: University of Chicago Press.

Thorne, John and Hannah Stuart (2008). *Islam on Campus: A Survey of UK Student Opinions*. London: Centre for Social Cohesion. http://henryjacksonsociety.org/wp-content/uploads/2013/01/islam-on-campus-new.pdf.

Vidino, Lorenzo (2011). 'The Muslim Brotherhood in the West: evolution and Western policies'. International Centre for the Study of Radicalisation and Political Violence (ICSR), London. http://icsr.info/wp-content/uploads/2012/10/1300106834ICSRTheNewMBintheWest.pdf.

Wilson, Tom (2017). *Mend: "Islamists Masquerading As Civil Libertarians"*. London: Henry Jackson Society. http://henryjacksonsociety.org/wp-content/uploads/2017/10/HJS-Mend-Report.pdf.

Index